Sudden and Disruptive Climate Change

Sudden and Disruptive Climate Change

Exploring the Real Risks and How We Can Avoid Them

Edited by

Michael C. MacCracken, Frances Moore and
John C. Topping, Jr

London • Sterling, VA

First published by Earthscan in the UK and USA in 2008

Hardback ISBN-13:   978-1-84407-477-8
Paperback ISBN-13:   978-1-84407-478-5

Typeset by JS Typesetting Ltd, Porthcawl, Mid Glamorgan
Printed and bound in the UK by Cromwell Press, Trowbridge
Cover design by Susanne Harris

For a full list of publications please contact:

Earthscan
8–12 Camden High Street
London, NW1 0JH, UK
Tel: +44 (0)20 7387 8558
Fax: +44 (0)20 7387 8998
Email: earthinfo@earthscan.co.uk
Web: **www.earthscan.co.uk**

22883 Quicksilver Drive, Sterling, VA 20166-2012, USA

Earthscan publishes in association with the International Institute for Environment and
Development

A catalogue record for this book is available from the British Library

Library of Congress Cataloging-in-Publication Data

Sudden and disruptive climate change : exploring the real risks and how we can avoid
them / edited by Michael C. MacCracken, Frances Moore and John C.
Topping, Jr.
        p. cm.
    ISBN-13: 978-1-84407-477-8 (hardback)
    ISBN-10: 1-84407-477-3 (hardback)
    ISBN-13: 978-1-84407-478-5 (pbk.)
    ISBN-10: 1-84407-478-1 (pbk.)
    1. Climate changes–Social aspects. 2. Climate changes–Environmental
aspects. I. MacCracken, Michael C. II. Moore, Frances. III. Topping, John C.
    QC981.8.C5S87 2007
    551.6–dc22
                                                                    2007034786

Mixed Sources
Product group from well-managed
forests and other controlled sources
www.fsc.org Cert no. TT-COC-2082
© 1996 Forest Stewardship Council

FSC

Contents

List of Figures, Tables and Boxes

Figures

Tables

Boxes

List of Acronyms and Abbreviations

ACIA	Arctic Climate Impact Assessment
ADCIRC	Advanced Circulation Model for Coastal Ocean Hydrodynamics
AGW	anthropogenic greenhouse warming
AMO	Atlantic Multidecadal Oscillation
AOSIS	Alliance of Small Island States
ASU	Arizona State University
CEST	Coastal and Estuarine Storm Time
CFL	Compact Fluorescent Light
CHP	combined heat and power
CICEANA	Centro de Información y Comunicación Ambiental de Norte América
CZM	Coastal Zone Management
DE	distributed energy
DMSP	Defense Meteorological Satellite Program
EESI	Energy and Environment Security Initiative
ENSO	El-Niño Southern Oscillation
ESMR	Electrically Scanning Microwave Radiometer
FEMA	Federal Emergency Management Agency
FIU	Florida International University
GISS	Goddard Institute of Space Studies
GSEII	Global Sustainable Energy Island Initiative
HGCI	Harvard Green Campus Initiative
ICEsat	Ice Cloud and Land Elevation Satellite
IHRC	International Hurricane Research Center
InSAR	Interferometric Synthetic Aperture Radar
IPCC	Intergovernmental Panel on Climate Change
LIDAR	light detection and ranging
MODIS	Moderate Resolution Imaging Spectroradiometer
MSL	mean sea level
MSX	Multinucleated sphere X
NAELS	National Association of Environmental Law Societies

NFIP	National Flood Insurance Program
NY-NJ	New York-New Jersey
PSU-NCAR	Penn State – National Center for Atmospheric Research
RGGI	Regional Greenhouse Gas Initiative
SMMR	Scanning Multichannel Microwave Radiometer
SSMI	Special Sensor Microwave Imager
SST	sea surface temperature
T&D	transmission and distribution
TRP	The Regeneration Project
UNIDO	United Nations Industrial Development Organization
WAIS	West Antarctic Ice Sheet

Foreword

One thing that is very striking in the UK and across Europe, and I wonder if it is true also in the US, is the public are well ahead of governments on the question of climate change. They are increasingly alarmed by what they hear from the scientists, and they would like governments to respond with a greater sense of emergency, ambition and coherence. And, in some cases, they would even be willing to change their personal choices as part of a collective effort, if they see strong leadership in government. A reflection of that in the UK is that the leader of the Conservative Party has made a very deliberate choice to make climate change one of the defining issues for his political platform. He has assessed that this is something the public wants to hear and will respond to. And all of that means that, in addition to the very strong and very clear personal commitment that Britain's [former] leaders have, Tony Blair and Margaret Beckett in particular, there is a deeper current in the British public mind, which means that the effort that is devoted to it is bound to intensify. This is not a passing phase; this is something that is going to intensify.

When I took on the role of being Special Representative for Climate Change for Foreign Secretary Margaret Beckett, she was very clear in telling me what she wanted me to do. She did not particularly want me to concentrate or spend too much of my time trying to make current policies marginally better, within the current limits of the possible. She was very clear that we cannot deal with this problem within those limits. So, she asked me to work with her and her colleagues to try to expand the political limits that currently constrain us. This is about building stronger coalitions of interest and mobilizing much more political energy than is currently available in support of their response.

Ringing in my ears is the message that is now coming from the front lines of the scientific community. I was with John Holdren, President of the American Association for the Advancement of Science in New York one Saturday, and he said very clearly that we should no longer speak of avoiding dangerous climate change. That is yesterday's issue. We have dangerous climate change already; what we now need to focus on is avoiding catastrophic climate change. And John, as many of you know, is not a sensationalist. That's a very measured judgment and a judgment you will find coming from most of the senior scientific figures who are taking a serious look at this issue.

There is an enormous gap that is opening up, and which is getting wider at the moment, between those people who are looking at the possible futures that an unstable climate will create (and what they think is the maximum that we should tolerate), and the assessment being made by the people who are rooted in the policy community, and the economics and political communities, around the world about what is the best that we can do. What the policy community thinks is the best that we can do is nowhere near what the people on the front lines say is what we have to do. And that's just another way of stating this problem.

I think, and this is supported by the major study, published in October 2006, carried through by Sir Nicholas Stern, who is the British government's chief economist, and who was the Chief Economist of the World Bank. He was commissioned by Tony Blair and Gordon Brown to take a comprehensive look at the economics of climate change. This study is, I think, the most rigorous and wide-ranging assessment that has ever been devoted to that subject, and it is certainly having a major impact on the economic debate. He says two things, in essence. One, that we have a window of opportunity in which we can still shift the massive flows of private investment that are building the world's energy infrastructure, so that it builds us a low carbon, or actually a zero carbon, energy infrastructure in the next 25 years. We can do that, and the cost of that will be an affordable cost. And second, if we don't do that, there will be costs that will not be within our means; they will be astronomical costs. So, fixing this problem will not cost us the Earth, whereas not fixing it will certainly cost us the Earth. And we know enough now about the impacts of climate change so that we could expect to understand that; it is a very powerful message.

While addressing climate change is mainly about climate investment, the problem for governments is how to use public policy to shift the flow of private investment. What we must attempt to do is to build the world's most ambitious public–private partnership. That is what the challenge is. In order to bring that effort to light, we will have to mobilize a much greater quantity of political energy than is currently available.

I just want to conclude by mentioning one dimension of that, which again connects back to my role, because I would not be in this job and it would not have been created if it were not for the fact that British politicians do not view this as an environmental issue. Climate change is not primarily an environmental issue; it is a security issue. Climate change is a security issue because, if we do not respond effectively, it will impose overwhelming difficulties in our efforts to achieve national security and achieve economic security. And a security issue is an imperative. It is an issue that you respond to by doing what you need to do as cost effectively as possible, rather than doing what you think you can do subject to the pressures of other priorities, and subject to the – in this area – misleading information that we get if we apply the traditional environmental policy tool of cost–benefit analysis. There is no plausible cost–benefit analysis we can carry out for the climate problem.

But climate change is a security issue, and it is a very integral part of the question of how we build a secure future in a world of high and rapidly increasing interdependence. Climate change creates a situation in which our security is becoming intertwined not only with the condition of the climate, but also with what I call the other three pillars of resource security: water security, food security and energy security. You cannot have one of these components of resource security without having the other three; they are all interlinked. If we want to build a stable and secure international system, we need to address all of them much more effectively than we have so far, starting with climate change.

My colleagues and their American colleagues and their colleagues in the international community are desperately trying to find a way of improving the conditions in Darfur. The primary reason there is a problem in Darfur and Sudan – and it is a very complex situation and there are many other factors in place – is related to changes in the climate. There would not be a problem to start with were it not for the fact that a community of nomadic herders started to move onto the land of a neighboring community of settled agriculturalists because of the fundamental shift in rainfall that has taken place in that part of Sudan. And this is just a little foretaste; it is just a little illustration, right at the leading edge of this problem, of the kind of situation that we can expect on a much larger scale if we do not immediately address the climate change issue.

As I said earlier, we need to shift the limits of what is possible. The UK is looking to build not only alliances and shared frameworks, but also shared ways of thinking about this problem that will reach into the many constituencies who control the flow of political power and, therefore, the scope for responding. The reason I am here is to begin some of the conversations that will enable us to do that, starting with the people who are thinking about the roots of security.

I thank the Climate Institute and you, John Topping, for giving me this opportunity, and I wish you a very successful proceedings.

Ambassador John Ashton
UK Foreign Secretary's Special Representative for Climate Change
UK Foreign and Commonwealth Office
19 September 2006

Introduction

Michael C. MacCracken and John C. Topping, Jr

Heat waves. Drenching rains. Disappearing glaciers and retreating Arctic sea ice. Drought and extensive wildfires in the western US. Ice shelf collapse. Melting near the top of the Greenland Ice Sheet. Unprecedented occurrence of powerful hurricanes causing extensive coastal erosion. An increased rate of sea level rise. Deforestation, land cover change and loss of species. Headline after headline reporting on global warming and the changing climate. Are we experiencing just natural fluctuations, or are human activities at least in part, and perhaps in large part, responsible for these events? What more can lie ahead?

In celebration of its 20th Anniversary, the Climate Institute organized the Washington Summit on Climate Stabilization (hereafter, the Summit) to assess the likelihood that human activities are tipping, or near to tipping, the world towards abrupt and highly disruptive climate change. On 19–20 September 2006, with additional workshops on the preceding and following days, the Summit brought together approximately 150 experts in the fields of climate change, environmental and societal impacts, adaptation, and technological, institutional and societal mitigation options. Throughout the Summit, participants explored the present and projected implications of human activities on the environment and reviewed a number of the creative responses that, if implemented more widely, could help the world avoid potentially catastrophic changes in the climate and our environment.

Scientific studies, summarized and evaluated most comprehensively and credibly in the periodic assessments prepared by the UN-sponsored Intergovernmental Panel on Climate Change (IPCC), project that continuing reliance on fossil fuels to supply most of the world's energy will lead to an increase in the global average surface temperature of roughly 1.4 to 5.5°C (about 2.5 to 10°F) by the year 2100, adding to the observed increase of about 0.6°C (about 1.1°F) over the 20th century.

Given that the fall of 2006 (and 2007) were several degrees warmer than normal over much of the US, why should the world be so concerned about a projected global average temperature increase of 'only' a few degrees over the course of the 21st century? Are not climatic conditions that the world will face in 100 years similar to the conditions that prevail several hundred miles to the south? Why should we be concerned if the climate of Washington DC becomes like that of Atlanta, or even Miami? With daily temperature variations being roughly 10°C (18°F) or more, and winter-to-summer differences in the daily average temperature being about 20°C or more (roughly 36°F), can societies not, over time, redesign their buildings and infrastructure to readily adapt to a few degree rise in the annual average temperature? Why is there so much concern?

The first reason for concern is that, while the projected increase in average temperature may seem small in comparison to everyday experience, it is large in the context of past changes in the global climate. Over the time span of human civilization, decadal average surface temperature has varied by relatively small amounts, and these changes were generally quite slow and often only regional in extent; by contrast, the global average temperature rose by about 0.6°C over the 20th century and the increase was larger than this in some regions. The changes in climate and temperature over the next 100 years are likely to be several times larger than the changes in climate and temperature that took place between the last ice age (about 20,000 years ago) and the beginning of the 20th century. The warming is expected to be larger in the middle to high latitudes than in the tropics, larger over land areas than over oceans, and larger in winter than in summer (except in areas that are dried out by summer warming). Significant impacts on natural and managed ecosystems and on water resources are likely in many critical regions. While adaptation to such changes in one place or for one year may be possible, just as the US and Europe survived the heat of the 2006 summer, a multitude of changes simultaneously occurring around the world and persisting for decades (and longer) will create a very challenging situation.

The second reason for concern is the accelerating pace of change, because this acceleration increases the likelihood that various climate thresholds will be crossed before emissions are brought under control. If we could be assured that changes in climate and the associated impacts would occur only slowly and steadily, the potential would exist for orderly, gradual adaptation, even if this became expensive. The problem is that accelerating fossil fuel emissions increases the risk that changes will not be smooth, slow or always as we expect them to occur. Climatic history provides a number of indications that some types of changes can occur abruptly and suggests that 'tipping points' may exist that could lead to very large impacts occurring over years to decades, once thresholds are crossed or particular conditions arise.

The scientific objectives of this Summit were two-fold: first, to explore a number of these potential risks; and second, to evaluate the societal vulnerability, especially in the event of the changes occurring at an accelerated rate or in an abrupt manner. The policy-related objectives of this Summit were to explore the ability of society to deal with possible nonlinearities in environmental systems that could result in unexpectedly rapid rates of change in response to human-induced global warming, and to identify and encourage creative ways of reducing emissions, beginning now or in the very near term. These kinds of rapid, near-term emissions reductions are critical because without them, the risk of rapid and disruptive change increases sharply.

The sections of this book are organized around topics where science and experience are suggesting quite rapid change could occur – either negative changes resulting from sudden climate impacts, or positive changes from effective adaptation or mitigation efforts. Thus, the sections of this book, each starting out with a brief overview from the chair of that session of the Summit, cover the following areas:

Part 1 focuses on *the pace of climate change*. Scientific studies over the past 25 years have made clear that the responsiveness of the global climate to higher concentrations of CO_2 and other greenhouse gases is unlikely to be less than the lower bound of what has been incorporated into the IPCC's estimates, but could well be greater than the upper bound that has been used. Recognizing that much warmer climates have existed in the Earth's distant past, the three chapters (1–3) in this section explore the risk that climate change and its direct health impacts on society will be greater than is generally perceived.

Part 2 focuses on factors that affect *the pace of sea level rise*. Global sea level is estimated to have risen almost 0.2 m during the 20th century, and recent satellite records suggest that the rate of rise has increased to over 0.3 m per century, presumably as a result of more rapid ocean warming (causing greater thermal expansion) and accelerated melting of mountain glaciers and the edges of the Greenland Ice Sheet. The recent collapse of the Larsen-B ice shelf, and the consequent acceleration of glacial streams that the ice shelf was buttressing, suggest that the loss of grounded ice can occur much faster than has traditionally been assumed. With the Greenland and West Antarctic ice sheets each containing the equivalent of about 6 m (20 feet) of sea level rise, the three chapters (4–6) in this section explore the potential for warming to prompt accelerating changes in the Earth's cryosphere.

Part 3 focuses on the increasing potential for *damaging impacts in coastal regions*. Coastal wetlands, marshes and estuaries are the breeding grounds and hatcheries for a vast array of marine and terrestrial species, some of which are located there throughout the year, but many of which migrate through in their seasonal pursuit of food and habitats for their young. These regions are vital to the health of the global ecosystem and provide important food and resources for society. Proximity to the resources of both the land and the ocean has led to many of the world's largest cities being located on the coast, often serving as ports, transportation hubs, and centers of trade and commerce. In addition, because the coast is aesthetically attractive, permanent and vacation communities now cover the barrier islands and coastal bluffs in many regions of the world, accepting the risk and damage that comes from existing levels and intensities of storms and storm surges. Climate change, however, will create new stresses, including more powerful tropical cyclones, higher sea levels and higher storm surges. The five chapters (7–11) in this section explore the risk of increasing damage and the steps that may be possible to limit the most severe impacts.

Part 4 focuses on the pace of *ecosystem transformation*. From southeastern and northeastern forests to the grasslands of the Great Plains and deserts of the southwest, the climate determines the prevailing ecosystem and, to a large extent, the potential for agriculture. As the climate changes, it is often suggested that existing systems will slowly move or seamlessly evolve into new systems with no disruption in the services the ecosystems provide. However, increasing evidence is emerging that pests, disease and fire accelerate the changeover from one system to another. With evidence indicating that the loss of ecosystems, or at least their key species, can occur much more rapidly than their reestablishment, the three chapters (12–14) in this section explore the potential for rapid changes in ecosystems to significantly disrupt biological diversity and the other ecosystem services that society depends on.

Part 5 focuses on the potential for *accelerating action to limit climate change*. Recognizing that climate change is underway and has the potential to cause damaging impacts for generations into the future, a growing number of efforts are underway to limit its pace. The early enthusiasm for dealing with the climate change issue that led to negotiation of the UN Framework Convention on Climate Change in 1992 and international acceptance of the need to limit 'anthropogenic interference with the climate system' has been replaced by an international process that is struggling to take steps so limited that continuing on this path is likely to produce at least dangerous, and quite possibly catastrophic, consequences. Recognizing this, a distributed and, in many cases, bottom–up effort has started with the intent of saving the world by changing it. The nine chapters (15–23) in this section describe a number of very positive efforts that are getting underway to slow the pace of climate change, proving that the Earth's climate can be stabilized because change is not only possible, but is justified, necessary, and, in many cases, cost effective.

Those who participated in the Summit came away enthusiastic and excited about what could be done, and committed to making changes happen through their efforts and through their collaborations and participation with the many other organizations and efforts of which they were and are a part. It was their enthusiasm and requests that led us to assemble the perspectives offered at the Summit into this book. We hope that the following collection of articles, which cover topics across the spectrum of climate science, environmental and societal impacts, and actions and programs to limit emissions, will inspire others to join the effort to limit climate change and do what needs to be done.

Already the Summit has begun to bear fruit in both Latin America and in small island nations. Just as the Summit opened, the Director General of Mexico's National Instituto Nacional de Astrofisica, Optica y Electronica (INAOE) wrote to the Climate Institute inviting it to join in building a High Altitude Climate Observatory in Pico De Orizaba National Park near the Large Millimeter Telescope operated by INAOE. Led by the efforts of Luis Roberto Acosta of the Climate Institute, plans and funding have solidified for this effort, and construction is expected to begin in the summer of 2007 with the High Altitude Climate Center operational by mid-2008. Co-location of the climate observatory and the radio telescope greatly increased interest in climate change in the Mexican news media. The Climate Institute's office in Mexico City is now working closely with the environmental awareness group, CICEANA (Centro de Información y Comunicación Ambiental de Norte América), to launch a national climate awareness campaign focused on actions that individuals can take to reduce energy use and greenhouse emissions. Wal-Mart, which has 2.6 million daily customers in Mexico, has indicated its willingness to disseminate public service messages on internal store video systems, and Televisa, Mexico's largest television network, has agreed to incorporate these public service messages into its programming. Two major museums in Mexico City are also now working with the Climate Institute to develop exhibits that will communicate the urgency and importance of climate change and practical steps individuals and society can take to respond to it.

This effort extends well past consciousness-raising to encompass practical steps in scientific cooperation, anticipatory adaptation, building design and siting, and energy use and design. The International Leadership Alliance for Climate Stabilization, the public–private partnership announced at the Washington Summit, is working to set up a flexible framework for North–South cooperation in creatively adapting to climate change and reducing greenhouse gas emissions. Already the Dominican Republic and Mexico's State of Quintana Roo appear eager to participate in the Leadership Alliance. Iceland, the Government of Mexico City and several English-speaking small island nations in the Caribbean appear interested in similar cooperative endeavors. Among the possible areas of cooperation would be an island-to-island initiative in which smaller island nations could learn from the success of Iceland in geothermal and hydropower development and the promising beginnings of the Dominican Republic in bioenergy, adaptation of the state-of-the-art storm surge mapping developed by the International Hurricane Research Center in Miami for use in vulnerable island nations or states such as Quintana Roo, use of vetiver grass to preserve beaches and roads from erosion and destruction in severe storms, and development of building practices to optimize energy use and survivability. A key to success in both adaptation and greenhouse emissions reduction is thinking smart from the outset. Some of these measures may in fact provide not only sizable reductions in greenhouse gas emissions, but also yield cost savings to industry and consumers.

The success of the Summit was built on the efforts of many people, to all of whom we offer our sincere thanks. These include the speakers and session chairs, whose names are indicated in the Table of Contents and whose brief biographies appear in an appendix, those who came and participated in the very lively discussions in and around the conference, those who helped to fund the Summit and its related events, and especially those individuals who helped to organize the conference. Details on many of these individuals and institutions are provided in the Acknowledgements section in the appendices.

For 20 years, the Climate Institute has sought to increase awareness of the climate change issue and to propose and encourage positive approaches to addressing it – ways around which we can all come together to treasure the world that we have and to create a society that lives more sustainably. The Climate Institute will be continuing these efforts over coming decades, and we invite everyone to join in – check for information about our ongoing activities at www.climate.org.

Part 1

The Potential for Rapid Changes to the Weather and Climate

Introduction to Part 1

Michael C. MacCracken

For nearly- 100 years following 1897, when Svante Arrhenius first made a quantitative estimate of how human-caused emissions of carbon dioxide (CO_2) would affect the climate, the presumption was that changes in the climate would occur slowly and that, therefore, society would have decades to develop the policies to slow and then stop climate change. When the President's Science Advisory Council advised President Lyndon Johnson in 1965 that climate change was an important emerging issue, there was no urgency expressed to deal with it. Similarly, assessments by the US National Academy of Sciences and various US government agencies summarized scientific understanding in the 1970s and 1980s, changes in climate that could make a difference to the environment and society seemed many decades off, especially in that observations were not convincingly showing any climatic response to the increasing concentrations of CO_2 and other greenhouse gases.

That the Earth's climate could change significantly over quite short periods, however, became particularly evident as a result of analyses of high-resolution ice cores from the Greenland Ice Sheet. Not only did these cores document the long-term changes that were seen in the low-resolution cores drilled in ocean sediments, but they suggested that abrupt changes in climate (at least over Greenland and the North Atlantic) were not even rare events, at least during times when there was substantial glacial ice and meltwater that could, in ways not yet completely understood, lead to rapid changes in ocean conditions.

At the same time, detection and attribution studies aimed at identifying the human 'fingerprint' of climate change found that, indeed, the climate was changing in ways that could only be explained by human activities. Studies brought together in the assessments of the Intergovernmental Panel on Climate Change (IPCC) made clear that both human-caused increases in the atmospheric loading of sulfate aerosols and natural variations in solar radiation and volcanic aerosols were actually countering the warming influences of the increasing concentrations of greenhouse gases, delaying observation of their strong warming influence. What these studies are suggesting is that there is a stronger potential for changes in the climate (and, in that climate is simply the average of the weather, for changes in the weather) than has been recognized in past scientific assessments.

The three chapters in this section explore various aspects of this issue. In Chapter 1, countering the oft-heard criticisms of media-hyped naysayers that the IPCC's estimates of climate change are too high, Dr A. Barrie Pittock presents ten reasons, each much more soundly argued than the criticisms, that the model-based projections of climate change summarized by the IPCC are likely to be *underestimating* the amount of climate change we can expect. In Chapter 2, Dr Judith Curry summarizes the observational evidence indicating that tropical cyclones (i.e. hurricanes and typhoons) are becoming more intense and destructive than projections with relatively coarse grid models have indicated, suggesting that the pace of increasing damage in coastal regions could continue to accelerate rapidly. In Chapter 3, with the pace of temperature change and of storm intensity both seeming likely to increase more rapidly than had been indicated, Dr Devra Davis and John Topping describe the types of health impacts that the accelerating pace of climate change is likely to cause, making clear that significant effort will need to be put towards enhancing public health infrastructure and practices in order to satisfactorily limit increasing societal vulnerability.

These findings and others from around the world are making it more and more clear that there is an increasing risk that the pace of climate change is accelerating, and that, because of the high degree of environmental and societal vulnerability, the potential for very serious impacts is becoming more and more likely.

1

Ten Reasons Why Climate Change
May be More Severe than Projected[1]

A. Barrie Pittock

Uncertainties in climate change science are inevitably large. They arise from questions of data quality, inadequate understanding of the climate system and its representation in climate models, and uncertainties about future emissions of greenhouse gases resulting from socio-economic and technical developments. Policies therefore must be based on risk management; that is, on consideration of the probability times the magnitude of any deleterious outcomes for different scenarios of human behavior (Schneider, 2001; Jones, 2004; Kerr, 2005a; Pittock, 2005). We do not insure our house for the coming year because we are certain it will burn down, but because there is a small chance that it might, with serious consequences for our finances. Better flood protection for New Orleans should have been built before 2005 (Fischetti, 2001), not because it was certain New Orleans *would* be flooded in 2005, but because it *might* have been.

When taken together, the ten areas of concern described below, each based on observations and modeling studies, strongly suggest that the risk of more serious outcomes is greater than was understood previously.

New evidence suggesting more rapid climate change

1. The climate sensitivity may be larger than has been traditionally estimated

In its Third Assessment Report (IPCC, 2001) the IPCC assumed that the climate sensitivity (the global warming after a doubling of the pre-industrial CO_2 concentration) is in the range of 1.5°C to 4.5°C. However, recent estimates of the climate sensitivity, mostly based on modeling, constrained by recent or paleoclimatic data, suggest a higher range of around 2°C to 6°C (Murphy et al,

2004; Piani et al, 2005; Stainforth et al, 2005; Annan and Hargreaves, 2006; Hegerl et al, 2006; Torn and Harte, 2006). The only exception is a paper by Forster and Gregory (2006), which provides one of the lowest estimates of climate sensitivity, 1.0°C to 4.1°C. However, it is based on only 11 years of data from the Earth Radiation Budget Experiment, and the results may not be representative of longer time scales at which some major feedback mechanisms come into play.

Overall, these estimates throw doubt on the low end of the IPCC (2001) assumed range and suggest a much higher probability of global average surface warmings by 2100 exceeding the midlevel estimate of 3.0°C above pre-industrial that many scientists consider may lead to 'dangerous' levels of climate change (Schellnhuber et al, 2006).

2. Global dimming is large but decreasing

Atmospheric particles (aerosols) reduce the amount of sunlight at the Earth's surface. The resulting 'global dimming' has delayed warming of the oceans (Delworth et al, 2005), especially in the Northern Hemisphere. With stricter controls leading to reductions in emissions of particles and precursor compounds (Bellouin et al, 2005; Pinker et al, 2005; Wild et al, 2005), the decreasing atmospheric loading of aerosols is leading to a decreasing cooling influence on the climate. Because aerosols have a short lifetime in the atmosphere, this cooling effect of aerosols is highly responsive to reductions in sulfur emissions (Andreae et al, 2005). In that the highest aerosol loading is in the Northern Hemisphere, reductions in global dimming are likely to have asymmetric effects, leading to greater warming in the Northern Hemisphere and to changes in cross-equatorial flows such as the Australian monsoon (Rotstayn et al, 2006) and the circulation in the Atlantic Ocean (Cai et al, 2006).

By contrast, emissions of CO_2 and other greenhouse gases exert a long-term warming influence because of their long lifetimes and the resulting cumulative effect on their concentrations. As a result, reductions in global dimming will lead in the short term to greater warming even if the emissions of greenhouse gases are cut back.

3. Permafrost melting and albedo changes

Observations show rapid melting of permafrost, or frozen ground (Nelson, 2003; Arctic Climate Impact Assessment, 2004; Overland, 2006), which is expected to increase (Lawrence and Slater, 2005). Melting changes the reflectivity, or albedo, of the surface (Chapin et al, 2005; Foley, 2005), and this will likely lead to emissions of CO_2 and methane previously stored in frozen soils. These are positive feedback effects that may have been underestimated. Where permafrost is replaced by swampland, methane is likely to be emitted, but where it is replaced by dry soil, CO_2 is more likely to be emitted. Changes wrought by global warming in the Arctic are complex and pervasive (Hinzman et al, 2005). Increased vegetation cover will tend to further reduce the albedo, especially when there is snow on the ground, but may take up more CO_2 from the atmosphere, at least until the carbon is released by fire.

Satellite data over the period 1984–1999 indicate a significant decreasing trend in surface albedo over high latitudes in the North American region, but this trend is not simulated in climate models (Wang et al, 2006). This suggests that the representation of surface albedo feedbacks in these climate models might be too weak, at least in the studied region.

4. Biomass feedbacks are kicking in

Saturation of terrestrial carbon sinks and potential destabilization of large biospheric carbon pools are possible (Canadell et al, 2007). Observations of soil and vegetation acting as sources rather than sinks of greenhouse gases (Bellamy et al, 2005; Raupach et al, 2006) suggest an earlier-than-expected (Friedlingstein et al, 2001; Matthews et al, 2005) positive feedback in the terrestrial carbon cycle (Gruber et al, 2004; Scheffer et al, 2006). Angert et al (2005) attribute an observed decreased summer uptake of CO_2 in middle and high latitudes to hotter and drier conditions, which cancels out increased uptake in warmer springtimes. This net loss in carbon has been observed at ground level in some regions under extreme warm conditions (Ciais et al, 2005), and such conditions are expected to occur more frequently in the future (Stott et al, 2004).

Other factors that may lead to a more rapid global warming include reduced sequestration of root-derived soil carbon (Heath et al, 2005), overestimates of responses to ambient CO_2 increases (Kilronomos et al, 2005), and forest and peat fires (Page et al, 2002; Aldhous, 2004; Langmann and Heil, 2004; Westerling et al, 2006) exacerbated by land clearing and draining of swamps. Based on data from one forest fire in Alaska, Randerson et al (2006) suggest that increased surface albedo following boreal forest fires may in fact outweigh the increase in radiative forcing due to the CO_2 emitted in the fires. However, the general applicability of this result remains highly uncertain.

The recent high growth rates in the atmospheric CO_2 concentration reported by Francey (2005) appear to be persisting through 2004–2005 (David Etheridge, CSIRO, personal communication, 2006) and may be linked to the regional surface observations (Langenfelds et al, 2002). Present indications are that emissions, sea level rise and global surface temperatures are all tracking along the highest of the range of estimates from the IPCC's Third Assessment Report (Rahmstorf et al, 2007).

5. Arctic sea ice is retreating rapidly

Rapid recession of arctic sea ice has been observed, leading to an acceleration of global warming as reduced reflection of sunlight increases surface heating (Gregory et al, 2002; Comiso and Parkinson, 2004; Lindsay and Zhang, 2005; NASA, 2005; Stroeve et al, 2005; NSIDC, 2005, 2006; Comiso, 2006; Overland, 2006; Serreze and Francis, 2006; Wang et al, 2006). Some scenarios have the summertime Arctic Ocean becoming ice-free by the end of the century. Comiso (2006) notes that the average area of perennial ice has recently been declining at a rate of 9.9 per cent per decade, with large inter-annual variability of ice cover. There have also been longer seasonal melt periods, for the sea ice as well as the Greenland Ice Sheet and other land areas, especially since 2002. Serreze and Francis (2006) argue that the Arctic is presently in a state of 'preconditioning', setting the stage for larger changes in coming decades. They state that 'extreme sea ice losses in recent years seem to be sending a message: the ice-albedo feedback is starting'.

How serious and irreversible this and other potential 'tipping points' in the climate system may be is a complex question, discussed thoughtfully in a review by Walker (2006). If a positive ice-albedo feedback kicks in to accelerate regional or global warming, it might contribute to other parts of the climate system also reaching critical points, notably the Greenland Ice Sheet and the North Atlantic thermohaline circulation (see below).

6. Changes in air and sea circulation in middle and high latitudes

Different rates of warming at low and high latitudes in both hemispheres have led to increasing sea level pressure in the middle latitudes and a poleward movement of the middle latitude westerlies (that is, a more positive 'northern or southern annular mode') (Cai et al, 2003; Gillett et al, 2003; Marshall, 2003). This partly explains the observed and projected drying trends in winter rainfall regimes in Mediterranean-type climatic zones in both hemispheres (Pittock, 2003).

This change has also strengthened the major surface ocean circulations, including the Antarctic Circumpolar Current (Cai et al, 2005; Cai, 2006; Fyfe and Saenko, 2006). These changes will significantly affect surface climate, including sea surface temperatures and storminess (Fyfe, 2003), and may already have accelerated melting in Antarctica (Carril et al, 2005; Marshall et al, 2006) and preconditioned the South Atlantic for the formation of tropical cyclones (Pezza and Simmonds, 2005).

The strengthening of the annular modes, if due to enhanced greenhouse gas forcing alone, appears to have been under-predicted in climate models (Gillett, 2005), but may be explained by the additional forcing effects of stratospheric ozone depletion (Cai and Cowan, 2007) that has now leveled off and may decline on a timescale of several decades.

7. Rapid changes in Antarctica

Rapid disintegration of ice shelves around the Antarctic Peninsula, and subsequent acceleration of outlet glaciers point to the role of surface meltwater in ice shelf disintegration (Scambos et al, 2000; Rignot et al, 2004; Thomas et al, 2004; Cook et al, 2005; Dupont and Alley, 2006) and to the role of ice shelves in retarding glacier outflow. The Larsen B Ice Shelf collapsed spectacularly in 2002, following Larsen A and the Prince Gustav Channel Ice Shelf, which both collapsed in 1995. Satellite observations clearly document that the sequence of the Larsen B Ice Shelf collapse involved the sudden disappearance of surface meltwater pools, followed immediately by the opening of crevasses and the break-up of the ice shelf over a period of a few weeks. Paleo-data indicate no previous collapse of the Larsen B Ice Shelf in the Holocene (the period since the last glaciation) although some other small ice shelves have shown earlier retreats (Hodgson et al, 2006).

Warm intermediate-depth water may also be penetrating below ice shelves and outlet glaciers such as Pine Island Glacier in West Antarctica, melting the ice from the bottom, weakening the floating ice, and reducing resistance to glacier outflow (Bindschadler, 2006).

Strengthening and warming of the Antarctic Circumpolar Current (Cai et al, 2005; Carril et al, 2005; Fyfe and Saenko, 2006) may accelerate Antarctic ice sheet disintegration by enhancing local warming, preventing sea ice formation, and undercutting ice shelves (Goosse and Renssen, 2001; van den Broeke et al, 2004; Carril et al, 2005). This hypothesis is supported by an observed link between the Southern Annular Mode (which is responding to anthropogenic forcing) and local warming, especially along the east coast of the Antarctic Peninsula (Marshall et al, 2006).

Recent modeling of the effect of global warming on the West Antarctic Ice Sheet does not appear to incorporate any of the above mechanisms (Greve, 2000; Gray et al, 2005).

Some indirect observations suggest that Antarctic sea ice extent is already in decline (Curran et al, 2004), although shorter direct observations are less clear. Radar observations (Zwally et al, 2005) and satellite gravity surveys show Antarctica to be losing mass (Velicogna and Wahr, 2006), while a major recent study suggests that the expected increase in snowfall in central Antarctica due to greater moisture in the lower atmosphere (Krinner et al, 2007), which might have contributed to a slowing of sea level rise, has not occurred (Monaghan et al, 2006). This is despite observed warming of the Antarctic winter troposphere (Turner et al, 2006).

8. Rapid melting and faster outlet glaciers in Greenland

The Greenland Ice Sheet is at a generally lower latitude than Antarctica and has widespread marginal surface melting in summer. The area of surface melting has rapidly increased in recent years, notably since 2002 (NASA, 2003, 2006). Penetration of this meltwater through moulins (crevasses and tunnels in the ice) to the lower boundary of the ice is thought to have lubricated the flow of ice over the bedrock and led to accelerated glacier flow rates (Alley et al, 2005; Fountain et al, 2005; Hansen, 2005; Dowdeswell, 2006; Kerr, 2006; Rignot and Kanagaratnam, 2006; Thomas et al, 2006). Melting of tidewater glaciers from the bottom, pushing back the grounding line, may also be contributing to acceleration of flow (Bindschadler, 2006; Kerr, 2006).

Outlet glaciers have accelerated rapidly in recent years, with Rignot and Kanagaratnam (2006) reporting from satellite radar interferometry that widespread acceleration occurred south of 66°N between 1996 and 2000, expanding to 70°N in 2005. Accelerated discharge in the west and, particularly, in the east more than doubled the outflow from 90 to 220 cubic kilometers per year. Thomas et al (2006), using laser altimeter measurements, report that net mass loss from Greenland more than doubled between 1993/4–1998/9 and 1998/9–2004.

These observational results indicate mass losses considerably faster than were modeled by glaciologists using models that did not take account of the recently identified mechanisms of meltwater lubrication and tidewater glacier undercutting (Huybrechts and de Wolde, 1999; Greve, 2000; Ridley et al, 2005). Indeed, Hansen (2005) suggests that various other positive feedbacks may come into play as the ice sheet slumps, most notably that more precipitation on the ice sheet interior will fall in summer as rain rather than snow, thereby accelerating the effect of surface melting and bottom lubrication. At present, marginal areas are slumping, but the high plateau is still accumulating mass. This may change in the future.

Simulations and paleo-climatic data indicate that Greenland and Antarctica together contributed several meters to sea level rise at 130,000 to 127,000 years ago, a time when global temperatures were about the same as presently projected for 2100 (Overpeck et al, 2006; Otto-Bliesner et al, 2006). Overpeck et al (2006) conclude that peak rates of sea level rise may well exceed 1 m per century, and that this may be strongly related to warming of the upper 200 m of the ocean, producing rapid thinning of ice shelves (and, presumably, tidewater glacier outlets) from below.

9. Tropical cyclones may already be more intense

Some observational analyses point to a rapid intensification of tropical cyclones over recent decades (Emanuel, 2005a; Webster et al, 2005; Hoyos et al, 2006). However, modeling of tropical cyclone behavior under enhanced global warming conditions (Knutson and Tuleya, 2004; Walsh et al, 2004) suggests only a slow increase in intensity that would not yet be detectable given natural variability. This is more in line with the analysis by Trenberth (2005).

The record hurricane season of 2005 in the Caribbean region has prompted debate on whether the modeling or more extreme observational analyses are more likely correct (Emanuel, 2005b; Kerr, 2005b; Pielke et al, 2005; American Meteorological Society, 2006; Anthes et al, 2006; Klotzbach, 2006; Witze, 2006). While the observations have their limitations (Landsea, 2005; Pielke, 2005), and have been revised in new analyses, it is also clear that the modeling to date has not been at sufficient horizontal resolution to capture the details of tropical cyclone behavior (Schrope, 2005), nor perhaps the effects of subsurface warming of the ocean. According to Pezza and Simmonds (2005), the first recorded South Atlantic hurricane may be linked to global warming.

10. Variations in North Atlantic Ocean circulation and salinity

The North Atlantic has a complex current system, with the largely wind-driven Gulf Stream splitting into the North Atlantic Current that heads north-east into the Norwegian Sea, and a subtropical recirculating arm, known as the Azores and Canary Currents, that turns south. Relatively warm, but highly saline, surface water in the northern arm tends to sink to a depth of several kilometers in three regions – the Labrador Sea, south of Iceland, and between Greenland and Norway. The north-flowing arm transports heat from low latitudes to high latitudes, tending to warm northwestern Europe.

Bryden et al (2005) report a significant slowing of this regional sinking, or 'meridional overturning' circulation, supporting other observations discussed by Quadfasel (2005), Schiermeier (2006) and Levi (2006), although these commentators raise questions about the representativeness of the limited data set used by Bryden et al (2005). Bryden et al found that the northward transport in the Gulf Stream at 25°N was unaltered, but there was an increase in the southward flowing surface waters and a corresponding decrease in the southward flowing North Atlantic Deep Water between 3000 and 5000 m in depth.

However, Bryden is reported (Kerr, 2006) as later finding that there were other large variations in flow, suggesting that the earlier reported slowing might in fact be part of the natural variability of the system (see also Bryden et al, 2006).

Any slowdown occurred despite the impact of aerosol-induced cooling, which acts to protect the overturning. The Cai et al (2006) and Delworth and Dixon (2006) studies suggest that without the 'protective' effect of aerosols the slowdown would be 10 per cent greater, indicating a future acceleration of slowdown as aerosols decrease.

Such changes have long been projected in climate models, but most models suggest that significant slowing or collapse of this heat transport system is not likely until well into the 21st or 22nd centuries (Kerr, 2005a), if at all. The slowdown in overturning could be related to observed significant freshening of the surface waters in the Arctic Ocean (Curry et al, 2003) due to increased precipitation

(Josey and Marsh, 2005), increased river inflow (Peterson et al, 2002; Labat et al, 2004), and recently increased ice-melt from Greenland and other glaciers (Rignot and Kanagaratnam, 2006; Swingedouw et al, 2006; Thomas et al, 2006).

Paleo-climatic records, and records over the last millennium (Lund et al, 2006) suggest that a tight linkage exists between the Atlantic Ocean circulation, temperatures in the North Atlantic region and the hydrologic cycle.

Discussion

The above lines of evidence (supported by well over 100 recent scientific papers), while not definitive and, in some cases controversial, suggest that the balance of evidence may be swinging toward more extreme global warming and sea-level rise outcomes. While some of the observations may be due merely to natural fluctuations, their conjunction and, in some cases, positive feedbacks (from permafrost melting, biomass changes, arctic sea ice retreat and melting of Greenland) are causes for concern. Some of the links between major elements of the climate system are shown in Figure 1.1. Several of these links indicate positive feedbacks. Overall, they illustrate the need to consider the whole system, not just its individual parts in isolation.

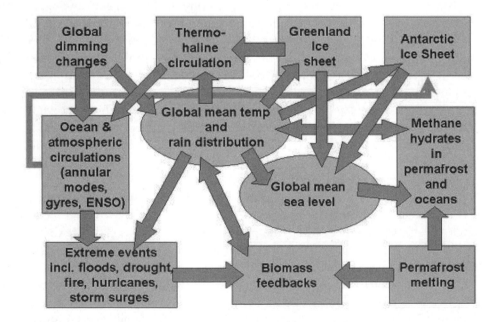

Figure 1.1 Links between parts of the climate system, including feedbacks that may accelerate climate change and its impacts

The observations and linkages suggest that critical levels of global warming may occur at even lower greenhouse gas concentrations and/or anthropogenic emissions than was considered justified in the IPCC (2001) report. The observed changes in Greenland and Antarctica suggest that a more rapid rise in sea level may be imminent, as has been observed in recent years (Church and White, 2006; Rahmstorf, 2007). Indeed, Rahmstorf et al (2007) find that emissions, global surface temperature and sea level rise are all increasing at rates at the very highest end of the IPCC range. Several of the points above suggest rapidly occurring regional impacts are imminent. Taken together, these recent developments increase the urgency of further improving climate models, and of taking action to reduce emissions in order to avoid the risk of unacceptable levels of climate change (see also National Research Council, 2002; Pittock, 2006; Schellnhuber et al, 2006; Steffen, 2006; *Time Magazine*, 2006).

A responsible risk management approach demands that scientists describe and warn about seemingly extreme or alarming possibilities, for any given scenario of human behavior (such as greenhouse gas emissions), if they have even a small probability of occurring. This is recognized in engineering design (for instance, for the safety of dams and bridges) and in military planning (where large resources are devoted to guarding against, and deterring, hopefully unlikely threats) and this practice is also commonplace in the insurance sector. The objective of policy-relevant advice must be to avoid unacceptable outcomes, not to determine the most likely outcome.

The recent developments discussed above might simply mean that the science is progressing. However, it also may suggest that up until now many scientists have consciously or unconsciously downplayed the more extreme possibilities at the high end of the uncertainty range in an attempt to appear moderate and 'responsible' (that is, to avoid scaring people). However, true responsibility requires providing evidence of what must be avoided: to define, quantify and warn against possible dangerous or unacceptable outcomes.

Notes

1.   This paper is an expansion of an article published in *EOS*, 'Are scientists underestimating climate change?', vol 87 (34, 22 August 2006) © American Geophysical Union.

References

Aldhous, P., 2004: Borneo is burning, *Nature*, **432**, 144–146
Alley, R. B., P. U. Clark, P. Huybrechts and I. Joughlin, 2005: Ice-sheet and sea-level changes, *Science*, **310**, 456–460

American Meteorological Society, 2006: Is global warming impacting, or expected to impact, hurricanes?, *Science Seminar Series*, October 20, 2006, see www.ametsoc.org/atmospolicy/environmentalsssarchives.html

Andreae, M. O., C. D. Jones and P. M. Cox, 2005: Strong present-day aerosol cooling implies a hot future, *Nature*, **435**, 1187–1190

Angert, A., S. Biraud, C. Bonfils, C. C. Henning, W. Buermann, J. Pinzon, C. J. Tucker, and I. Fung, 2005: Drier summers cancel out the CO_2 uptake enhancement induced by warmer springs, *Proc. Natl. Acad. Sci.*, **102**, 10,823–10,827

Annan, J. D. and J. C. Hargreaves, 2006: Using multiple observationally based constraints to estimate climate sensitivity, *Geophys. Res. Lett.*, **33**, L06704, doi:10.1029/2005 GL025259

Anthes, R. A., R. W. Corell, G. Holland, J. W. Hurrell, M. C. MacCracken and K. E. Trenberth, 2006: Hurricanes and global warming – Potential linkages and consequences, *Bull. Am. Meteorol. Soc.*, **87**, 623–628

Arctic Climate Impact Assessment, 2004: *Impacts of a Warming Arctic*, Cambridge University Press, New York (available at www.acia.uaf.edu)

Bellamy, P. H., P. J. Loveland, R. I. Bradley, R. M. Lark and G. J. D. Kirk, 2005: Carbon losses from all soils across England and Wales 1978–2003, *Nature*, **437**, 245–248

Bellouin, N., O. Boucher, J. Haywood and M. S. Reddy, 2005: Global estimate of aerosol direct radiative forcing from satellite measurements, *Nature*, **438**, 1138–1141

Bindschadler, R., 2006: Hitting the ice where it hurts, *Science*, **311**, 1720–1721

Bryden, H. L., H. R. Longworth and S. A. Cunningham, 2005: Slowing of the Atlantic meridional overturning circulation at 25°N, *Nature*, **438**, 655–657, doi:10.1038/nature04385

Bryden, H. L. et al, 2006: Variability in the Atlantic meridional overturning circulation at 25°N, see www.noc.soton.ac.uk/rapid/rapid2006/

Cai, W., 2006: Antarctic ozone depletion causes an intensification of the Southern Ocean supergyre circulation, *Geophys. Res. Lett.*, **33**, L03712, doi:10.1029/2005GL024911

Cai, W. and T. Cowan, 2007: Trends in Southern Hemisphere circulation in IPCC AR4 models over 1950–1999: Ozone-depletion vs. greenhouse forcing, *J. Clim.*, **20**, 681–693

Cai, W., D. Bi, J. Church, T. Cowan, M. Dix and L. D. Rotstayn, 2006: Pan-oceanic response to increasing anthropogenic aerosols: Impacts on the Southern Hemisphere oceanic circulation, *Geophys. Res. Lett.*, **33**, L21707, doi:10.1029/2006GL027513

Cai, W., G. Shi, T. Cowan, D. Bi and J. Ribbe, 2005: The response of the Southern Annular Mode, the East Australian Current, and the southern midlatitude ocean circulation to global warming, *Geophys. Res. Lett.*, **32**, L23706, doi:10.1029/2005GL024701

Cai, W., P. H. Whetton and D. J. Karoly, 2003: The response of the Antarctic Oscillation to increasing and stabilized atmospheric CO_2, *J. Clim.*, **16**, 1525–1538

Canadell, J. G., D. E. Pataki, R. Gifford, R. A. Houghton, Y. Luo, M. R. Raupach, P. Smith and W. Steffen, 2007: Saturation of the terrestrial carbon sink, in Canadell, J. G., D. Pataki and L. Pitelka (eds) *Terrestrial Ecosystems in a Changing World*, Springer-Verlag, Berlin Heidelberg

Carril, A. F., C. G. Menéndez, and A. Navarra, 2005: Climate response associated with the Southern Annular Mode in the surroundings of Antarctic Peninsula: A multimodel ensemble analysis, *Geophys. Res. Lett.*, **32**, L16713, doi:10.1029/2005GL023581

Chapin, F. S., III, M. Sturm, M. C. Serreze, J. P. McFadden, J. R. Key, A. H. Lloyd, A. D. McGuire, T. S. Rupp, A. H. Lynch, J. P. Schimel, J. Beringer, W. L. Chapman, H. E. Epstein, E. S. Euskirchen, L. D. Hinzman, G. Jia, C.-L. Ping, K. D. Tape, C. D. C. Thompson, D. A. Walker and J. M. Welker, 2005: Role of land-surface changes in Arctic summer warming, *Science*, **310**, 657–660

Church, J. A. and N. J. White, 2006: A twentieth-century acceleration in global sea level rise, *Geophys. Res. Lett.*, **33**, L01602, doi:10.1029/2005GL024826

Ciais, P. et al, 2005: Europe-wide reduction in primary productivity caused by the heat and drought in 2003, *Nature*, **437**, 529–533

Comiso, J. C., 2006: Arctic warming signals from satellite observations, *Weather*, **61**, 70–76

Comiso, J. C. and C. L. Parkinson, 2004: Satellite-observed changes in the Arctic, *Phys. Today*, Aug. 38–44

Cook, A. J., A. J. Fox, D. G. Vaughan and J. G. Ferrigno, 2005: Retreating glacier fronts on the Antarctic Peninsula over the past half-century, *Science*, **308**, 541–547

Curran, M. A. J., T. D. van Ommen, V. I. Morgan, K. L. Phillips and A. S. Palmer, 2004: Ice core evidence for 20% decline in Antarctic sea ice extent since the 1950s, *Science*, **302**, 1203–1206

Curry, R., B. Dickson and I. Yashayaev, 2003: A change in the freshwater balance of the Atlantic Ocean over the past four decades, *Nature*, **426**, 826–829

Delworth, T. L. and K. W. Dixon, 2006: Have anthropogenic aerosols delayed a greenhouse gas-induced weakening of the North Atlantic thermohaline circulation? *Geophys. Res. Lett.*, **33**, L02606, doi:10.1029/2005GL024980

Delworth, T. L., V. Ramaswamy and G. L. Stenchikov, 2005: The impacts of aerosols on simulated ocean temperature and heat content in the twentieth century, *Geophys. Res. Lett.*, **32**, L24709, doi:10.1029/2005GL024457

Dowdeswell, J. A., 2006: The Greenland Ice Sheet and global sea-level rise, *Science*, **311**, 963–964

Dupont, T. K. and R. B. Alley, 2006: Role of small ice shelves in sea-level rise, *Geophys. Res. Lett.*, **33**, L09503, doi:10.1029/2005GL025665

Emanuel, K., 2005a: Increasing destructiveness of tropical cyclones over the past 30 years, *Nature*, **436**, 686–688

Emanuel, K., 2005b: Emanuel replies, *Nature*, **438**, doi:10.1038/nature04427

Fischetti, M., 2001: Drowning New Orleans, *Scientific American*, October, 68–77

Foley, J. A., 2005: Tipping points in the tundra, *Science*, **310**, 627–628

Forster, P. M. D. and J. M. Gregory, 2006: The climate sensitivity and its components diagnosed from Earth radiation budget data, *J. Clim.*, **19**, 39–52

Fountain, A. G., R. W. Jacobel, R. Schlechting and P. Janssen, 2005: Fractures as the main pathways of water flow in temperate glaciers, *Nature*, **433**, 618–621

Francey, R. J., 2005: Recent record growth in atmospheric CO_2 levels, *Environ. Chem.*, **2**, 3–5

Friedlingstein, P., L. Bopp, P. Ciais, J.-L. Dufresne, L. Fairhead, H. LeTreut, P. Monfray and J. Orr, 2001: Positive feedback between future climate change and the carbon cycle, *Geophys. Res. Lett.*, **28**, 1543–1546

Fyfe, J. C., 2003: Extratropical Southern Hemisphere cyclones: Harbingers of climate change? *J. Clim.*, **16**, 2802–2805

Fyfe, J. C. and O. A. Saenko, 2006: Simulated changes in the extratropical Southern Hemisphere winds and currents, *Geophys. Res. Lett.*, **33**, L06701, doi:10.1029/2005GL025332

Gillett, N. P., 2005: Northern Hemisphere circulation, *Nature*, **437**, 496

Gillett, N. P., F. W. Zwiers, A. J. Weaver and P. A. Scott, 2003: Detection of human influence on sea-level pressure, *Nature*, **422**, 292–294

Goosse, H. and H. Renssen, 2001: A two-phase response of the Southern Ocean to an increase in greenhouse gas concentrations, *Geophys. Res. Lett.*, **28**, 3469–3472

Gray, L., I. Joughin, S. Tulaczyk, V. B. Spikes, R. Bindschadler and K. Jezek, 2005: Evidence for subglacial water transport in the West Antarctic Ice Sheet through three-dimensional satellite radar interferometry, *Geophys. Res. Lett.*, **32**, L03501, doi:10.1029/2004GL021387

Gregory, J. M., P. A. Stott, D. J. Cresswell, N. A. Rayner, C. Gordon and D. M. H. Sexton, 2002: Recent and future changes in Arctic sea ice simulated by the HadCM3 AOGCM, *Geophys. Res. Lett.*, **29**(24), 2175, doi:10.1029/2001GL014575

Greve, R., 2000: On the response of the Greenland Ice Sheet to greenhouse climate change, *Clim. Change*, **46**, 289–303

Gruber, N., P. Friedlingstein, C. B. Field, R. Valentini, M. Heimann, J. F. Richey, P. Romero, E.-D. Schulze and A. Chen, 2004: The vulnerability of the carbon cycle in the 21st century: An assessment of carbon-climate-human interactions, in C. B. Field and M. Raupach (eds) *Global Carbon Cycle: Integrating Human, Climate, and the Natural World*, Island Press, Washington DC

Hansen, J., 2005: A slippery slope: How much global warming constitutes 'dangerous anthropogenic interference'?, *Climate Change*, **68**, 269–279

Heath, J., E. Ayres, M. Possell, R. D. Bardgett, H. I. J. Black, H. Grant, P. Ineson and G. Kerstiens, 2005: Rising atmospheric CO_2 reduces sequestration of root-derived soil carbon, *Science*, **309**, 1711–1713

Hegerl, G. C., T. J. Crowley, W. T. Hyde and D. J. Frame, 2006: Climate sensitivity constrained by temperature reconstructions over the past seven centuries, *Nature*, **440**, 1029–1032

Hinzman, L. D. et al, 2005: Evidence and implications of recent climate change in northern Alaska and other Arctic regions, *Climate Change*, **72**, 251–298

Hodgson, D. A., M. J. Bentley, S. J. Roberts, J. A. Smith, D. E. Sugden and E. W. Domak, 2006: Examining Holocene stability of Antarctic Peninsula ice shelves. *EOS*, **87**(31), 305 and 308

Hoyos, C. D., P. A. Agudelo, P. J. Webster and J. A. Curry, 2006: Deconvolution of the factors contributing to the increase in global hurricane intensity, *Science*, **312**, 94–97

Huybrechts, P. and J. de Wolde, 1999: The dynamic response of the Greenland and Antarctic Ice Sheets to multiple-century climatic warming, *J. of Climate*, **12**, 2169–2188

IPCC (Intergovernmental Panel on Climate Change), 2001: *Climate Change 2001: Synthesis Report – Contribution of Working Groups I, II and III to the IPCC Third Assessment Report*, Cambridge University Press, New York (available at www.ipcc.ch)

Jones, R. A., 2004: Incorporating agency into climate change risk assessment, *Climate Change*, **67**, 13–36

Josey, S. A. and R. Marsh, 2005: Surface freshwater flux variability and recent freshening of the North Atlantic in the eastern subpolar gyre, *J. Geophys. Res.*, **110**, C05008, doi:10.1029/2004JC002521

Kerr, R. A., 2005a: Confronting the bogeyman of the climate system, *Science*, **310**, 432–433

Kerr, R. A., 2005b: Is Katrina a harbinger of still more powerful hurricanes? *Science*, **309**, 1807

Kerr, R. A., 2006: A worrying trend of less ice, higher seas, *Science*, **311**, 1698–1701

Kilronomos, J. N., M. F. Allen, M. C. Rillig, J. Plotrowski, S. Makvandi-Nejad, B. E. Wolfe and J. R. Powell, 2005: Abrupt rise in atmospheric CO_2 overestimates community response in a model plant-soil system, *Nature*, **433**, 621–624

Klotzbach, P. J., 2006: Trends in global tropical cyclone activity over the past 20 years (1986–2005), *Geophys. Res. Lett.*, **33**, L10805, doi:10.1029/2006GL025881

Knutson, T. R. and R. E. Tuleya, 2004: Impact of CO_2-induced warming on simulated hurricane intensity and precipitation: Sensitivity to the choice of climate model and convective parameterization, *J. Clim.*, **17**, 3477–3495

Krinner, G., O. Magand, I. Simmonds, C. Genthon and J. L. Dufresne, 2007: Simulated Antarctic precipitation and surface mass balance at the end of the twentieth and twenty-first centuries, *Climate Dynamics*, **28**, 215–230

Labat, D., Y. Godderis, J. L. Probst and J. L. Guyot, 2004: Evidence for global runoff increase related to global warming, *Adv. Water Resour.*, **27**, 631–642

Landsea, C. W., 2005: Hurricanes and global warming, *Nature*, **438**, E11–E12, doi:10.1038/nature04477

Langenfelds, R. L., R. J. Francey, B. C. Pak, L. P. Steele, J. Lloyd, C. M. Trudinger and C. E. Allison, 2002: Interannual growth rate variations of atmospheric CO_2 and its $\delta^{13}C$, H_2, CH_4, and CO between 1992 and 1999 linked to biomass burning, *Global Biogeochem. Cycles*, **16**(3), 1048, doi:10.1029/2001GB001466

Langmann, B. and A. Heil, 2004: Release and dispersion of vegetation and peat fire emissions in the atmosphere over Indonesia 1997-1998, *Atmos. Chem. Phys.*, **4**, 2145–2160

Lawrence, D. M. and A. G. Slater, 2005: A projection of severe near-surface permafrost degradation during the 21st century, *Geophys. Res. Lett.*, **32**, L24401, doi:10.1029/2005GL025080

Levi, B. G., 2006: Is there a slowing in the Atlantic Ocean's overturning circulation?, *Physics Today*, April, 26–28

Lindsay, R. W. and J. Zhang, 2005: The thinning of Arctic sea ice, 1988–2003: Have we passed the tipping point?, *J. Clim.*, **18**, 4879–4894

Lund, D. C., J. Lynch-Stiegler and W. B. Curry, 2006: Gulf Stream density structure and transport during the past millennium, *Nature*, **444**, 601–604

Marshall, G. J., 2003: Trends in the Southern Annular Mode from observations and reanalysis, *J. Clim.*, **16**, 4134–4143

Marshall, G. J., A. Orr, N. P. M. van Lipzig and J. C. King, 2006: The impact of a changing Southern Hemisphere Annular Mode on Antarctic Peninsula summer temperatures, *J. Clim.*, **19**, 5388–5404

Matthews, H. D., A. J. Weaver and K. J. Meissner, 2005: Terrestrial carbon cycle under recent and future climate change, *J. Clim.*, **18**, 1609–1628

Monaghan, A. J., D. H. Bromwich, R. L. Fogt, S.-H. Wang, P. A. Mayewski, D. A. Dixon, A. Ekaykin, M. Frezzoti, I. Goodwin, E. Isaksson, S. D. Kaspari, V. I. Morgan, H. Oerter, T. D. Van Ommen, C. J. Van der Veen and J. Wen, 2006: Insignificant change in Antarctic snowfall since the International Geophysical Year, *Science*, **313**, 827–831

Murphy, J. M., D. M. H. Sexton, D. N. Barnett, G. S. Jones, M. J. Webb, M. Collins and D. A. Stainforth, 2004: Quantification of modelling uncertainties in a large ensemble of climate change simulations, *Nature*, **430**, 768–772

NASA, 2003: Vanishing ice, features, 7 May (available at: http://earthobservatory.nasa. gov/Study/vanishing/)

NASA, 2005: Satellites continue to see decline in Arctic sea ice in 2005, news release, 28 September (available at http://nasa.gov/centers/goddard/news)

NASA, 2006: Greenland ice loss doubles in past decade, raising sea level faster, news release, 16 February (available at http://earthobservatory.nasa.gov/Newsroom/NasaN ews/2006/2006021621775.html)

National Research Council, 2002: *Abrupt Climate Change: Inevitable Surprises*, Washington DC (available at http://newton.nap.edu/books/)

NSIDC (National Snow and Ice Data Center), 2005: Sea ice decline intensities, National Snow and Ice Data Center, news release, Boulder, CO, 28 September (available at http://nsidc.org/news/press/20060404-winterrecovery.html)

NSIDC, 2006: Winter sea ice fails to recover, down to record low, National Snow and Ice Data Center, news release, Boulder, CO, 5 April (available at http://nsidc.org/news/ press/20060404-winterrecovery.html)

Nelson, F. E., 2003: (Un)frozen in time, *Science*, **299**, 1673–1675

Otto-Bliesner, S. J., S. J. Marshall, J. T. Overpeck, G. H. Miller, A. Hu and CAPE Last Interglacial Project members, 2006: Simulating Arctic climate warmth and icefield retreat in the last interglacial, *Science*, **311**, 1751–1753

Overland, J. E., 2006: Arctic change: multiple observations and recent understanding, *Weather*, **61**, 78–83

Overpeck, J. T., S. J. Otto-Bliesner, G. H. Miller, D. R. Muhs, R. B. Alley and J. T. Kiehl, 2006: Paleoclimatic evidence for future ice-sheet instability and rapid sea-level rise, *Science*, **311**, 1747–1750

Page, S. E., F. Siegert, J. O. Rieley, H.-D. V. Boehm, A. Jaya and S. Limin, 2002: The amount of carbon released from peat and forest fires in Indonesia during 1997, *Nature*, **420**, 61–65

Peterson, B. J., R. M. Holmes, J. W. McClelland, C. J. Vorosmarty, R. B. Lammers, A. I. Shiklomanov, I. A. Shiklomanov and S. Rahmstorf, 2002: Increasing river discharge to the Arctic Ocean, *Science*, **298**, 2171–2173

Pezza, A. B. and I. Simmonds, 2005: The first South Atlantic hurricane: Unprecedented blocking, low shear and climate change, *Geophys. Res. Lett.*, **32**, L15712, doi:10.1029/ 2005GL023390

Piani, C., D. J. Frame, D. A. Stainforth and M. R. Allen, 2005: Constraints on climate change from a multi-thousand member ensemble of simulations, *Geophys. Res. Lett.*, **32**, L23825, doi:10.1029/2005GL024452

Pielke, R. A., Jr, 2005: Are there trends in hurricane destruction?, *Nature*, **438**, doi:10.1038/nature04426

Pielke, R. A., Jr, C. Landsea, M. Mayfield, J. Laver and R. Pasch, 2005: Hurricanes and global warming, *Bull. Am. Meteorol. Soc.*, **86**, 1571–1575

Pinker, R. T., B. Zhang and E. G. Dutton, 2005: Do satellites detect trends in surface solar radiation?, *Science*, **308**, 850–854

Pittock, A. B., 2003: *Climate Change: An Australian Guide to the Science and Potential Impacts*, Australian Greenhouse Office, Canberra, see www.greenhouse.gov.au/science/pubs/science-guide.pdf

Pittock, A. B., 2005: *Climate Change: Turning Up the Heat*, Commonwealth Scientific and Industrial Research Organisation, Melbourne, Victoria (available at http://publish.csiro.au/pid/4992.htm)

Pittock, A. B., 2006: Are scientists underestimating climate change?, *EOS*, **87**(34), 22 August

Quadfasel, D., 2005: The Atlantic heat conveyor slows, *Nature*, **438**, 565–566

Rahmstorf, S., (2007), A semi-empirical approach to projecting future sea-level rise, *Science*, **315**, 368-370

Rahmstorf, S., A. Cazenave, J. A. Church, J. E. Hansen, R. F. Keeling, D. E. Parker, and R. C. J. Somerville, 2007: Recent Climate Observations Compared to Projections, *Science*, **316**, 709

Randerson, J. T. et al, 2006: The impacts of boreal forest fire on climate warming, *Science*, **314**, 1130–1132

Raupach, M., P. Briggs, E. King, M. Schmidt, M. Paget, J. Lovell and P. Canadell, 2006: Impacts of decadal climate trends on Australian vegetation, paper presented at the Earth Observation Symposium, Commonwealth Scientific and Industrial Research Organisation, Canberra, 15–16 February

Ridley, J. K., P. Huybrechts, J. M. Gregory and J. A. Lowe, 2005: Elimination of the Greenland Ice Sheet in a high CO_2 climate, *J. Clim.*, **18**, 3409–3427

Rignot, E. and P. Kanagaratnam, 2006: Changes in the velocity structure of the Greenland Ice Sheet, *Science*, **311**, 986–990

Rignot, E., G. Casassa, P. Gogineni, W. Krabill, A. Rivera and R. Thomas, 2004: Accelerated ice discharge from the Antarctic Peninsula following the collapse of Larsen B ice shelf, *Geophys. Res. Lett.*, **31**, L18401, doi:10.1029/2004GL020697

Rotstayn, L. D., W. Cai, M. R. Dix, G. D. Farquhar, Y. Feng, P. Ginoux, M. Herzog, A. Ito, J. E. Penner, M. L. Roderick and M. Wang, 2006: Have Australian rainfall and cloudiness increased due to remote effects of Asian anthropogenic aerosols? *J. Geophys. Res.*, **112**, D09202, doi:10.129/2006JD007712

Scambos, T. A., C. Hulbe, M. Fahnestock and J. Bohlander, 2000: The link between climate warming and break-up of ice shelves in the Antarctic Peninsula, *J. Glaciol.*, **46**, 516–530

Scheffer, M., V. Brovkin and P. M. Cox, 2006: Positive feedback between global warming and atmospheric CO_2 concentration inferred from past climate change, *Geophys. Res. Lett.*, **33**, L10702, doi:10.1029/2005GL025044

Schellnhuber, H. J., W. Cramer, N. Nakicenovic, T. Wigley and G. Yohe (eds), 2006: *Avoiding Dangerous Climate Change*, Cambridge University Press, New York (available at www.defra.gov.uk/environment/climatechange/internat/dangerous-cc.htm)

Schiermeier, Q., 2006: A sea change, *Nature*, **439**, 256–260

Schneider, S. H., 2001: Can we estimate the likelihood of climatic changes at 2100?, *Nature*, **411**, 17–19

Schrope, M., 2005: Winds of change, *Nature*, **438**, 21–22

Serreze, M. C. and J. A. Francis, 2006: The Arctic on the fast track of change, *Weather*, **61**, 65–69

Stainforth, D. A., T. Aina, C. Christensen, M. Collins, N. Faull, D. J. Frame, J. A. Kettleborough, S. Knight, A. Martin, J. M. Murphy, C. Piani, D. Sexton, L. A. Smith, R. A. Spicer, A. J. Thorpe and M. R. Allen, 2005: Uncertainty in predictions of the climate response to rising levels of greenhouse gases, *Nature*, **433**, 403–406

Steffen, W., 2006: *Stronger Evidence But New Challenges: Climate Change Science 2001–2005*, Dep. of Environ. and Heritage, Aust. Greenhouse Off., Canberra (available at http://greenhouse.gov.au)

Stott, P. A., D. A. Stone and M. R. Allen, 2004: Human contribution to the European heat wave of 2003, *Nature*, **432**, 610–614

Stroeve, J. C., M. C. Serreze, F. Fetterer, T. Arbetter, W. Meier, J. Maslanik and K. Knowles, 2005: Tracking the Arctic's shrinking ice cover: Another extreme September minimum in 2004, *Geophys. Res. Lett.*, **32**, L04501, doi:10.1029/2004GL021810

Swingedouw, D., P. Braconnot and O. Marti, 2006: Sensitivity of the Atlantic meridional overturning circulation to the melting from northern glaciers in climate change experiments, *Geophys. Res. Lett.*, **33**, L07711, doi:10.2029/2006GL025765

Thomas, R., E. Rignot, G. Casassa, P. Kanagaratnam, C. Acuna, T. Atkins, H. Brecher, E. Frederick, P. Gogineni, W. Krabill, S. Manizade, H. Ramamoorthy, A. Rivera, R. Russell, J. Sonntag, R. Swift, J. Yungel and J. Zwally, 2004: Accelerated sea-level rise from West Antarctica, *Science*, **306**, 255–258

Thomas, R., E. Frederick, W. Krabill, S. Manizade and C. Martin, 2006: Progressive increase in ice loss from Greenland, *Geophys. Res. Lett.*, **33**, L10503, doi:10.1029/2006GL026075

Time Magazine, 2006: Special report: Global warming, 3 April

Torn, M. S. and J. Harte, 2006: Missing feedbacks, asymmetric uncertainties, and the underestimation of future warming, *Geophys. Res. Lett.*, **33**, L10703, doi:10.1029/2005GL025540

Trenberth, K., 2005: Uncertainty in hurricanes and global warming, *Science*, **308**, 1753–1754

Turner, J., T. A. Lachlan-Cope, S. Colwell, G. J. Marshall and W. M. Connolley, 2006: Significant warming of the Antarctic winter troposphere, *Science*, **311**, 1914–1917

van den Broeke, M., N. van Lipzig and G. Marshall, 2004: On Antarctic climate and change, *Weather*, **59**, 3–7

Velicogna, I. and J. Wahr, 2006: Measurements of time-variable gravity show mass loss in Antarctica, *Science*, **311**, 1754–1756

Walker, G., 2006: The tipping point of the iceberg, *Nature*, **441**, 802–805

Walsh, K. J. E., K.-C. Nguyen and J. L. McGregor, 2004: Fine-resolution regional scale model simulations of the impact of climate change on tropical cyclones near Australia, *Clim. Dyn.*, **22**, 47–56

Wang, S., A. P. Trishchenko, K. V. Khlopenkov and A. Davidson, 2006: Comparison of International (sic) Panel on Climate Change Fourth Assessment Report climate model simulations of surface albedo with satellite products over northern latitudes, *J. Geophys. Res*, **111**, D21108, doi:10.1029/2005JD006728

Webster, P. J., G. J. Holland, J. A. Curry and H.-R. Chang, 2005: Changes in tropical cyclone number, duration, and intensity in a warming environment, *Science*, **309**, 1844–1846

Westerling, A. L., H. G. Hidalgo, D. R. Cayan and T. W. Swetnam, 2006: Warming and earlier spring increases western U.S. forest wildfire activity, *Science*, **313**, 940–943

Wild, M., H. Gilgen, A. Roesch, A. Ohmura, C. N. Long, E. G. Dutton, B. Forgan, A. Kallis, V. Russak and A. Tsvetkov, 2005: From dimming to brightening: Decadal changes in solar radiation at Earth's surface, *Science*, **308**, 847–850

Witze, A., 2006: Bad weather ahead, *Nature*, **441**, 564–566

Zwally, H. J., M. B. Giovinetto, J. Li, H. G. Cornejo, M. A. Beckley, A. C. Brenner, J. L. Saba and D. Yi, 2005: Mass changes of the Greenland and Antarctic ice sheets and shelves and contributions to sea-level rise 1992–2002, *J. Glaciol.*, **51**, 509–527

2

Potential Increased Hurricane Activity in a Greenhouse Warmed World

Judith A. Curry

The prospect of increased hurricane intensity in a greenhouse warmed world is arguably the greatest short-term risk from greenhouse warming. With observations of increased hurricane activity emerging, the risk appears to be increasing even more rapidly than has been expected based on the initial studies.

That the situation was more serious than had been thought became clear during 2005, both because of the record-breaking North Atlantic hurricane season and because of papers published by Emanuel (2005) and Webster et al (2005) that demonstrated an increase in hurricane intensity that has been associated with an increase in tropical sea surface temperature. Webster et al (2005) examined global hurricane activity since 1970 (the advent of reliable satellite data). The most striking finding from their study was that while the total number of hurricanes has not increased globally, the number and percentage of category 4–5 hurricanes has nearly doubled since 1970 (see Figure 1).

Scientists are debating the quality of the data upon which these analyses are based. The most reliable data are on tropical cyclones in the North Atlantic. The HURDAT data prepared by the National Hurricane Center go back to 1851. Prior to 1944, only surface-based data were available (for example, land-falling storms and ship observations). Since 1944, aircraft reconnaissance flights have been made into nearly all of the North Atlantic tropical cyclones. Since 1970, satellite observations have made observing and monitoring tropical cyclones more accurate.

Figure 2.2 shows the time series in the North Atlantic of the numbers of named storms (tropical cyclones), hurricanes and category 4–5 hurricanes (NCAT45; NCAT45 is not shown prior to 1944 owing to concerns about data accuracy). To highlight the decadal and longer-term variability, the data have been smoothed (11-year running mean) to eliminate the year-to-year variability. A nominal 70-year cycle is evident, with peaks in about 1880 and 1950, and minima in about

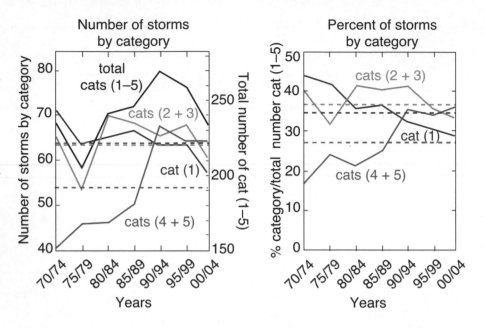

Figure 2.1 Intensity of global hurricanes according to the Saffir-Simpson scale (categories from 1 to 5, or least to most intense), in 5-year periods, showing the total number of storms (left) and percentage of total number of hurricanes in each category class (right)

Source: After Webster et al, 2005.

1915 and 1985. However, the most striking aspects of the time series are the overall increasing trend since 1970 and the high level of activity since 1995.

Linkage to increased tropical sea surface temperature

The increase in global hurricane intensity since 1970 has been associated directly with a global increase in tropical sea surface temperature (Emanuel, 2005; Webster et al, 2005; Hoyos et al, 2006). Figure 2.3 shows the variation of tropical sea surface temperature (SST) in each of the ocean regions where tropical cyclone storms form. In each of these regions, SST has increased by approximately 0.5°C (or 1°F) since 1970. The causal link between SST and hurricane intensity was established over 50 years ago, when it was observed that tropical cyclones do not form unless the underlying SST exceeds 26.5°C and that warm SSTs are needed to supply the energy to support development of hurricane winds. The role of SST in determining hurricane intensity is now generally understood and is supported by case studies of individual storms and by the theory of potential intensity.

   While globally the number of tropical cyclones has not increased (Figure 2.1), there has been an increase in the number of tropical cyclones in the North

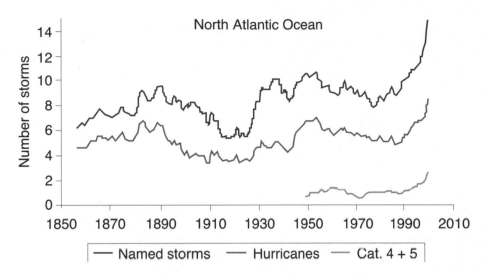

Figure 2.2 Number of total named storms, hurricanes and category 4–5 storms since 1851, filtered by an 11 year running mean

Note: Based on data obtainable from www.aoml.noaa.gov/hrd/hurdat/. Intensity of major hurricanes prior to 1970 is adjusted following Landsea.
Source: Courtesy of J. Belanger.

Atlantic. Figure 2.4 shows the time series of total named storms and the average SST in the main development region of the North Atlantic. Comparison of the two time series shows coherent variations of the number of storms and the SST for periods greater than 20 years. In particular, the period 1910–1920 with low storm activity is associated with anomalously cool SSTs.

Attribution of the increased hurricane activity

The data show that the tropical SST increase is global in nature and occurs consistently in each of the ocean basins (Figure 2.3). The surface temperature trends over the last century have been extensively studied, as summarized in the Third Assessment Report of the IPCC (IPCC, 2001). Detection-attribution studies comparing observations with climate model simulations clearly indicate that the global surface temperature trend since 1970 (including the trend in tropical SSTs) cannot be reproduced in climate models without inclusion of the effects of anthropogenic greenhouse gases. The climate model simulations are the basis for attributing the increase in tropical SSTs to anthropogenic greenhouse warming.

A number of natural internal oscillations of the atmosphere/ocean system have been found to have a large impact on SST (for example, El Niño, North

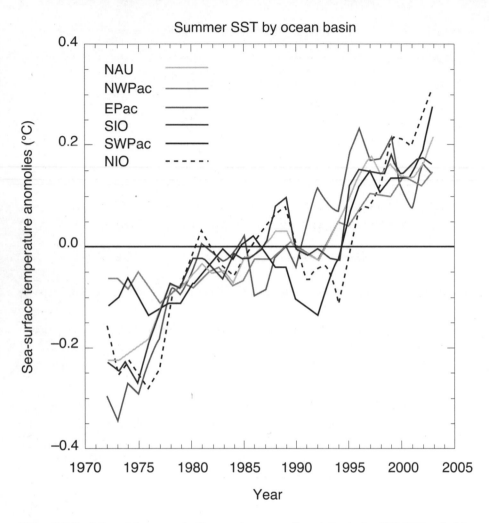

Figure 2.3 Evolution of the sea surface temperature anomalies relative to the 1970–2004 period for the North Atlantic, Western Pacific, East Pacific, South Indian Ocean, Southwest Pacific and North Indian Ocean Basins

Source: Curry et al, 2006.

Atlantic Oscillation), and some scientists have argued that the increase in tropical cyclone intensity since 1970 can be explained by such natural variability. However, decadal-scale oscillations tend to be specific to each ocean basin and are often anti-correlated from one basin to another. In particular, there have been repeated assertions from the National Hurricane Center that the recent elevated hurricane activity is associated with natural variability, particularly the Atlantic Multidecadal Oscillation (AMO). Figures 2.2 and 2,4 suggest that natural modes of multidecadal variability, notably the AMO (~70 year cycle), do have an influence on North Atlantic hurricane activity. However, recent examination of the data by Mann and Emanuel (2006) suggests that the impact of the AMO on tropical SST and hurricane activity has been overestimated owing to the convolution of the AMO with the temperature changes resulting from global forcing (natural plus anthropogenic). They found that analyses that rely solely on SST to identify the AMO might have aliased the phase and amplitude of the AMO signal. If the AMO analyses are correct, the next peak of the AMO is anticipated in about 2020. The strength of the tropical cyclone activity during the period 1995–2005 (50 per cent greater than the previous peak period in about 1950; see Figure 2.2), which is at least a decade before the expected peak of the current AMO cycle, suggests that the AMO alone cannot explain the elevated tropical cyclone activity observed in the North Atlantic over the last decade.

What can we conclude from the above analysis regarding the global increase in hurricane intensity and the increase in the North Atlantic of the total number of tropical cyclones? The arguments that natural variability can explain the increase run counter to the known range of natural variability in the past record and the absence of a natural mechanism that would explain the global increase in both oceanic temperatures and the frequency of intense hurricanes. The best available evidence instead supports the hypothesis that greenhouse warming is contributing to the increase in hurricane activity, although the evidence is not yet conclusive.

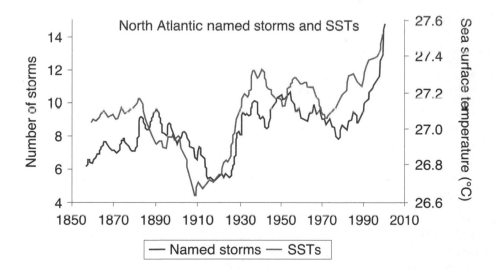

Figure 2.4 Number of total named storms in the North Atlantic and the average sea surface temperature in the main development region, filtered by an 11-year running mean

Note: Data obtained from www.aoml.noaa.gov/hrd/hurdat/
Source: Courtesy of J. Belanger.

The primary issue is whether the magnitude of the observed increase in hurricane intensity is as large as that observed by Webster et al (2005) and Emanuel (2005), given concerns about the quality of the data. As previously stated, a reanalysis of the global hurricane data set is needed to create a robust and homogeneous climate data record. Current efforts to use very high resolution coupled climate models to examine the impact of global warming on hurricane characteristics can also be expected to shed new light on the subject once these models are capable of simulating realistic tropical cyclones.

Projections of future hurricane activity in the North Atlantic

While scientists that support the natural variability explanation and those that support the global warming contribution both predict that hurricane activity in the North Atlantic will remain elevated for some years, their projections for hurricane activity for the rest of the century are quite different. Analyses based on the hypothesis that natural variability has been the cause of the high level of hurricane activity in the North Atlantic since 1995 project a forthcoming downturn in hurricane activity. For example, the analysis by Goldenberg et al (2001) implies a downturn in 10–40 years, and Gray (2006) anticipates a downturn in 3–8 years associated with a global cooling that he predicts will also result from ongoing natural variability.

If our hypothesis is correct that greenhouse warming is causing an increase in hurricane intensity globally and also an increased number of storms in the North Atlantic, what does this imply for future hurricane activity as SSTs continue to rise as a result of greenhouse warming? The following analysis addresses specifically the projection of North Atlantic tropical cyclone activity. We develop a range of projections using two different approaches: climate model responses to the increasing concentrations of greenhouse gases, and linear projections based upon the historical data record. Our projections are for average conditions in the years around 2025 (such that high frequency fluctuations from short-term oscillations such as El Niño are ignored), corresponding to an increase in tropical SST of 1°F (0.56°C) that would result from greenhouse gas-induced warming.

The Webster et al (2005) observations scale to a 6 per cent increase in maximum wind speeds for a 1°F SST increase. By contrast, high-resolution climate model simulations (Knutson and Tuleya, 2004; Oouchi et al, 2006) have found a 2 per cent increase in intensity when scaled for a 1°F SST increase, which is a factor of three smaller than that determined from the observations. Oouchi et al (2006) also found that the number of North Atlantic tropical cyclones increased by 30 per cent for a 4.5°F (2.5°C) increase in SST, which scales to an increase of one tropical cyclone per 1°F increase in SST. By contrast, based upon the historical data record in the North Atlantic (see Figure 2.4), an increase of 1°F in tropical SST implies an additional five tropical storms per season, which is a factor of five greater than the number inferred from climate model simulations.

Projections of future changes in hurricane variability must include both natural variability and greenhouse warming. Estimates of the magnitude of the impact of the AMO on the total number of tropical cyclones per year range from zero (no effect) to four to six (the AMO explains the entire magnitude of the trough to peak variability in Figure 2.1). Assuming that the AMO continues with a 70-year periodicity, the peak of the next cycle would be expected in 2020 (70 years after the previous 1950 peak). So, 2025 would be very near the peak of the AMO cycle. Proponents of the natural variability explanation refer to active and quiet phases rather than actual cyclic behavior; their analyses indicate that we are currently in an active phase that will last another 10 to 40 years, and that the level of activity in 2025 will be similar to the activity of the past decade.

Based upon these assumptions, consider the following simple statistical model. The average annual number of North Atlantic tropical cyclones for the past decade has been 14.4. Assuming that the effects of greenhouse warming and the AMO are separable and additive, Table 2.1 compares simple statistical projections based on the projected effects of both anthropogenic greenhouse warming (AGW) and AMO, of AGW only, and of AMO only. The range of projections given in Table 2.1 provides some broad constraints on the conceivable elevation of North Atlantic tropical cyclone activity in coming decades. The combination of AGW+AMO would result in the greatest elevation in the number of named storms, and an unprecedented level of tropical cyclone activity. The different assumptions lead to estimates of an increase of 0 to 6.5 named storms per year. In terms of the intensity of the storms, Figure 2.1 suggests that the distribution of storm intensity is changing with warming, such that the increase in the number of tropical storms is in the number of category 4–5 storms (NCAT45) rather than in the number of weaker hurricanes. Even if, as some suggest, the AMO begins its descending mode about 2020, continued warming makes it doubtful that we will ever again see the low levels of hurricane activity of the 1980s; instead, it seems

Table 2.1 *Projections for the average total number of North Atlantic tropical cyclones (named storms) for 2025*

Situation	AGW+AMO	AGW only	AMO only
Average last decade	14.4	14.4	14.4
Global warming increases SST 1°F	+1 to +5	+1 to +5	0
Continued increase of AMO	+1.5	0	0
Total	16.9 to 20.9	15.4 to 19.4	14.4

Note: AGW refers to anthropogenic greenhouse warming; AMO refers to Atlantic Multidecadal Oscillation.

likely that we can expect a leveling off rather than a significant decrease in activity until the next ascending phase of the AMO.

Impacts and policy responses

Hurricane-induced economic losses have increased steadily in the US over the past 50 years, with estimated total losses averaging US$35.8 billion per year during the last five years (see, for example, Pielke et al, 2005). The 2005 season was exceptionally destructive, with damages from Hurricane Katrina exceeding US$100 billion. During 2004 and 2005, nearly 2000 deaths were attributed to land-falling hurricanes in the US. Presently, 50 per cent of the US population lives within 50 miles of a coastline and the physical infrastructure along the Gulf and Atlantic coasts represents an investment of over US$3 trillion; over the next several decades this investment is expected to double. The combination of coastal demographics with the increased hurricane activity is therefore very likely to continue to escalate the socio-economic impact of hurricanes.

The risk of elevated hurricane activity arguably represents the most devastating near-term impact of global warming, particularly for the US, Caribbean and Central American regions that are impacted by North Atlantic hurricanes. How should policy makers and other decision makers react to the risk of elevated hurricane activity associated with global warming in the face of the scientific uncertainties?

To address the short-term (decadal) impacts of elevated hurricane activity, decreasing our vulnerability to damage from hurricanes will require a comprehensive evaluation of coastal engineering, building construction practices, insurance, land use, emergency management and disaster relief policies. Any conceivable policy for reducing CO_2 emissions or sequestering CO_2 is unlikely to have a noticeable impact on sea surface temperatures and hurricane characteristics over the next few decades; rather, any such mitigation strategies would only have the potential to impact the longer-term effects of global warming. On the time scale of a century, sea level rise will compound the impact of increased hurricane activity by increasing vulnerability to storm surge. By 2100, a sea level rise of 0.3–0.6 m (or even more) is plausible. Hurricane prone regions in the US at greatest risk from storm surge enhancement associated with greenhouse warming include New Orleans, South Florida and portions of the mid-Atlantic coast.

Looking globally, Bangladesh is particularly vulnerable to the combination of increased hurricane intensity and sea level rise; several hundred million people live in the southern part of the country where the elevation is only a few feet above sea level, and three tropical cyclones during the 20th century each killed over 100,000 people. In Central America, there is substantial vulnerability associated with landslides, and the vulnerability is exacerbated by deforestation; Hurricane

Mitch in 1998 resulted in more than 75 inches of rain and catastrophic landslides that killed more than 11,000 people. The vulnerability of the developing world to increased hurricane activity and sea level rise raises not only the obvious humanitarian and economic issues, but also the potential for regional instabilities and international security concerns that could be associated with mass migrations of refugees.

References

Curry, J. A., P. J. Webster and G. J. Holland, 2006: Mixing politics and science in testing the hypothesis that greenhouse warming is causing a global increase in hurricane intensity, *Bull. Amer. Meteorol. Soc.*, in press

Emanuel, K., 2005: Increasing destructiveness of tropical cyclones over the past 30 years, *Nature*, **436**, 686–688

Goldenberg, S. B., C. W. Landsea, A. M. Mestas-Nuñez and W. M. Gray, 2001: The recent increase in Atlantic hurricane activity: Causes and implications, *Science*, **293**, 474–479

Gray, W. M., 2006: Global warming and hurricanes, 27th American Meteorological Society Conference on Tropical Meteorology, Monterey, CA, paper 4C.1, http://ams.confex.com/ams/pdfpapers/107533.pdf

Hoyos, C. D., P. A. Agudelo, P. J. Webster and J. A. Curry, 2006: Deconvolution of the factors contributing to the increase in global hurricane intensity, *Science*, **312**(5770), 94–97

IPCC (Intergovernmental Panel on Climate Change), 2001: *Climate Change 2001. The Scientific Basis*, J. T. Houghton, Y. Ding, D. J. Griggs, M. Noguer, P. J. van der Linden, X. Dai, K. Mansell and C. A. Johnson (eds), Cambridge University Press, New York and Cambridge (available at www.ipcc.ch)

Knutson, T. R. and R. E. Tuleya, 2004: Impact of CO_2-induced warming on simulated hurricane intensity and precipitation: Sensitivity to the choice of climate model and convective parameterization, *J. Clim.*, **17**, 3477–3495.31

Mann, M. E. and K. A. Emanuel, 2006: Atlantic hurricane trends linked to climate change, *EOS*, **87**, 233–244

Oouchi, K., J. Yoshimura, H. Yoshimura, R. Mizuta, S. Kusunoki and A. Noda, 2006: Tropical cyclone climatology in a global-warming climate as simulated in a 20 km-mesh global atmospheric model: Frequency and wind intensity analyses, *J. Meteorol. Soc. Japan*, **84**(2), 259

Pielke, R. A., Jr, C. Landsea, M. Mayfield, J. Laver and R. Pasch, 2005: Hurricanes and global warming, *Bull. Amer. Meteorol. Soc.*, **86**, 1571–1575

Webster, P. J., G. J. Holland, J. A. Curry and H.-R. Chang, 2005: Changes in tropical cyclone number, duration, and intensity in a warming environment, *Science*, **309**, 1844–1846

Chapter 3

Potential Effects of Weather Extremes and Climate Change on Human Health

Devra Lee Davis and John C. Topping, Jr

Projected extremes and variations in weather associated with long-term climate change pose a number of chronic and acute risks for human health. With sufficient advance warning and relatively gradual rates of change, public health systems, even in poorer developing countries, might adapt to such changes to limit their adverse impacts. Much of the evidence advanced by climate experts writing in this book suggests that the abruptness of climate change is likely to limit the effectiveness of any adaptation strategies. We may see an interplay of a variety of factors: significantly higher temperatures producing more frequent and prolonged heat waves along with associated deterioration of air quality; more extreme weather events (storms, floods and droughts); coastal inundation and salt water intrusion into fresh water supplies, water treatment plants, landfills and hazardous waste facilities; and increased ranges for the survival of pests and other disease vectors as a result of warmer winters and earlier onset of spring temperatures. Rapid rates of change will profoundly alter habitats, changing some forests to grasslands (with the pace of change often accelerated by wildfire), squeezing out many wetlands, and shifting distributions of flora and fauna. Projecting the impacts of such changes on human health and well-being remains somewhat speculative, however, there are a number of reasons to anticipate some rude surprises.

Climate change will lead to a wide diversity of direct and indirect effects on human health and well-being. These include: threats to food security; increased incidence of heat stress and air pollution; changes in the frequency and intensity of extreme events such as flooding, droughts and severe storms; changes in the incidence and magnitude of water and food-borne diseases; changes in the incidence and distribution of diseases borne by insects, rodents and other wildlife; and ripple effects of large-scale displacements of people and ecosystems projected as a result of extreme events and failures in food production. The implications of climate change are global, although this chapter focuses primarily on the public health implications of the current build-up of greenhouse gases for nation states in North America and the Caribbean.

Although there remains considerable uncertainty on the magnitude and specific regional distribution of impacts, some generalizations on the relationship between climate change and public health can be drawn with a modest degree of confidence. These findings, together with those reported by the IPCC and others, indicate that policies that will reduce greenhouse gas emissions in the long term can be expected to also have significant benefits for public health and the environment in the near term.

Impacts on nutrition and the food supply

The IPCC has tended to see the positive and negative effects of climate change on agricultural production, if the warming were to occur at a moderate pace, as close to even in terms of overall global food production, but with some regional variations that might harm local food security (IPCC, 2001). Generally, the areas of the globe most vulnerable to climate-related stress on food production are poorer countries in lower latitudes. Not only do these nations have limited capacity to adapt, but their food distribution systems, as we have seen in several of the African famines, are also poorly positioned to disseminate food aid, should it be sent. To date, the greatest human health disasters, on a par with global pandemics such as influenza, plagues or tuberculosis, have been famines.

A huge wild card in the climate equation is the possibility of increased meteorological volatility as the world warms. This would cause more intense precipitation at irregular intervals (meaning more floods and droughts) and would lead to a decrease in soil-moisture content for many agricultural regions, especially because there will be higher rates of evaporation due to the warmer temperatures. This, in turn, could lead to poor food security and increased political volatility. Thus, ethnic and tribal strife in Darfur have resulted, in part, from famines in the region that have created persistent conflicts over the region's sparse natural resources, killing or forcing from their homes many thousands of people.

Total world grain reserves amount to only enough to cover about 57 days of consumption (Brown, 2006). Increased spatial and temporal volatility of seasonal climate regimes could result in severely curtailed production in the same year in several food-exporting regions (for example, North America, Australia and Argentina). This would not only raise food prices worldwide but would also significantly raise the costs for rich nations to ship food to poorer nations that might be affected. The recent severe weather of 2006 caused significant losses in the agricultural bastions of California and the Midwest, underscoring the potential fragility of global food security.

Health impacts from heat stress and air pollution

Model projections clearly predict more frequent and more intense summertime heat waves, along with greater instability of weather patterns, much like the searing temperatures in the summer of 2006 in the US and Europe. Heat stress is likely to increase morbidity and mortality and lead to adverse impacts on food production. At the same time, adverse impacts from exposure to cold temperatures are likely to decline. Societies can adapt in ways that can limit significant damage to public health by, for example, increasing the availability of air conditioning (and providing funding for their use by the poor) and providing public facilities to shelter vulnerable populations. In Western Europe in 2003, over 30,000 people died from heat stress (Battacharya, 2003). The worst heat-related public health episode in the US in recent years occurred in Chicago in July 1995 when 485 people died over a 17-day period from heat stress, according to medical examiner reports (Donoghue et al, 2003). Yet deaths attributable to severe heat go well beyond numbers that a medical examiner will certify. Epidemiological evidence suggests that mortality and morbidity from cardiovascular and respiratory disease rises significantly during heat waves and that heat-related deaths from these causes are consistently underestimated.

Weather extremes tied to overall climate change will affect both mortality and morbidity, including hospital admissions and sick days away from work due to air pollution. We should also recognize that the combustion of fossil fuels, which generates greenhouse gases and contributes to climate warming, is also the principal source of air pollution. Even though the US has one of the most stringent sets of air pollution control regulations on the planet, it is estimated that at least 30,000 Americans die prematurely each year from exposure to air pollution, especially fine particulate matter (Ali et al, 2004). Control strategies to lower greenhouse gas emissions are likely to also produce lowered mortality from air pollution (Davis, 1997; Cifuentes, 2001). Conversely, without emission controls, the warming itself is likely to have several adverse effects. Although the situation will vary across air quality regions, warming will change and generally accelerate the photochemical reactions that produce ground-level ozone. This may produce increased mortality and other adverse health effects. It also may exact a large economic penalty, as many of the gains in ozone attainment won at great economic cost will be counteracted by an acceleration of ozone photochemistry. Another adverse effect that is likely to increase mortality and morbidity is an interaction between temperature stress and air pollution. Higher ozone levels and temperature stress may compound the risks for those with cardiovascular and respiratory disease.

Impacts on water and food-borne diseases

Climate-related effects on water and food-borne diseases are likely to be a much more significant factor in developing countries than in the US. The El-Niño Southern Oscillation (ENSO) cycle is already associated with large fluctuations in incidence of cholera in Peru (Pascual et al, 2000). Although climate change may affect the overall availability of water in the US, it does not seem likely to compromise the safety of drinking water. Higher temperatures may, however, heighten risk of salmonella in the US, and hotter, less-mixed estuaries may lead to more frequent contamination of fish and shellfish. Effects on food production and distribution and on water supply systems in the US are likely to have a much greater effect on cost than on human health. Exceptions to this generalization might occur as a result of major storm disasters such as Hurricane Katrina, when populations are ripped away from water and health infrastructure, and when heavy precipitation causes storm runoff to overload sewage treatment plants.

An increase in temperatures, especially winter temperatures that are typically low enough to kill off many pest populations, is expected to exacerbate the proliferation of pests such as insects and rodents. Climate warming, particularly if it occurs rapidly, is likely to change ecosystems, affecting predator–prey relationships and allowing some populations of disease-bearing pests to proliferate. The hanta virus outbreak in the southwestern US a few years ago, caused by an abnormally large rodent population, was a manifestation of this kind of risk. Warming and associated changes in water availability, evaporation, soil moisture and habitat may also change the areas in which diseases such as malaria, West Nile virus and dengue fever can thrive. While the US' public health infrastructure is sufficiently strong that these disease risks should be manageable, except when there have been massive disruptions such as in severe hurricanes or floods, Americans traveling overseas are likely to experience less adequate controls.

Health impacts resulting from international interconnections

Large-scale climatic disruptions in nearby nations such as Mexico or the Caribbean island nations may also have spillover effects on health systems in the US. This might occur in several ways: a rapid surge in illegal migration as people flee storm-ravaged or sun-parched regions to earn a living, or simply an outbreak of disease in fetid urban slums that spreads across borders. New immigrants, especially those who come to the US illegally, may have a higher incidence of some diseases such as tuberculosis that are rare today in the US. It is very hard to make projections of what these impacts are likely to be. Public health officials will, however, need to be on the lookout for a wider variety of diseases as climates change and the mobility of peoples and other disease-carriers increases.

Conclusion

A well-planned response to the risks to human health from large-scale climate change will have two dimensions. First, is slowing the rate of change in order to increase time for measured preparation. For this we depend on the wisdom and will of world leaders in laying out a policy framework and the innovation of industry in achieving a viable path to stabilizing the atmospheric concentration of greenhouse gases. Second, we in the public health community need to develop better monitoring systems to assess emerging risks that may increase as the climate warms. We should advise governments at all levels on how to minimize the chance of epidemics and small outbreaks, and other short-term impacts of weather extremes.

References

Ali, H. M., J. S. Marks, D. F. Stroup and J. L. Gerberding, 2004: Actual causes of death in the United States, *Journal of the American Medical Association*, **291**, 1238–1245

Battacharya, S., 2003: European heat-wave caused 35,000 deaths, *New Scientist.com*, 10 October, www.newscientist.com/article.ns?id=dn4259, accessed 26 March 2007

Brown, L., 2006: World grain stocks fall to 57 days of consumption: Grain prices starting to rise, *Energy Bulletin*, 15 June, www.energybulletin.net/17261.html, accessed 26 March 2007

Cifuentes, L., V. H. Borja-Aburto, N. Gouveia, G. Thurston and D. L. Davis, 2001: Hidden health benefits of greenhouse gas mitigation, *Science*, **293**, 1257–1259

Davis, D. L., T. Kjellstrom, R. Sloff, A. McGortland, D. Atkinson, W. Borbour, W. Hohenstein, P. Nagelhout, T. Woodruff, F. Divita, J. Wilson, L. Deck and J. Schwartz, 1997: Short-term improvements in public health from global-climate policies on fossil-fuel combustion: An interim report, *Lancet*, **350**, 1341–1349

Donoghue, E. R., J. T. Nelson, G. Rudis, J. T. Watson, G. Huhn and G. Luber, 2003: Heat-related deaths – Chicago, Illinois, 1996–2001, and United States, 1979–1999, *MMWR Weekly*, **52**, 610–613

IPCC, 2001: *Climate Change 2001: Impacts, Adaptation and Vulnerability*, J. J. McCarthy, O. F. Canziani, N. A. Leary, D. J. Dokken and K. S. White (eds) Cambridge University Press, New York and Cambridge

Pascual, M., X. Rodo, S. P. Ellner, R. Colwell and M. J. Bouma, 2000: Cholera dynamics and El Niño – Southern Oscillation, *Science Magazine*, **289**, 1766–1769

Part 2

The Potential for Rapid Melting of Ice and Amplification of Sea Level Rise

Introduction to Part 2

Robert W. Corell

Twenty thousand years ago, during the Last Glacial Maximum when the global average surface temperature was roughly 4–5°C (about 7–9°F) colder than at present, sea level was about 130 m (nearly 400 ft) below its current level due to the glacial build-up. This ice, which was piled 2 km (over a mile) deep over much of northern North America and Europe, melted away over 6000–10,000 years, so roughly at a rate of 1–2 m (about 3–6 ft) per century.

During the Eemian, which was the last interglacial and was centered about 127,000 years ago, sea level, as estimated from the elevations of beaches on a number of tropical islands, was about 4–6 m (13–20 ft) higher than at present. Reconstructions of the global average surface temperature suggest that it was perhaps 1–2°C (2–4°F) warmer than at present (perhaps a bit more in high northern latitudes) during this interglacial period, which was of quite short duration, and estimates indicate that the pace of sea level rise leading to that point was also near 1 m (3 ft) per century, and perhaps even a bit faster. Based on ice core evidence, it appears that Greenland was covered with only half as large an ice sheet as at present, suggesting that a significant fraction of the West Antarctic Ice Sheet must also have melted.

The last time that global average temperature was roughly 5°C (9°F) higher than at present was roughly 20 million years ago. At that time, there was virtually no ice stored on land, and sea level must therefore have been nearly 70 m (roughly 225 ft) above its present level (over 7 m from Greenland, 61 m from the West Antarctic and the rest from mountain glaciers). While some of this change was likely related to the continents being in different locations, that the IPCC projections of warming through the 21st century range from about 1–6°C suggests that society faces the risk of rises in sea level that will be much greater than the 0.15–0.2 m experienced during the 20th century. Indeed, over the last decade, the first global satellite estimate has sea level currently rising at a rate of about 0.3 m per century.

So, what about the future? In IPCC's Third Assessment Report, it was projected that sea level would rise between 0.09 and 0.88 m from 1990 to 2100. The most recent IPCC assessment, published in early 2007, based on improved estimates of the effects of warming on thermal expansion of ocean waters and melting of mountain glaciers, and the effects of altered balances in the build-up and decay of ice and snow, narrowed the range to 0.18–0.59 m, depending upon emission scenario and climate sensitivity. While it is important to note that the minimum estimate doubled, little reassurance should be taken from the upper estimate being lower because the IPCC, in each of these estimates, notes that it has left out some important terms. What IPCC has done in generating its estimate is to focus only on the terms that it believes can be effectively estimated, and it has left out the terms that climate models cannot yet represent well. As it turns out, these are just the terms that could cause rapid loss of mass from the ice sheets by (a) meltwater carving tunnels in the ice sheet and changing its density, and (b) meltwater lubricating the base of the glaciers and allowing faster rates of flow. IPCC suggests that these terms could add to the pace of sea level rise, but there is uncertainty about how much this might be, and so the terms were left out of the numerical estimates.

The three papers in Part 2 address a number of aspects of this issue, including evaluating the potential that the pace of change could speed up. In Chapter 4, Dr Claire Parkinson focuses on the increasing pace of reduction in the amount of sea ice, which, although this will not directly affect sea level, could dramatically affect the climate that would, in turn, affect the conditions experienced by mountain glaciers, ice caps and ice sheets, the melting of which would affect sea level. In Chapter 5, Dr Eric Rignot provides the latest information on the state of the Greenland Ice Sheet, indicating that it is losing mass at an increasing rate. In Chapter 6, Dr Robert Bindschadler reports on the state of the Antarctic Ice Sheet, also indicating that it seems poised for change.

While the newest IPCC estimate suggests that we likely have some time to deal with the climate change issue before significant sea rise occurs, the deteriorating state of the Greenland and West Antarctic ice sheets, the increasing pace of warming in high latitudes due to the retreat of sea ice, and the rapid rates of sea level rise evident in the geological record make it quite plausible that human-induced climate change could now be committing the world to much more rapid and greater sea level rise than had been considered likely less than a decade ago.

4

Changes in Polar Sea Ice Coverage

Claire L. Parkinson

Sea ice is an integral component of the polar climate system, both affecting and responding to key processes in the polar oceans and atmosphere. In both polar regions, sea ice spreads over vast areas, with the wintertime sea ice areal extent in each hemisphere exceeding one and a half times the area of the US.

Both polar regions show considerable interannual variability, but both also show statistically significant trends in sea ice extent. The long-term trends have been greatest in the Arctic, where the annually averaged sea ice extent has been decreasing at a rate of about 3 per cent per decade. This equates to a loss, on average, of about 35,000–40,000 km² of ice per year, a trend that will potentially have severe consequences on Arctic ecosystems should it continue. The Antarctic case, however, has been quite different, showing a sharp decline in the early and mid-1970s and an increasing trend of about 1 per cent per decade since then.

As the evidence for global warming and its impacts has accumulated, records of changes in sea ice have produced abundant data ripe for highlighting by both sides of the global warming debate. The Arctic sea ice decreases are firmly in line with the increasing Arctic temperatures, whereas the increases in Antarctic sea ice over the past quarter century are less easily placed in the global warming context.

The extent and influence of polar sea ice

Sea ice influences the rest of the polar climate system in multiple ways: limiting ocean/atmosphere exchanges of heat, mass and momentum; reflecting solar radiation back toward space; and exerting a wide range of influences on polar weather and polar ecosystems (see, for example, Parkinson, 2004; Serreze and Barry, 2005). Sea ice spreads over a significant area of each polar region, globally exceeding the 17.8 million km² area of South America throughout the year (see Figures 4.1 and 4.2 and Plates 1 and 2). Because of this large spatial expanse and the absence of permanent settlements on the ice, there was no feasible means of

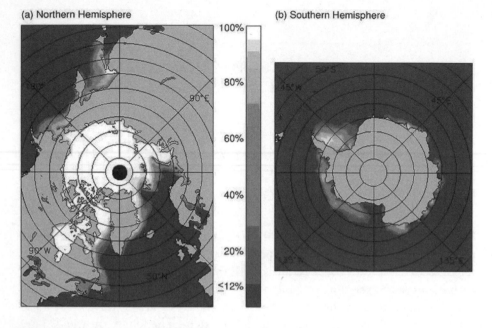

Figure 4.1 February sea ice coverage averaged over the 26 years 1979–2004, for (a) the Northern Hemisphere, and (b) the Southern Hemisphere (see Plate 1 for color version)

Note: Mid-winter in the Northern Hemisphere and mid-summer in the Southern Hemisphere, February, averaged over 1979–2004, had sea ice covering 15.2 million km² of the north polar region and 3.0 million km² of the south polar region, for a global total of 18.2 million km², exceeding the 17.8 million km² area of South America. The sea ice concentration (per cent areal ice coverage) is derived from data from the satellite-borne SMMR and SSMI passive-microwave instruments. No data are available poleward of 87.6°N from either sensor, and only the SSMI data are available between 84.6°N and 87.6°N; hence the former region is presented in black, representing missing data, and the latter region only incorporates data for the 17 years 1988–2004.

obtaining frequent, large-scale records of sea ice coverage before the satellite era. As a result, our consistent large-scale sea ice records extend back only to the 1970s, greatly limiting the database available for climate studies.

On the positive side, the satellite record of sea ice is particularly robust. This is because sea ice is well observed from space with a technology, specifically passive-microwave radiometry, that allows near-global data coverage almost daily, irrespective of sunlight conditions and of most cloud conditions. The multichannel satellite passive-microwave data record extends back to late October 1978, with some lesser-quality, single-channel data also available for much of the period 1973–1976.

The key satellite passive-microwave instruments used for examining sea ice changes in the Arctic and Antarctic since the late 1970s are the Scanning

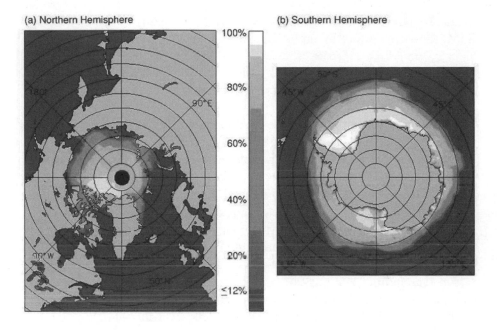

Figure 4.2 August sea ice coverage averaged over the years 1979–2004, for (a) the Northern Hemisphere, and (b) the Southern Hemisphere (see Plate 2 for color version)

Note: Mid-summer in the Northern Hemisphere and mid-winter in the Southern Hemisphere, August, averaged over 1979–2004, had sea ice covering 7.5 million km² of the north polar region and 17.5 million km² of the south polar region, for a global total of 25.0 million km², exceeding the 24.3 million km² area of North America. The sea ice concentration is derived from data from the satellite-borne SMMR and SSMI passive-microwave instruments. No data are available poleward of 87.6°N from either sensor, and only the SSMI data are available between 84.6°N and 87.6°N; hence the former region is presented in black, representing missing data, and the latter region only incorporates data for the 17 years 1988–2004.

Multichannel Microwave Radiometer (SMMR) and the Special Sensor Microwave Imager (SSMI). The SMMR was launched in October 1978 on NASA's Nimbus 7 satellite and collected data through mid-August 1987, and the first SSMI was launched in June 1987 on a satellite of the Defense Meteorological Satellite Program (DMSP), with subsequent SSMIs launched on other DMSP satellites. The SMMR/SSMI combination provides a sea ice record from late 1978 until at least 2007. The earlier, single-channel passive-microwave data are primarily from the Electrically Scanning Microwave Radiometer (ESMR), which was launched in December 1972 on the Nimbus 5 satellite and collected data for much of the period 1973–1976. Technical details regarding the ESMR record can be found in Zwally et al (1983) for the Antarctic and in Parkinson et al (1987) for the Arctic; details regarding the SMMR record can be found in Gloersen et al (1992); and details regarding the SMMR/SSMI record and the linking of the SMMR and SSMI time series can be found in Cavalieri et al (1999).

The Arctic record

The Arctic sea ice record is one of the primary 'poster children' for demonstrating that the Earth's climate is undergoing warming, at least in the North Polar Region. Although the record exhibits considerable interannual and regional variability, the evidence for decreasing Arctic sea ice coverage is extremely strong (see Figure 4.3) and has been extensively reported and discussed. This decrease has been most frequently presented as a decrease in Arctic sea ice extent (see, for example, Parkinson and Cavalieri, 1989; Johannessen et al, 1995, 2004; Maslanik et al, 1996; Bjørgo et al, 1997; Parkinson et al, 1999; Walsh and Chapman, 2001; Comiso, 2006), but the record also shows a decrease in the length of the sea ice season (Parkinson, 1992, 2000b), an increase in the length of the melt season (Smith, 1998), and, from in situ and submarine data, thinning of the sea ice cover (Rothrock et al, 1999; Wadhams and Davis, 2000; Yu et al, 2004).

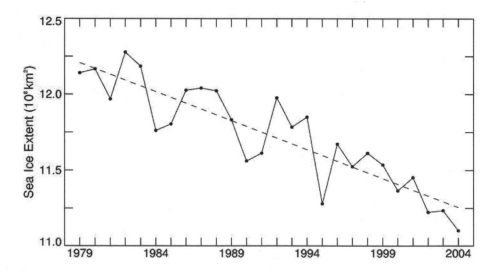

Figure 4.3 Annual average sea ice extent in the Northern Hemisphere, 1979–2004, as derived from data from the satellite-borne SMMR and SSMI instruments

Note: Ice extent is the sum of all grid cells (each approximately 25 km × 25 km) with ice concentration of at least 15 per cent. The dashed line is the linear least-squares fit through the data points.

The Arctic sea ice decrease is not uniform temporally (see Figure 4.3) or regionally (see Figure 4.4). For instance, the ice cover in the Seas of Okhotsk and Japan largely decreased, on an annual average basis, from 1979 to 1997, then increased until 2001 and then decreased again, while the sea ice cover of the Bering Sea instead started in 1979 at one of its lowest annually averaged extents for the entire 26-year record and had its highest extent in 1999, although still showing a negative trend overall from 1979 through 2004 (see Figure 4.4). The differing sea ice changes in the Bering Sea and the Seas of Okhotsk and Japan have been linked to the North Pacific Oscillation and the positioning of the Aleutian Low atmospheric pressure system (Cavalieri and Parkinson, 1987), and other regional contrasts throughout the Arctic have been similarly linked to various atmospheric circulation patterns and large-scale oscillations in the climate system. Considerable attention has been given to possible connections of the Arctic sea ice with the North Atlantic Oscillation (see, for example, Hurrell and van Loon, 1997; Johannessen et al, 1999; Kwok and Rothrock, 1999; Deser et al, 2000; Kwok, 2000; Parkinson, 2000a; Vinje, 2001), although some attention has also been given to connections with the Arctic Oscillation (Deser et al, 2000; Wang and Ikeda, 2000), the Arctic Ocean Oscillation (Polyakov et al, 1999; Proshutinsky et al, 1999; Rigor et al, 2002), and an unnamed interdecadal Arctic climate cycle (Mysak et al, 1990; Mysak and Power, 1992).

Still, despite the non-uniformity of the sea ice decrease and the possible connection with various oscillatory patterns, the long-term decreasing trend for the Northern Hemisphere as a whole is quite apparent, both visually (see Figure 4.3) and statistically. The trend value for the yearly averaged ice extents in Figure 4.3 is $-38,100 \pm 4200$ km^2/yr (-3.1 ± 0.34 per cent per decade), which is statistically significant at the 99+ per cent confidence level. Furthermore, the negative trend is apparent, from the SMMR/SSMI data, in every month of the year. The strongest trend is a decrease of $51,300 \pm 10,800$ km^2/yr (6.9 ± 1.5 per cent per decade) for the month of September, but even the weakest monthly trend (for February) is still significant at $27,500 \pm 5800$ km^2/yr (1.8 ± 0.4 per cent per decade).

The September Arctic ice decrease has garnered particular attention in recent years (see, for example, Maslanik et al, 1996; Comiso, 2002; Stroeve et al, 2005), not only because it is the largest of the monthly decreases, but also because of speculation that the September decrease could result in a late-summer ice-free Arctic, perhaps by the middle to end of the 21st century. Although the lesser wintertime decreases have also been reported previously (see, for example, Parkinson et al, 1999), recently they have been further highlighted because of particularly low winter sea ice coverage in both 2005 and 2006 (Comiso, 2006).

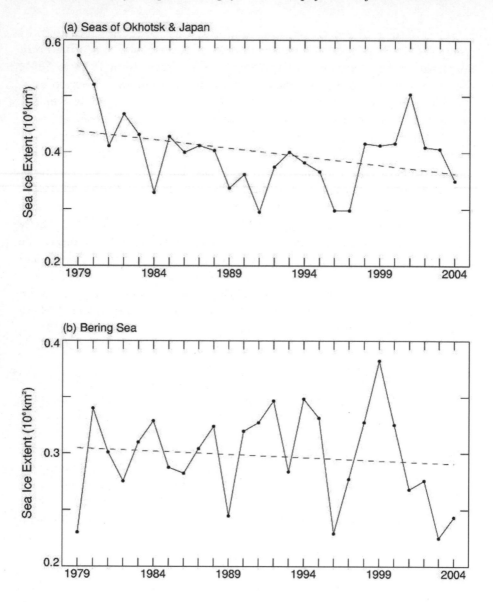

Figure 4.4 Annual averaged sea ice extent for 1979–2004, as derived from data from the satellite-borne SMMR and SSMI instruments, for (a) the Seas of Okhotsk and Japan and (b) the Bering Sea

Note: The dashed lines are the linear least-squares fits through the respective data points.

The Antarctic record

In terms of demonstrating a long-term pattern reflective of global warming, the Antarctic sea ice record is not nearly as convincing as the Arctic record. This was not the case in 1981, when Kukla and Gavin (1981) published a paper showing a striking decrease in Antarctic sea ice coverage that occurred in the 1970s. At the time, this Antarctic sea ice decrease was heralded as perhaps the first really strong geophysical evidence of global warming. The ice decrease of the 1970s, however, has not continued.

As with the Arctic record, the satellite record of Antarctic sea ice shows considerable interannual (see Figure 4.5) and regional (see Figure 4.6) variability. The overall trend since 1979, however, shows increasing rather than decreasing sea ice coverage (see Figure 4.5). The trend magnitude is not nearly as large as for the Arctic sea ice decrease, but, at 14,000 ± 5200 km²/yr (1.24 ± 0.46 per cent per decade), it is still substantial and is statistically significant at the 99 per cent confidence level. The increasing Antarctic sea ice coverage since the late 1970s has been reported by Stammerjohn and Smith (1997), Watkins and Simmonds (2000), and Zwally et al (2002), for the periods 1979–1994, November 1978–December 1996, and November 1978–December 1998, respectively.

Regional studies of Antarctic sea ice frequently divide the Southern Ocean into five regions. Of these, the Ross Sea, immediately north of the Ross Ice Shelf, shows the strongest trend towards increasing sea ice coverage over the 1979–2004 period (Figure 4.6(b)), while the region of the Bellingshausen and Amundsen Seas, between the Ross Sea on the west and the Antarctic Peninsula on the east, is the only region with a decreasing 1979–2004 sea ice cover (see Figure 4.6(a)).

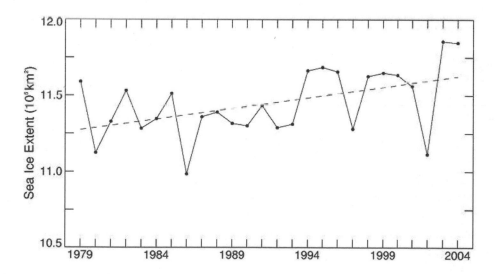

Figure 4.5 Annual averaged sea ice extent in the Southern Hemisphere, 1979–2004, as derived from data from the satellite-borne SMMR and SSMI instruments

Note: The dashed line is the linear least-squares fit through the data points.

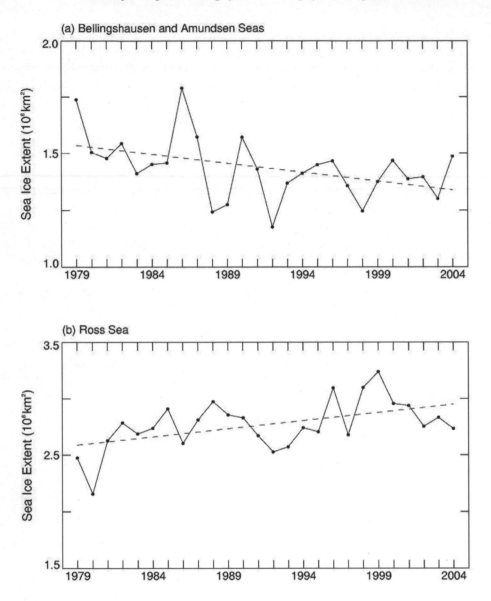

Figure 4.6 Annual averaged sea ice extent for 1979–2004, as derived from data from the satellite-borne SMMR and SSMI instruments, for (a) the Bellingshausen and Amundsen Seas and (b) the Ross Sea

Note: The dashed lines are the linear least-squares fits through the respective data points.

The sea ice increase in the Ross Sea is statistically significant at the 99 per cent confidence level, and the sea ice decrease in the Bellingshausen and Amundsen Seas is statistically significant at the 95 per cent confidence level.

The regional sea ice contrasts in the Antarctic correspond well with the known Antarctic atmospheric temperature record. The one region of the Antarctic with a strong record of temperature increases is the Antarctic Peninsula (Hansen et al, 1999; Vaughan et al, 2003), which extends north toward South America and lies immediately to the east of the decreasing sea ice coverage in the Bellingshausen and Amundsen Seas (see Figure 4.6(a)). Furthermore, the greater spatial detail provided by maps of trends in the length of the sea ice season shows that the decreasing sea ice coverage occurs not just to the west of the Antarctic Peninsula, but also to the immediate east, in the far western Weddell Sea (Parkinson, 2002). In fact, the pattern of change in the length of the sea ice season throughout the Southern Ocean has been found to correlate well with the pattern of temperature changes, with warming conditions found in conjunction with shortening sea ice seasons and cooling conditions found in conjunction with lengthening sea ice seasons (Vaughan et al, 2003).

Discussion

The Arctic region has experienced an array of environmental changes over the past few decades that, overall, reflect a consistent pattern of increasing air temperature, increasing water temperature, increasing precipitation, rising river flows, declining sea ice, declining lake and river ice, declining snow cover, melting glaciers, a declining Greenland Ice Sheet and thawing permafrost (see, for example, Morison et al, 2000; Serreze et al, 2000; ACIA, 2005). These are well documented in a variety of reports, most notably the Arctic Climate Impact Assessment (ACIA, 2005), which details, in 1042 pages, these physical changes and the related biological changes and impacts on indigenous peoples.

Sea ice is an important element of the changing environmental conditions in the Arctic. As the ice cover decreases (see Figure 4.3), its highly reflective white surface is replaced by a far less reflective liquid ocean, so that more solar radiation is absorbed within the ocean/atmosphere system, encouraging further warming and its attendant impacts. Reduced sea ice coverage also allows increased ocean–atmosphere exchange of heat and moisture and has significant ecosystem impacts. These impacts include a reduction in the primary hunting grounds and the length of the seal-hunting season for polar bears, which stand atop the Arctic marine food chain (Stirling and Derocher, 1993; Derocher et al, 2004), a reduction in the habitat for organisms that are at the bottom of the food chain and live within the ice itself (Gradinger, 1995), and a variety of positive and negative impacts on species throughout the food chain (Melnikov, 1997; Croxall et al, 2002). In fact, the ice is so important to polar bears that questions have been raised regarding whether the species can survive if the Arctic sea ice decrease continues to the point where the late-summer Arctic Ocean is ice-free, a scenario projected by some as plausible by the middle or end of the 21st century.

Reduced Arctic sea ice cover is also likely to lead to some benefits, most notably a greater ease of shipping in the Arctic region. However, even this perceived benefit could prove more harmful than advantageous as it could lead to increased pollution, increased disruption of native wildlife, and increased political tensions caused by issues of sovereignty and access to various polar resources.

On the opposite side of the planet, the Antarctic sea ice cover is just as important to the Antarctic climate system (see, for example, White and Peterson, 1996; Yuan and Martinson, 2000; Venegas et al, 2001; Hall and Visbeck, 2002; Raphael, 2003; Stammerjohn et al, 2003; Parkinson, 2004) and to Antarctic ecosystems (see, for example, Ainley et al, 2003; Arrigo and Thomas, 2004). As an illustrative example, penguin distributions are changing markedly in the Bellingshausen Sea region as the local sea ice cover decreases, with a major increase in the chinstrap penguin population but a decrease in the Adélie penguin population, reflecting the chinstrap penguin's preference for open water and the Adélie's dependence on sea ice (Smith et al, 1999; Parmesan, 2006). In fact, the Adélie population on Anvers Island along the Antarctic Peninsula, where sea ice is decreasing, has decreased by well over half in recent decades, whereas the Adélie population on Ross Island, in the midst of increasing sea ice, has thrived (Parmesan, 2006).

By August and September of 2007, the basic sea ice trends established from the 1979–2004 satellite record (Figures 4.3 and 4.5) were clearly continuing, as the Arctic sea ice cover reached a new record minimum ice extent and the Antarctic ice cover reached a new record maximum, August and September being late summer in the Northern Hemisphere and late winter in the Southern Hemisphere. The Arctic minimum is particularly noteworthy because it fell well below any previous minimum during the period of the satellite record. In fact, the extreme nature of the Arctic ice reductions in 2007 was such that the ice had reached a new record minimum, exceeding that established in late September 2005, by mid-August 2007, with several weeks remaining in the 2007 melt season, during which the extents continued to decrease. The magnitude of the decreases in 2007 has increased speculation that an ice-free Arctic may occur not only sometime this century but perhaps well within the first half of the century.

The sea ice cover in both polar regions is a critical determinant of polar climates. Both the Arctic and Antarctic sea ice covers are well monitored from space, and both are changing in ways that are partly, but not fully, understood. Because significant regions in both hemispheres fluctuate each year from having no sea ice in late summer to having extensive sea ice in late winter, it is extremely unlikely that a 'tipping point' exists with respect to the areal extent of sea ice (i.e. such that once the ice extent is reduced below some point, it will be unable to recover). Nonetheless, there might well be tipping points in other elements of the polar climate system (for example, involving ice shelf stability and ice sheet grounding lines) that, if reached, could have marked impacts on sea ice cover and the regional climate in general. Any resulting changes in sea ice would necessarily propagate further through the rest of the polar climate system.

Acknowledgements

The author greatly appreciates Nick Di Girolamo for his assistance in the generation of the figures and the Cryospheric Processes Program at NASA Headquarters for funding the work.

References

ACIA, 2005: *Arctic Climate Impact Assessment*, Cambridge University Press, Cambridge

Ainley, D. G., C. T. Tynan and I. Stirling, 2003: Sea ice: A critical habitat for polar marine mammals and birds, in D. N. Thomas and G. S. Dieckmann (eds) *Sea Ice: An Introduction to Its Physics, Chemistry, Biology and Geology*, Blackwell Science, Oxford

Arrigo, K. R. and D. N. Thomas, 2004: Large scale importance of sea ice biology in the Southern Ocean, *Antarctic Science*, **16**(4), 471–486

Bjørgo, E., O. M. Johannessen and M. W. Miles, 1997: Analysis of merged SMMR-SSMI time series of Arctic and Antarctic sea ice parameters 1978–1995, *Geophys. Res. Ltrs.*, **24**(4), 413–416

Cavalieri, D. J. and C. L. Parkinson, 1987: On the relationship between atmospheric circulation and the fluctuations in the sea ice extents of the Bering and Okhotsk seas, *J. Geophys. Res.*, **92**(C7), 7141–7162

Cavalieri, D. J., C. L. Parkinson, P. Gloersen, J. C. Comiso and H. J. Zwally, 1999: Deriving long-term time series of sea ice cover from satellite passive-microwave multisensor data sets, *J. Geophys. Res.*, **104**, 15,803–15,814

Comiso, J. C., 2002: A rapidly declining perennial sea ice cover in the Arctic, *Geophys. Res. Ltrs.*, **29**(20), 1956, doi:10.1029/2002GL01560

Comiso, J. C., 2006: Abrupt decline in the Arctic winter sea ice cover, *Geophys. Res. Ltrs.*, **33**, L18504, doi:10.1029/2006GL027341

Croxall, J. P., P. N. Trathan and E. J. Murphy, 2002: Environmental change and Arctic seabird populations, *Science*, **297**, 1510–1514

Derocher, A. N., N. J. Lunn and I. Stirling, 2004: Polar bears in a warming climate, *Integrative and Comparative Biology*, **44**, 163–176

Deser, C., J. E. Walsh and M. S. Timlin, 2000: Arctic sea ice variability in the context of recent atmospheric circulation trends, *J. Clim.*, **13**, 617–633

Gloersen, P., W. J. Campbell, D. J. Cavalieri, J. C. Comiso, C. L. Parkinson and H. J. Zwally, 1992: *Arctic and Antarctic Sea Ice, 1978–1987: Satellite Passive-Microwave Observations and Analysis*, NASA SP-511, National Aeronautics and Space Administration, Washington DC

Gradinger, R., 1995: Climate change and biological oceanography of the Arctic Ocean, *Philosophical Transactions of the Royal Society of London*, Series A, **352**, 277–286

Hall, A. and M. Visbeck, 2002: Synchronous variability in the Southern Hemisphere atmosphere, sea ice, and ocean resulting from the annular mode, *J. Clim.*, **15**, 3043–3057

Hansen, J., R. Ruedy, J. Glascoe and M. Sato, 1999: GISS analysis of surface temperature change, *J. Geophys. Res.*, **104**(D24), 30,997–31,022

Hurrell, J. W. and H. van Loon, 1997: Decadal variations in climate associated with the North Atlantic Oscillation, *Climatic Change*, **36**(3), 301–326

Johannessen, O. M., M. Miles and E. Bjørgo, 1995: The Arctic's shrinking sea ice, *Nature*, **376**(6536), 126–127

Johannessen, O. M., E. V. Shalina and M. W. Miles, 1999: Satellite evidence for an Arctic sea ice cover in transformation, *Science*, **286**, 1937–1939

Johannessen, O. M., L. Bengtsson, M. W. Miles, S. I. Kuzmina, V. A. Semenov, G. V. Alekseev, A. P. Nagurnyi, V. F. Zakharov, L. P. Bobylev, L. H. Pettersson, K. Hasselmann and H. P. Cattle, 2004: Arctic climate change: Observed and modelled temperature and sea-ice variability, *Tellus*, **56**A(4), 328–341

Kukla, G. and J. Gavin, 1981: Summer ice and carbon dioxide, *Science*, **214**(4520), 497–503

Kwok, R., 2000: Recent changes in Arctic Ocean sea ice motion associated with the North Atlantic Oscillation, *Geophys. Res. Ltrs.*, **27**(6), 775–778

Kwok, R. and D. A. Rothrock, 1999: Variability of Fram Strait ice flux and North Atlantic Oscillation, *J. Geophys. Res.*, **104**(C3), 5177–5189

Maslanik, J. A., M. C. Serreze and R. G. Barry, 1996: Recent decreases in Arctic summer ice cover and linkages to atmospheric circulation anomalies, *Geophys. Res. Ltrs.*, **23**(13), 1677–1680

Melnikov, I. A., 1997: *The Arctic Sea Ice Ecosystem*, Gordon and Breach Science Publishers, Amsterdam

Morison, J., K. Aagaard and M. Steele, 2000: Recent environmental changes in the Arctic: A review, *Arctic*, **53**(4), 359–371

Mysak, L. A. and S. B. Power, 1992: Sea-ice anomalies in the western Arctic and Greenland-Iceland Sea and their relation to an interdecadal climate cycle, *Climatological Bulletin/ Bulletin Climatologique*, **26**(3), 147–176

Mysak, L. A., D. K. Manak and R. F. Marsden, 1990: Sea-ice anomalies observed in the Greenland and Labrador Seas during 1901–1984 and their relation to an interdecadal Arctic climate cycle, *Climate Dynamics*, **5**, 111–133

Parkinson, C. L., 1992: Spatial patterns of increases and decreases in the length of the sea ice season in the north polar region, 1979–1986, *J. Geophys. Res.*, **97**(C9), 14,377–14,388

Parkinson, C. L., 2000a: Recent trend reversals in Arctic sea ice extents: Possible connections to the North Atlantic Oscillation, *Polar Geography*, **24**(1), 1–12

Parkinson, C. L., 2000b: Variability of Arctic sea ice: The view from space, an 18-year record, *Arctic*, **53**(4), 341–358

Parkinson, C. L., 2002: Trends in the length of the Southern Ocean sea-ice season, 1979–99, *Annals of Glaciology*, **34**, 435–440

Parkinson, C. L., 2004: Southern Ocean sea ice and its wider linkages: Insights revealed from models and observations, *Antarctic Science*, **16**(4), 387–400, doi:10.1017/S0954102004002214

Parkinson, C. L. and D. J. Cavalieri, 1989: Arctic sea ice 1973–1987: Seasonal, regional, and interannual variability, *J. Geophys. Res.*, **94**(C10), 14,499–14,523

Parkinson, C. L., J. C. Comiso, H. J. Zwally, D. J. Cavalieri, P. Gloersen and W. J. Campbell, 1987: *Arctic Sea Ice, 1973–1976: Satellite Passive-Microwave Observations*, NASA SP-489, National Aeronautics and Space Administration, Washington DC

Parkinson, C. L., D. J. Cavalieri, P. Gloersen, H. J. Zwally and J. C. Comiso, 1999: Variability of the Arctic sea ice cover 1978–1996, *J. Geophys. Res.*, **104**, 20,837–20,856

Parmesan, C., 2006: Ecological and evolutionary responses to recent climate change, *Annual Review of Ecology, Evolution, and Systematics*, **37**, 637–669

Polyakov, I. V., A. Y. Proshutinsky, and M. A. Johnson, 1999: Seasonal cycles in two regimes of Arctic climate, *J. Geophys. Res.*, **104**(C11), 25,761–25,788

Proshutinsky, A. Y., I. V. Polyakov and M. A. Johnson, 1999: Climate states and variability of Arctic ice and water dynamics during 1946–1997, *Polar Research*, **18**(2), 135–142

Raphael, M. N., 2003: Impact of observed sea-ice concentration on the Southern Hemisphere extratropical atmospheric circulation in summer, *J. Geophys. Res.*, **108**(D22), 4687, doi:10.1029/2002JD003308

Rigor, I. G., J. M. Wallace and R. L. Colony, 2002: Response of sea ice to the Arctic Oscillation, *J. Clim.*, **15**, 2648–2663

Rothrock, D. A., Y. Yu and G. A. Maykut, 1999: Thinning of the Arctic sea-ice cover, *Geophys. Res. Ltrs.*, **26**(23), 3469–3472

Serreze, M. C. and R. G. Barry, 2005: *The Arctic Climate System*, Cambridge University Press, Cambridge

Serreze, M. C., J. E. Walsh, F. S. Chapin III, T. Osterkamp, M. Dyurgerov, V. Romanovsky, W. C. Oechel, J. Morison, T. Zhang and R. G. Barry, 2000: Observational evidence of recent change in the northern high-latitude environment, *Climatic Change*, **46**(2), 159–207

Smith, D. M., 1998: Recent increase in the length of the melt season of perennial Arctic sea ice, *Geophys. Res. Ltrs.*, **25**, 655–658

Smith, R. C., D. Ainley, K. Baker, E. Domack, S. Emslie, B. Fraser, J. Kennett, A. Leventer, E. Mosley-Thompson, S. Stammerjohn and M. Vernet, 1999: Marine ecosystem sensitivity to climate change, *BioScience*, **49**(5), 393–404

Stammerjohn, S. E. and R. C. Smith, 1997: Opposing Southern Ocean climate patterns as revealed by trends in regional sea ice coverage, *Climatic Change*, **37**(4), 617–639

Stammerjohn, S. E., M. R. Drinkwater, R. C. Smith, and X. Liu, 2003: Ice-atmosphere interactions during sea-ice advance and retreat in the western Antarctic Peninsula region, *J. Geophys. Res.*, **108**(C10), 3329, doi:10.1029/2002JC001543

Stirling, I. and A. E. Derocher, 1993: Possible impacts of climate warming on polar bears, *Arctic*, **46**(3), 240–245

Stroeve, J. C., M. C. Serreze, F. Fetterer, T. Arbetter, W. Meier, J. Maslanik and K. Knowles, 2005: *Geophys. Res. Ltrs.*, **32**, L04501, doi:10.1029/2004GL021810

Vaughan, D. G., G. J. Marshall, W. M. Connolley, C. Parkinson, R. Mulvaney, D. A. Hodgson, J. C. King. C. J. Pudsey and J. Turner, 2003: Recent rapid regional climate warming on the Antarctic Peninsula, *Climatic Change*, **60**, 243–274

Venegas, S. A., M. R. Drinkwater and G. Shaffer, 2001: Coupled oscillations in Antarctic sea ice and atmosphere in the South Pacific sector, *Geophys. Res. Ltrs.*, **28**, 3301–3304

Vinje, T., 2001: Anomalies and trends of sea-ice extent and atmospheric circulation in the Nordic Seas during the period 1864-1998, *J. Clim.*, **14**, 255–267

Wadhams, P. and N. R. Davis, 2000: Further evidence of ice thinning in the Arctic Ocean, *Geophys. Res. Ltrs.*, **27**(24), 3973–3975

Walsh, J. E. and W. L. Chapman, 2001: 20th-century sea-ice variations from observational data, *Annals of Glaciology*, **33**, 444–448

Wang, J. and M. Ikeda, 2000: Arctic Oscillation and Arctic Sea-Ice Oscillation, *Geophys. Res. Ltrs.*, **27**(9), 1287–1290

Watkins, A. B. and I. Simmonds, 2000: Current trends in Antarctic sea ice: The 1990s impact on a short climatology, *J. Clim.*, **13**(24), 4441–4451

White, W. B. and R. G. Peterson, 1996: An Antarctic circumpolar wave in surface pressure, wind, temperature and sea ice extent, *Nature*, **380**, 699–702

Yu, Y., G. A. Maykut and D. A. Rothrock, 2004: Changes in the thickness distribution of Arctic sea ice between 1958–1970 and 1993–1997, *J. Geophys. Res.*, **109**, C08004, doi:10.1029/2003JC001982

Yuan, X. and D. G. Martinson, 2000: Antarctic sea ice extent variability and its global connectivity, *J. Clim.*, **3**, 1697–1717

Zwally, H. J., J. C. Comiso, C. L. Parkinson, W. J. Campbell, F. D. Carsey and P. Gloersen, 1983: *Antarctic Sea Ice, 1973–1976: Satellite Passive-Microwave Observations*, NASA SP-459, National Aeronautics and Space Administration, Washington DC

Zwally, H. J., J. C. Comiso, C. L. Parkinson, D. J. Cavalieri and P. Gloersen, 2002: Variability of Antarctic sea ice 1979–1998, *J. Geophys. Res.*, **107**(C5), 10.1029/2000JC000733

5

Changes in the Greenland Ice Sheet and Implications for Global Sea Level Rise

Eric Rignot

The Greenland Ice Sheet is changing rapidly in response to climate warming. Even though snowfall slightly increased in the interior, coastal regions are melting and sliding to the sea faster than before, which causes sea level to rise. Between melting, snowfall and faster sliding, the acceleration of glaciers to the sea contributes two-thirds of the mass loss; that is, it dominates the ice sheet response to climate warming. Over the last decade, the mass deficit of the ice sheet doubled, and in 2005 it exceeded 200 cubic kilometers of ice per year (50 cubic miles per year), a rate that would be sufficient to raise sea level by 0.6 mm per year (0.25 inches per year). Because warming will cause more glaciers to speed up and ice will continue to thin further inland, this rate of mass loss will increase as climate continues to warm. Global climate models project roughly 1–2 ft of sea level rise by 2100, but these models do not include a complete description of glacier mechanics and cannot explain current observations. At present, we do not have models capable of predicting the future state of the Greenland Ice Sheet. Other considerations, based on air temperature and paleoclimatic evidence, suggest that sea level could rise by as much as 1–3 m (3–10 ft) by 2100.

Knowing what the ice sheet is doing today and how it will behave in the future is a problem of considerable societal and scientific importance. There is enough ice left in Greenland to raise global sea level by roughly 7 m (about 21 ft). Complete melting of Greenland is unlikely, however, unless enormous warming takes place (Gregory et al, 2004). During the last interglacial about 127,000 years ago, when air temperatures in the region of the Greenland Ice Sheet were only 2–3°C warmer than today, the ice sheet got considerably smaller and likely contributed roughly 3 m (about 10 ft) to global sea level rise (Otto-Bleisner et al, 2006; Overpeck et al 2006).

As recently as the early 1990s, little was known about the balance between the input of snow to the ice sheet versus the discharge of ice into the ocean as icebergs and meltwater, the so-called mass balance of the ice sheet. The situation

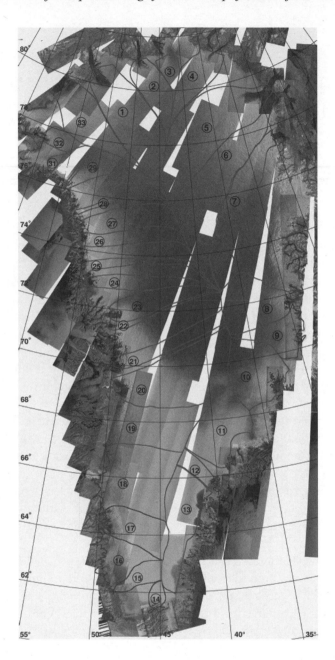

Figure 5.1 Ice velocity mosaic of the Greenland Ice Sheet assembled from year 2000 Radarsat-1 interferometry data, color coded on a logarithmic scale from 1 m/yr (brown) to 3 km/yr (purple), overlaid on a map of radar brightness from ERS-1/Radarsat-1/Envisat radar images (see Plate 3 for color version)

Note: Drainage boundaries are shown in red and blue. Kangerdlugssuaq Glacier is 10, Helheim Glacier is 11, southeast Greenland glaciers are 12 and 13, Jakobshavn Isbrae is 20, Rinks Isbrae is 23, northwest Greenland glaciers are 26–31.

has improved considerably over the last decade due to the widespread application of airborne and satellite techniques combined with in-situ data collection. At the same time, major glaciological changes took place in Greenland (see Figure 5.1, Plate 3), most of which were not expected, and challenged prevailing views on the evolution of the ice sheet (Rignot and Kanagaratnam, 2006).

Ice sheet changes

In the late 1990s, repeat-pass airborne laser altimetry measurements revealed that the Greenland Ice Sheet was nearly in balance in the interior, but was thinning along its periphery, with deterioration concentrated along the channels occupied by outlet glaciers (Krabill et al, 1999). Overall, the ice sheet was thinning because the coastal changes dominated the balance. This result was consistent with a recent warming in air temperature and an increase in summer melt intensity and extent in Greenland compared to the 1980s. The larger rates of thinning on glaciers, however, suggested that thinning from changes in glacier dynamics could be significant (Abdalati et al, 2001). In the interior, shallow ice cores revealed large interdecadal variations in snowfall, but no clear long-term trend in snowfall.

Subsequent surveys conducted in the late 1990s and early 2000s confirmed the mass loss of the ice sheet, but also revealed that the mass loss was increasing with time (Krabill et al, 2004). Air temperatures were also on the rise. In addition, several glaciers were starting to change behavior. Jakobshavn Isbrae, the largest discharger of ice on the Greenland's west coast, saw its floating section collapse in 2000–2003, accompanied by a doubling in glacier speed (Joughin et al, 2004). The mass loss consecutive to the glacier acceleration was much larger than that caused by the melting of ice and snow.

In the southeast sector of Greenland, where snowfall is the highest and ten times that of the dry north, glaciers were significantly out of balance in the 1990s (Rignot et al, 2004). Few of these glaciers have been studied in any sort of detail; most of them are unnamed. They flow through narrow passages in a complex alpine landscape. Ice thinning was detected all the way to the ice divide in the early 1990s (Krabill et al, 1999), at more than 2000 m elevation. Glacier velocities were more than 50 per cent too large to maintain the ice sheet in a state of mass balance. In 1996, this sector was already contributing the largest mass loss from the Greenland Ice Sheet into the ocean.

More changes took place between 2000 and 2005, which progressively altered the velocity structure of the entire Greenland Ice Sheet (Rignot and Kanagaratnam, 2006). The glaciers in southeast Greenland accelerated 30 per cent on average between 1996 and 2000, and another 57 per cent in 2000–2005, to bring their mass balance even more into the negative. In 2004–2005, Jakobshavn Isbrae was still receding and profusely calving, with a speed stabilized at about twice its former value, and an ice front well inland of anything the glacier had experienced since 1850s, including a warm period in the 1940s. On the east coast, two of the largest glaciers accelerated almost at the same time: Kangerdluqssuaq Glacier in the north and Helheim Glacier in the south. In the case of the former, we had no evidence for any major flow change since at least the 1960s (Thomas et al, 2000). But the glacier suddenly accelerated 250 per cent in 2004, its surface dropped by more than 100 m, and its calving front retreated 5 km (Rignot and Kanagaratnam, 2006). Figure 5.2 (Plate 4) shows how the catastrophic retreat left remnants of ice stranded on the side mountains. Helheim Glacier, 200 km south, sped up 60 per cent and its ice front retreated several kilometers. The mass loss caused by the speed up of these two large glaciers was sufficient to double the mass deficit from east Greenland. In 2006, the two glaciers slowed down near the front, but the thinning wave was propagating inland and the mass loss remained significant (Howat et al, 2007). Similarly, the glaciers in the southeast coast slowed down 10–20 per cent in 2006 but remain largely out of balance with interior accumulation.

Figure 5.2 The ice front of Kangerdlugssuaq Glacier, East Greenland in 2005 (see Plate 4 for color version)

Note: The photograph shows massive calving activity at the ice front as well as elevated ice margins (red arrow) compared to the glacier center as a result of the massive drawdown of the ice surface caused by the doubling in speed of the glacier.
Source: courtesy of J. Sonntag.

Few large glaciers exist along the southern tip and southwest coast of Greenland because of its large ablation area and shallower slopes, which, together, have the effect of causing the loss of most of the ice before the glaciers reach the ocean even though this fast loss allows modest flow speeds. This sector experienced higher snowfall in the 1980–1990s, which triggered partial advance of ice fronts (Weidick, 1995), except for tidewater glaciers that have been retreating steadily since the Little Ice Age. Over the last few years, glacier acceleration was detected in that sector as well. For instance, Kangiata-nunata Glacier accelerated 38 per cent in 1996–2006.

North from Jakobshavn Isbrae, few glaciers were observed to speed up, but many glaciers were already out of balance and discharging more ice to the sea than required to maintain mass balance in the 1990s. If and when these glaciers will undergo a major speed up, they will add considerably to the mass deficit of Greenland because they are responsible for some of the largest discharge of ice in Greenland.

Mass balance estimates

Combining ice thickness data, ice velocity measured with satellite imaging radars on nearly all the glaciers in Greenland, and a melt and accumulation model for snow/ice referenced to the 1960s, we calculated the ice sheet mass balance and its change through time caused by glacier acceleration. The result, which is the contribution of changes in ice dynamics to the mass balance, showed that the ice sheet lost 56 ± 30 km^3 of ice per year in 1996, increasing to 167 ± 40 km^3 of ice per year in 2005. Added to that, there were changes in snow/ice melt and snowfall, or surface mass balance of the glaciers. Changes in the surface balance calculated by Hanna et al (2005) added to the loss from ice dynamics because ice melt has increased faster and removed more ice than the increase in snowfall in the interior was able to supply. This increased the estimated mass deficit to 91 ± 31 km^3 in 1996 and 224 ± 41 km^3 of ice per year in 2005 (i.e. nearly 50 cubic miles of ice per year).

Other techniques employed to survey the ice sheet have confirmed these estimates or yielded lower values. Lower values are obtained by airborne surveys because these surveys do not cover all glaciers and only include one or two laser profiles on each one (Krabill et al, 2004; Thomas et al, 2006). The observed trend in mass loss, however, agrees quite well with the mass flux technique. The airborne surveys were also able to reveal the enormous rates of ice thinning that are affecting the glaciers, up to a 50 m drop in ice elevation on Kangerdluqssuaq Glacier in 2003–2004. Another technique, satellite radar altimetry, gives lower numbers and even ice sheet growth (Zwally et al, 2005). But this instrument was designed to sample the flat surface of oceans and is not well adapted to survey the steep margins of an ice sheet, and especially narrow glaciers surrounded by mountains (Thomas et al, 2005). The resulting estimates are therefore mostly characteristic of the vast interior, but not of the entire ice sheet.

Gravity surveys from the GRACE satellite mission are providing another set of independent estimates of the mass balance, with a spatial resolution of about 400 km, but without having to make an assumption about snow/firn density because this technique directly samples changes in mass of the ice sheet. Many corrections must be applied to the data, however, before analyzing the results in order to account for the influences of ocean variability, atmospheric variability and post-glacial rebound. The results also vary with time and the GRACE satellites were only launched in 2002, at a time when the Greenland Ice Sheet was changing rapidly. Despite these limitations, the GRACE data confirmed a large mass loss from Greenland and an acceleration of the loss over the last few years (Chen et al, 2006; Luthcke et al, 2006; Velicogna and Wahr, 2006).

Overall, observations suggest that the ice sheet is contributing to an increase in global sea level of about 0.3–0.6 mm/yr since the 1990s. This represents a significant fraction of the observed global sea level rise of 3 mm/yr that has been observed since about 1993 with satellites. At this rate, sea level will increase by 6 cm (over 2 inches) by 2100 due to the loss of ice from Greenland alone.

There are, however, no physical reasons why the present rate should not continue to increase. As warming continues and propagates along the northern shores, the mass deficit will increase, with estimates that it could double in the next decade. The central question is no longer to determine whether the ice sheet is losing mass to the ocean or not, but how fast it will lose ice over the next hundred years and beyond.

What is causing these changes?

Air temperatures have warmed by 2–3°C along the coast of southeast and southwest Greenland since the 1980s (see Figure 5.3), which is a large forcing. As temperature records show, there is a strong coherence in the warming trends affecting east and west stations. This symmetry breaks down further north. As a result, further glacier acceleration will likely progress in an erratic manner in the north, for the reasons below.

The increase in air temperature has four consequences:

1. Warming increases the melting of snow and ice, hence the mass deficit of the ice sheet. As the ice sheet thins and becomes lower, melting increases, even if air temperatures remain the same, a phenomena known as topography feedback. The removal of the upper level of fresh snow also reduces the ice sheet albedo, which further increases melting and the spatial extent of melting.

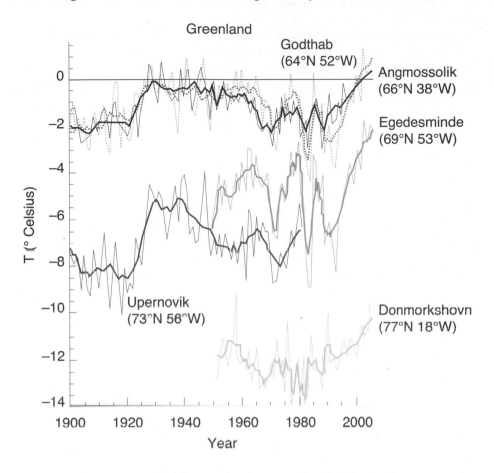

Figure 5.3 Air temperature records for several stations around Greenland showing the strong warming since the 1980s (Angmassalik and Godthab), and a shorter period of warming in the 1930s

2. Warming allows more melt water to reach the glacier beds. When more water lubricates the bed, glaciers flow faster, especially as subglacial water pressure increases and lifts the glaciers off their beds. Recent GPS surveys (Zwally et al, 2002) revealed that even areas not associated with glaciers accelerate by 30–50 per cent in the summer, on short time scales, meaning that melt water goes rapidly from the surface to the glacier base and accelerates ice flow. Natural pathways for that transition are provided by moulins, which guide rivers of melt water down to the ice sheet bottom, or pre-existing networks of crevasses and micro-fractures connecting to the bed. Increased subglacial water pressure or lubrication enhances glacier flow. The rates of speed up remain modest, however, when averaged over the whole year. For instance, we measured an 8–10 per cent speed up over the summer months compared to the winter months over a wide latitudinal range of glaciers in Greenland,

almost regardless of the amount of melt water produced. Enhanced sliding from more melt water is therefore not the primary response of the ice sheet to warming.

3.   Rather than percolating through the bottom, melt water may pond and form large supraglacial lakes that either freeze in or drain to the bottom of the ice sheet. When they drain to the sea, these lakes send large pulses of melt water, which may travel quickly (1km/hr) over large distances and lift the glacier above its bed, thereby allowing fast flow. Little is known about the effect of these lakes because most of them cannot be seen from the surface, but they certainly play an important role in controlling ice flow.

4.   Ice thinning near the glacier's front edge progressively disconnects the glaciers from the ground below, equivalent to removing a part of the glacier that would normally buttress its upstream flow. The thinning of the frontal plug helps glaciers flow faster. Model studies suggest that the effect on speed is enormous, i.e. an order of magnitude larger than that associated with an increase in melt water. This was indeed first illustrated in the Antarctic (Thomas et al, 2004), where melt water is not a factor. Ice front thinning is the main reason for the abrupt and enormous speed up of the southeast Greenland glaciers (Howat et al, 2005). As glaciers re-advance, the speed up may diminish, as observed on Helheim and Kangerdlugssuaq in 2006 (Howat et al, 2007). But the process is unlikely to reverse entirely because the glacier speed up has significantly and almost irreversibly altered the force balance of the glaciers. We come back to that point later in the discussion.

What can be predicted?

We know the root causes of the change (warmer climate) and how it exerts its control (ice front buttressing and sliding at the bed), but many details elude observations and understanding. The first map of Greenland showing glacial velocities was published in 2006. The first revised map of ice thickness was assembled in 2001, with many glaciers not yet surveyed, i.e. we do not know how deep the beds are near the coast of many of these glaciers. We do not know the distribution of water at the glacier beds, where it accumulates, where it drains, and how it affects ice flow, although it certainly does. Human and financial resources dedicated to the ice sheet problem are woefully inadequate. Closing the gap between numerical models and reality is glaciology's next challenge. In the last few years, we learned two lessons: first, existing numerical models are not reliable enough to predict the future contribution to sea level from Greenland; and second, ice sheet changes are taking place on much shorter time scales than previously thought.

Numerical models of ice sheet evolution do not include ice shelf buttressing as a control (Huybrechts and Wolde, 1999). In Greenland, the rapid speed up of large glaciers cannot be explained by these models because they do not include glacier dynamics. The reasons for that are multiple:

- The physics is not adequately understood (for instance, what controls glacier sliding? where is the dominant resistance to flow? how subglacial water controls flow and so on).
- The mathematical treatment is difficult, requiring full 3-dimensional non-linear Navier-Stokes equations with non-linear rheology and computer resources that are not typical of what is usually available to glaciologists.
- Observations of glacier changes (for example, glacier thickness) required to constrain the models have only been available recently and are still incomplete.

Existing numerical models excel at modeling the surface mass balance of ice sheets and ice sheet flow (under the shallow ice approximation) over time scales of millennia (Huybrechts and Wolde, 1999; Hanna et al, 2005). The real world revealed by satellites, however, shows a more dynamic landscape and time scales of variability measured in decades, years, months and even hours – all much closer to our own time scale. Such abrupt changes are not well understood or treated in numerical analyses.

Are these changes significant over the longer term?

Are the glaciers going to run out of steam, slow down and return to normal? Are the changes going to propagate far inland and do so rapidly? We do not have an answer to these questions. Yet we know that the changes taking place now in Greenland are unlikely to have had any precedent this century. It was warmer in Greenland during the 1930s and 1940s, and glaciers were losing mass rapidly at that time, but Jakobshavn Isbrae, Helheim Gletscher and Kangerdlugssuaq Gletscher did not undergo a major speed up, ice shelf collapse and several kilometer retreat as a result of warming. The warming of the 1930s was rapid but of finite duration. The warming that we are experiencing since the 1980s is longer and will not end next year.

Analogs to Greenland glaciers exist. They correspond to the warm tidewater glaciers of Alaska. These glaciers reach states of equilibrium almost independent of climate, but climate change can trigger them out of equilibrium, at which point their behavior is more guided by the glacier geometry, in particular, how deep below sea level they are grounded, than climate. As they retreat into deeper waters, they produce larger icebergs, more rapidly, and continue to retreat. In Greenland, glaciers ending on a shoal in deep water and grounded well below sea level upstream, will retreat abruptly and rapidly for a long period of time into the interior before they may eventually stabilize on higher grounds. Jakobshavn Isbrae, for instance, is grounded below sea level over several hundred kilometers into the interior. It has maintained high flow speeds, and the effects of its speed up are now felt more than 100 km inland, with no sign of reversal. In contrast, Rinks Glacier, a few hundred kilometers north, is grounded well above sea level, and has been stable since the 1960s.

Until numerical models catch up with the real world – as they probably will – we are limited to observations to figure out what may come next. Because the ice sheet changes are rapid, we will learn fast. It is incomparably easier to study the dynamics of a changing system than those of a static system. Major progress will take place in the coming years from the coupling of satellite observations with numerical models, especially now that this problem has drawn urgent interest beyond the world of glaciology.

A recent study (Rahmstorf, 2007) proposed an alternative prediction of sea level rise in the future, without requiring sophisticated numerical models of ice sheet flow, which is illuminative of the current uncertainties in predicting the future of ice sheets. A simple regression between global temperature and sea level rise suggests that sea level will rise 1 m (about 3 ft) by 2100 (Rahmstorf, 2007), or twice more than asserted by the IPCC. At the other extreme, during the Eemian interglacial (127,000 years ago), the Greenland Ice Sheet was smaller than at present, not completely melted, but enough to have raised sea level by 3 m (about 10 ft) (Overpeck et al, 2006). Depending on how fast global temperature rises, sea level may or may not be driven up by 1–3 m (about 3–10 ft) by 2100. So, there is no reason to panic at this point, but also no basis for providing reassurance.

Conclusions

Enormous progress has been made in the last decade in our knowledge of the evolution of ice sheets in a warmer climate, but it is perhaps ironic that this progress took place over a time period when significant changes were taking place as a result of global climate change. Hence, the simple answers we were seeking with modern tools changed as we got better able to research them. This will ultimately provide unprecedented, novel understanding of the evolution of ice sheets in a changing climate, but we are not in a good position at present to predict what may come next. Most advances revealed how little we know about the dynamics of ice sheets and how long of a road it will be before realistic numerical predictions can be made. At the same time, modern observation techniques are extremely powerful and will continue to provide tremendous scientific insights into the physical processes that control ice sheet dynamics.

It is now certain that the ice sheet as a whole is losing mass to the ocean and contributing to sea level rise. It is certain that the mass deficit is increasing with time, and that the mass deficit is a response to a warmer climate, especially in the southern part of Greenland. It is equally certain that the most significant changes are taking place along the coast, and that those rapid changes will not stop tomorrow, because climate is not going to cool down tomorrow. Glaciers are not only beautiful natural features, but they also exert tremendous control on ice sheet evolution, which, in turn, exerts control on ocean circulation, sea level and global climate.

Conservative models, which do not include glacier dynamics, predict that the ice sheet is doomed over the next 1000 years (Gregory et al, 2004). In light of recent observations, we might be less certain that it will take this long. At the current rate, it could happen two to three times faster (Rahmstorf, 2007), or even faster if the Eemian interglacial is an appropriate analog (Overpeck et al, 2006). In the last ten years, the margins of uncertainty in predicting ice sheet evolution have grown larger rather than smaller. Enormous progress in our understanding will be required in years to come, which require that we keep observing systems in place and build new ones, capable of more precise and comprehensive observations. Bold initiatives and ideas will be encouraged, explored and actively pursued in order to break new frontiers in our understanding of the evolution of ice sheets and obtain timely answers for scientists, educators, politicians and the general public.

References

Abdalati, W., W. Krabill, E. Frederick, S. Manizade, C. Martin, J. Sonntag, R. Swift, R. Thomas, W. Wright and J. Yungel, 2001: Outlet glacier and margin elevation changes: Near-coastal thinning of the Greenland Ice Sheet, *J. Geophys. Res.*, **106**(D24), 33729–33741

Chen, J., C. Wilson and B. Tapley, 2006: Satellite gravity measurements confirm accelerated melting of the Greenland ice sheet, *Science*, **313**, 1958–1960

Gregory, J., P. Huybrechts and S. Raper, 2004: Climatology: Threatened loss of the Greenland Ice Sheet, *Nature*, **428**, 616–616

Hanna, E., P. Huybrechts, I. Janssens, J. Cappelen, K. Steffen and A. Stephens, 2005: Runoff and balance of the Greenland Ice Sheet: 1958–2003, *J. Geophys. Res.*, **110**, D13108

Howat, I., I. Joughin, S. Tulaczyk and S. Gogineni, 2005: Rapid retreat and acceleration of Helheim Glacier, east Greenland, *Geophys. Res. Lett.*, **32**, L22502

Howat, I., I. Joughin and T. Scambos, 2007: Rapid changes in ice discharge from Greenland outlet glaciers, *Science Express*, 1138478, 8 February

Huybrechts, P. and J. de Wolde, 1999: The dynamic response of the Greenland and Antarctic ice sheets to multiple-century climatic warming, *J. Climate*, **12**, 2169–2188

Joughin, I., W. Abdalati and M. Fahnestock, 2004: Large fluctuations in speed on Greenland's Jakobshavn Isbrae glacier, *Nature*, **432**(7017), 608–610

Krabill, W., E. Frederick, S. Manizade, C. Martin, J. Sonntag, R. Swift, R. Thomas, W. Wright and J. Yungel, 1999: Rapid thinning of parts of the southern Greenland ice sheet, *Science*, **283**, 1522–1524

Krabill, W., E. Hanna, P. Huybrechts, W. Abdalati, J. Cappelen, B. Csatho, E. Frederick, S. Manizade, C. Martin, J. Sonntag, R. Swift, R. Thomas and J. Yungel, 2004: Greenland ice sheet: increased coastal thinning, *Geophys. Res. Lett.*, **31**(24), L24402

Luthcke, S., J. Zwally, W. Abdalati, D. Rowlands, R. Ray, R. Nerem, F. Lemoine, J. McCarthy and D. Chinn, 2006: Recent Greenland ice mass loss by drainage system from satellite gravity observations, *Science*, **314**(5803), 1286–1289

Otto-Bleisner, B., S. Marshall, J. Overpeck, G. H. Miller, A. Hu and CAPE Last Interglacial Project members, 2006: Simulating Arctic climate warmth and icefield retreat in the last interglaciation, *Science*, **311**, 1751–1753

Overpeck, J. T., B. L. Otto-Bliesner, G. H. Miller, D. R. Muhs, R. B. Alley and J. T. Kiehl, 2006: Paleoclimatic evidence for future ice-sheet instability and rapid sea-level rise, *Science*, **311**, 1747–1750

Rahmstorf, S., 2007: A semi-empirical approach to projecting future sea-level rise, *Science*, **315**, 368–370

Rignot, E. and P. Kanagaratnam, 2006: Changes in the velocity structure of the Greenland Ice Sheet, *Science*, **311**(5763), 986–990

Rignot, E., D. Braaten, S. Gogineni, W. B. Krabill and J. R. McConnell, 2004: Rapid ice discharge from southeast Greenland glaciers, *Geophys. Res. Lett.*, **31**(10), L10401

Thomas, R., W. Abdalati, T. Akins, B. Csatho, E. Frederick, S. Gogineni, W. Krabill, S. Manizade and E. Rignot, 2000: Substantial thinning of a major east Greenland outlet glacier, *Geophys. Res. Lett.*, **27**(9), 1291–1294

Thomas, R., E. Frederick, W. Krabill, S. Manizade, C. Martin and A. Mason, 2005: Elevation changes on the Greenland ice sheet from comparison of aircraft and ICESAT laser-altimeter data, *Ann. Glaciol.*, **42**, 77–82

Thomas, R., E. Frederick, W. Krabill, S. Manizade and C. Martin, 2006: Progressive increase in ice loss from Greenland, *Geophys. Res. Lett.*, **33**(10), L10503

Thomas, R., E. Rignot and P. Kanagaratnam, 2004: Force-perturbation analysis of Pine Island Glacier, Antarctica suggests cause for recent acceleration, *Ann. Glaciol.*, **39**, 133–138

Velicogna, I. and J. Wahr, 2006: Acceleration of Greenland ice mass loss in spring 2004, *Nature*, **443**, 329–331

Weidick, A., 1995: *Satellite Image Atlas of Glaciers of the World*, U.S. Geological Survey, Prof. Paper *1386C*, C1–C105

Zwally, J., W. Abdalati, T. Herring, K. Larson, J. Saba and K. Steffen, 2002: Surface melt-induced acceleration of Greenland ice-sheet flow, *Science*, **297**(5579), 218–222

Zwally, J., M. B. Giovinetto, J. Li, H. G. Cornejo, M. A. Beckley, A. C. Brenner, J. L. Saba and D. Yi, 2005: Mass changes of the Greenland and Antarctic ice sheets and shelves and contributions to sea-level rise: 1992–2002, *J. Glaciol.*, **51**(175), 509–527

6

Why Predicting West Antarctic Ice Sheet Behavior is so Hard: What We Know, What We Don't Know and How We Will Find Out

Robert Bindschadler

One million years of paleoclimatic data tell a consistent and convincing story – a warmer Earth contains less ice. Given that the IPCC Fourth Assessment Report predicts a temperature increase of 1.1–6.4°C over the next century, we can expect the amount of ice on the planet to decrease. Just how fast this decrease will occur, however, is still not well established as scientists are working to understand the mechanisms that control how fast the ice sheets will melt. What we do know is that records of sea level in ancient coral show that, as the ice sheets retreated at the end of the last glaciation, sea level rose at a rate up to 30 times faster than the present rate of rise, suggesting that once ice sheets begin to melt, extended episodes of ice loss can be relatively rapid. Understanding what this would mean for the Antarctic Ice Sheet, particularly the West Antarctic Ice Sheet that is grounded below sea level, is the focus of this chapter.

Sea level rise is very much a 'wild card' when it comes to predicting the effects of climate change. Approximately a third of the world's population lives within about 50 km of the coast, with many living much closer. As a result, any rise in sea level could have significant social and economic consequences that would occur in addition to the environmental impacts. Even a relatively modest rise would begin to inundate low-lying regions, accelerate coastal erosion, increase the vulnerability of coastal cities to hurricanes, storm surges and other extreme events, and begin to force relocation of coastal communities and infrastructure. The cost to those in the US of a 1 m rise in sea level, occurring over a century, has been estimated at approximately US$400 billion (Titus et al, 1991). If the rate of rise is more rapid or occurs in increments as storms pound the coastline, the impacts could be much greater. The rate of future sea level rise remains difficult to predict, largely because the impacts of warming on the behavior of the Greenland and West Antarctic Ice Sheets cannot yet be accurately modeled, makes planning along the world's coastlines particularly problematic.

Understanding ice sheet behavior

Ice sheets, namely the Greenland and the West and East Antarctic Ice Sheets store 75 per cent of the planet's fresh water – enough to raise sea level by approximately 65 m. Data from ocean sediment cores and from cores drilled through the ice sheets themselves are providing a rich trove of information about past behavior of the ice sheets. The record indicates that, over the roughly hundred thousand-year cycle of Pleistocene ice ages (the Pleistocene is the geological epoch covering the last glacial period from about 1.8 million to about 11,000 years ago), there have been repeated, slow build-ups of ice sheets, followed by relatively rapid retreats. Ice sheet waning by accelerating ice flow is an easy explanation for the asymmetric behavior, but the details of when, where and how this happens are far from adequately understood, and this is particularly troubling. The time histories suggest that what matters most is what is happening around the edges of the ice sheets. It appears that the dynamics of ice sheet movement, processes that are at present poorly represented in ice sheet models, are the likely mechanisms behind rapid retreat and that, once initiated, these processes rapidly overwhelm the potential for ice build-up from any increase in snowfall rates.

While evident in the geological and cryospheric record, any credible skill in models of reproducing or predicting these dynamic processes remains absent, although achieving skill is currently the main focus of research by many groups. So far, the IPCC assessments have suggested that the pace of change will be modest and smooth, even though glacial history suggests that there could be meltwater pulses and relatively rapid change.

Until recently, the lack of data from the polar regions has meant that scientists had only a rough idea of how the ice sheets would respond over extended periods to climate change. Now better access to these areas for scientific expeditions and new observations from near-polar orbiting satellites have helped show scientists the complexity of the polar environment and how it is already responding to climate change.

State of the ice sheets

Unlike the Arctic, which is an ocean surrounded by land, Antarctica is land surrounded by ocean. While both the Greenland and West Antarctic Ice Sheets are changing in similar ways, the changes do not match expectations (see Chapter 5 for a discussion of the changes currently happening in Greenland).

Satellite monitoring of the West Antarctic Ice Sheet (WAIS) has revealed several changes in recent decades that seem to be responses to direct interaction with the surrounding ocean, facilitated by atmospheric changes that are ultimately the result of climate warming. These observations include ice sheet thinning near the coast (measured by satellite altimetry), ice stream acceleration (measured by InSAR[1]), grounding line retreat (measured using photographic records from the Landsat), and increased calving of large icebergs (measured by MODIS[2]), all of which could signal the beginnings of disintegration (see Figure 6.1, Plate 5).

Other more direct indications that climate change is already affecting Antarctica come from the collapse of ice shelves along the Antarctic Peninsula. Because this peninsula extends northward toward the southern tip of South America, scientists expected that the effects of global warming on Antarctica would be seen first. This prediction was confirmed by the 1995 collapse of the northernmost section of the Larsen A ice shelf, followed in 2002 by the collapse of Larsen B – an ice shelf that had been in place for at least the last 12,000 years (see Figure 6.2, Plate 6). As warming continues, we should expect similar dramatic changes further south

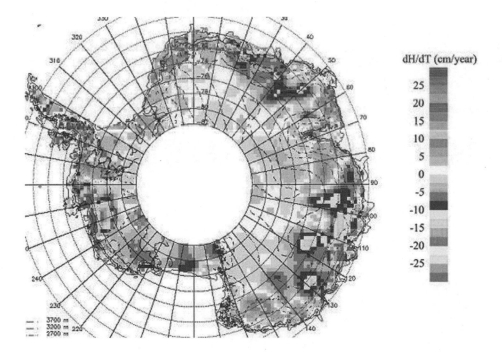

Figure 6.1 Map of Antarctica showing annual change in height of various locations of the ice sheet see Plate 5 for color version)

Note: The areas in blue show that extensive thinning is occurring in the coastal areas of the West Antarctic Ice Sheet.

Figure 6.2 Satellite image of the Antarctic Peninsula, showing the rapid break-up of the Larsen B ice shelf over about five weeks in 2002 (see Plate 6 for color version)

Note: The ice shelf had been in place for approximately 12,000 years. Following the disintegration, grounded ice streams that had been flowing into the ice shelf accelerated substantially.

(poleward) on the Antarctic Peninsula and even later on the main body of the Antarctic continent.

Feedback mechanisms that could accelerate melting

One of the reasons that the future behavior of the WAIS is so hard to predict is the existence of complex interactive mechanisms that link changes in the atmosphere and ocean to changes on the ice sheet, which can act to amplify the effects of warming. For example, as the circumpolar atmospheric circulation increases, the strength of the westerly Antarctic Circumpolar Current in the Southern Ocean increases. This response, along with the compensating easterly boundary current, combines to increase upwelling of warmer Circumpolar Deep Water onto the continental shelf. This additional heat is eventually delivered to the underside of the floating ice shelf and the ice sheet grounding line, driving faster ice flow and retreat of the grounding line.

Another important process results from warmer air temperatures, which produce meltwater ponds that act to speed up ice sheet disintegration in several ways. First, the pools of meltwater (such as those recently observed on the Greenland Ice Sheet) have a lower albedo than the ice itself and so absorb more radiation, further warming the surface. Second, when extensive meltwater occurs on an ice shelf, it can also act as a wedge, slicing the ice shelf into tall, thin icebergs that, like falling dominoes, push each other into the open ocean (a process thought to be responsible for the very rapid collapse of the Larsen B ice shelf).

Third, meltwater can travel through cracks and crevasses in the ice surface to the base of the ice sheet, a process that both warms deeper ice much faster than ordinary conductive warming and provides a lubricant that helps the ice flow faster over underlying rock. Recently, NASA's Ice Cloud and Land Elevation Satellite (ICEsat) has shown the existence of an extensive network of connected lakes under the WAIS ice streams (Fricker et al, 2007). These large volumes of water appear to move relatively rapidly under the ice, supporting the expectation that meltwater plays an important role in controlling ice sheet movement.

A final feedback mechanism involves the disintegration of the ice shelves, which are thought to 'buttress' on-land glaciers. The collapse of ice shelves removes this buttressing effect, accelerating the glaciers and leading to a net loss of grounded ice. This is happening now, for example, in the Amundsen Sea area.

Discussion

The complexity of these, and possibly other feedback mechanisms that have yet to be identified, makes predicting the future of the WAIS very difficult. Glaciological models do not yet capture many of these feedback processes, and yet researchers are increasingly finding that they are crucial in controlling how ice sheets behave. What we do know is that most ice streams along the northern edge of the WAIS have been thinning and accelerating, and that there is currently a net loss of mass from the Antarctic Ice Sheet (Zwally et al, 2006).

Other elements of the cryosphere are also already responding to global warming: Arctic sea ice extent has decreased dramatically over recent decades and the late-summer Arctic Ocean could be ice-free even before 2050; mountain glaciers are in retreat around the world and this retreat appears to be accelerating; springtime snow cover in the Northern Hemisphere has decreased by approximately 10 per cent in the last 50 years; and permafrost in the Arctic is melting over large areas.

It is clear that the polar regions are reacting to climate change faster than the rest of the planet, and the presence of multiple positive feedback mechanisms will likely maintain this disproportionate response. While we do not yet have the capability to simulate the reaction of the West Antarctic Ice Sheet to warming, we can expect that increasing greenhouse emissions are likely to continue, and probably will accelerate loss of ice from the region and, correspondingly, contribute to further increases in the rate of sea level rise.

Notes

1. Interferometric Synthetic Aperture Radar (InSAR) is a satellite-based instrument that allows very precise observations of changes in the height of the surface and its character (see http://quake.usgs.gov/research/deformation/modeling/InSAR/whatisInSAR. html).
2. MoDIS (or Moderate Resolution Imaging Spectroradiometer) is a satellite-based instrument that provides data in 36 wavelength bands. These data can be used to improve understanding of the surface changes and characteristics of land and ocean sites (see http://modis.gsfc.nasa.gov/about/).

References

Fricker, H. A., T. A. Scambos, R. Bindschadler and L. Padman, 2007: An active subglacial water system in West Antarctica mapped from space, *Science*, **315**, 1544 (doi: 10.1126/science.1136897)

Titus, J. G., R. A. Park, S. P. Leatherman, J. R. Weggel, M. S. Greene, P. W. Mausel, S. Brown, G. Gaunt, M. Trehan and G. Yohe, 1991: Greenhouse effect and sea level: The cost of holding back the sea, *Coastal Management*, **19**, 171–204

Zwally, H. J., M. B. Giovenetto, J. Li, H. G. Cornejo, M. A. Beckley, A. C. Brenner, J. L. Saba and D. Yi, 2006: Mass changes of the Greenland and Antarctic ice sheets and shelves and contributions to sea level rise: 1992–2002, *Journal of Glaciology*, **51**, 509–527

Part 3

The Potential for Dramatic
Changes in Coastal Regions

Introduction to Part 3

The Honorable Tom Roper

Oceans cover about 70 per cent of the Earth's surface, abut most of the world's nations and surround thousands of inhabited islands. The IPCC's 2001 assessment suggests that approximately a fifth of the world's population lives within 30 km of the sea and nearly double that within 100 km. The proportion is growing, particularly with rapid urbanization.

Oceans pose a number of threats to coastal environments and communities, the most significant of which has been storms. In mid- to high latitudes, the strongest storms are often in winter; in low to mid-latitudes, the strongest storms are typically in summer. Both can result in high winds, creating damaging storm surges, causing coastal erosion and high amounts of precipitation. This is particularly true for tropical cyclones, which draw their power from warm ocean waters and intensify into hurricanes, creating winds and rains that destroy coastal settlements and forests, inundate agriculture, and cause serious flooding and mudslides. Although improved warning of such events has led to reduced death rates, evacuations and damage typically create significant disruption.

While there is considerable debate about the extent of climate change impacts on coasts, the differences are about degree, not direction. Warmer ocean waters, melting glaciers and perhaps ice sheets are raising sea level above its long-term level – and prospects are for up to 1 m rise during the 21st century. Rachel Warren of the UK's Tyndall Centre and James Hansen of NASA point to potentially much greater rises with ice melt in Antarctica and Greenland.

The 2001 IPCC Report states that many coastal systems would experience:

- increased levels of inundation and storm flooding;
- accelerated coastal erosion;
- seawater intrusion into fresh groundwater;

- encroachment of tidal waters into estuaries and river systems;
- elevated sea surface and ground temperatures;
- threats to coral and mangroves.

It is also predicted that the number of extreme events will increase. There may or may not be more hurricanes and typhoons, but it is expected that they will become more powerful and, consequently, more destructive. Ecosystem resilience will be reduced by a combination of human and climate impacts.

Millions more are likely to be flooded regularly, particularly in the mega-deltas of Asia and Africa and in the especially vulnerable small islands, as described in repeated IPCC assessments. In Nigeria, for instance, 25 million people live along the coastal zone. A sea level rise of 0.5 m would displace 1.5 million people and result in the loss of 200,000 jobs in Alexandria, Egypt, alone.

While the atolls in small island developing states such as the Maldives, Marshalls, Tuvalu and Kiribati are the most vulnerable, and even may vanish as geographical areas and nations, almost all small island developing states have most of their social and economic activity and capital investment less than 2 m above sea level. As a result of the 2004 Indian Ocean tsunami, the Maldives suffered the effects of a century of sea level rise in an afternoon, with 10 per cent of the habitable land lost and the ongoing salinization of scarce fresh water supplies and food gardens.

Part 3 describes three vulnerable coastal situations in the US that are typical of situations worldwide. These examples show the need and potential for taking action to protect lives and properties in many areas vulnerable to sea level rise. In Chapter 7, Professor Michael Kearney details the potential for significant impacts on Chesapeake Bay, the largest estuary in the US and typical of large estuaries worldwide. In Chapter 8, Dr Virginia Burkett outlines the situation along the Gulf Coast and Mississippi River delta, which is typical of many low-lying coastal areas that are protected by barrier islands and wetlands. In Chapter 9, Professor Malcolm Bowman describes the situation facing the New York metropolitan area, which has major development right up to the coastal edge and is extremely vulnerable to powerful storms, the effects of which will be exacerbated by sea level rise and climate change. In Chapter 10, Dr Bruce Douglas and Professor Stephen Leatherman depict the worsening situation facing many of the world's coastlines from rising sea levels, intensifying storms, coastal erosion and intense development, and then outline the near-term steps needed to address these concerns. In the final chapter in this section, Admiral Loy, former Commandant of the US Coast Guard, presents the urgently needed actions required to protect the lives of people living in coastal areas.

Although there have always been risks for coastal residents, they are worsening, creating situations for which neither coastal ecosystems nor communities are prepared. Attention must be devoted to prepare for what seem to be inevitable challenges and changes while simultaneously taking action, as we are doing in the Global Sustainable Energy Islands Initiative, to reduce greenhouse gas emissions and slow and then stop the intensifying pace of climate change. It is too late to stop serious deleterious impacts to our coastlines. Hopefully, there is still time to prevent catastrophic change.

7

The Potential for Significant Impacts on Chesapeake Bay from Global Warming

Michael S. Kearney

Chesapeake Bay is the largest estuarine system in North America. Like other such estuaries around the world, it will face a number of significant impacts during the 21st century that are directly related to global warming. These impacts will affect people in ways that have not been witnessed since the first English settlers came to the region in 1607. In addition, the effects of global climate change will, in many cases, augment trends associated directly or indirectly with human activities, which have already produced a perilous situation in which fundamental ecosystem components or processes could be irretrievably damaged. As a result, these challenges cannot be put off to future generations and their elected representatives; the sea level future of the Chesapeake Bay in many cases is already upon us. Decisions people make today can lay a firm groundwork for understanding and planning for changes that, otherwise left unaddressed, are likely to leave few options for their solution by the end of this century.

Sea level rise and its impacts

The Chesapeake Bay, like all estuaries, owes its existence to global sea level rise. It was formed as the Susquehanna River valley was drowned as water poured back into ocean basins beginning about 18,000 years ago when the great ice sheets of the last glacial ice age (Wisconsin in North America) began to melt. The period between 18,000 and 12,000 years ago (late Glacial) witnessed most of the 130 m global rise in sea level that occurred as the continental ice sheets retreated worldwide. At this time, a series of ancestral Chesapeake bays transgressed across the outer and inner continental shelves from where the ancient Susquehanna River emptied directly in the Atlantic Ocean basin during the Glacial Maximum. The annual rate of sea level rise clearly varied over the centuries during this early phase, but, overall, likely averaged at least 2 cm per year (2 m or 6.6 ft per century), or

10 times the global trend of the latter half of the 20th century (see Douglas et al, 2001).

It is difficult to imagine what these proto-Chesapeake bays looked like since erosion of the shelves as sea level rose removed all but occasional traces of their sediments, even after sea level reached the inner continental shelf and the rate of global sea level rise had slowed considerably (Kraft et al, 1987). It is certain, however, that they must have appeared very different from the Chesapeake Bay we see today. For one, coastal marshes and sea grasses would have largely been absent, as the best estimates available suggest rates of sea level rise around 1 m per century may be the upper limit that they can survive. It is also almost certain that rates of shore erosion and land submergence were probably such that every decade saw wholesale changes. The paucity of preserved sediments from this period attests to the extraordinary beveling of the coastal features and sediments.

The little information that has been gleaned about ancestral Chesapeake bays of the late Glacial period gives indications of what a very rapid sea level rise – on the order of meters per century – could mean for the present bay: an impoverished system with large gaps in the range of ecosystem services that it now provides. The impacts on people around the Bay's shores (and for a considerable distance away from those past shorelines) are without historical precedent and can only be imagined.

The potential for such catastrophic change in the future cannot be considered totally out of the realm of possibility. What if outlet glaciers of the Greenland Ice Sheet become unstable, leading to rapid thinning of this major ice mass, and there is a concurrent wholesale ablation of the West Antarctic Ice Sheet (WAIS)? Though the 2007 report of Working Group I of the IPCC projects rates of rise of global sea level during this century of between 23 and 38 mm, this projection is based on largely steric (thermal or volume) expansion of ocean water down to perhaps 1000 m and includes relatively limited additions of water mass from glacial melting. The estimates also do not allow for any major melting of the largest ice masses on the planet, despite recent radar and LIDAR data suggesting much more rapid surface ablation than has been predicted (see Chapter 6). The prospect of massive melting of the largest ice masses on the planet is indeed disquieting.

At present, there is no telling whether the estimates for global sea level rise will ultimately prove far too conservative. We can, as an initial analysis, evaluate the potential impacts of a 23–38 mm (9–15 inches) rise in global sea levels for Chesapeake Bay. Over the last millennium, climatic conditions in this region have shifted from the cold of the Little Ice Age – an obvious candidate for perhaps the coldest period in the last 5000 years – to a period of warming beginning around the mid-19th century, which most scientists agree today continues to be driven increasingly by anthropogenic greenhouse gases. Though there exists no universal curve for the sea level record of the past 1000 years – unlike the 'hockey stick' for global temperatures of Mann et al (1999) – sufficient data are available (see Kearney, 2001) to portray a period when steric contraction of surface ocean waters and growth of mountain ice masses (mainly in the Northern Hemisphere) produced a flat, if periodically falling, sea level. In Chesapeake Bay, sea level stood approximately 70 cm (2.3 ft) below present about the time of the beginning of the Little Ice Age (c. 1300–1450 AD) (Kearney, 1996). Prior to about 1850 AD, sea level in the Bay rose only around 35 inches over a period going back to the early 14th century (about 500 years). Within the last 150 years, it has risen a little over 40 cm (16 inches) (Kearney, 1996), almost its rise since the first half of the past millennium. Since 1960, the trend has been particularly steep (Kearney et al, 2002). The overall sea level trend for the Chesapeake Bay for the last 1000 years is shown in Figure 7.1, and the trend since 1900 in Figure 7.2.

Submergence, shore erosion, storm flooding and waves

The upshot of the changes in Bay sea level rise during the last 150 years has, in many cases, been a dramatic transformation of shorelines and once distinctive islands. Clearly, the first Europeans living in the region would see a Chesapeake Bay that has been obviously changed. Physical and cultural landmarks they once knew would in many cases have disappeared; large islands once supporting plantations known for generations have vanished (Kearney and Stevenson, 1991); elsewhere, shorelines have migrated roughly 100 m (300–400 ft) landward of former positions; and former upland forests have now become marshlands (Figure 7.3 illustrates the fate of Sharps Island). In fact, it is likely that their grandchildren living in the middle 19th century were probably the first people to have witnessed the onset of changes wrought by rising sea level, though the rate of change may have been slow at first as sea level rise only really began to accelerate after 1850 AD, the conventional end of the Little Ice Age. Since then, sea level has continued to rise globally; most scientists are now in agreement that anthropogenic greenhouse warming during the 20th century has contributed significantly to this trend. In the Chesapeake Bay, rates of sea level rise are presently the highest they have been for at least 1000 years (Kearney, 1996) (see Figure 7.1).

Because the Chesapeake Bay region is subsiding (having been pushed upwards 20,000 years ago by the vast continental ice sheet to the north), it is especially vulnerable to increases in sea level. With a 'built-in' sea level rise of 1.6–2.0 mm per year (Kearney, 1996) – about equal to the present global rate (Douglas et al, 2001) – sharp upward departures in world sea level will become magnified along the shores of Chesapeake Bay. For the low-lying shorelines of the Eastern Shore of the Bay, outright submergence will be the fate of many areas. From southern Dorchester County in Maryland down to the Virginia Eastern Shore, land elevations rise almost imperceptibly away from the mean high water mark. It is not uncommon to be only a foot above mean tide level 2 km (over a mile)

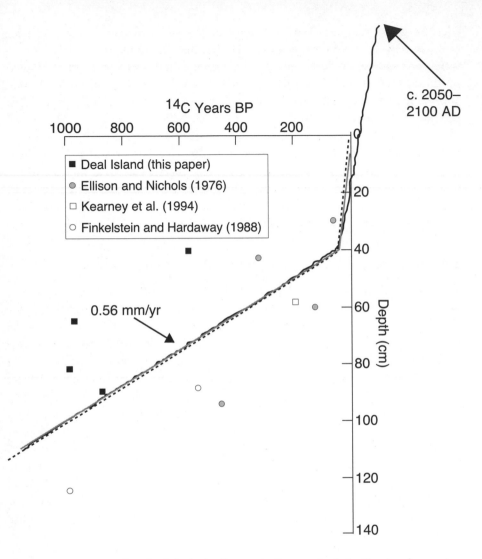

Figure 7.1 Reconstructed sea level rise in the Chesapeake Bay over the last millennium from various radiocarbon dates and other data

Note: The black line shows the general trend extended through the latter half of the 21st century based on the mean sea level rise projections in the Fourth Assessment Report of the IPCC.

landward of mean tide level. The physical expression of this nearly flat coastal profile is an extremely broad intertidal zone that is characterized by the largest marsh systems in the Bay. The 'rise to run' of such profiles can be small, 1:2500, meaning that you rise 1 unit above mean sea level for every 2500 units away from the shoreline. It is thus easy to see how vulnerable such a coast is to the possible

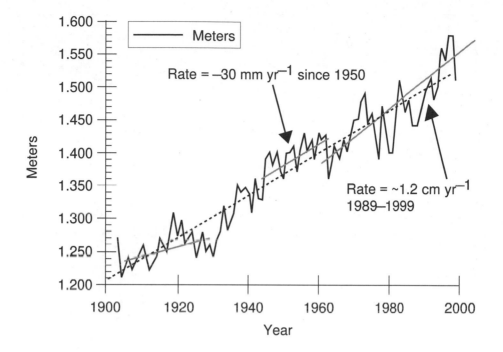

Figure 7.2 The Baltimore tide gauge data for sea level change in the Chesapeake Bay during the 20th century

Note: The superimposed lines on the general curve show the approximate mean trend for different time periods. Note the steep trend for the last 40 years.
Source: Kearney et al, 2002.

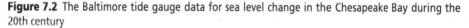

global changes in sea level rise proposed in the Fourth Assessment Report of the IPCC. It is also not surprising that some of the first LIDAR surveys for detailed elevation estimates undertaken in Maryland focused on the low-lying Eastern Shore. It is here where the greatest change from an accelerated rate of sea level rise resulting from global warming will occur. There is a realistic possibility that the shoreline in some areas could migrate over 1 km (roughly a mile) from its present position (see Figure 7.4, Plate 7).

For the high cliff shorelines of the western shore and the low cliff shorelines of the northern eastern shore, greatly accelerated shore erosion will be the main consequence. Many people remain incredulous upon being told that Bay shorelines are eroding much faster than on nearby barrier islands, often a difference of meters per year for the Bay compared to a few centimeters per year for Assateague Island. The incredulity stems from the fact that observations indicate that open

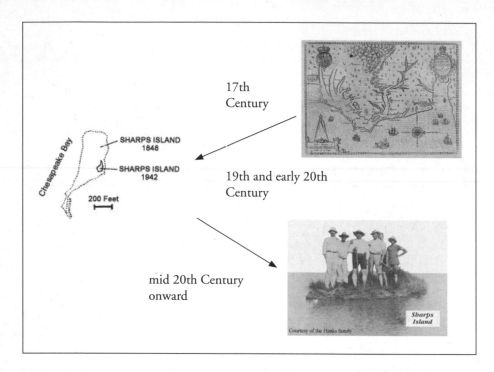

Figure 7.3 Changes in Sharps Island since the 17th century

Note: The island, once a prominent feature at the mouth of the Choptank River on the Maryland Eastern Shore, was the site of a large hotel as late as 1900–1910. The photograph shows the remnants of the island in about 1950. Today, all that remains is a shoal, with only the late 19th century caisson Sharps Island Light to mark its passing. The arrow shows the island's depiction on a late 17th century map, with a symbol for a plantation.
Source: Stevenson and Kearney, 1996.

coast should be eroding faster since storms there are often more ferocious and their waves much bigger than those in the estuary. But, such observations do not take into account that along the open coast the large storm waves of winter are countered by the long swell waves from the southeast in summer, which move back on shore much of the sediment eroded earlier in the year. In estuaries this does not happen. Therefore, while the waves in the Chesapeake Bay are generally much smaller, reflecting its relative shallowness and narrow width (fetch), they are much more effective at eroding the coastline.

On barrier islands along the open coast, the Bruun Rule provides a useful estimate of how much shore erosion is likely to occur with sea level rise. Zhang et al (2002) demonstrate that the Bruun Rule predicts a 1:150 ratio for recession of the shoreline from sea level rise. In essence, a 1 m rise in sea level would result in a 450 m (about 1500 ft) retreat. The Fourth Assessment mean expected increase

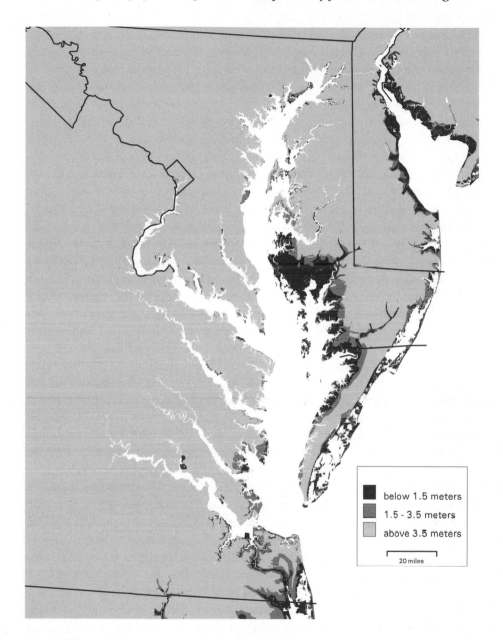

Figure 7.4 Mean elevations above mean sea level for the Chesapeake Bay region, showing the likelihood that areas will be flooded for different levels of sea level rise induced by global warming (see Plate 7 for color version)

Source: Courtesy of J. G. Titus. See also Titus and Richmond (2001).

of 17 cm, adjusted for subsidence in the Bay region, thus suggests that Assateague Island could sustain about 42 m (about 139 ft) of shoreline retreat this century from erosion, regardless of submergence.

While this is astounding enough, it is likely that the same 1 m rise would produce a substantially greater amount of shoreline retreat from erosion in Chesapeake Bay. Unfortunately, the Bruun Rule simply does not work in estuaries, or along coasts composed of materials other than sand – both of which characterize the Bay. However, if the figures of 30–200 m of retreat from erosion in the Chesapeake Bay since 1850 AD, with an approximate rise of 0.3 m, are scaled up for a rise of 37 cm (the mean IPCC estimate plus mean subsidence rate of 2 mm yr^{-1} for the Chesapeake Bay), erosion of 37–240 m (122–792 ft) could occur in the Bay.

The heightened rates of shore erosion that will occur with accelerated sea level rise in the Chesapeake Bay will not only threaten structures within the potential zone of erosion, but will also make flooding and wave damage to property close to the shoreline much more likely, even though the properties are now relatively secure from storm impacts. Potentially damaging storms include not only hurricanes and nor'easters that make landfall within the Bay region, but 'backdoor' storms that come ashore in the eastern Gulf of Mexico and transverse up the spine of the Appalachians, passing out to the Atlantic Ocean across the Chesapeake Bay. Such storms are far more common in the Bay than people realize (Stevenson and Kearney, 2005). In fact, the flood of record within the last 40 years in the estuary resulted from Tropical Storm Agnes in 1972, a large Gulf of Mexico hurricane that moved up the Appalachians into the Susquehanna River drainage basin; it dumped so much rain that the flood wave eventually submerged downtown Norfolk under 1.8 m (6 ft) of water (US Army Corps of Engineers, 1990).

An additional large liability of becoming ever closer to the shoreline as erosion occurs is to come within striking distance of waves. At the very least, being within the zone of wave impacts will increase flooding risk as a result of both how far floodwaters penetrate landward and increasing water depth. Two processes are involved: wave run-up and wave set-up. Wave run-up is by far the most important, allowing storm waves to reach farther landward and even overtop shore protection structures like bulkheads. However, it is the power of large waves that is devastating. Large waves are one of nature's most powerful phenomena, exerting forces both due to their mass (hydrostatic force) and momentum (hydrodynamic force). The power of large waves was indelibly demonstrated by the Galveston Hurricane of 1900 when 9–12 m (30–40 ft) waves came crashing over Galveston, probably moving close to 50 miles per hour. The storm surge of around 5 m (17 ft) facilitated the waves reaching the island, although by itself, it would not have caused the tremendous destruction and loss of life produced by the storm, because the rise in sea level was only about 1.5 m (5 ft) higher than average elevation of the center of Galveston (see Figures 7.5 and 7.6).

Figure 7.5 Hearst newspaper reconstruction of Galveston Island about 3 pm, 8 August 1900

Source: Courtesy of J. G. Titus. See also Titus and Richmond (2001).

Ecological impacts

Coastal marsh loss and its effects

Nicholls et al (1999), using estimates for global sea level rise based on the Hadley Centre climate model, predicted that existing coastal marshes worldwide could be inundated by 2080 AD. For Chesapeake Bay, like many microtidal coasts (i.e., 0–2 m mean tidal range), this dire prediction could come true much earlier. Marsh loss has been occurring in the Bay since at least the 1920s (Stevenson et al, 1985), and by 1993 nearly 50 per cent of the marshes in the estuary had become degraded, being unable to keep pace with the past rate of sea level rise (Kearney et al, 2002). This situation parallels that which has characterized the brackish marshes in the Mississippi River Delta (see Boesch et al, 1994). Typically, the degradation is associated with the growth of large open water areas, or ponds in interior marsh sites ('interior ponding'), with erosion of shoreline areas being a considerably less significant process (Stevenson et al, 1985; Stevenson and Kearney, 1996). Mendelssohn et al (1981) described the underlying mechanism

Figure 7.6 Large waves demolishing docks and boathouses at the Virginia Institute of Marine Sciences during Hurricane Isabel in 2003

Source: Virginia Institute of Marine Science.

as involving depletion of dissolved oxygen in waterlogged surface marsh sediments (anoxia) as the upward growth of marsh surface is outpaced by rising sea levels. The resulting plant dieback leads to break up of the marsh from collapsing of the root mass. The process may be triggered by events like storms, after which an increasing number of small open water areas (ponds) coalesce into larger ponds. Eventually, the formation of ever-larger ponds reaches a point where pond size (about 2.5 hectares) is large enough that wave erosion of the pond edge accelerates pond enlargement (Kearney et al, 1988; Stevenson and Kearney, 1996).

Compounding the problem of accelerated marsh loss is the fact that some of the biggest and ecologically most important marshes in the Chesapeake Bay may be especially predisposed to rapid loss. For biogeochemical reasons that are not fully understood, older organic materials buried below the root zone can undergo further (so-called 'refractory') degradation. By this process, larger structures like roots and rhizomes that keep the sediments together are broken down to a finely divided, relatively loose organic mass (Stevenson et al, 1985), resulting in a sequence of materials that is readily eroded if the marsh peat becomes fragmented. The loose materials below the shallow surface peat make them quake when walked over, and rise and fall slightly with the tide. They are uniquely fragile and, unfortunately, marshes of this type are probably more common in the Chesapeake Bay than is realized. An even more sobering thought is that presently, stable tidal freshwater marshes and very slightly brackish marshes (salinities of around 5 parts per 1000 salt) could be transformed by rising sea level into these highly vulnerable semi-quaking marshes. It is believed that sulfates from seawater are the agent behind the biogeochemical processes that cause the older peat to become essentially ooze. A rapid rise in sea level, moreover, could catch salt intolerant plants in these marshes before they were able to migrate naturally inland, with a massive die-off within a few years. Such a scenario has been occurring in freshwater parts of the Blackwater Wildlife Refuge, where a natural marsh 'dike' of brackish plants historically kept the high salinity waters of this part of the Bay from reaching a large freshwater cattail marsh more landward. In the late 1990s, the marsh dike broke, probably as a consequence of sea level rise, and very brackish water began pouring into the cattail marsh, killing the plants within a few years (see Figure 7.7, Plate 8).

Recent studies (Kearney et al, 2002) of marsh 'health' in the Chesapeake Bay have indicated that they may be poised for a rapid dieback as a result of not keeping pace for most of the 20th century with sea level rise. The trigger for such a catastrophe could be sea level rise itself, especially an episode like the decade long 'ramp up' in rate that occurred in the 1990s, which saw dramatic increases in rates of loss. Or, it could be a very hot summer, which would exacerbate the low dissolved oxygen problem further – or both factors combined with a drought, which causes inadequate flushing of sulfides that hinder the necessary uptake of nitrogen by the plants.

However, whatever the precise trigger that exploits conditions promoted by decades of rapid sea level rise, it will likely happen when least expected and sooner rather than later. The consequences will be losses and severe degradation of fundamental coastal ecosystems that sustain animals ranging from waterbirds and crabs to finfish, as well as providing a buffer to storm surges and waves in many areas. Unfortunately, these impacts, though having the potential to change fundamentally the Chesapeake's ecology and ecosystem services, may not be the only ones. Wicks (2005) found that eroding marshes leave a sea bottom not conducive to the establishment of sea grasses, which often are found just seaward of marshes. As sea level rises, and the sea grasses must migrate to shallower water to survive, in many cases there may be no place for them to go.

Impacts of increasing water temperatures and salinity

The struggle to control the pernicious effects of excess nutrients (nitrogen and phosphorus) flooding into the Chesapeake Bay has held center stage among the environmental concerns of the region for more than a quarter of a century.

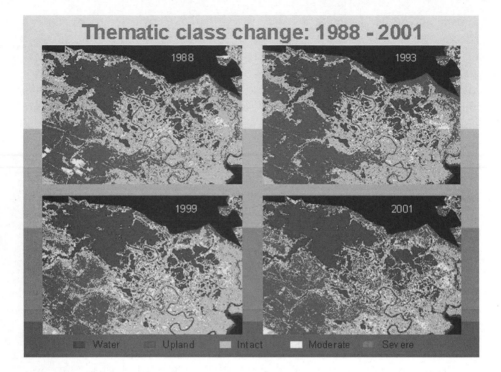

Figure 7.7 Marsh loss at Blackwater Wildlife Refuge on the Maryland Eastern Shore from 1988–2001 as derived from satellite data (see Plate 8 for color version)

Note: This marsh system, once the largest in the Chesapeake Bay, has lost more than 5000 acres of marsh since the late 1930s, with much of the marsh area that is left in severely degraded condition. It can be seen in the images that losses between 1999 and 2001 were greater than those between 1993 and 1999, showing the increasing effects of a sea level rise of over 1cm per year for most of the 1990s on the Chesapeake Bay region.

Some successes in mitigating the effects of this problem have been achieved, most notably in the return of sea grasses to many areas of the Bay (though this may indeed be offset by marsh loss as described above). Burgeoning population growth in the Chesapeake Bay watershed still remains the major threat to the Bay's ecology, with all the pollutants (such as nutrients) that the development produces. Nevertheless, future warming of the Bay waters during the summer as a result of global warming, coupled with more rainfall in the Susquehanna watershed (Fisher, 2000), could contribute to curtailing any further remediation. Warmer water has less capacity to hold dissolved oxygen, and the flushing of increasing amounts of nutrients from future development during spring floods into the Bay's tributaries could dramatically forestall any scenario for successful management of the Bay's living resources. At the very least, expectations for improvement in overall estuarine health may have to be revised, or even more stringent controls for nutrient influxes put into effect.

A greater unknown is the long-term impact of increasing salinity as ocean waters intrude into the system. An estuary represents a delicate balance between the mixing of freshwater from a river (in the case of the Bay, principally the Susquehanna) and saltwater from the ocean. Organisms correspondingly adjust to local variations in this balance, and even short-term large shifts in salinity up and down the system (i.e., longitudinal changes) can exact major repercussions. The intrusion of oyster parasites such as *Haplosporidium nelsoni* (which causes Multinucleated Sphere X (MSX) disease) into the middle and upper Bay, which are generally held in check by lower salinities, is a recent example. Salinities in the Chesapeake Bay have, of course, changed over time, as sea level rose and ocean waters intrude further inland. But whether organisms, especially those that tolerate only a narrow range of brackish water (i.e., salinities less than those of ocean water), can adjust to rapid, large-scale and persistent salinity changes is an open question. Aspects of competition for space in an ever-narrowing zone of appropriate salinity for bottom dwellers (benthic species) have yet to be examined in detail. Nonetheless, this could be the wild card in the mix of ecological changes that arise from sea level rise and global warming, with effects that could prove more lasting than any other.

The challenge of global warming to the Chesapeake Bay

Rapid sea level rise will be the most important agent of global warming in changing the physical characteristics and ecological functioning of the Chesapeake Bay. It will also enhance very significantly the hazards of building and living around the Bay's shores. Nonetheless, though the changes may be unavoidable to a large degree; how the region and the nation – the Chesapeake Bay is certainly a national resource – respond, could allay the disquiet that surrounds what the future holds.

Environmental hazards posed by future sea level rise from a scientific and engineering standpoint may be the easiest to address. The science has converged on figures for global sea level rise that between the Third and Fourth Assessments changed comparatively little compared to the range of trends predicted in the 1980s. These figures ultimately may prove woefully too conservative if the Greenland Icecap and WAIS collapse, but at present this is an imponderable that must await further research. In the mean time, with better data on coastal elevations in low-lying areas from technologies such as LIDAR, better storm surge models more able to address the high spatial resolution required for a complex coast, better estimates of shoreline erosion rates, and better storm wave models, uncertainties can be addressed about flood risks and damage. Such work is already being undertaken in the Chesapeake Bay, and in the immediate future could prove a boon to coastal landowners concerned about whether large private insurers will continue to underwrite their homes and property.

What will be more intractable is a formulation of a coast-wide policy to minimize threats from sea level rise. Principles of English Common Law and political and economic realities inevitably wend their way through such discussions, and consensus can be hard to achieve. There is nevertheless ample precedent on strategies such as setback regulations, economic incentives and disincentives, land acquisition programs, and the like (see Klee, 1998) to provide a basis for decision making. It is certain that no one approach can apply to all of the Chesapeake Bay, as the risks from sea level rise in the Tidewater Virginia region – a low-lying, sprawling mix of port, major recreational and government land uses exposed to the full force of hurricanes making landfall in the Bay – are considerably different from those of Baltimore, where a more compact port facility is juxtaposed with more traditional city development. The differing impacts of Hurricane Isabel exemplified these differences.

The question of planning for ecological impacts poses greater scientific challenges because the science is less developed. For example, we have only in the last couple of decades begun to tease out the details of eutrophication in the Chesapeake Bay, its relations to land use, interannual and intraannual variations in nutrient inputs relative to rainfall, and aspects of bioprocessing (organisms modifying nutrient inputs) within the system. Although we expect global warming to yield generally warmer Bay waters and possibly greater rainfall in the Chesapeake's watershed, the landscapes and streams that mediate the sources of nutrients into the estuary will also be affected by such changes, and our grasp of how these integral components of the Bay system operate in the present context needs significant refinement if these considerations are to be taken into account in addressing a changing climate.

Similarly, the impacts of increasing salinity in the Chesapeake Bay are also difficult to gauge, especially apart from general impacts on tidal freshwater marshes, or sessile (i.e., attached to the sea bottom) organisms like oysters. What is particularly worrying is how the lower trophic levels (i.e., the lower levels of the food chain) might be impacted, especially planktonic species. The broad outlines are known of where oligohaline (essentially freshwater to very slightly brackish), mesohaline (brackish) and polyhaline (higher salinity brackish to open ocean) species are organized longitudinally up the Bay's waters, however, the historical baseline is slim. As a result, it is not yet clear what would happen if irreversible systemic changes occur; for example, it is unclear what would happen if salinities increased dramatically and permanently rather than temporarily shifted as occurs as a result of droughts or periods of high rainfall. Ultimately, such changes could strike at the heart of the Bay's ecology – as would also be the case in other estuaries – and such irreversible changes might cause the most damaging impacts of all.

References

Boesch, D. F., M. N. Josselyn, A. J. Metha, J. T. Morris, W. K. Nuttle, C. A. Simenstad and D. J. P. Swift, 1994: Scientific assessment of coastal wetland loss, restoration and management in Louisiana, *Journal of Coastal Research*, Special Issue No. 20

Douglas, B. C., M. S. Kearney and S. P. Leatherman (eds), 2001: *Sea Level Rise: History and Consequences*, Academic Press, New York

Fisher, A., 2000: Mid-Atlantic region: Preparing for a changing climate, *Acclimations* (newsletter US National Assessment of the Potential Consequences of Climate Variability and Change), May/June 2000 issue (see www.usgcrp.gov/usgcrp/Library/nationalassessment/newsletter/2000.06/midatl.html)

Kearney, M. S., 1996: Sea-level change during the last thousand years in Chesapeake Bay, *Journal of Coastal Research*, **12**, 977–983

Kearney, M .S., 2001: Late Holocene sea level variation, in B. C. Douglas, M. S. Kearney and S. P. Leatherman (eds) *Sea Level Rise: History and Consequences* Academic Press, New York

Kearney, M. S. and J.C. Stevenson, 1991: Island land loss and marsh vertical accretion rate evidence for historical sea-level changes in Chesapeake Bay, *Journal of Coastal Research*, **7**, 403–416

Kearney, M. S., R. E. Grace and J. C. Stevenson, 1988: Marsh loss in the Nanticoke Estuary, Chesapeake Bay, *Geographical Review*, **78**, 205–220

Kearney, M. S., A. S. Rogers, J. R. G. Townshend, J. C. Stevenson, J. Stevens, E. Rizzo and K. Sundberg, 2002: Landsat imagery shows decline of coastal marshes in Chesapeake and Delaware Bays, *EOS, Transactions American Geophysical Union*, **83**(16), 173, 177–178

Klee, G. A., 1998: *The Coastal Environment*, Prentice Hall, Upper Saddle River, New Jersey

Kraft, J. C., M. J. Chrzastowski, D. F. Belknap, M. A. Toscano and C. H. Fletcher, 1987: Morphostratigraphy, sedimentary sequences and response to relative sea level rise along the Delaware coast, in D. Nummedal, O. H. Pilkey and J. D. Howards (eds) *Sea Fluctuation and Coastal Evolution*, Society of Economic Paleoentologists and Mineralogists, Special Publication No. 41

Larson, E., 2000: *Isaac's Storm: A Man, a Time, and the Deadliest Hurricane in History*, Random House, New York

Mann, M. E., R. S. Bradley and M. K. Hughes, 1999: Northern Hemisphere temperatures during the past millennium: Inferences, uncertainties, and limitations, *Geophysical Research Letters*, **26**(6), 759–762

Mendelssohn, I. A., K. L. McKee and W. H. Patrick, Jr, 1981: Oxygen deficiency in *Spartina alterniflora* roots: Metabolic adaptation to anoxia, *Science*, **214**, 439–441

Nicholls, R. J., F. M. J. Hoozemans and M. Marchand, 1999: Increasing flood risk and wetland losses due to global sea-level rise: Regional and global analyses, *Global Environmental Change*, **9**, S69–S8

Stevenson, J. C. and M. S. Kearney, 1996: Shoreline dynamics on the windward and leeward shores of a large temperate estuary, in K. F. Nordstrom and C. T. Roman (eds) *Estuarine Shores: Hydrological, Geomorphological and Ecological Interactions*, John Wiley & Sons, New York

Stevenson, J. C. and M. S. Kearney, 2005: Dissecting and classifying the impacts of historic hurricanes on estuarine systems, in K. Sellner (ed.) *Hurricane Isabel in Perspective*, Conference Proceedings, Chesapeake Bay Research Consortium, Edgewater, MD

Stevenson, J. C., M. S. Kearney and E. C. Pendleton, 1985: Sedimentation and erosion in a Chesapeake Bay brackish marsh system, *Marine Geology*, **67**, 213–235

Titus, J. G. and C. Richman, 2001: Maps of lands vulnerable to sea level rise: Modeled elevations along the US Atlantic and Gulf Coasts, *Climate Research*: **18**, 1–14

US Army Corps of Engineers, 1990: *Chesapeake Bay Shoreline Erosion Study*, Vol. 2. Baltimore District, Baltimore, Maryland

Wicks, E. C., 2005: The effect of sea level rise on seagrasses: Is sediment adjacent to retreating marshes suitable for seagrass growth?, Ph.D. dissertation, Marine, Estuarine and Environmental Science Program, University of Maryland, College Park, Maryland

Zhang K., W. K. Huang, B. C. Douglas and S. P. Leatherman, 2002: Shoreline position variability and long-term trend analysis, *Shore and Beach*, **70**, 31–36

8

The Northern Gulf of Mexico Coast: Human Development Patterns, Declining Ecosystems and Escalating Vulnerability to Storms and Sea Level Rise

Virginia Burkett

The northern Gulf of Mexico coastal zone has some of the highest rates of coastal erosion and wetland loss in the world. The Gulf Coast region also ranks highest in the number of US billion dollar weather-related disasters and flood insurance claims. The high vulnerability of this low-lying coastal zone to land loss and flooding is generally attributed to the combined effects of human development activity, sea level rise, hurricanes and other tropical storms, and a natural physical setting that is sensitive to subtle changes in the balance of marine, coastal and onshore processes. Human-induced climate change has the potential to greatly enhance this vulnerability by increasing the intensity of tropical storms, altering precipitation and runoff, and accelerating sea level rise. The threshold-type responses that have been observed in some Gulf Coast systems suggest that changes in climatic variables could have rapid, widespread impacts during coming decades. Retreat of the coastal shoreline and inundation of adjacent lowlands, coupled with losses of life and property during recent hurricanes, have also stimulated public concerns about the sustainability of some Gulf Coast ecosystems and the human communities that depend upon them, as the climate warms.

Gulf Coast physiographic setting

The US Gulf Coast physiographic region extends from Brownsville, Texas to the Florida Keys and encompasses the coastal plain, low hills, barrier islands, estuaries and river deltas of the northern Gulf of Mexico. Sediments consist of coastal plain deposits and thick land-derived sediments on the outer continental shelf that, ultimately, transition to evaporite and carbonate deposits in deep offshore waters. While the coastal margin is considered tectonically stable, its geomorphic features are subject to natural processes that alter the landscape at time scales ranging from millennia to days.

At the eastern end of the coastline in Florida, sediments are underlain by limestone at varying depths from the surface. Sinkholes, caves and freshwater springs are common features where the limestone is nearest the surface, particularly in the coastal plain from Tallahassee southward to Tampa Bay. Quartz sands, clayey sands and clays in this region occur as a surface veneer about 10 m thick or as elongated ridges that may be over 30 m thick. The ridges are relict shorelines created over the past several million years by the Pliocene-Pleistocene sea level cycles (Cooke, 1945; White, 1970). Most of the Florida landscape, however, is characteristically flat (Scott, 2001).

Sediments in the central Gulf Coast are dominated by thick fluvial deposits of the Mississippi and smaller rivers that deliver eroded sediments from the mainland. Deposited in coalescing river floodplains, the sediments of the Mississippi, Alabama and Louisiana coastal zone are dominated by marshes, floodplain forests, natural river levees and barrier islands. The barrier islands in Mississippi and Alabama are relatively recent features (less than 5000 years old) that are nurtured by sand carried alongshore by wave transport from the Florida panhandle and Alabama. They have all diminished in size since the mid-1880s with the greatest erosion on their east end (Morton, 2007). The barrier islands of Louisiana are remnants of Mississippi River deltas created and abandoned over the past 7000 years (Coleman et al, 1998; Gosselink et al, 1998). The Louisiana barrier islands are all retreating and diminishing in size, with the most significant breaching and retreat occurring during storms and frontal passages.

The Mississippi River has had a pronounced influence on the development of the central Gulf of Mexico coast. The Mississippi River delta covers an area of roughly 30,000 km² in Louisiana and accounted for 41 per cent of the coastal wetlands in the US in 1998 (Coleman et al, 1998). Large volumes of sediment transported by the Mississippi River during the Tertiary period (from about 2–65 million years before present) created a major basin with prolific oil and gas reservoirs (Gosselink, 1984). The current landscape of south Louisiana was shaped by the Mississippi River as it built a series of overlapping delta lobes during the Holocene (see Figure 8.1). Offshore sand shoals and barrier islands are erosional features of the oldest delta lobes. The formation of the present Mississippi Delta plain and most of the other large deltas of the world during the past 7000 years has been linked with low rates of sea level rise (Nicholls et al, 2007). For millions of years sea level has determined whether the Mississippi River delta front was transgressing or regressing across the continental shelf (Fisk, 1944; Winker, 1991). The current combination of storms and high rates of relative sea level rise are

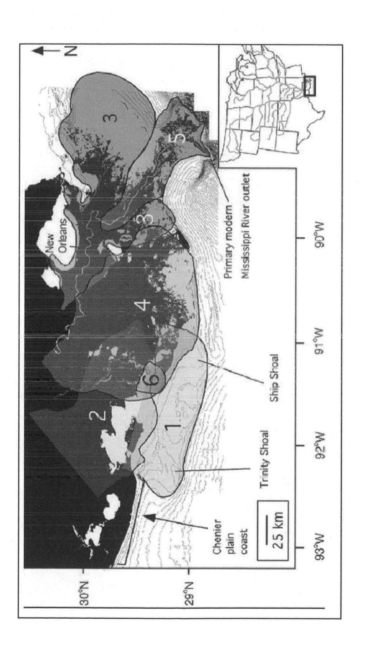

Figure 8.1 Location of the six major deltas of the Mississippi River that have developed during the past 9000 years

Note: In order from oldest to youngest, the six deltas are the (1) Maringouin, (2) Teche, (3) St. Bernard, (4) Lafourche, (5) Modern (Plaquemines–Balize), and (6) Atchafalaya lobes.

Source: Draut et al, 2005, modified from Penland and Ramsey, 1990, based on radiocarbon dating work of Frazier, 1967. Reprinted from *Continental Shelf Research* 25, A. E. Draut, G. C. Kineke, D. W. Velasco, M. A. Allison and R. J. Prime, Influence of the Atchafalaya River on recent evolution of the chenier-plain inner continental shelf, northern Gulf of Mexico, 2005, pp91–112, with permission from Elsevier.

responsible for the high rate of shoreline retreat and barrier island disintegration in the Mississippi River deltaic plain (Coleman et al, 1998).

The Chenier Plain of southwest Louisiana and southeast Texas is characterized by recessional beach ridges ('cheniers') that represent former positions of the Gulf of Mexico shoreline. Reworked sediments from Mississippi River deltas are thought to be the main source of sediments of the sand and shell fragment ridges that parallel the shoreline in this region between Vermillion Bay and the tip of Texas Bolivar Peninsula. The westward drift and deposition of sediments along this part of the Gulf of Mexico shoreline coincides with periods when Mississippi River deltas were being constructed or abandoned (and eroded) in the western delta plain. Lake, marsh and bay deposits in the Chenier Plain are highly interconnected, and small changes in rates of sea level rise can convert a marsh to a bay within a relatively short time (Gosselink et al, 1979).

West of the Chenier Plain, the Gulf coastline is characterized by long, sandy barrier islands (such as Mustang and Padre Islands), sandy mainland beaches and dunes, river mouth accretions, sheltered bays and lagoons, and fringing wetlands. The barrier islands between Aransas Pass and Mansfield Channel formed several thousand years ago and they have continued to enlarge as a result of abundant sand supplied by the along-shore currents (Morton, 1994). Because the tide range

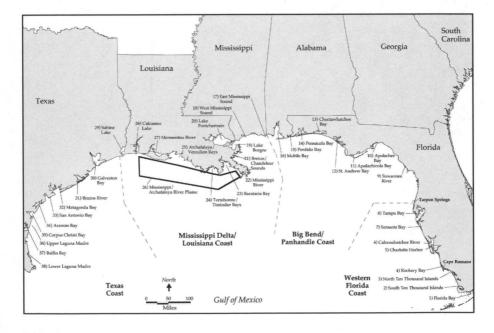

Figure 8.2 Estuarine systems located along the US coastline of the Gulf of Mexico

Source: NOAA, 1997.

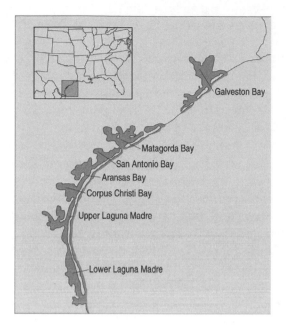

Figure 8.3 Laguna Madre of Texas

Source: Onuf, 1995.

in the western Gulf of Mexico is so low and sand supply in the littoral system is so high, there are only a few natural tidal inlet positions (for example, Aransas Pass and Packery Channel) along the Texas coast. In some areas, such as the northern part of Padre Island National Seashore, sand dunes have migrated across the barrier island and into adjacent Laguna Madre (Morton and Peterson, 2006). Estuaries (formed when the fresh water from rivers flows into coastal embayments and mixes with the salt water from the ocean) are common along the entire Gulf Coast. Salinity in Gulf Coast estuaries generally grades from marine to fresh water along a continuum beginning at the mouth of the estuary and extending landward from the Gulf shoreline. The morphology of tidal inlets and barrier islands, water levels and tidal flushing rates, and fresh water inflows determine the environmental gradients and vegetation zonation in the estuaries and wetlands of the region. The 30 large estuaries in the Gulf Coast region account for 42 per cent of US total estuarine acreage (NOAA, 1997) (see Figure 8.2). The Laguna Madre is a unique feature of the western Gulf Coast that extends southward into Mexico (see Figure 8.3). The hypersalinity of the Laguna Madre (averaging 50–100 parts per 1000) is dependent upon the balance of evaporation, fresh water runoff from the mainland, and inflows from the Gulf of Mexico, the salinity of which averages 35 parts per 1000.

Human development activities and impacts

Human development activity during the past century had more of an impact than climate change on most coastal regions (Scavia et al, 2002; Nicholls et al, 2007). The Gulf Coast region comprises some of the most valuable and heavily populated coastal landscape in North America. The total population of the coastal counties in the five Gulf Coast states has roughly doubled since 1950 and is projected to grow another 40 per cent or more by 2025, compared with an average of 23 per cent for the entire US (Twilley et al, 2001; Census Bureau, 2000).

Natural resources in the region are under intense pressure from navigation and flood control projects, and from large-scale land use change associated with industrial, agricultural and municipal development. In addition, this coastal region is being impacted by the development of its oil, gas and mineral resources. The northern Gulf of Mexico Outer Continental Shelf produces roughly one quarter of US domestic oil and gas, and Gulf coastal counties receive 60 per cent of the nation's oil imports (EIA, 2005). The Texas and Louisiana coasts are heavily impacted by oilfield access canals, navigation channels and onshore facilities that support oil and gas development in state and federal waters. Elevation has not been a constraint to development and climate change and, with rare exception, is not currently a consideration in coastal infrastructure planning. Approximately 25 per cent of the roads, 72 per cent of the port facilities and 9 per cent of the rail lines in the coastal counties between Mobile and Galveston are on land below 1.5 m in elevation (Savonis et al, in review).

The large and growing pressures of development are responsible for most of the current stresses on Gulf Coast natural resources, which include: water quality and sediment pollution, increased flooding, loss of barrier islands and wetlands, declining fisheries and other factors that are altering biodiversity, productivity and the resilience of coastal habitats (EPA, 1999). Human alterations to freshwater inflows through upstream dams and impoundments, dredging of natural rivers and man-made waterways, and flood control levees have also affected the quantity of water and sediment delivered to the Gulf coastal zone. The pressure on freshwater resources was particularly evident in the summer drought of 2000, when cities and agricultural water users suffered from salt-water intrusion and reduced availability of water resources (Twilley et al, 2001). In contrast to salt-water intrusion, which is a problem in the central and eastern Gulf region, human activity has led to a lowering of salinity in the Laguna Madre since 1949. The dredging of the Gulf Intracoastal Waterway (which allowed less saline Gulf waters to enter the lagoon) and increased drainage from agricultural lands has shifted seagrass species from the highly salt-tolerant shoalgrass (*Halodule wrightii*) to manatee grass (*Syringodium filiforme*), which has a lower salinity tolerance (Quammen and Onuf, 1993).

Roughly 80 per cent of US coastal wetland losses have occurred in the Gulf Coast region since 1940, and predictions of future population growth portend increasing pressure on Gulf Coast communities and their environment. Upper Mobile Bay marshes, for example, have declined by 34 per cent since the 1950s due to commercial and residential development, disposal of dredged material from navigation projects, industrial development, erosion and subsidence (Roach et al, 1987). Wetland loss in south Louisiana is the highest in the region and is attributed to a combination of human activity and natural factors including sediment and fresh water deprivation due to the construction of levees and dams along the Mississippi River and its tributaries, groundwater and oil and gas withdrawals, drainage of organic soils, natural compaction and dewatering of deltaic sediments, dredge and fill operations, channelization of wetlands and waterways, and sea level rise. The net effect of these various stressors has been the loss of over 1565 km² of intertidal coastal marshes and adjacent lands to open water between 1978 and 2000 (Barras et al, 2003; and for a popular account, see Tidwell, 2003).

Increased urbanization, industrialization and agricultural land use have significantly altered coastal water quality in all five Gulf Coast states. Over 25 per cent of the Gulf Coast's shellfish growing areas are closed during an average year due to pollution (EPA, 1999), and increased nutrient loading of the Mississippi River can lead to hypoxia in a near-shore area of the Gulf of Mexico covering roughly 15,000–20,000 km² and chronic algal blooms in many of the regions inshore coastal waters (Rabalais et al 1996). Salt-water intrusion is a serious problem threatening water supplies in some parts of the region, such as Houma, Louisiana.

Sea level rise and subsidence

The formation and maintenance of shorelines, wetlands, barrier islands, estuaries and lagoons of the Gulf Coast are intimately linked with sea level. Geologic records indicate that global sea level has risen about 120 m since the Last Glacial Maximum approximately 20,000 years ago. Sea level rose rapidly (averaging almost 0.9 m per century) between 20,000 and 6000 years before present and slowed to about 0.02 m per century or less during the past 3000 years (IPCC, 2001). From the mid-19th century through much of the 20th century, the average rate of global sea level rise increased to between 0.17 m and 0.18 ±0.05 m per century, and satellite data for the last decade suggest that the contemporary rate is as much as 0.3 m per century (IPCC, 2007). Most atmosphere–ocean general circulation model simulations project that sea level rise will accelerate during the 21st century and beyond due to human-induced warming. If the rate of sea level rise increases as projected, the Gulf Coast and other low-lying coastal mainlands, barrier islands and wetlands that are not experiencing significant uplift or high rates of sediment accretion will be seriously impacted. Most of the Mississippi, Louisiana and Texas coastline has been classified by the US Geological Survey as 'highly vulnerable' to erosion due to sea level rise (Thieler and Hammar-Klose, 2000).

Relative sea level change at any coastal location is determined by the combination of eustasy (global sea level rise) and local processes that affect elevation of the land surface, such as tectonism, isostasy (glacial rebound) and subsidence (sinking of the land surface). Subsidence is the predominant direction of elevation change in the Gulf Coast region. Subsidence is highest in southeast Louisiana due to its geologic age and structure. Subsidence generally decreases westward and eastward of the Mississippi delta. The western Mississippi coastline is experiencing higher subsidence rates than to the east in Alabama and Florida, but subsidence has been observed in the marshes of Grand Bay, Mississippi (Schmid, 2001) and Mobile Bay, Alabama (Roach, undated).

Tide gauge records for the region indicate that relative sea level rise during the 20th century was greatest in the Mississippi River Deltaic Plain and in southeast Texas (NOAA, 2001). The linear mean relative sea level trend at the tide gauge at Grand Isle, Louisiana (established in 1947) indicates relative sea level rise of 9.85 mm/yr. The two tide gauges in the vicinity of Galveston, Texas (established in 1908 and 1957) indicate an average rate of relative sea level rise of 6.9 mm/yr. The contribution of global sea level rise at these gauges during the past century could be estimated at the global average rate of 1.7 mm/yr. However, the rate of sea level rise is not uniform spatially due to differences in ocean basin geometry, depth/heat uptake, circulation and other factors that influence ocean volume. Twentieth century tide gauge records and satellite altimetry data since 1993 indicate that the rate of sea level rise in the Gulf of Mexico is higher than many other parts of the world ocean (see Figure 8.4, Plate 9). Hence, assessments of sea level rise impacts that are based on the global average rate may underestimate impacts in the Gulf Coast region.

Deltas have long been recognized as highly sensitive to sea-level rise (Coleman et al, 1998; Woodroffe, 2003). Rates of relative sea level rise in many of the world's deltas are at least double the current global average rate of rise (Saito, 2001; Waltham, 2002) because of human activities and the fact that deltas are generally compacting under their own weight. The heavy sediment load deposited by the Mississippi River during the past several million years has caused high rates of natural subsidence that were offset to some degree by delta building processes during much of the Holocene. Sea level has an important influence on Mississippi River deltaic processes. During periods of falling sea level, sediment deposition shifts seaward and the deltaic land mass is built on the continental shelf; during times of rising sea level, the delta deposition shifts landward and, depending upon the rate of sea level rise, may cease to deposit sediments above mean sea level. Sediment inputs to shallow waters of the deltaic plain have been curtailed by the closing of distributary channels (for example, Bayou La Fourche in 1904) and the construction of levees, upstream dams, deep-water channels and other engineering works during the past century.

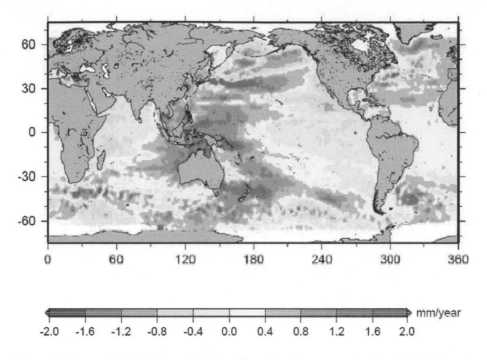

Figure 8.4 Geographic distribution of short-term linear trends in mean sea level for 1993–2003 based on TOPEX/Poseidon satellite altimetry (see Plate 9 for color version)

Source: IPCC, 2007, updated from Cazenave and Nerem, 2004.

Subsidence as a result of both hydrocarbon and groundwater extraction has been recognized as a problem in the Texas Gulf Coast since the mid-1920s. Subsidence caused by ground-water extraction has led to substantial and expensive problems in areas such as Houston, Baytown and Galveston. Subsidence in the vicinity of the Port Neches oil and gas field resulted in wetland losses that can be related to fault reactivation as a result of hydrocarbon production. State and local organizations (such as the Harris-Galveston Coastal Subsidence District) have implemented regulations that have reduced the rate of subsidence while helping to maintain ground-water supplies.

Sea level rise will generally increase marine transgression on natural estuarine shorelines (Pethick, 2001) and the frequency of barrier island overwash during storms, with effects most severe in habitats that are already stressed and deteriorating. Salt-water intrusion and increased mean water levels will lead to a change in plant and animal communities. In coastal Florida, for example, sea level rise has been identified as a causal factor in the die-off of cabbage palm (*Sabal palmetto*) (Williams et al, 1999). Salt-water intrusion has destroyed large tracts of coastal bald cypress (*Taxodium disticum*) forests in Louisiana (Krauss et al, 1998, 2000; Melillo et al, 2000). One effect of rising sea level in the Laguna Madre of

Texas will be greater water depths and increased tidal exchange, which will further reduce salinity in the lagoon (Nicholls et al, 2007).

Sea level rise does not necessarily lead to loss of saltmarshes because some marshes accrete sufficient sediments vertically to maintain their elevation with respect to sea level rise (Cahoon et al, 2006). The threshold at which coastal wetlands and other intertidal habitats are inundated by sea level rise varies widely depending upon local morphodynamic processes. Sediment inputs, even from frequent hurricanes, have not been able to compensate for subsidence and sea level rise effects in the rapidly deteriorating marshes of the Mississippi River delta (Rybczyk and Cahoon, 2002).

Tropical storms

The most extensive flooding, shoreline erosion and wetland loss in the Gulf Coast region occurs during hurricanes and lesser tropical storms. An increase in the frequency or intensity of tropical storms entering the Gulf of Mexico could have serious consequences for human settlements and natural ecosystems along this low-lying coastal margin. During Hurricanes Katrina and Rita in 2005, for example, about 300 km² of land in south Louisiana were converted to open water, according to preliminary surveys (Barras, 2006) (see Figure 8.5, Plate 10). Over 1800 people lost their lives during Hurricane Katrina and the economic losses totaled more than US$100 billion (Graumann et al, 2006). While a single storm cannot be attributed to climate change, the impacts of Hurricanes Katrina and Rita in 2005 illustrate the types of impacts that it is projected would occur more frequently if the Gulf Coast were to experience more category 4 and 5 hurricanes in the future.

An increase in sea surface temperature is considered an important indicator of climate change, and sea surface temperature plays a dominant role in determining the intensity and frequency of hurricanes (Santer et al, 2006). While factors such as wind shear, moisture availability and atmospheric stability also influence tropical cyclone genesis and evolution, increasing sea surface temperature has been correlated with hurricane intensity in the Atlantic tropical cyclogenesis regions where Gulf Coast hurricanes are formed (Emanuel, 2005).

The precise contribution of increasing sea surface temperature to tropical cyclone formation during recent decades is the subject of several recent scientific studies. Some analyses indicate that the increasing intensity of hurricanes since 1970 is driven by natural multidecadal variability (Pielke, 2005, Landsea et al, 2006), but most recent studies support the hypothesis that hurricanes are increasing in the Atlantic cyclogenesis region as a result of sea surface temperature increases related to anthropogenic warming (Emanuel, 2005; Webster et al, 2005; Hoyos et al, 2006; Mann and Emanuel, 2006; Trenberth and Shea, 2006). Some

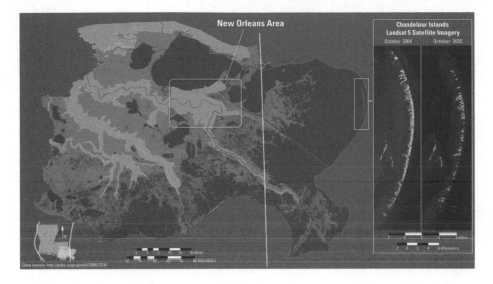

Figure 8.5 The Mississippi delta, including the Chandeleur Islands (see Plate 10 for color version)

Note: Areas in red were converted to open water during Hurricanes Katrina and Rita. Yellow lines in index map show the track of Hurricane Katrina on right and Hurricane Rita on left.
Source: US Geological Survey, Lafayette, Louisiana, modified from Barras, 2006.

studies conclude that the increase in recent decades is due to the combination of natural, cyclic fluctuations and human-induced increases in sea surface temperature (for example, Elsner, 2006). Sea surface temperature has increased significantly in the main hurricane development region of the North Atlantic during the past century (Bell et al, 2007) (see Figure 8.6) as well as in the Gulf of Mexico (Smith and Reynolds, 2004) (see Figure 8.7). Based on modeling, theory and published empirical studies, the IPCC (2007) concludes that the observed increase in intense tropical cyclone activity in the North Atlantic since about 1970 correlates with a concomitant increase in tropical sea surface temperature. The IPCC further projects that tropical cyclone activity is likely to increase during the 21st century.

The greatest damages from hurricanes are caused by the large mass of water pushed ashore by the storms high winds, known as the storm surge. If a category 3, 4 or 5 hurricane makes landfall along the shallow Gulf of Mexico coastal margin when the tide is high and barometric pressure is low, the effects can be particularly severe. An increase in sea surface temperature is likely to increase the probability of higher sustained winds and surge levels per tropical storm circulation (Emanuel, 1987; Holland, 1997; Knutson et al, 1998). Analyses of sea surface temperature, air temperature, wind speed and dew point data from NASA satellites and NOAA buoys in the Gulf of Mexico indicate that Hurricane Katrina reached

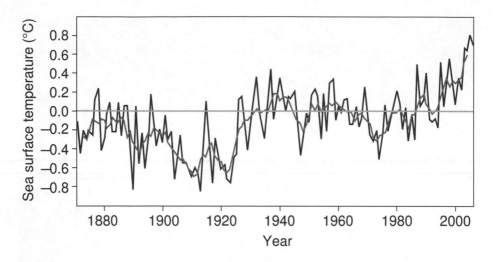

Figure 8.6 Sea surface temperature trend in the main hurricane development region of the North Atlantic during the past century

Note: Dark gray line shows the corresponding five-year running mean. Anomalies are departures from the 1971–2000 period monthly means.
Source: Bell et al, 2007.

peak intensity when the difference between sea surface temperatures and air temperatures was greatest (Kafatos et al, 2006). Surge during Hurricane Katrina peaked at approximately 8.5 m in coastal Mississippi (Graumann et al, 2006). An increase in storm surge associated with hurricanes that make landfall in the Gulf Coast region could affect the sustainability of natural systems and human developments in Gulf Coast counties because the land surface in most areas is less than 6 m in elevation (see Figure 8.8, Plate 11).

Conclusions

While either accelerated sea level rise or an increase in the intensity of tropical storms could significantly increase the potential for coastal disasters in the Gulf Coast region, it is likely that both will occur. Even if hurricanes do not increase in frequency or intensity over the next century, flooding is likely to increase along much of the low-lying Gulf of Mexico shoreline due to ongoing sea level rise and land surface subsidence, which is presently greater than the current rate of sea level rise in some regions. The projected acceleration in the rate of sea level rise will increase the current rate of loss of land and the widespread, episodic flooding that is already challenging the sustainability of some ecosystems and human settlements in the region. As climate change intensifies, the natural flood defenses (for example, barrier islands and forests) of the region will decline more rapidly,

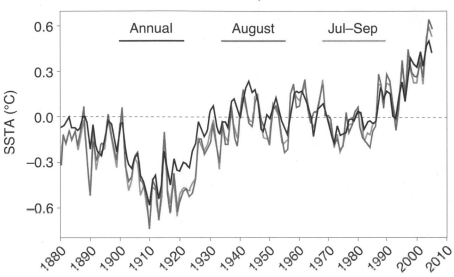

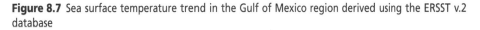

Figure 8.7 Sea surface temperature trend in the Gulf of Mexico region derived using the ERSST v.2 database

Note: The plot displays the sea surface temperature anomalies averaged annually, as well as the anomalies determined from the averages for August only and for the July–September peak of the hurricane season.
Source: Smith and Reynolds, 2004.

Figure 8.8 Land surface elevation and roads in the central Gulf Coast region (see Plate 11 for color version)

Note: Areas in red are all below 6 m in elevation.
Source: Elevation data from US Geological Survey, National Wetlands Research Center. Road data from US Department of Transportation, Bureau of Transportation Statistics.

thereby serving as a positive (amplifying) feedback to the effects of climate change on coastal systems. That is, the deterioration of natural coastal environments caused by sea level rise and storm surge increases the potential for more intense flooding and land loss due to sea level rise and storm surge in the future.

The likelihood that tropical storms will increase in intensity and the unavoidability of future sea level rise conflicts with present-day development patterns on the Gulf Coast. Historical damage due to flooding is high in the Gulf Coast region compared to many other US coastal areas because of the elevation relative to sea level, intensity and proximity of development to the shoreline, deterioration of natural coastal defenses, and the lack of infrastructure design features that would accommodate a changing environment. In addition to the direct impacts of human development on coastal ecosystems, the buildings, roads, seawalls, flood control levees and revetments that have been constructed along the Gulf Coast will prevent the natural inland migration of coastal landforms in response to sea level rise. Another consequence of intensive development in this low-lying coastal zone is the exposure of human communities and infrastructure to storm surge and increasing mean water levels. Exposure to flooding is virtually certain to increase in most Gulf Coast counties if sea level rise accelerates and tropical storms intensify. Damages will likely be most severe in places that are lowest in elevation, have insufficient natural or engineered features to buffer against storm surge, and are already deteriorating due to factors other than climate change.

Collectively, the effects of human development, accelerated sea level rise and increased tropical storm activity in the Gulf Coast region have important implications for coastal landforms, the natural habitats that they support, and the human communities that depend upon them. Other aspects of climate change will affect the ecological structure and sustainability of coastal habitats globally, such as the effects of increasing temperature on coastal plant communities and the effects of changing rainfall patterns on runoff. In the Gulf Coast region, however, increasing sea level rise and tropical storm activity appear to be the most important climate-related factors affecting the sustainability of ecosystem services and human settlements.

References

Barras, J. A., 2006: *Land Area Change in Coastal Louisiana After the 2005 Hurricanes: A Series of Three Maps*, US Geological Survey, National Wetlands Research Center, Lafayette, Louisiana, Open-File Report 2006-1274 (available at http://pubs.usgs.gov/of/2006/1274/, accessed 18 October 2006)

Barras, J., S. Beville, D. Britsch, S. Hartley, S. Hawes, J. Johnston, P. Kemp, Q. Kinler, A. Martucci, J. Porthouse, D. Reed, K. Roy, S. Sapkota and J. Suhayda, 2003: *Historical and Projected Coastal Louisiana Land Changes: 1978–2050*, US Geological Survey, National Wetlands Research Center, Lafayette, Louisiana, Open-File Report 03–334

Bell, G. D., E. Blake, C. W. Landsea, M. Chelliah, R. Pasch, K. C. Mo and S. B. Goldenberg, 2007: Tropical Cyclones: Atlantic Basin, in A. Arguez (ed.) *State of the Climate in 2006, Bulletin of the American Meteorological Society*, **88**, S1–S135

Cahoon, D. R., P. F. Hensel, T. Spencer, D. J. Reed, K. L. McKee and N. Saintilan, 2006: Coastal wetland vulnerability to relative sea-level rise: Wetland elevation trends and process controls, in J. Verhoeven, D. Whigham, R. Bobbink, and B. Beltman (eds) *Wetlands as a Natural Resource, Vol. 1: Wetlands and Natural Resource Management*, Springer Ecological Studies series, Heidelberg, Germany

Cazenave, A. and R. S. Nerem, 2004: Present-day sea level change: Observations and causes, *Reviews of Geophysics*, **42**, 10.1029/2003RG000139

Census Bureau, 2000: *Census 2000*, US Department of Commerce, Washington DC

Coleman, J. M., H. H. Roberts and G. W. Stone, 1998: The Mississippi River Delta: An Overview, *Journal of Coastal Research*, **14**, 698–716

Cooke, C. W., 1945: *Geology of Florida*, Bulletin 29, Florida Geological Survey, Tallahassee

Draut, A. E., G. C. Kineke, D. W. Velasco, M. A. Allison and R. J. Prime, 2005: Influence of the Atchafalaya River on recent evolution of the chenier-plain inner continental shelf, northern Gulf of Mexico, *Continental Shelf Research*, **25**, 91–112

EIA, 2005: *Hurricane Impacts on the US Oil and Natural Gas Markets*, US Energy Information Administration, Washington DC (available at http://tonto.eia.doe.gov/oog/special/eia1_katrina.html, accessed 5 June 2007)

Elsner, J. B., 2006: Evidence in support of the climate change-Atlantic hurricane hypothesis, *Geophysical Research Letters*, **33**, L16705

Emanuel, K., 1987: The dependence of hurricane intensity on climate, *Nature*, **326**, 483–485

Emanuel, K., 2005: Increasing destructiveness of tropical cyclones over the past 30 years, *Nature*, **436**, 686–688

EPA, 1999: *Ecological Condition of Estuaries in the Gulf of Mexico*, US Environmental Protection Agency, Office of Research and Development, National Health and Environmental Effects Research Laboratory, Gulf Ecology Division, Gulf Breeze, FL, EPA-620-R-98-004

Fisk, H. N., 1944: *Geological investigations of the alluvial valley of the lower Mississippi River*, US Army Corps of Engineers, Mississippi River Commission, Vicksburg, Mississippi

Frazier, D. E., 1967: Recent deposits of the Mississippi River, their development and chronology, *Transactions – Gulf Coast Association of Geological Societies*, **17**, 287–315

Gosselink, J. G., 1984: *The Ecology of Delta Marshes of Coastal Louisiana: A Community Profile*, FWS/OBS-84/09, US Fish and Wildlife Service, Slidell, Louisiana

Gosselink, J. G., J. M. Coleman and R. E. Stewart, Jr, 1998: Coastal Louisiana, in M. J. Mac, P. A. Opler, C. E. Puckett Haecker and P. D. Doran (eds) *Status and Trends of the Nation's Biological Resources*, 2 Vols, US Department of the Interior, US Geological Survey, Reston, Va.

Gosselink, J. G., C. L. Cordes and J. W. Parsons, 1979: *An Ecological Characterization Study of the Chenier Plain Coastal Ecosystem of Louisiana and Texas*, Volume 1: FWS/OBS-78/9, US Fish and Wildlife Service, Slidell, Louisiana

Graumann, A., T. Houston, J. Lawrimore, D. Levinson, N. Lott, S. McCown, S. Stephens and D. Wuertz, 2006: Hurricane Katrina: A Climatological Perspective, updated August 2006, Technical Report 2005-01, NOAA National Climate Data Center, Asheville, North Carolina (www.ncdc.noaa.gov/oa/reports/tech-report-200501z.pdf)

Holland, G. J., 1997: The maximum potential intensity of tropical cyclones, *Journal of Atmospheric Sciences*, **54**, 2519–2541

Hoyos, C. D., P. A. Agudelo, P. J. Webster and J. A. Curry, 2006: Deconvolution of the factors contributing to the increase in global hurricane intensity, *Science*, **312**, 94–97

IPCC (Intergovernmental Panel on Climate Change), 2001: Changes in sea level, in J. J. McCarthy, O. F. Canziani, N. A. Leary, D. J. Dokken and K. S. White (eds) *Climate Change 2001, The Scientific Basis*, Cambridge University Press, Cambridge and New York

IPCC, 2007: *Climate Change 2007: The Physical Science Basis*, Contribution of Working Group I to the Fourth Assessment Report of the Intergovernmental Panel on Climate Change, Geneva

Kafatos, M., D. Sun, R. Gautam, Z. Boybeyi, R. Yang and G. Cervone, 2006: Role of anomalous warm gulf waters in the intensification of Hurricane Katrina, *Geophysical Research Letters*, **33**, L1780

Knutson, T. R., R. E. Tuleya and Y. Kurihara, 1998: Simulated increase of hurricane intensities in a CO_2-warmed climate, *Science*, **279**, 1018–1020

Krauss, K., J. L. Chambers and J. A. Allen, 1998: Salinity effects and differential germination of several half-sib families of baldcypress from different seed sources, *New Forests*, **15,** 53–68

Krauss, K. W., J. L. Chambers, J. A. Allen, D. M. Soileau, Jr and A. S. DeBosier, 2000: Growth and nutrition of baldcypress families planted under varying salinity regimes in Louisiana, USA, *Journal of Coastal Research*, **16,** 153–163

Landsea, C. W., B. A. Harper, K. Hoarau and J. A. Knaff, 2006: Can we detect trends in extreme tropical cyclones?, *Science*, **313**, 452–454

Mann, M. E. and K. A. Emanuel, 2006: Atlantic hurricane trends linked to climate change, *EOS: Transactions of the American Geophysical Union*, **87**(24), 233–244

Melillo, J. M., A. C. Janetos, T. R. Karl, R. W. Corell, E. J. Barron, V. Burkett, T. F. Cecich, K. Jacobs, L. Joyce, B. Miller, M. G. Morgan, E. A. Parson, R. G. Richels and D. S. Schimel, 2000: *Climate Change Impacts on the United States: The Potential Consequences of Climate Variability and Change, Overview*, Cambridge University Press, Cambridge

Morton, R. A., 1994: Texas barriers, in R. A. Davis (ed.) *Geology of Holocene Barrier Islands*, Springer-Verlag, Berlin

Morton, R. A., 2007: *Historical Changes in the Mississippi-Alabama Barrier Islands and the Roles of Extreme Storms, Sea Level, and Human Activities*, Open File Report 2007-1161, US Geological Survey, St Petersburg, Florida

Morton, R. A. and R. L. Peterson, 2006: *Coastal Classification Atlas, Central Texas Coastal Classification Maps – Aransas Pass to Mansfield Channel*, Open File Report 2006-1096, US Geological Survey, St Petersburg, Florida

Nicholls, R. J., P. P. Wong, V. Burkett, J. Codignotto, J. Hay, R. McLean, S. Ragoonaden and C. Woodroffe, 2007: Coastal Systems and Low-lying Areas, in IPCC, *Climate Change Impacts, Adaptations and Vulnerability*, Intergovernmental Panel on Climate Change Fourth Assessment Report, IPCC Secretariat, Geneva, Switzerland, in press.

NOAA, 1997: *Volume 4: Gulf of Mexico Estuarine Eutrophication Survey*, Office of Ocean Resources Conservation and Assessment, National Ocean Service National Oceanic and Atmospheric Administration, US Department of Commerce, Washington DC

NOAA, 2001: *Sea level variations of the Unites States, 1854–1999*, US National Oceanic and Atmospheric Administration, National Ocean Service, Silver Spring, Maryland

Onuf, C. P. 1995: The seagrass meadows of the Laguna Madre of Texas, in E. T. LaRoe, G. S. Farris and P. T. Doran (eds) *Our Living Resources: A Report to the Nation on the Distribution, Abundance and Health of U. S. Plants, Animals and Ecosystems*, US Department of Interior, National Biological Service, Washington DC

Penland, S. and K. E. Ramsey, 1990: Relative sea-level rise in Louisiana and the Gulf of Mexico: 1908–1988, *Journal of Coastal Research*, **6**, 323–342

Pethick, J., 2001: Coastal management and sea-level rise, *Catena*, **42**, 307–322

Pielke, R. A., Jr, 2005: Meteorology: Are there trends in hurricane destruction? *Nature*, **438**, E11

Quammen, M. L. and C. P. Onuf, 1993: Laguna Madre: Seagrass changes continue decades after salinity reduction, *Estuaries*, **16**, 302–310

Rabalais, N. N., R. E. Turner, Q. Dortch, W. J. Wiseman and B. K. Sen Gupta, 1996: Nutrient changes in the Mississippi River and System responses on the adjacent continental shelf, *Estuaries*, **19**(2B), 386–407

Roach, E. R., M. C. Watzin and J. D. Scurry, 1987: Wetland changes in coastal Alabama, in T. A Lowery (ed.) *Symposium on the Natural Resources of the Mobile Bay Estuary*, Alabama Sea Grant Extension Service, Mobile, AL, MASGP-87-007

Roach, R., (Undated): *Partners for Fish and Wildlife Program Alabama*, US Fish and Wildlife Service, Daphne, AL (available at www.fws.gov/southeast/pubs/facts/apacon. pdf).

Rybczyk, J. M. and D. R. Cahoon, 2002: Estimating the potential for submergence for two subsiding wetlands in the Mississippi River delta, *Estuaries*, **25**, 985–998

Saito, Y., 2001: Deltas in Southeast and East Asia: Their evolution and current problems, *Proceedings of the APN/SURVAS/LOICZ Joint Conference on Coastal Impacts of Climate Change and Adaptation in the Asia – Pacific Region*, 14–16 November 2000, Kobe, Japan, Asia Pacific Network for Global Change Research, 185–191

Santer, B. D., T. M. L. Wigley, P. J. Gleckler, C. Bonfils, M. F. Wehner, K. AchutaRao, T. P. Barnett, J. S. Boyle, W. Bruggemann, M. Fiorino, N. Gillett, J. E. Hansen, P. D. Jones, S. A. Klein, G. A. Meehl, S. C. B. Raper, R. W. Reynolds, K. E. Taylor and W. M. Washington, 2006: Forced and unforced ocean temperature changes in Atlantic and Pacific tropical cyclogenesis regions, *Proceedings National Academy of Sciences*, **103**, 13905–13910

Savonis, M., V. R. Burkett and J. Potter, In Review: Impacts of climate change and variability on transportation systems and infrastructure: Gulf Coast Study, Phase 1, US Department of Transportation, Washington DC and US Geological Survey, National Wetlands Research Center, Lafayette, LA

Scavia, D., J. C. Field, D. F. Boesch, R. W. Buddemeier, D. R. Cayan, V. Burkett, M. Fogarty, M. Harwell, R. Howarth, C. Mason, D. J. Reed, T. C. Royer, A. H. Sallenger and J. G. Titus, 2002: Climate change impacts on U.S. coastal and marine ecosystems, *Estuaries*, **25**(2), 149–164

Schmid, K., 2001: *Shoreline Erosion Analysis of Grand Bay Marsh*, Mississippi Department of Environmental Quality, Office of Geology, Jackson

Scott, T. M., 2001: *The Geologic Map of Florida*, Florida Geological Survey, Tallahassee, Florida, Open File Report No. 80

Smith, T. M. and R. W. Reynolds, 2004: Improved extended reconstruction of SST (1854–1997), *Journal of Climate*, **17**, 2466–2477

Thieler, E. R. and E. S. Hammar-Klose, 2000: *National Assessment of Coastal Vulnerability to Sea-Level Rise: Preliminary Results for the U.S. Gulf of Mexico Coast*, US Geological Survey, Woods Hole, Massachusetts, Open-File Report 00-179, 1 sheet (available at http://pubs.usgs.gov/of/of00-179)

Tidwell, M., 2003: *Bayou Farewell: The Rich Life and Tragic Death of Louisiana's Cajun Coast*, Pantheon, New York

Trenberth, K. E. and D. J. Shea, 2006: Atlantic hurricanes and natural variability in 2005, *Geophysical Research Letters*, **33**, L12704

Twilley, R. R., E. Barron, H. L. Gholz, M. A. Harwell, R. L. Miller, D. J. Reed, J. B. Rose, E. Siemann, R. G. Welzel and R. J. Zimmerman, 2001: *Confronting Climate Change in the Gulf Coast Region: Prospects for Sustaining Our Ecological Heritage*, Union of Concerned Scientists, Cambridge, MA and Ecological Society of America, Washington DC

Waltham, T., 2002: Sinking cities, *Geology Today*, **18**, 95–100

Webster, P. J., G. J. Holland, J. A. Curry and H. Chang, 2005: Changes in tropical cyclone number, duration, and intensity in a warming environment, *Science*, **309**, 1844–1846

Williams, K. L., K. C. Ewel, R. P. Stumpf, F. E. Putz and T. W. Workman, 1999: Sea-level rise and coastal forest retreat on the west coast of Florida, *Ecology*, **80**, 2045–2063

Winker, C. D., 1991: Summary of Quaternary framework, northern Gulf of Mexico, *Gulf Coast Section of Economic Paleontologists and Mineralogists 12th Annual Research Conference Proceedings*, 280–284

White, W. A., 1970: The Geomorphology of the Florida Peninsula, Geological Bulletin No. 51, Bureau of Geology, Florida Department of Natural Resources, Tallahassee, FL

Woodroffe, C. D., 2003: *Coasts: Form, Process and Evolution*, Cambridge University Press, Cambridge

9

Threats and Responses Associated with Rapid Climate Change in Metropolitan New York

Malcolm Bowman, Douglas Hill, Frank Buonaiuto, Brian Colle, Roger Flood, Robert Wilson, Robert Hunter and Jindong Wang

Metropolitan New York is vulnerable to coastal flooding and widespread damage to urban infrastructure, commercial structures and residential neighborhoods from both seasonal hurricanes and extra-tropical storms. A significant portion of the metropolitan area lies less than 3 m above mean sea level; in total covering an area of about 260 km^2 (see Figure 9.1). Many types of structures are located within this low-lying region, including commercial properties and financial institutions, apartment buildings and private dwellings, hospitals, police and fire stations, marine transportation terminals, three major airports, heliports, numerous underground railroad and subway lines (with associated station entrances and ventilation shafts), highways, bridge access roads, tunnels, power plants, the underground steam district heating system, electrical and communication networks, landfills, 14 waste water treatment facilities and 770 combined sewer overflows with their tide gate regulators discharging near or at sea level (Zimmerman, 1996).

Recent storms have already revealed the intrinsic potential for disaster in this region. For example, the nor'easter of December 1992 flooded the entrance of the Hoboken train station with seawater, short-circuiting the electric trains and city subways and shutting down the underground public transportation system for up to ten days. The Brooklyn–Battery tunnel experienced serious flooding as did the FDR Highway on Manhattan's east side. Fortunately, no lives were lost, but there would have been fatalities if the sea had risen another 30 cm (US Army Corps of Engineers et al, 1995). During the 21st century, rising sea level will aggravate the effects of storm surges and wave damage along the Metropolitan New York, Long Island and northern New Jersey coastlines, leading to more severe and more frequent flooding. An abrupt acceleration in the pace of climate change would accelerate sea level rise and make infrastructure protection measures and emergency planning imperatives even more urgent.

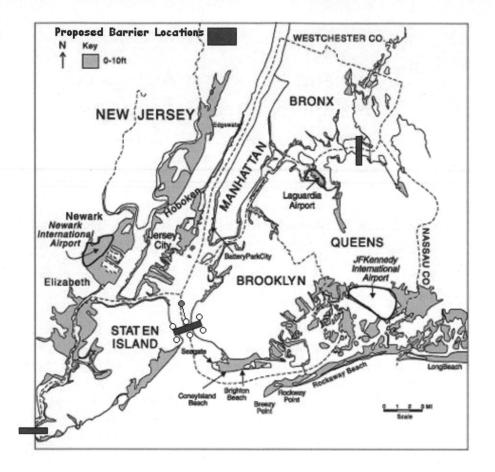

Figure 9.1 Map of Metropolitan New York showing inundation predictions for a 100-year flood at present mean sea level

Note: The proposed locations for storm surge barriers discussed in this chapter are shown as dark gray bars.
Source: adapted from Gornitz, 2001.

Characteristics of tropical and extra-tropical storms in the Metropolitan region

The height and reach of storm surges and flooding along low-lying coastlines are influenced by a variety of factors, including offshore morphology, coastline geometry, astronomical tides and both the regional and local wind and pressure fields. Tropical (for example, hurricanes) and extra-tropical (for example, nor'easters) storm systems are associated with different wind and pressure fields, and these produce characteristically different storm surges. Extra-tropical storms cover a larger geographical extent and often elevate water level across the entire shelf, whereas tropical storms are geographically smaller. However, their strong winds can drive large local surges that propagate with the eye of the storm.

The waterways surrounding New York City are particularly prone to flooding because of the gentle topography, indented coastline and shallow bathymetry of the region (both inside the New York-New Jersey (NY-NJ) harbor estuary and on the inner continental shelf). The orientation of the axis of Long Island Sound positions it as a natural funnel for strong northeasterly winds driving storm surges down to the western Sound, through the East River and into New York harbor. Northeasterly winds blowing parallel to the southern coast of Long Island also drive surges against the south shore of Long Island that then penetrate into the harbor's Upper Bay through the Verrazano Narrows, the main entrance to the Port of New York. This is explained by the Ekman effect due to the rotation of the Earth, where in the Northern Hemisphere, surface waters veer to the right of the wind direction.

The onset and duration of storm surges differ significantly between hurricanes and winter nor'easters. As illustrated in Figure 9.2, the oscillating surge from a hurricane typically lasts only a few hours, but rises and falls very rapidly. The extent of flooding, therefore, depends critically upon the state of the astronomical

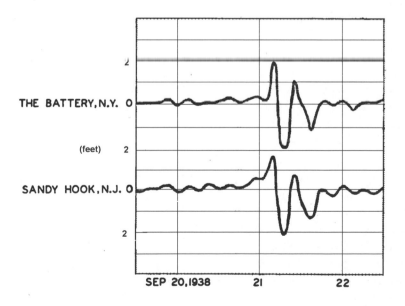

Figure 9.2 Storm surge of the 21–22 September 1938 hurricane

Note: Typically, a hurricane storm surge oscillates rapidly but lasts only a few hours. Dates are shown at noon EST.
Source: Pore and Barrientos, 1976.

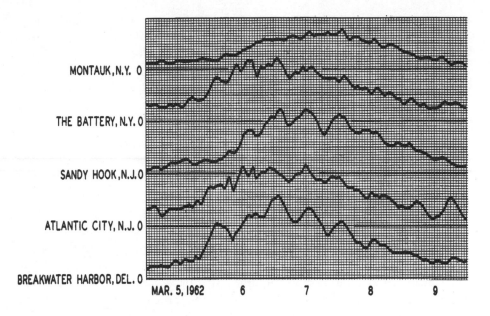

Figure 9.3 Storm surge of the 5–8 March 1962 nor'easter

Note: Typically, the storm surge of a nor'easter rises slowly but lasts several days. Dates are shown at noon EST.
Source: Pore and Barrientos, 1976.

tide at the time of landfall. For nor'easters, by contrast, the surge typically rises more slowly but lasts a few days (see Figure 9.3), running the risk of flooding with each high tide (Pore and Barrientos, 1976).

Previous investigations have shown the flooding susceptibility of Metropolitan New York associated with hurricanes of varying intensity. Figure 9.4 (Plate 12) is a digital terrain map of Metropolitan New York with elevation contours shown (in feet) in various shades of green and earth tones. Superimposed in shades of blue are estimates of inundation zones as calculated by the SLOSH storm surge model (see www.nhc.noaa.gov/HAW2/english/surge/slosh.shtml) that would be caused by a direct hit by hurricanes of categories 1 to 4 on the Saffir-Simpson scale (Simpson and Riehl, 1981).

The SLOSH model is based on the characterization of the effects of a synthetic storm core vortex, defined by location, translation speed, radius and intensity of maximum winds. It is a useful planning tool for emergency managers, but its predictions are necessarily approximate (accurate to within ± 20 per cent) and are highly dependent on how the computational grid is set up. However, the possibility of a major flooding catastrophe is obvious even for a category 2 hurricane.

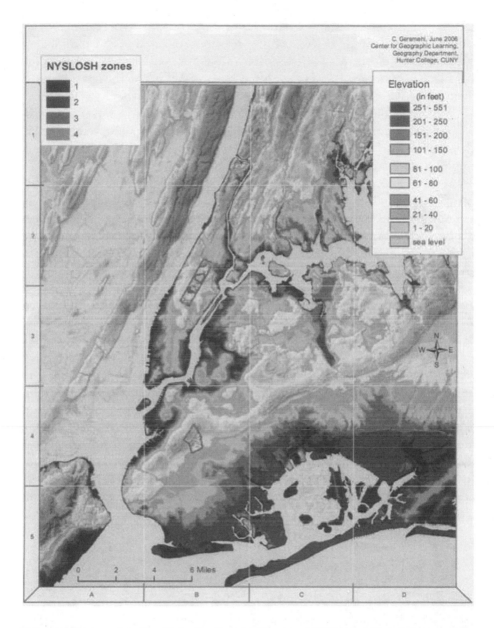

Figure 9.4 Metropolitan New York elevations, landforms and SLOSH model inundation zones for category 1 to 4 hurricanes (see Plate 12 for color version)

Source: courtesy of C. Gersmehl.

Significant sections of the lower west and east sides of Manhattan Island, Queens and Brooklyn boroughs and the east coast of Staten Island are vulnerable. Jamaica Bay and environs (cell C5) are clearly at risk, as is JFK airport on the eastern shores of the Bay. Twenty-five subway stations in Brooklyn alone have entrances at or below 10 m above mean sea level (MSL). Not shown in Figure 9.4 are the flooding predictions for northern New Jersey, which would be considerable, including the Hackensack Meadows, Port Elizabeth and Newark Airport on the left side of the figure, as well as the ocean coast of New Jersey. Figure 9.5 (Plate 13) illustrates how all of the south shore of Long Island, plus the two eastern forks, are at risk of inundation from storm surges. Protecting Long Island poses a second major challenge, but beyond the scope of this contribution. Coastal New Jersey faces a similar predicament.

Sea level as recorded at the NOAA Battery primary tide station at the southern tip of Manhattan Island has risen inexorably over the past one and a half centuries at a rate of about 30 cm (1 ft) per century. In the metropolitan region as a whole, sea level increased by 23–38 cm (9–15 inches) during the 20th century. The statistical return periods of storm surge-related flooding events decrease with sea level rise, independent of any global warming effects on the weather itself, so getting a handle on the future rate of rise is very important.

Extrapolating the current trend, global sea level would be expected to rise by another 0.3 m (1 ft) by the 2090s. As a result, surge-related floods would be higher, cover a wider area and occur more often. Future storm surges would ride on this elevated base level, so the potential damage inflicted by a future 30-year event would be expected to be equivalent to that of a present-day 100 year storm.

However, the pace of global warming is expected to intensify unless very sharp limitations in emissions occur (see Figure 9.6), and the vulnerability and threats of inundation of the New York metropolitan region will correspondingly increase. Projections based on climate change simulations made in 2001 suggest that, excluding the contributions from dynamical ice flow of the Greenland and the West Antarctic ice sheets, sea level will rise by 10–30 cm (4–12 inches) in the next 20 years, 18–60 cm (7–24 inches) by the 2050s, and 25–110 cm (10–42

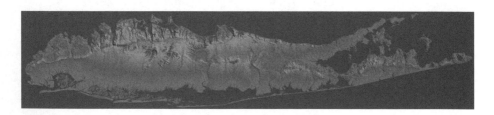

Figure 9.5 Digital terrain map of Long Island, NY (see Plate 13 for color version)

Note: This illustrates the extent of low-lying land and the inherent difficulty of protecting Long Island against major storm surge events and rising sea level. Approximate elevation scale: blue 0–8 m, green 8–50 m, orange 50–80 m and red 80–130 m.
Source: Courtesy G. Hanson http://pbisotopes.ess.sunysb.edu/reports/dem_2/

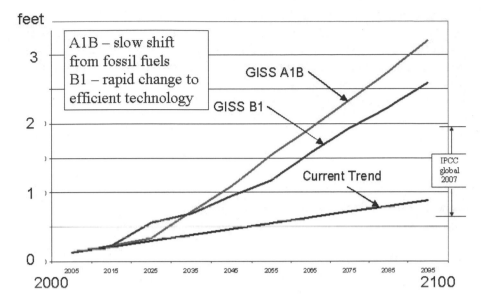

Figure 9.6 Goddard Institute of Space Studies projected sea level rise for New York City to the year 2100 using IPCC scenarios A1B and B1

Note: The current trend is the extrapolated secular rise in sea level as recorded at the Battery tide station over the last 150 years and is not primarily associated with global warming, but with isostatic adjustment of the continent following the last glaciation. See earthobservatory.*nasa*. gov/Newsroom/*NASA*News/2006/2006102523436.html

inches) by the 2080s (Gornitz, 2001). More recent projections for these terms (i.e., other than from significant deterioration of the polar ice sheets) are slightly lower than those estimated in the Third Assessment Report of the IPCC. For example, recent analyses by C. Rosenzweig and V. Gornitz using the version of the Goddard Institute of Space Studies (GISS) Atmospheric-Ocean Model global climate model used to estimate the effects of warming on sea level rise for the newest IPCC assessment, project a sea level rise of 38–48 cm (15–19 inches) by the 2050s in New York City (see http://earthobservatory.*nasa*.gov/Newsroom/ *NASA*News/2006/2006102523436.html). However, there are early signs that the Greenland and West Antarctic ice sheets are starting to lose mass (see Chapters 5 and 6), so higher levels of sea level rise continue to be quite plausible. For the highest estimate of sea level rise by the 2090s, which is roughly 1.6 m (3.8 ft), the return period of a 100-year equivalent-damage storm may drop to every other year (Bowman et al, 2005).

In a worst-case scenario envisioned in the Metro New York Hurricane Transportation Study (US Army Corps of Engineers et al, 1995), hurricane winds striking New York's skyscrapers would result in debris falling onto the streets from broken windows and dislodged masonry. Pedestrians would seek shelter in the subways from severe winds, rain and the falling debris. Hurricane surge waters would quickly fill the subway tunnels, even if the elevation at the surface were above potential flood levels, drowning those underground. No estimate was made of the likely number of casualties.

Short-term fixes have already been undertaken, such as fitting moveable gates at the entrances to the PATH train station in Hoboken (which was inundated with seawater during the 1992 nor'easter). However, to protect the myriad individual structures with seawalls or, where feasible, by raising subway entrances and ventilation shafts above grade, would become increasingly difficult and would end up, presumably, with seawalls being constructed along the several hundred miles of shoreline in the metropolitan region.

Possible responses to increasing risk from accelerating sea level rise

There are several conceivable approaches for dealing with the threat of rising sea level:

- *The do nothing approach.* The do-nothing approach is based on a wait-and-see attitude by coastal planners in the hope that nothing catastrophic will happen on their watch. Many risk analyses and cost–benefit studies are completed, but in the end, insufficient political will or funds are available to proceed with raising large amounts of money to build urban coastal defenses for catastrophic storm surge events that may never happen. This is the most common scenario for nations without a strong tradition or commitment to spend federal monies for regional coastal protection against natural hazards.
- *The iterative approach.* This centers on fixing problems on a case-by-case basis as they arise, for example, patching up and strengthening leaky seawalls, modifying transportation routes, raising airport runways and building new seawalls around facilities, raising subway entrances and ventilation shafts prone to flooding, protecting other underground infrastructure related to energy and communications, pumping out backed-up sewers and so forth. This approach is analogous to patching up potholes on the highway – the basic roadway is in good repair, but weak spots showing signs of wear and upheaval due to adverse weather keep popping up and must be repaired to eliminate or minimize safety hazards. This method is the most responsive to relatively modest amounts of municipal funds becoming available from time to time and that must be spent or be lost from the budget.
- *The regional approach.* At times, the iterative approach may become large scale in nature. For example, the Dutch have been busily reclaiming and

protecting their lowlands for centuries by creating an intricate network of dikes surrounding low-lying tracts of land known as polders, then pumping out the sea and turning the land into useful pasture and even cities. Amsterdam, the capital city of The Netherlands, whose urban area is home to 1.2 million residents, in places is built on land as much as 5.5m (18 ft) below mean sea level. One half of the country's land area is now reclaimed from the sea. After a devastating flood that took 3000 lives in 1953, the Delta Project was begun, and a series of large barriers were constructed around the southeastern coast, connected by high seawalls. Clearly, once a decision has been made to protect a city or state against storm surges and rising sea level with moveable barriers, levies and seawalls, there is no going back. The commitment is forever. The Dutch made that commitment centuries ago and have a highly professional and established engineering, marine hydraulics and governmental infrastructure dedicated to building, maintaining and improving the country's coastal defenses against the sea.

Storm surge barriers for Metropolitan New York

In contrast to the innumerable local flood measures that would be required to protect vulnerable infrastructure, it seems possible to protect the core of the city and northern New Jersey docks and transportation facilities with three storm surge barriers and associated embankments constructed at strategic locations. These structures would be placed at: (1) the Verrazano Narrows; (2) the mouth of Arthur Kill near Perth Amboy; and (3) across the upper East River near the Whitestone Bridge (see Figure 9.1). Protecting southern Brooklyn, Queens, Jamaica Bay and JFK airport would require a fourth barrier across Rockaway Inlet and extensive seawall extensions.

Based on current NASA GISS projections of sea level rise to the year 2100 (see Figure 9.6) and SLOSH modeling (see Figure 9.4), each barrier would need to be about 15 m in height with associated seawalls stretching to higher ground. But this is a first estimate. Given the high uncertainty in projected rates of sea level rise and changes in weather patterns, more careful calculations based on the improved surge models that are under development and the best climate models are needed. Planning must take into account the worst case that could ever be contemplated over the life of the barriers (say 200 years); anything less would be inviting disaster.

The barriers would normally be kept in the fully opened position. During unusually powerful tropical storms and hurricanes, the barriers would be closed for periods of hours to block the associated surge. For nor'easters, the barriers might be closed only during high tides, and opened intermittently over a few days as opportunities arose near low tide to release impounded water.

The surprise is that the feasibility of this concept to protect the NY-NJ metropolitan area has not yet been established. While there would be many engineering challenges to be overcome, there can be little doubt that such structures could be built, the questions are:

*   How physically and cost effective would barriers be in protecting the city core?
*   Would such barriers amplify surges on the weather (ocean) side to an unacceptable degree?
*   Would the rivers swollen with rainfall lead to flooding within the barriers anyway?
*   Would there be sufficient protection and greater cost-effectiveness with partial blockage at some of the barrier locations?

The Stony Brook storm surge models

In order to better understand regional and local meteorology and oceanography, and to advance storm surge science, the Stony Brook Storm Surge Group has been developing modern, integrated weather/storm surge hind-casting and predictive models, typically running with 60-hour time horizons. We analyze both historical and current surge events for coastal New York, Long Island Sound, the NY-NJ Harbor estuary system, and northern New Jersey (Bowman et al, 2005; Colle et al, in review). (See http://stormy.msrc.sunysb.edu for further details.)

Our models utilize surface winds and sea level pressures derived from the Penn State - National Center for Atmospheric Research (PSU-NCAR) MM5 mesoscale model (see www.mmm.ucar.edu/mm5/) running at 12 km resolution to drive the Advanced Circulation Model for Coastal Ocean Hydrodynamics (ADCIRC) (see www.adcirc.org/). ADCIRC is run on an unstructured grid whose resolution ranges from about 75 km far offshore down to around 5 m in inland waterways. Further details are given in Bowman et al (2005) and Colle et al (in review). We avoid using synthetic wind and sea level pressure predictions used in models such as SLOSH, but, rather, depend on predictions derived from modern mesoscale research models like MM5 and WRF (see www.wrf-model.org/index.php).

The skill of our models is presently being evaluated against significant historical weather situations (for example, hurricanes and nor'easters) and associated archived surge data gathered over the last 50 years, as well as current events as they occur. These data also support a real-time Web-based storm surge warning system being developed for the New York metropolitan region and Long Island (see http://stormy.msrc.sunysb.edu).

Using these models, our responses to the four questions regarding the efficacy of storm surge barriers are (Bowman et al, 2005):

- Closing the barriers in sequence at local slack water near low tide before the arrival of the surge and keeping the barriers closed for the duration of the surge would indeed work as expected.
- The two ocean barriers would lead to only a negligible rise (a few centimeters) in sea level outside (to the south of) the barriers, but the third barrier in the upper east River could lead to an increase in surge levels outside (to the east) of the barrier by around 30 cm, depending upon its location (tested for conditions observed during the 25 December 2002 nor'easter).
- Entrapped river water, precipitation and runoff inside the barriers would be within safety limits even during the annual peak of Hudson River discharge in late winter.
- Partial blockage with only one or two barriers operational would not be sufficient.

The models are also being used to:

- improve the quality of coastal surge-related flooding predictions in the metropolitan region (but not of precipitation-induced inland flooding), both for the present era and for a future milieu of rapid climate change and rising sea level;
- further investigate the hydrologic feasibility of establishing a valid scientific basis for deciding whether to further consider the construction of a set of retractable storm surge barriers;
- establish the hydrologic performance requirements (as contrasted with a civil engineering or cost analysis) of such barriers; for example, most effective locations to protect the core city, their efficacy, effects on circulation and water quality during deployment and during normal out-of-service conditions, and so on.

It is not our intent to present candidate barrier designs for discussion, although much has been learned from European and New England experiences, to be discussed below. Our general approach has been to apply our storm surge models to the bathymetry and topography of the metropolitan region, and determine the flooding that would result – inside and outside the barriers – under extreme storm conditions, with/without barriers, singly/in combination, and now/future scenarios.

Storm surge barriers: The European experience

The notion of storm surge barriers is not unique to New York – they are being tried in a number of other locations.

Thames River Barrier, London

London has been periodically flooded since records began back in 1099, with water levels reaching as high as 2.38 m (7.8 ft). In 1953, a particularly disastrous flood occurred in which the tide rose by 2 m (6.5 feet) above its predicted normal level, 300 people drowned and about 65,000 hectares (160,000 acres) near the mouth of the Thames River were covered with seawater.

The Thames River barrier has been constructed to protect London. It is located on the Woolwich Reach, 14 km east of London Bridge. Construction commenced in 1974 and the barrier was opened in 1984. As shown in Figure 9.7, it spans the 520 m river width with four large navigation openings and six smaller flood control openings. Four main rotatable (about a horizontal axis) gates, 61 m wide, span the main navigation channels. Their design is based on Tainter gates (referred to as 'rising sector gates'), steel structures with a radius of curvature of 12 m (66 ft). The gates are hollow so that water can drain into and out of them as they are closed and opened. They are designed to be stored underwater when the gates are open, flush with the sill depth of 9 m (30 ft), so that there is unlimited overhead clearance for ships. There are also four 30 m gates, which, being normally stored in the overhead position, are called falling radial gates. The 9 piers on which the gates are mounted occupy 17 per cent of the span. As shown in Figure 9.8, each of the main gates can be raised to an overhead position for maintenance. They can also be partially opened near the river bottom to the

Figure 9.7 Thames River barrier with the gates partially open in the undershot position for flushing away accumulated sediments

Source: http://alumweb.mit.edu/clubs/uk/Events/Barrier.jpg.

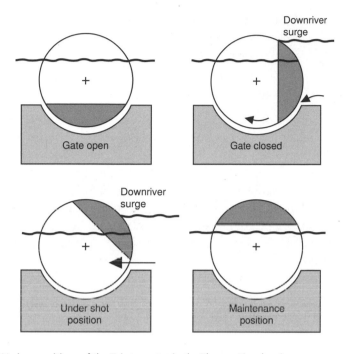

Figure 9.8 Various positions of the Tainter gates in the Thames River barrier

Source: Holloway et al, 1978.

undershot position to use river currents to scour out any accumulated sediment. The Thames Barrier was given an attractive architectural appearance, which has helped to make it something of a tourist attraction.

The Thames Barrier is the world's second largest movable flood barrier (the largest is the Oosterscheldekering in The Netherlands). It is designed to withstand a 1000-year return flood with a very low upstream water level (Clark and Tappin, 1978). When conditions indicate that a tidal surge is building downstream to a dangerous level, an early warning is sounded that is normally several hours in advance of the order to close the barrier. In certain circumstances, however, the warning time could be as short as one hour. Therefore, the machinery is designed to close each gate in 15 minutes and the complete barrier within 30 minutes (Fairweather and Kirton, 1978).

Since 1982, the Thames Barrier has been closed over 100 times. The barrier now has to be closed as often as 12 times a year, compared to 4 or 5 times when first commissioned. This has recently led the Greater London Authority to reexamine the revised estimates of global warming and the effects of climate change that the city is likely to experience in the next century and to consider whether the barriers need to be strengthened or rebuilt entirely. In 2005, a suggestion that it might become necessary to supersede the Thames Barrier with a much more ambitious 16 km (10 miles) long barrier across the Thames Estuary from Sheerness in Kent to Southend in Essex was made public.

Delta Project, The Netherlands

A series of flood protection barriers and seawalls known as the Delta Project were built in The Netherlands after more than 1800 people were drowned during the same 1953 North Sea storm that ravaged southeast England. Work began soon after and finished in 1997 with the completion of the storm surge barrier across the 360 m wide Nieuwe Waterweg (see Figure 9.9). This barrier has two hinged, floating Tainter gates that are swung out to meet each other, then filled with seawater and dropped onto a supporting sill before an impending North Sea storm makes landfall. It protects greater Rotterdam's 1 million inhabitants and seaport from flooding.

The barrier was designed to be capable of withstanding forces and actions that have a probability of occurring once in every 4000 years (a 5.3 m surge plus another 4.5 m wave run-up at the present stand of MSL). The design life of the barrier is 200 years (Ypey, 1982).

Figure 9.9 The Netherlands' Nieuwe Waterweg (New Waterway) storm surge barriers, spanning the 360 m width of the river, were opened in 1997

Source: http://images.encarta.msn.com/xrefmedia/sharemed/targets/images/pho/t902/T902 898A.jpg.

Figure 9.10 A second example of Dutch engineering is the Eastern Scheldt barrier, completed in 1986

Note: Stretched over a width of 3 km, 66 piers are built on 45 m centers with 40m wide gates. The height of the gates is 6–12 m. This barrier, built across the Scheldt estuary does not allow the passage of ships.

Source: www.safetyengineering.nl/servic6.jpg.

To build a second storm surge barrier across the mouth of the Eastern Scheldt estuary was enormously difficult (see Figure 9.10). The tidal volume at the mouth is over 10^9 m³ during ebb or flood tide; the main channels are almost 40 m deep. Over 0.5×10^6 m³ of prefabricated pre-stressed concrete were needed, and 11 specialized ships had to be designed and built to assist in the construction.

Venice Lagoon, Italy

Venice suffers from chronic flooding that now threatens the integrity of many of its historic structures. After several decades of controversy, the installation of 79 storm surge barriers across the 3 inlets (Lido, Malamocco and Chiiogia) of the Venice Lagoon was finally approved in 2002; construction began shortly thereafter. So-called Project Moses follows a novel design of three groups of submerged, hinged gates, as sketched in Figure 9.11. The idea of a barrier first arose in 1966, after the disastrous 2 m flood that brought thousands of volunteers to Venice to help to save priceless art treasures. The cost of Moses has nearly doubled since it was approved (see www.veniceinperil.org/news_articles/newsarticles1.htm).

In the face of an approaching storm, air will be pumped into the hollow caissons, normally lying flat on the floors of the three inlet channels, to allow them to rotate up to and penetrate the surface (see www.smit.com/sitefactor/public/downloads/pdf/Marine%20Projects/Venice%20flood%20barrier.pdf). The sum of the three barrier widths is 1600 m. The individual gates measure about 30 m high, 20 m wide and 4–5 m thick. The barriers are expected to cost between US$3–4 billion and the target completion date is 2011.

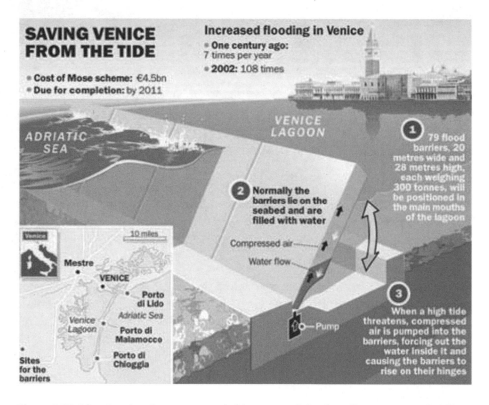

Figure 9.11 After decades of controversy, a decision was made by the Italian government in 2002 to construct three inflatable storm surge barriers across the entrances of the lagoon separating the city of Venice from the Adriatic Sea

Source: www.veniceinperil.org/images/Moses-Barrier.jpg.

St Petersburg, Russia

The city of St Petersburg, with 5 million residents, is located on the delta of the Niva River at the eastern end of the Gulf of Finland of the Baltic Sea. The city floods regularly, often once a year, and has suffered from floods with surges greater than 1.6 m about 300 times in recorded history, including 3 catastrophic floods in 1777 (3.2 m), 1824 (4.2 m) and 1924 (3.8 m). Begun in the Soviet era but never completed, the project was resurrected in 2002 and is presently under final construction. The barrier is 25 km long and is composed of 11 earth and rock dam sections, six water exchange sluice gates and two navigation passages, the larger of which is 940 m in width.

A sketch of the project including the six sluice gates, shipping entrance/barrier and the elevated city ring road extension is shown in Figure 9.12 (Plate 14). Of all the European examples, St Petersburg's pertinent characteristics are most similar to those of New York: a large city of great commercial and cultural significance, built on a flood plain delta with gentle topography at the mouth of a navigable river (third largest in Europe) with strong seasonal flow variations, and with an indented or semi-enclosed coastline susceptible to surge amplification.

Figure 9.12 Sketch of the storm surge barrier and seawall system that is presently under construction to protect the city of St Petersburg, Russia (see Plate 14 for color version)

Source: www.oceansatlas.org/unatlas/-ATLAS-/IMAGES/HIGH/i241-1.jpg.

Storm surge barriers: The New England experience

Although dwarfed in scale by the European barriers, three New England barriers constructed during the 1960s have some design features and operating characteristics that might be relevant to the New York metropolitan region. Barriers across open waterways exist at three locations: Stamford CT, Providence RI and New Bedford MA. The construction of hurricane-flood protection for the region was authorized by Congress in the Flood Control Act of 5 July 1958 (Public Law 85-500, 85th Congress). The settings are quite different in these three locations, and three different types of barriers were constructed (Wiegel, 1993; Bowman et al, 2005).

Stamford, Connecticut

In Stamford CT, the 1938 Long Island Express hurricane surge peaked at approximately 4 m. Between 1965–1968, a hurricane barrier was built across East Branch, above Stamford Harbor, at a cost then of US$14.4 million (see

Figure 9.13 Stamford CT hurricane barrier in a partially closed position

Source: Courtesy of Richard C. Carlson, New England District of Corps of Engineers, Department of the Army.

Figure 9.13). At the bottom of the opening, resting on a sill 4.3 m deep, is a flap gate – a hollow barrier structure about 30 m wide and 11 m high. Triggered by a storm surge threshold of 2 m, hydraulic arms raise the gate to the surface, taking 20 minutes to close. The interior of the gate can be pumped out so that the gate is able to float during maintenance operations.

Providence, Rhode Island

The Providence area has a history of storm flooding dating back to 1635. In more recent times, Providence was also hit by the Long Island Express (hurricane) in September 1938, with surges cresting at 5 m, leaving in its wake 600 dead and causing US$400 million damage. Then Hurricane Carol roared by on 31 September 1954, creating another 5 m surge, killing a total of 60 persons and causing US$300 million in damage.

After engineering and economic studies were completed in the late 1950s, a hurricane barrier was built across the 300 m entrance to Providence Harbor between 1961 and 1966 at a cost then of US$15 million. Seawalls 3–5 m high extend out from the ends of the barrier 250 m in one direction and 430 m in the other. A view of the Providence barrier (horizontal axis Tainter gate design) is shown in Figure 9.14.

Figure 9.14 Horizontal axis Tainter gates built across Providence RI Harbor

Source: Douglas Hill.

New Bedford, Massachusetts

The 1938 hurricane reached a flood level of 4 m at New Bedford. The hurricane barrier (not shown) separating New Bedford Harbor from Buzzards Bay was built from 1962–1966 at a cost then of US$18.6 million. Protecting 560 hectares (1400 acres), the barrier at New Bedford spans the 1500 m mouth of the harbor between New Bedford and Fairhaven MA. The 7 m seawall consists of packed clay core faced with large boulders, with a 50 m opening toward its eastern end. The opening consists of a reinforced concrete structure with two opposing steel Tainter vertical axis sector gates, each with a radius of 30 m, which can rotate to close the opening. The 20 m high sector gates weigh 440 tons, and rest on a concrete sill 13 m below MSL. There is no overhead restriction, and the New Bedford fishing fleet and pleasure craft routinely pass through the opening.

Since its construction, the New Bedford barrier has protected the harbor from many storm surges, including the 2.5 m surge of Hurricane Bob (August 1991) and the 2 m surge from an unnamed coastal storm in January 1997.

According to the New England District, US Army Corps of Engineers, none of the three New England harbors has experienced sedimentation problems attributable to the presence of the gates nor have any related dredging projects been necessary. A small amount of dredging was needed at the Stamford barrier in the mid-1990s to remove unrelated sediment deposits.

What can we learn from experiences of existing barriers?

Experiences to date provide some information potentially relevant to protecting New York harbor.

Would storm surge barriers be cost effective?

Table 9.1 lists comparative costs for two representative European barriers plus a hypothetical East River tidal gate designed for water pollution control. Given that water damage resulting from a major hurricane event colliding with New York City has been estimated in the many hundreds of billions of dollars, it is obvious from the table that barriers would be very cost effective, even for one major storm event alone.[1]

How high would the barriers and seawalls need to be? How long would they be designed to last?

The Dutch have taken the view that their extensive barrier/seawall defenses must be able to withstand a 1000-year storm and have a useful working lifetime of

Table 9.1 *Comparative barrier costs in 2006 US$, updated using the US Bureau of Reclamation Construction Cost Trends Composite Trend*

Barrier	Dates	Cost	Exchange rate then	$ Cost then	Cost index*	2006 cost
Eastern Scheldt	1979–1986	3 billion guilders	3.32 guilders/$	$900 million	299/159	$1.7 billion
Thames River	1973–1984	600 million £	$1.328/£	$800 million	299/153	$1.6 billion
East River	1993	$1 billion	–	$1 billion	299/190	$1.6 billion
TOTAL						$5.0 billion

Source: Delta Barrier Symposium, 1982; Abrahams and Matlin, 1994.

200 years. It is our position that such a high standard is also appropriate for Metropolitan New York. In determining the height for the barrier, wave heights, which can add several meters to the total rise, and a safety factor must be added to the storm surge height. Based on estimates for storm surge height from the SLOSH model (see Table 9.2), we have adopted a 15 m barrier as our working height for worst-case scenarios.

Table 9.2 *SLOSH-estimated storm surges in meters (feet in parentheses) associated with a direct hit of hurricanes of various intensities*

Location	Category 1	Category 2	Category 3	Category 4
Fort Hamilton, Brooklyn	2.8 (9)	4.6 (15)	6.4 (21)	8.3 (27)
Willets Point, Queens	13.0 (8)	3.5 (11)	5.6 (18)	7.0 (23)
Amboy, New Jersey	3.3 (11)	6.0 (19)	7.3 (24)	8.2 (27)

Source: US Army Corps of Engineers et al, 1995.

Are storm surge barriers reliable and fail-safe?

They have to be. Obviously storm surge barriers would need to be 100 per cent reliable; otherwise catastrophic flooding could result. The misery of the New Orleans experience highlights the need for a substantially greater vision of what coastal storm surge protection of low-lying urban areas demands in an era of climate change. Once again, the Dutch experience is worth examining. They possess a bold vision and enduring courage to have built their nation below sea level and are clearly committed to its protection as a central issue of national security. The US has the engineering and oceanographic expertise to design and build storm surge barriers that will function efficiently over a design life of 200 years. It can be done, but the challenge needs to be approached with a much more substantial political and financial commitment than has typically been evident, and with an order of magnitude stronger design features than the city of New Orleans ever possessed.

What are the downsides of an engineering solution? Are we only delaying the inevitable catastrophe?

The downside of an engineering solution to rising sea level and increased threats of severe storms is the fear that the barriers will eventually fail and that the final catastrophe will be far worse than if we decided as of today to:

- modify building codes to prohibit unwise and unsafe shoreline development;
- harden local infrastructure as necessary;
- begin planning for the eventual retreat of the city from the coastline (K. Jacob, personal communication).

When might the City of New York start planning for barriers?

Apart from the Hollandse Ijessel barrier, for the other six examples analyzed in Table 9.3, several decades typically passed before governments completed the debates, legislation, surveys, design, permitting, construction, testing and commissioning of major barrier works. In the absence of a major natural disaster in the next few years, there is little reason to be optimistic that New York City could proceed more quickly than its European counterparts.

Conclusions

The existing storm surge barriers in New England and Europe were built after devastating floods that did enormous damage and cost hundreds, even thousands, of lives. Considering the projected multibillion costs for metropolitan New York, regrettably it may take a similar disaster for a decision to be made to build storm surge barriers to protect the metropolitan region.

With the increasing likelihood of more frequent flooding due to climate change and the possibility of rapid sea level rise, such a delay should clearly be minimized. There is still no broad public awareness of the problem and thus no political concern. We conclude, therefore, that it is incumbent upon the professional community – scientists and engineers inside and outside government – to take the initiative to move forward with an evaluation of the feasibility of building storm surge barriers to protect the core region of metropolitan New York.

Table 9.3 *Comparative delays between serious flooding events and final completion of storm surge barriers for seven locations*

Barrier	Flood	Delay (years)	Start	Construction time (years)	Completion
Providence	1938	23	1961	5	1966
New Bedford	1938	24	1962	4	1966
Stamford	1938	27	1965	4	1969
Hollandse Iiessel	1953	1	1954	4	1958
Eastern Scheldt	1953	14–26	1967–1979	7	1986
Maeslant	1953	36	1989	8	1997
Venice	1966	37	2003	8	(2011)

Nobody alive knows what the climate and weather will be like 500 years from now. We don't know if civilization as we know it will endure that long. But we can plan for a 200-year time horizon; it seems that we can, and should, start planning for storm surge barriers, and start now.

Acknowledgements

This research was supported by New York Sea Grant, HydroQual, Inc., New York City Department of Environmental Protection, and The Eppley Foundation for Research.

Note

1   V. Lankarge, in the Web article 'Top 10 Worst Places for an Extreme Hurricane to Strike', estimated the potential total economic losses in New York City and New Orleans to be US$53 billion and US$16.8 billion, respectively. Since the actual cost to New Orleans has proved to be in the order of US$100 billion or more, presumably the estimate for New York City should be similarly adjusted for inflation. See www.insure.com/home/disaster/worsthurricane.html.

References

Abrahams, M. J. and A. Matlin, 1994: East River Tidal Barrage, in D. Hill (ed.) *The East River Tidal Barrage*, Volume 742, Annals of the New York Academy of Sciences, New York Academy of Sciences, New York

Bowman, M. J., B. Colle, R. Flood, D. Hill, R. Wilson, F. Buonaiuto, P. Cheng and Y. Zheng, 2005: *Hydrologic Feasibility of Storm Surge Barriers to Protect the Metropolitan*

New York – New Jersey Region. Final Report, Marine Sciences Research Center, State University of New York, Stony Brook NY

Clark, P. J. and R. G. Tappin, 1978: Final design of Thames Barrier gate structure, in *Thames Barrier Design*, Proceedings of the conference held in London on 5 October 1977, The Institution of Civil Engineers, London

Colle, B. A., F. Buonaiuto, M. J. Bowman, R. E. Wilson, R. Flood, R. Hunter, A. Mintz and D. Hill, in review: Simulations of past cyclone events to explore New York City's vulnerability to coastal flooding and storm surge model capabilities, *Bulletin of the American Meteorological Society*

Delta Barrier Symposium, 1982: *Proceedings of the Delta Barrier Symposium*, Rotterdam, 13–15 October

Fairweather, D. M. S. and R. R. H. Kirton, 1978: Operating machinery, in *Thames Barrier Design*, Proceedings of the conference held in London on 5 October 1977, The Institution of Civil Engineers, London

Gornitz, V., 2001: Sea-level rise and coasts, in C. Rosenzweig and W. D. Solecki (eds) *Climate Change and a Global City: The Potential Consequences of Climate Variability and Change: Metro East Coast*, Columbia Earth Institute, New York

Holloway, B. G. R., G. Miller Richards, R. C. Draper, 1978. Basic concept of the rising sector gates, in *Thames Barrier Design. Proceedings of the conference held in London, 5 October, 1977*. The Institute of Civil Engineers, London, 1978, 202pp.

Pore, N. A. and C. S. Barrientos, 1976: *Storm Surge*, Marine Ecosystem Analysis Program, MESA New York Bight Atlas Monograph 6, New York Sea Grant Institute, New York

Simpson, R. H. and H. Riehl, 1981: *The Hurricane and Its Impact*, Louisiana State University Press, Louisiana

US Army Corps of Engineers, FEMA, National Weather Service, NY/NJ/CT State Emergency Management, 1995: *Metro New York Hurricane Transportation Study*, interim technical report, November, USACE

Wiegel, R.L., 1993: Hurricane and coastal storm surge barriers in New England, *Shore and Beach*, **61**, 30–49

Ypey, E., 1982: Design of gate structures: Gates, in *Eastern Scheldt Storm Surge Barrier*, Proceedings of the Delta Barrier Symposium, Rotterdam, 13–15 October

Zimmerman, R., 1996: Global warming, infrastructure, and land use in the metropolitan New York area, in D. Hill (ed.) *The Baked Apple? Metropolitan New York in the Greenhouse*. Vol. 790, Annals of the New York Academy of Sciences, Johns Hopkins University Press, New York

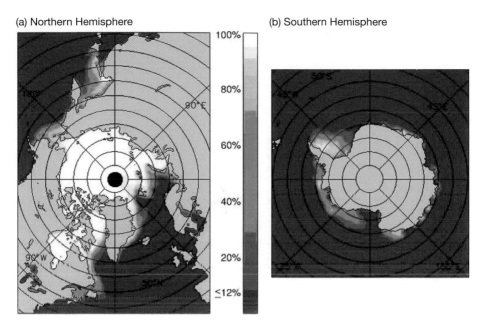

Plate 1 February sea ice coverage averaged over the 26 years 1979–2004, for (a) the Northern Hemisphere, and (b) the Southern Hemisphere

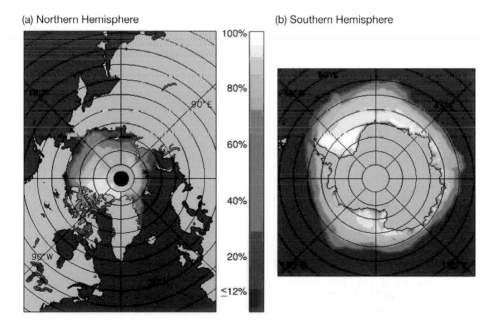

Plate 2 August sea ice coverage averaged over the years 1979–2004, for (a) the Northern Hemisphere, and (b) the Southern Hemisphere

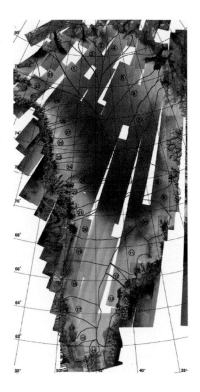

Plate 3 Ice velocity mosaic of the Greenland Ice Sheet assembled from year 2000 Radarsat-1 interferometry data, color coded on a logarithmic scale from 1 m/yr (brown) to 3 km/yr (purple), overlaid on a map of radar brightness from ERS-1/Radarsat-1/Envisat radar images

Plate 4 The ice front of Kangerdlugssuaq Glacier, East Greenland in 2005

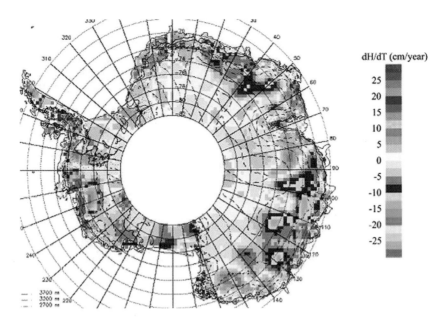

Plate 5 Map of Antarctica showing annual change in height of various locations of the ice sheet

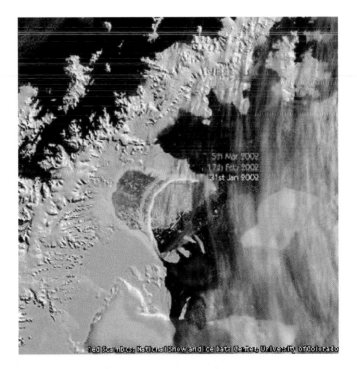

Plate 6 Satellite image of the Antarctic Peninsula, showing the rapid break-up of the Larsen B ice shelf over about five weeks in 2002

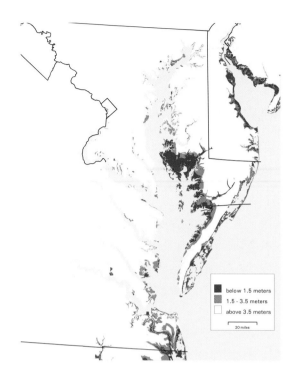

Plate 7 Mean elevations above mean sea level for the Chesapeake Bay region, showing the likelihood that areas will be flooded for different levels of sea level rise induced by global warming

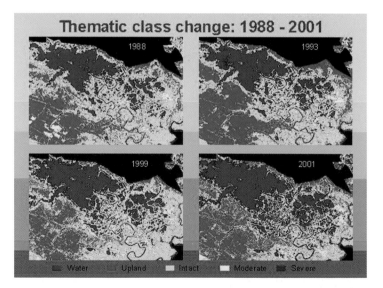

Plate 8 Marsh loss at Blackwater Wildlife Refuge on the Maryland Eastern Shore from 1988–2001 as derived from satellite data

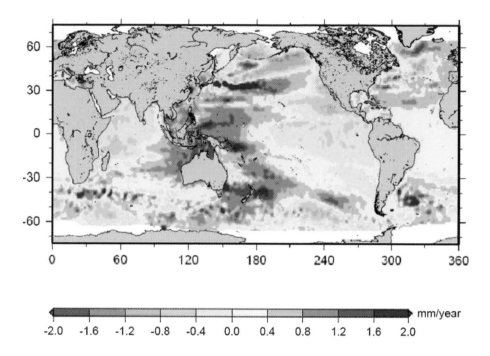

mm/year

-2.0   -1.6   -1.2   -0.8   -0.4   0.0   0.4   0.8   1.2   1.6   2.0

Plate 9 Geographic distribution of short-term linear trends in mean sea level for 1993–2003 based on TOPEX/Poseidon satellite altimetry

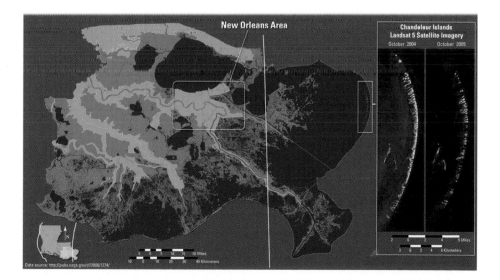

Plate 10 Digital terrain map of Long Island, NY

Plate 11 Land surface elevation and roads in the central Gulf Coast region

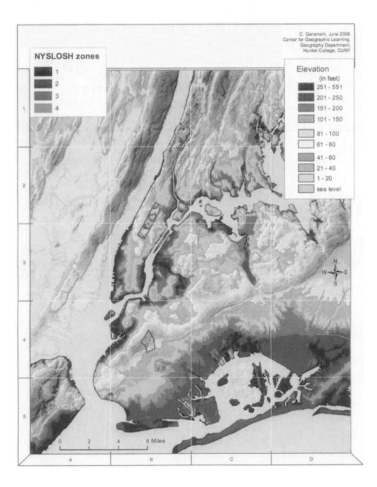

Plate 12 Metropolitan New York elevations, landforms and SLOSH model inundation zones for category 1 to 4 hurricanes

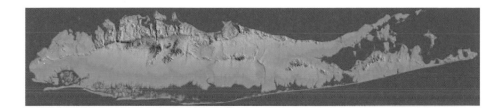

Plate 13 Digital terrain map of Long Island, NY

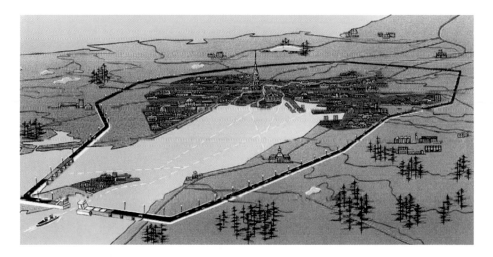

Plate 14 Sketch of the storm surge barrier and seawall system that is presently under construction to protect the city of St Petersburg, Russia

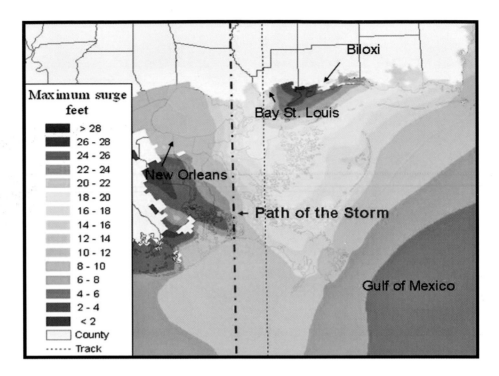

Plate 15 Storm surge height forecast from IHRC's CEST model for Hurricane Katrina

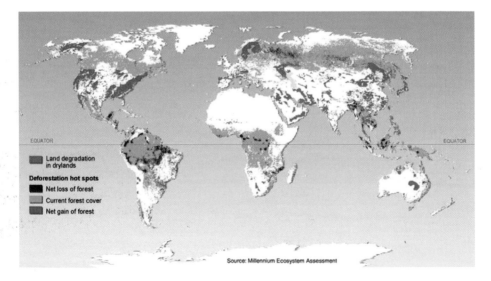

Figure 16 Main areas of deforestation and land degradation from 1980–2000

Ecosystem Models

Current Ecosystems

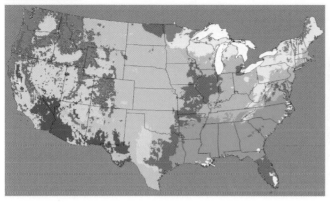

Tundra
Taiga / Tundra
Conifer Forest
Northeast Mixed Forest
Temperate Deciduous Forest
Southeast Mixed Forest
Tropical Broadleaf Forest
Savanna / Woodland
Shrub / Woodland
Grassland
Arid Lands

Canadian Model

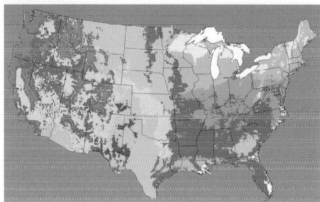

Tundra
Taiga / Tundra
Conifer Forest
Northeast Mixed Forest
Temperate Deciduous Forest
Southeast Mixed Forest
Tropical Broadleaf Forest
Savanna / Woodland
Shrub / Woodland
Grassland
Arid Lands

Hadley Model

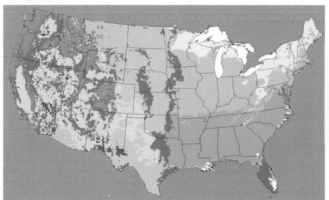

Tundra
Taiga / Tundra
Conifer Forest
Northeast Mixed Forest
Temperate Deciduous Forest
Southeast Mixed Forest
Tropical Broadleaf Forest
Savanna / Woodland
Shrub / Woodland
Grassland
Arid Lands

Plate 17 Distribution of ecosystems across the US at present and for two climate change scenarios based on projections to 2100 from results prepared for the US National Assessment

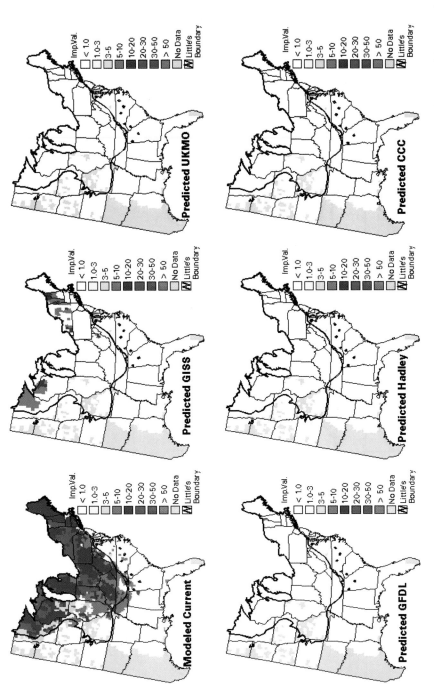

Plate 18 Present and projected distribution of sugar maple trees based on the results of five general circulation climate models assuming a doubling of the atmospheric CO_2 concentration

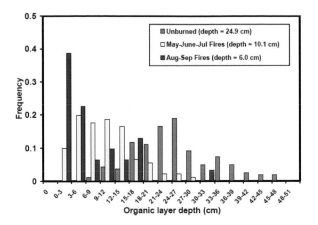

Plate 19 Distribution of organic layer depths measured in burned and unburned Alaskan black spruce forests

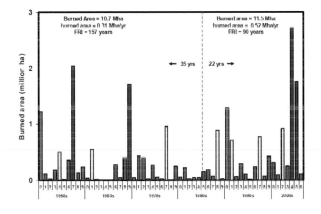

Plate 20 Historical patterns of annual burned area in Alaska

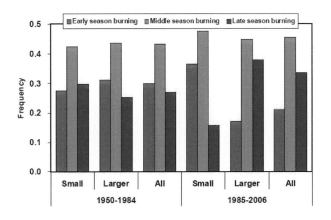

Plate 21 Seasonal patterns of burned area for two periods for small and larger fire years in Alaska

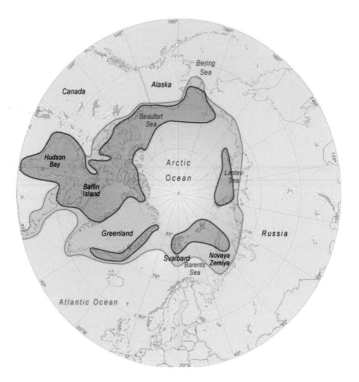

Plate 22 Circumpolar distribution of polar bears showing high and low density

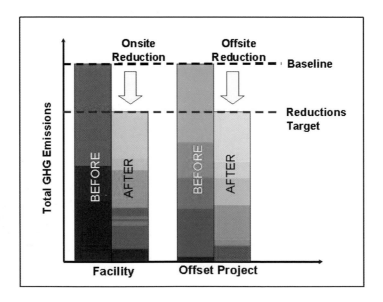

Plate 23 Equivalence of greenhouse gas reduction projects to onsite reductions

10

Increasing the Resilience of Our Coasts: Coastal Collision Course of Rising Sea Level, Storms, Coastal Erosion and Development

Bruce C. Douglas and Stephen P. Leatherman

More and more people are living near ocean and estuarine coasts. Coastal watershed counties are home to about 50 per cent of the US population, and 29 per cent of the US population lives in areas subject to the effects of sea level rise. It seems that everyone wants a waterfront view, and beachfront property has become some of the most expensive real estate in the country. Small beach cottages have given way in recent decades to luxurious multistory houses, and in South Florida some high-rise condominium complexes are approaching US$500 million valuations. The 'Gold Coast' of Florida alone, which runs along the southeastern coast between Palm Beach and Miami, has an appraised value exceeding US$1.3 trillion. At the same time, the coast is facing a number of threats. Hurricanes are a regular occurrence along the East and Gulf coasts of the US: during the 20th century, 167 tropical storms made landfall. In addition to the problems arising directly from coastal construction in areas where storms are routine, increasing sea level results in coastal erosion and wetlands loss. The result is that fixed structures are increasingly exposed to storm waves and surges (see Figure 10.1).

Hurricanes in recent years have been more active than average; some investigators[1] attribute the heightened activity to the Atlantic Multidecadal Oscillation (AMO), while Mann and Emanuel (2006) and others argue that global warming is making hurricanes more powerful. In any case, the increase of hurricane activity combined with the tremendous amount of coastal construction during the last few decades has greatly increased weather-related damage costs. According to the National Science Board (2007):

> *Hurricane-induced economic losses have increased steadily in the U.S. during the past 50 years, with estimated annual total losses (in constant 2006 dollars)*

Figure 10.1 Storm damage on the south shore of Long Island: Narrow beaches enable storm wave energy to reach fixed structures

Source: International Hurricane Research Center (IHRC), Florida International University, Miami, Florida.

averaging $1.3 billion from 1949-1989, $10.1 billion from 1990-1995, and $35.8 billion per year during the last 5 years. The 2005 season was exceptionally destructive, with Hurricane Katrina pushing annual damage loss over the $100 billion mark for the first time since records began. Added to this financial cost is the intolerable and unnecessary loss of life associated with hurricanes – 196 individuals perished from 1986–1995 and approximately 1,450 were lost in the past two years alone.

Wind and flood damage from hurricanes are not the only issues for coastal residents. Along the US West Coast, winter storms, the impacts of which are made worse on occasion by the periodic El Niño events that tend to elevate sea level, pound the coastline with waves and cause significant erosion. On the US East Coast, a great nor'easter can cause more erosion in a few days than many previous decades of normal erosion, with devastating impact upon coastal properties. In addition to storm-induced erosion, there is an underlying long-term background rate of erosion that is almost certainly related to sea level rise (Leatherman et al, 2000; Zhang et al, 2004). In total, erosion is affecting almost 90 per cent of the nation's sandy beaches. With many new buildings increasingly located right near the coast, it is not surprising that damage costs from hurricanes and winter storms has been rising.

Climate change and coastlines

Climate change is adding to coastal stresses in many ways. The rise in sea level during the 20th century is estimated to have been near 0.2 m (about 8 inches) (Douglas, 1991, 1997; Peltier, 2001; Church and White, 2006). Projections are that, as a result of thermal expansion and glacier and ice sheet melting, human-induced changes in the climate could result in an additional rise in global sea level of as much as 0.5 m (about 20 inches) and possibly much more by 2100 (IPCC, 2007). Satellite altimeter data for the past 15 years indicate that there has been a 50 per cent increase in the rate of sea level rise over this time (Church and White, 2006) as compared to the historic rate estimated from older tide gauge data. This rate of sea level rise will accelerate the loss of coastal wetlands and erosion if it is maintained.

Sea level rise has been shown to be a significant driver of beach erosion (Leatherman et al, 2000; Zhang et al, 2004); certainly beach erosion has been ubiquitous over the last century, a period during which sea level has risen at a faster rate than any time over the last several millennia (Woodworth, 1999). Along a low-lying sandy beach coastline, the rate of erosion can be up to two orders of magnitude greater than the rate of sea level rise, so that even small changes in sea level are likely to result in significant beach loss. If present trends continue without extensive coastal engineering projects, it is estimated that one in four buildings located within about 150 m (about 500 ft) of the US shoreline will be destroyed as a direct or indirect result of coastal erosion during the next 50–75 years (Heinz Center, 2000).

Many low lying mainland areas are protected by barrier islands from large oceanic waves along the US East and Gulf Coasts; coastal inundation and salt-water intrusion are the primary problems in these extremely low-sloping areas. Even a 1 m rise has the potential to inundate many kilometers inland (i.e. the ratio of the height of sea level rise to the distance of inland advance can be up to four orders of magnitude) — with storms serving to tip the ocean onto the land. These low-lying mainland areas are being densely developed because beachfront property is now so expensive. Clearly, growing coastal populations and development in low-lying coastal regions in the face of rising sea levels, shoreline recession and coastal storms have set the US on a coastal collision course.

In areas where the slope of the coastal plain is very gentle (for example, 1:10,000) with little sediment input, inundation destroys wetlands vegetation – the plants simply cannot keep up with the rapid change of sea level and drown. A preview of rapid wetlands loss can be seen in the Mississippi delta region (see also Chapter 8), where relative sea level rises by up to 1 cm per year (Douglas, 2005), largely because of subsidence. The resulting loss of wetlands is about 65 km^2 per year (Boesch et al, 1994). Since Louisiana coastal wetlands amount to 40 per cent of the national wetland area, the loss there is responsible for about 80 per cent of the total US annual wetland loss.

Even more moderate rates of sea level rise, however, will cause wetlands loss. The rate of sea level rise in Maryland is nearly 4 mm per year, about twice the average global rate over the last century. This high rate is a combination of the modern global rate of about 1.8 mm per year and land subsidence due to tectonic adjustments associated with past deglaciation (Peltier, 2001). At this elevated rate, which has existed only since the mid-19th century when global sea level rise began to increase to the modern rate, the plants in the coastal wetlands drown. Figure 10.2 shows the wetland loss at Blackwater Wildlife Refuge in Cambridge, Maryland between 1938 and 1988. That even a modest increase in the rate of sea level rise can have severe consequences for wetlands emphasizes the challenge being faced by many coastal regions.

In addition to problems of erosion and inundation, hurricanes may become more intense as a result of climate change (IPCC, 2007). Greater losses of life and property would also be expected from more intense winter storms. In Alaska, the retreat of sea ice that previously buffered the coast against winter storms is further amplifying coastal damage by allowing waves to pound the frozen barrier islands that have served as the home of Inuit and other indigenous groups for many millennia; so much erosion is occurring that villages are literally falling into the sea and have to be relocated inland at great expense (Arctic Climate Impact Assessment, 2004; Robertson, 2004).

Reducing coastal risk

With so many living on the coastal edge, how can society reduce the inevitable risks of living near the shore? Beach nourishment is seen by an increasing number of coastal communities as an alternative to forcing people to move from the coasts, even though many replenished beaches have lasted only a few years rather than decades; for most locations, this strategy cannot work in the long term. Armoring the beach with seawalls can stabilize the shore, but the monetary and aesthetic costs are very high and do not protect the beaches currently enjoyed by oceanfront properties. Structures of the sort that protect Galveston (see Figure 10.3) will increasingly be needed. This seawall was built following the disastrous 1900 hurricane and has served the city well, but the entire sandy beach has been lost.

By contrast, the Coastal Zone Management (CZM) Program offers states an incentive to better manage beachfront development. Unfortunately, best management practices have rarely been exercised (Leatherman and White, 2005),

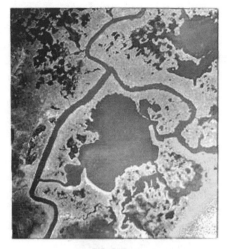

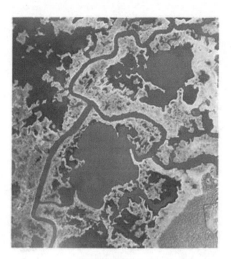

1938

1957

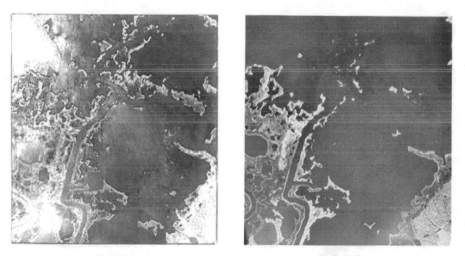

1972

1988

Figure 10.2 Wetlands loss at Blackwater, Maryland, since 1938, from aerial photographs

Source: IHRC.

and unless such management efforts include provisions for building levees around especially valuable regions or facilities and for ultimate retreat from the coastline, this approach has limited potential to work in a cost-effective manner.

With adequate steps to ensure coastal protection not yet taken, most of the burden of sustaining vulnerable (and increasingly damaged) coastal communities

Figure 10.3 The Galveston seawall has protected buildings and coastal infrastructure at the expense of the beach

Source: IHRC.

has fallen on the Federal Emergency Management Agency (FEMA) and its National Flood Insurance Program (NFIP). FEMA has taken an important step towards protecting coastal property by providing incentives to build new structures above the projected elevation of storm surges and to strengthen existing structures against windstorm damage. However, there has been no direct consideration of horizontal shoreline movement, specifically coastal erosion, nor planning to accommodate the accelerating pace of sea level rise and the likelihood of more intense storms (with their higher winds and larger storm surges). The lack of coordinated federal programs and policies is abundantly evident as the coastal building boom continues.

The flooding and destruction caused by storm surges are well known. Accurately predicting surge height and extent are critical for evacuation decisions. The National Weather Service's SLOSH model has served the country well for several decades, but it is now outdated and new models, such as AdCIRC, which was developed for the US Army Corps of Engineers, and the Coastal and Estuarine Storm

Time (CEST) model, which is being developed by the International Hurricane Research Center (IHRC) at Florida International University, are coming on line. The CEST model incorporates high-resolution Light Detection and Ranging (LIDAR) data that are gathered by an airborne LIDAR (laser) profiler, which can determine coastal elevations to an accuracy of a few centimeters. CEST also uses a 50 m grid size and a new overland flooding algorithm to provide superior results compared to the SLOSH model.

In advance of Hurricane Katrina's landfall, a 30 ft storm surge at Bay St Louis, Mississippi was predicted by the IHRC research team (see Figure 10.4 and Plate 15). The CEST model proved to be highly accurate as field measurements[2] confirmed the extremely high surge height and landward penetration. Katrina surpassed the previous storm surge record of 22.4 ft generated by Hurricane Camille in 1969 at Pass Christian, Mississippi.

The IHRC CEST model is presently undergoing further development with the goal of becoming a real-time forecast model for use by NOAA's National Hurricane Center and FEMA, perhaps along with other models of storm surge

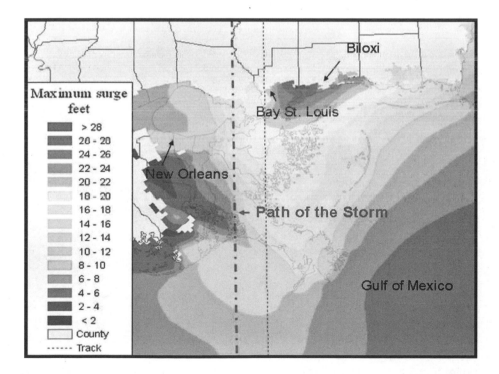

Figure 10.4 Storm surge height forecast from IHRC's CEST model for Hurricane Katrina (see Plate 18 for color version)

Source: IHRC.

height to produce a suite of forecasts, as is done for hurricane track and intensity. These advances will save lives during hurricanes while also allowing better mapping of coastal vulnerabilities and planning of the adaptations necessary to be prepared for increasingly severe coastal storms and rising sea level.

New technology to improve coastal resilience

An essential issue for coastal planning is survivability of coastal structures. This is a complex matter. For example, wind-driven rainwater can effectively ruin a house if the doors and windows are breached, even if the roof stays intact. Roof design, materials and construction methods need to be tested in a repeatable manner so that a scientifically based set of construction and upgrade standards can be developed. Essential to this effort is full-scale destructive testing analogous to the automobile crash testing done by the insurance industry and automobile manufacturers. The IHRC is developing an apparatus for first-of-its-kind, full-scale, destructive testing of houses and low-rise commercial structures. The 2-fan Wall of Wind (see Figure 10.5) generates 120 mph winds (low category 3) and

Figure 10.5 The IHRC 2-fan Wall of Wind apparatus, capable of generating 120 mph winds for destructive testing of houses

Note: A condemned house in Sweetwater, Florida is systematically destroyed during a test.
Source: IHRC.

includes a water injector to simulate horizontally flowing rainfall under hurricane conditions.

While wind tunnel testing of model houses has provided useful information, it also has many limitations – gravity cannot be scaled nor can roofing materials (shingles, tiles) be reduced to a miniature size and provide any useful understanding of wind dynamics and failure mode. Full-scale destructive testing of structures will likely change the public's perception of building safety, just as the visualization of car crash testing led to the adoption of air bags and many other safety features.

The IHRC research team is presently completing a larger and more powerful 6-fan Wall of Wind funded by Renaissance Reinsurance Holdings, Ltd (RenaissanceRe), the largest re-insurer of hurricane-prone areas in the world. The insurance industry is already recognizing the enormous potential of full-scale Wall of Wind testing in the midst of an emerging insurance crisis for coastal areas. The more powerful 6-fan RenaissanceRe Wall of Wind can generate 130–140 mph winds. It will be housed in a fully instrumented building at the FIU Engineering Center in Miami, Florida. This new technology is necessary in order to learn how to build more hurricane-resistant houses, which is paramount in the present situation, and before considering the probability of more powerful hurricanes in response to global warming in the future.

Conclusions

A national policy for shoreline management is vitally needed. Were the further effects of climate change not facing us, Florida's program for dealing with storm impacts and coastal erosion could, in principle, be replicated by others. However, with ongoing and accelerating climate change and sea level rise, the contradictory, or at least divergent, approaches to beachfront management must be replaced with a coordinated policy and streamlined process to address the nation's growing coastal hazard losses.

Acknowledgement

Bruce Douglas received support from the NASA Solid Earth and Natural Hazards Program. Dr Leatherman was supported by the Tom and Barbara Gale Foundation.

Notes

1.   See, for example, www.aoml.noaa.gov/phod/amo_faq.php.
2.   See www.fema.gov/pdf/hazard/flood/recoverydata/katrina/ms_overview.pdf.

References

Arctic Climate Impact Assessment, 2004: *Impacts of a Warming Arctic*, Cambridge University Press, Cambridge (see http://amap.no/acia/)

Boesch, D. F., M. N. Josslyn, A. J. Mehta, J. T. Morris, W. K. Nuttle, C. A. Simestad and D. J. Swift, 1994: Scientific assessment of coastal wetland loss, restoration and management in Louisiana, *J. Coastal Res.*, Special Issue, **20**, 103pp

Church, J. A. and N. White, 2006: A 20th century acceleration in global sea-level rise, *Geophysical Research Letters*, **33**, L01602, doi:10.1029/2005GL024826

Douglas, B. C., 1991: Global sea level rise, *J. Geophys. Res.*, **96**, 6981–6992

Douglas, B. C., 1997, Global sea (level) rise: A redetermination, *Surveys in Geophys.*, **18**, 279–292

Douglas, B. C., 2005: Gulf of Mexico and Atlantic Coast sea level change, in *Circulation in the Gulf of Mexico: Observations and Models*, Geophysical Monograph Series **161**, American Geophysical Union, Washington DC

Douglas, B. C. and M. Crowell, 2005: Long-term position prediction and error propagation for shoreline positions, *J. Coastal Res.*, **16**, 145–152

Heinz Center, 2000: *Evaluation of Erosion Hazards*, Heinz Center, Washington DC (see www.heinzctr.org/publications.shtml)

IPCC (Intergovernmental Panel on Climate Change), 2007: *Climate Change 2007: The Physical Science Basis – Summary for Policymakers*, Contribution of Working Group I to the Fourth Assessment Report of the Intergovernmental Panel on Climate Change, IPCC, Geneva (available at www.ipcc.ch/SPM2feb07.pdf)

Leatherman, S. P., K. Zhang and B. C. Douglas, 2000: Sea level rise shown to drive coastal erosion, *EOS Trans. AGU*, **81**(6), 55–57

Leatherman, S. P. and G. White, 2005: Living on the edge: The coastal collision course, *Natural Hazards Observer*, **30**(2), 5–6

Mann, M. E. and K. A. Emanuel, 2006: Atlantic hurricane trends linked to climate change, *EOS Trans. AGU*, **87**(24), 233, 238, 241

National Science Board, 2007: *Hurricane Warning: The Critical Need for a National Hurricane Research Initiative*, Report NSB-06-115, National Science Foundation, National Science Board, Arlington, VA (see also www.nsf.gov/nsb/committees/hurricane/initiative.pdf)

Peltier, W. R., 2001: Global glacial isostatic adjustment and modern instrumental records of relative sea level history, in B. C. Douglas, M. S. Kearney and S. P. Leatherman (eds) *Sea Level Rise: History and Consequences*, Academic Press, San Diego

Robertson, R. A., 2004: *Alaska Native villages: Villages Affected by Flooding and Erosion have Difficulty Qualifying for Federal Assistance*, GAO Report GAO-04-895T, US Government Accountability Office, Washington DC (see also www.gao.gov/new.items/d04895t.pdf)

Woodworth, P. L., 1999: High waters at Liverpool since 1768: The UK's longest sea level record, *Geophysical Research Letters*, **26**, 1589–1592

Zhang, K., B. C. Douglas and S. P. Leatherman, 2004: Global warming and coastal erosion, *Climatic Change*, **64**, 41–58

11

Preparing and Protecting American Families from the Onslaught of Catastrophe

Admiral James M. Loy

American families need to be better prepared for and protected from mega-catastrophes. Hurricane Katrina underscored this point with the same force and clarity that the savage attacks of 11 September 2001 crystallized our national awareness and galvanized our national thinking about the immediate need to improve and enhance our preparation and defenses with regard to terrorism.

The US needs the same resolve and commitment to a national effort to improve and enhance preparation, mitigation and education before the next natural catastrophe strikes, as well as the establishment of a national financial mechanism that will stand as a backstop to the private insurance industry to assure our families that the resources will be available to help them rebuild and recover in the aftermath of another mega-catastrophe.

ProtectingAmerica.org is committed to finding better ways to prepare for and protect American families from the devastation caused by natural catastrophes. I co-chair the organization with James Lee Witt, the former director of the Federal Emergency Management Agency, and our coalition members include the American Red Cross, other first responder groups, emergency management officials, insurers, municipalities, small businesses, Fortune 100 companies and private citizens. The membership is broad and diverse and includes members from virtually every state in the nation.

ProtectingAmerica.org was formed to raise the national awareness about the important responsibility we all have to prepare and protect consumers, families, businesses and communities from natural disasters. We are building a campaign to create a comprehensive, national catastrophe management solution that protects homes and property at a lower cost, improves preparedness and reduces the financial burden on consumers and taxpayers – all in an effort to speed recovery, protect property, save money and save lives when a significant natural disaster strikes.

Though we come from all walks of life, we share a common belief that the current system of destroy, rebuild and hope in the aftermath of extraordinary natural disasters is fatally flawed in two significant and dangerous ways.

We continue to face the likelihood of natural catastrophes

We as a country simply do not prepare well enough in advance for natural catastrophes. Fundamental to the current system is the vain belief that 'it won't happen here'. This denial, which is pervasive from homeowners to officeholders, has provided us all with the false comfort that, while we would like to prepare for the possibility of catastrophe, the likelihood of an event actually happening 'here' is so remote that we should spend our time and resources on other more immediate and pressing problems.

This denial undermines efforts to prepare in advance of catastrophe, which, naturally, leads to the other sweeping shortcoming, which is that the current system is a patchwork of after-the-fact responses with all of the inefficiencies that are inherent in a system dominated by crisis and confusion.

The simple fact is that natural catastrophes can and do occur virtually everywhere in this country. The urgent threat posed by natural catastrophe in America cannot be denied:

- The majority – in fact 57 per cent – of the American public lives in areas prone to catastrophes like major hurricanes, earthquakes or other natural disasters, and more and more families move into those areas every day.
- Seven of the ten most costly hurricanes in US history occurred in the last five years.
- Some of the most valuable real estate in this country is squarely in the path of a natural catastrophe – on the Atlantic, Gulf and Pacific coasts and on top of the New Madrid fault in the greater Mississippi Valley.

Natural catastrophe preparedness, prevention and recovery are not a challenge limited only to Florida and the Gulf Coast, nor to the earthquake zone of northern California:

- In the past 100 years, 11 hurricanes have made direct hits on New England; 6 have made direct hits on Long Island. The most famous of those hurricanes hit in 1938 and is known as the Long Island Express. It hit Long Island and ripped up into New England. Seven hundred people were killed; 63,000 were left homeless. Had it made landfall a mere 20 miles west, New York City would have been inundated.

- Although the Great San Francisco Earthquake of 1906 is the best-known earthquake in the US, in fact, the New Madrid series of earthquakes in the early 1800s covered a far greater area with a force every bit as strong as San Francisco's earthquake. The New Madrid earthquakes emanated from New Madrid, Missouri and struck over a three-month period in 1811 and 1812. They changed the course of the Mississippi River, shook the ground from Mississippi to Michigan and from Pennsylvania to Nebraska. Structures were damaged throughout the Mississippi Valley, landslides occurred from Memphis to St Louis. These earthquakes are largely unknown today because they struck at a time when the earthquake zone was largely wilderness. What was essentially the bulk of the Louisiana Purchase now encompasses major population centers across the Midwest and Midsouth.

Climatologists are united in their observation that surface water temperatures are up. There is some evidence that we are in a weather cycle that is likely to last for many years, possibly several decades, and will include hurricanes with greater force and frequency than even those we have experienced in recent years. An emerging view, however, is that the shifts toward more powerful and destructive hurricanes are a result of climate change, and will continue on and further intensify in the future. Whichever is the case, the US very likely faces an extended period of very severe hurricanes.

Seismologists are similarly united in their observation that we are overdue for a major earthquake along many of the fault lines that run along our Pacific Coast or, as in the case of the New Madrid Fault, transect the very heartland of this nation.

There should be no comfort in the notion that the great earthquakes and hurricanes that previously ravaged our country seem to have occurred in such a vastly different age and time that they are not likely to repeat. Is our modern society so sophisticated and our cutting-edge technology so advanced that Mother Nature will choose to strike in some remote and distant land? To wager our families' futures on that sort of conceit is a fool's bet.

Simply put, catastrophe can happen here, it has happened here and there is no doubt that it will happen again. It is a question not of 'if' a mega-catastrophe will strike, but 'when' it will strike and 'how hard' it will strike. The costs of any of the best-known natural catastrophes repeating themselves would be enormous:

- Disaster experts project that a replay of the San Francisco earthquake – same force at the same location – could result in more than US$400 billion in replacement and rebuilding costs.
- Were we to experience a replay of the 1938 Long Island Express hurricane, the damages could exceed US$100 billion. If that hurricane made landfall smack in the middle of Manhattan, the damages would be even more staggering.

The effect of such tremendous losses would be felt through our entire national economy.

Our preparedness for responding needs enhancement

When catastrophe strikes, our after-the-fact response programs and protocols do a remarkable job in getting victims into shelters and in mobilizing emergency supplies and personnel so that the situation does not worsen.

All Americans, whether or not they have been victimized by catastrophe, owe our first responders an enormous debt of gratitude and thanks. We are equally indebted to the people behind the scenes – the government employees who work around-the-clock to ensure that logistics are worked out, that supplies are ordered and that funding is delivered. These men and women are too often overlooked. Their service is invaluable.

The first responders in harm's way and the government workers in makeshift outposts perform exceptionally well in this crisis mode. But, as we all know, the crisis mode is hyper-stressful, both on a human level and on a system-wide level. It requires split-second triage and prioritization that can lead to inefficiencies and unfairness.

While little can be done to completely eliminate the crisis mode, ProtectingAmerica.org believes that it can, and must, be mitigated. Clearly, programs that would improve preparedness, increase public education, enhance prevention and mitigation programs, and augment support for first responder programs would improve our national capability to prepare and protect those of us who live in harm's way.

Public education programs would help homeowners to make necessary plans and be prepared in advance of an emergency. Mitigation programs such as strong building codes and effective retrofitting programs would improve the integrity of catastrophe-prone structures so that damage would be minimized if catastrophe strikes. Experts tell us that for every dollar spent on mitigation, we save US$5–7 in future losses. An increase in first responder funding would help finance these critical programs that too often get short-changed in the give-and-take of local budgeting.

Studies in the aftermath of Hurricane Katrina suggest that the current after-the-fact recovery funding for catastrophes results in an enormous taxpayer subsidy for uninsured and underinsured properties. In fact, a Brookings Institution study (Litan, 2006) published in March 2006 found that of the first US$85 billion in taxpayer dollars spent on Katrina recovery efforts, more than US$10 billion went to cover losses for uninsured or underinsured properties.

ProtectingAmerica.org believes that in addition to minimizing the extent of catastrophic losses through prevention and mitigation programs, we should also reduce the taxpayer subsidy of recovery efforts, ensure the adequacy of recovery dollars, and improve the delivery of those critical funds to homeowners.

ProtectingAmerica.org supports the establishment of a stronger public–private partnership as part of a comprehensive, integrated solution at the local, state and national levels. The solution would include privately funded natural catastrophe funds in catastrophe-prone states that provide more protection at lower cost to consumers. These funds would serve as a backstop to the private insurance market and would generate investment earnings that, in addition to helping to pay claims in the aftermath of a mega-catastrophe, would be used for mitigation, prevention, preparation and first responder programs in each state.

We also support the creation of a national catastrophe fund that would serve as a backstop to participating state catastrophe funds in the event of a natural mega-catastrophe. Those state catastrophe funds would be financed through mandatory contributions by insurance companies in each of those states in an amount that reflects the catastrophe risk of the policies that they write in each state. These are private dollars, not taxpayer funds. The state funds would be required to set aside a minimum of US$10 million up to a maximum of 35 per cent of investment income for prevention, mitigation and public education programs.

Those states that choose to create a natural disaster fund would be able to purchase reinsurance from the national program. Rates for this coverage would be actuarially based and self-sufficient, and would only be available to state programs that have established the prevention and mitigation funding as described above.

In the event that a catastrophe strikes, private insurers would be required to meet all of their obligations to their policyholders. Should catastrophic losses exceed those obligations, the state catastrophe fund would be utilized. In the event of an extraordinary mega-catastrophe, the national backstop program would provide benefits to the state and help pay remaining claims.

Because this is a state-by-state program based entirely on risk, the likelihood of a taxpayer subsidy is virtually eliminated. This approach requires pre-event funding and relies on private dollars from insurance companies in the states that are most exposed to catastrophe. Because this program relies on the traditional private market for paying claims, the inherent inefficiencies and bureaucracy in a government-run program are eliminated. Also, because the program requires states to fund meaningful prevention and mitigation programs, catastrophe planning, protection and preparation will take place *before* the onslaught of catastrophe and will be in a state of continuous and rigorous improvement.

Conclusion

Establishing a pro-active and integrated approach to natural catastrophe management needs to be a top national priority. Steps need to be taken now, before the next catastrophe strikes.

References

Litan, R. E., 2006: *Preparing for Future 'Katrinas'*, Policy Brief No. 150, Brookings Institute, Washington DC (available at www.brookings.edu/comm/policybriefs/pb150.htm)

Part 4

The End of Evolution?
The Potential for Rapid
Changes in Ecosystems

Introduction to Part 4

Paul C. Pritchard

Despite the societal infrastructure that we have built up over the years, humankind is still deeply dependent on the environment around us and the diverse services the environment provides. In fact, economists estimate that the natural environment, in addition to its intrinsic worth, provides goods and services to society that are comparable in value to those that we produce for ourselves. Thus, the environment cleans the air we breathe, purifies the water that we drink, generates compounds that make up our medicines, assists in growing the food and fiber that we depend on, and provides the beauty that inspires our souls and enriches our vacations. Everywhere people live, the environment is drawn upon and shapes our lives.

In turn, each region's environment has been shaped and determined by the climate in which it has evolved and the region's connections to the broader world that exist through the atmosphere, hydrosphere and biosphere. While some climatic zones spread over vast regions, others occupy very small niches, sometimes at the tops of mountains or the edges of continents where an ecosystem has precious little space to maneuver with more robust ecosystems occupying more space at their warmer edge and their inability to relocate if conditions change.

And now comes human-induced climate change – at a pace more rapid that has been experienced since at least the end of the last ice age and of a magnitude that may well exceed that degree of change, but on the warm side. Within a century or two, climatic conditions have the potential, if we do not act aggressively, to change the natural world more than it has changed in millions of years. The magnitude of the impact of these human-induced changes on ecosystems in every corner of the Earth is taking the world into a new age, an age of the end of evolution as the driver of species change and development. From classic 'mega-fauna' such as the polar bear to the smallest worm, from the great boreal forests to the smallest orchid, the significance of what is occurring is almost beyond comprehension, given the limited experiences of most of humanity. Yet these changes will further affect all life, including mankind. Chapter 12 by noted ecologist Dr Anthony Janetos gives an indication of the global pervasiveness of the changes that are underway.

Global climate change and the resulting changes to ecosystems are so vast, however, that its importance may be easier to comprehend by assessing the impacts on one region or on one species. The polar regions, like deserts, are excellent study areas because of their fragility and of the minimal human disruption, at least to date; although remote, however, their condition and influence are critical to life as we know it. In Chapter 13, Dr Eric Kasischke and Dr F. Stuart Chapin III describe the increasing vulnerability of Alaska's boreal forest as a result of climate change, especially due to increased pest infestations and increased likelihood of fire. In Chapter 14, Dr Andrew Derocher considers the impact of the warming Arctic on polar bears, which live in a food chain that depends on their environment remaining cold. We seldom think of the vulnerability of Arctic ecosystems and wild species because they are perceived as massive and self-reliant. But the opposite is in fact reality – each depends on a very narrow range of conditions to keep the balance and provide the conditions on which they depend.

These three chapters, while providing many insights, can only touch on the real magnitude of the devastating consequences that climate change is likely to induce – and in many cases has already started to induce. The recent assessment of the IPCC cites hundreds of indications that climate change is already adversely impacting the world's ecosystems and wildlife. As Nobelist Paul Crutzen has said, we are creating the 'Anthropocene', a new epoch whose conditions we can only roughly predict, but which will surely be very different than the past, and thus, almost certainly, very disruptive to not only the environment, but to society.

12

Where Will Ecosystems Go?

Anthony C. Janetos

Climate-induced changes in ecosystems have been both modeled and documented extensively over the past 15–20 years. Those changes occur in the context of many other stresses and interacting factors, but it is clear that many, if not most, ecosystems are sensitive to changing climate.

Recent results from a wide range of scientific assessments shed light both on what is currently being observed in terms of the response of ecosystems to climate variability and change-related impacts, and on the degree to which the response of ecosystems can be represented in numerical models. Capabilities are improving for identifying and evaluating climate-induced changes in ecosystems in the context of changes from many other sources of environmental stress, although much needs to be learned in order to improve understanding and modeling of the dynamics of sudden or discontinuous change. With climate change continuing, an increasingly important issue is becoming the degree to which ecosystems can naturally adapt and possible measures that can be taken to enhance adaptive capacity.

Background and context

The state of the Earth system has clearly been changing rapidly over the past several decades. The Fourth Assessment Report of Working Group I of the IPCC (IPCC, 2007a) has summarized the available scientific information on recent changes in the Earth's physical climate system, and concluded that a significant human influence on climate is unequivocal. It is no longer possible, for example, to model changes in climate during the 20th century without accounting for the influences of changes in human forcings from greenhouse gases and aerosols. This is powerful evidence that human actions are already affecting the climate system, and there is a very clear expectation that this influence will continue to increase, especially if emissions and atmospheric concentrations of greenhouse gases also continue to increase. IPCC's analyses of simulations carried out using a wide range of atmosphere–ocean general circulation models demonstrate clearly that, over the next century, the Earth is very likely to experience both rates of change and absolute magnitudes of change in the physical climate system that far surpass any that human societies have experienced, and indeed that surpass natural rates of change seen in hundreds of thousands of years.

At the same time, there have been equally dramatic changes in the Earth's complement of natural resources and ecosystems. The Millennium Ecosystem Assessment (MEA, 2005), which is the most recent and most comprehensive scientific assessment of the planet's natural resources, provides documentation of unprecedented changes in natural resources over the past 40–50 years. For example:

- more land has been converted to cropland since 1945 than during the 18th and 19th centuries combined;
- 20 per cent of the world's coral reefs have been lost and 20 per cent degraded over recent decades;
- 35 per cent of mangrove area has been lost over recent decades;
- the amount of water held in reservoirs has quadrupled since 1960;
- withdrawals of water from rivers and lakes have doubled since 1960.

From the standpoint of terrestrial ecosystems, one of the most dramatic changes in the status of ecosystems and natural resources is the dramatic land-cover change that has taken place over past decades. In the MEA (2005) and in Lepers et al (2005), the locations of deforestation and forest degradation, and of cropland expansion and contraction were carefully documented for the time period 1980–2000. Figure 12.1 (Plate 16) shows one of the results of this analysis, which required harmonizing regional and global datasets, and then portraying them on the same GIS grid so that the top 10 per cent of pixels in which changes were seen could be identified (more methodological details are available in Lepers et al, 2005).

The results of this analysis are very clear. Major areas of tropical and subtropical forests were lost over this time period in South America, Central America, Central and East Africa, and throughout Southeast Asia. However, in addition, there was substantial loss and degradation of forests across Russia, from its Eastern European borders to the Russian Far East. These regions include some of the most species-rich regions of the world (for example, the Amazon Basin), as well as the largest expanse of boreal forest. It is also important to note that many areas not showing change over this period were significantly transformed in prior periods.

During the same time period, there were also extensive changes in the land devoted to cropland. Significant expansions of croplands occurred in South America, Central and East Africa, and Southeast Asia, whereas cropland in East Asia actually decreased in area. Data for the US indicate a patchwork quilt of

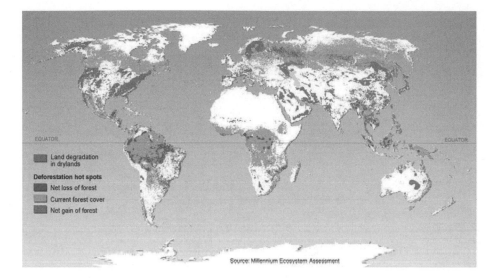

Figure 12.1 Main areas of deforestation and land degradation from 1980–2000 (see Plate 16 for color version)

Source: MEA, 2005.

increases and decreases, partially depending on the specific definitions of cropland used in the different data sets that were harmonized. The very beginnings of the large expansion of soy agriculture in South America were just beginning to be detected in the MEA analysis.

Marine ecosystems experienced similarly large and rapid changes. The MEA concluded that many of the major open ocean fish stocks have already been depleted from overfishing and are no longer being harvested in a sustainable manner.

Current observations of change related to climate

Research from the Commonwealth Scientific and Industrial Research Organisation (CSIRO) in Australia shows the relationship between sea surface temperatures and bleaching of several coral species in the Great Barrier Reef over the past 140 years, and projections into the future (see Figure 12.2). The data are clear that we are now in a transition period, when the frequency of conditions conducive to bleaching are increasing rapidly, and will soon be in a range where bleaching conditions occur annually. The link between high sea surface temperatures and bleaching of corals has been established unequivocally, and the phenomenon has been shown to be circumtropical in nature.

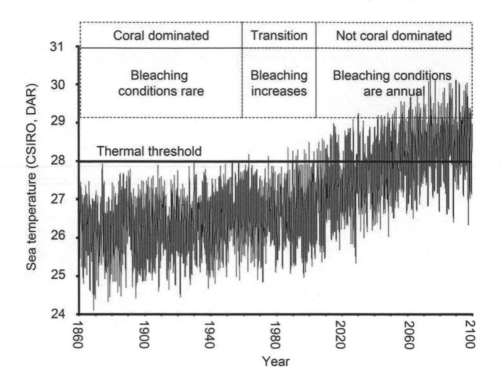

Figure 12.2 Projected outlook for coral reefs as ocean temperature rises as a result of climate change

Source: Hoegh-Guldberg, 2005.

The widespread occurrence of land-based glacial retreat is also well documented. Glaciers in both northern latitudes in North America, Europe and Asia are known to be receding. Moreover, glaciers at high elevations in mid-latitudes and in the subtropics and tropics are also receding. Widespread change in the climate system is the only forcing factor that can explain the simultaneity of these changes over such broad ranges of latitude and elevation. Some of these changes (for example, the retreat of Chacaltaya Glacier in Bolivia) have direct impacts on human well-being, in this case, reduction of one of the major water supplies for La Paz.

The most recent assessment by IPCC's Working Group II (IPCC, 2007b) has extensively documented a wide range of physical and ecological impacts that are clearly associated with changes in the physical climate system. These range from reductions in mountain snowpack in the US Pacific Northwest to the loss of Arctic sea ice and unexpectedly rapid break-up of several ice shelves in the Antarctic. In addition to these, there are more purely biological changes, such as the earlier migration of many species of birds and butterflies, and longer growing seasons in temperate latitudes. Over 1500 studies are documented by IPCC, and two extensive meta-analyses show conclusively that the ecological and biological changes that have been documented are consistent with changes in the climate system itself.

One marine ecosystem change that has recently been documented is also due to the accumulation of excess CO_2 in the atmosphere, although it is not directly related to changes in the climate system per se. Because the chemistry of ocean surface waters quickly comes into equilibrium with the changing atmospheric concentration of CO_2, a reduction in the average pH of surface ocean waters of about 0.1 pH units has been observed over the last 150 years. If concentrations of atmospheric CO_2 continue to rise at about the same rate as is occurring at present, ocean pH could drop another 0.1 units over the next several decades (see Figure 12.3).

It is already known that reductions in average ocean surface pH of this magnitude do not reflect the full range of pH losses in different ocean basins. In addition, the reactions by which marine organisms, including corals and free swimming plankton, extract calcium carbonate from solution in seawater to construct their skeletons are themselves pH-dependent. The reduction in oceanic pH results in those organisms being less capable of building their skeletons. While of obvious importance for corals and plankton, there are almost certainly going to be impacts from this phenomenon all through marine food chains. However, the consequences for fisheries and other marine organisms are not known at this time with any certainty.

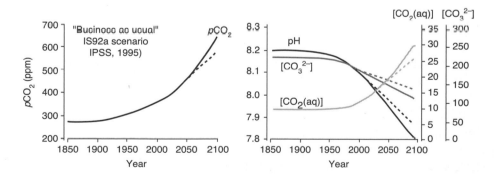

Figure 12.3 Past and projected changes in ocean chemistry as a result of the rising atmospheric CO_2 concentration

Source: Wolf-Gladrow et al, 1999.

There have also been significant increases in the number of major wild fires over the past 50 years (see Figure 12.4). As with many other phenomena, this pattern has multiple causes, including increases in the likelihood of persistent drought and the consequences of decades of fire suppression policy, which has acted to increase the fuel available for ignition. However, variations in fire frequency in forest ecosystems in western North America, at least, have been linked to variations and change in the climate system. This phenomenon parallels one of the most consistent, and apparently robust, model projections that has emerged over recent decades, namely, that there will be an increase in the risk of forest fire as a result of climate change.

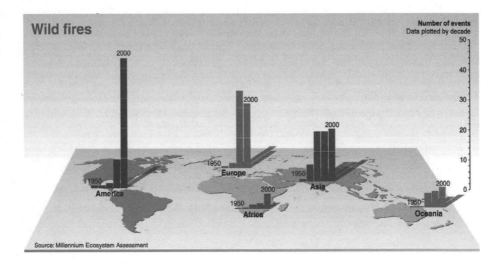

Figure 12.4 Number of major wild fires by continent and decade since 1950

Source: MEA, 2005.

Results from the US National Assessment

The most extensive investigation into the underlying vulnerability of ecosystems, natural resources, health, agriculture and coastal systems in the US was the US National Assessment of the Potential Consequences of Climate Variability and Change (NAST, 2000). This national process investigated, through a collection of sectoral and regional studies, the current sensitivities and potential changes to these sectors in the US, as they might occur as a result of several climate scenarios.

Some of the most important vulnerabilities occur in unmanaged ecosystems. Figure 12.5 (Plate 17) shows results from the MAPSS ecosystem model for two different climate scenarios generated through application of GCM models to

Ecosystem Models

Current Ecosystems

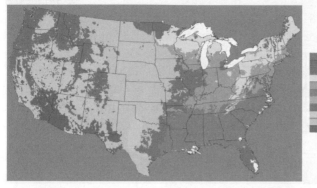

Canadian Model

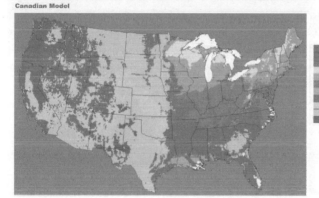

Hadley Model

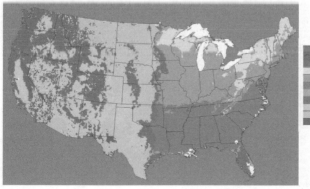

Figure 12.5 Distribution of ecosystems across the US at present and for two climate change scenarios based on projections to 2100 from results prepared for the US National Assessment (see Plate 17 for color version)

Note: Hadley = warm-moist; Canadian = hot-dry.
Source: NAST, 2000.

existing patterns of interannual and interdecadal variability. In these analyses, the warm-wet scenario generated by the Hadley second generation model resulted in a general northward migration of potential natural vegetation, but also led to significant break-up of the vegetation types of the arid Southwest. Alternatively, the hot-dry scenario generated from the results of the Canadian Climate Model not only showed similar patterns for the Southwest, but also showed the typical forest vegetation of the Southeast breaking up as a result of extensive fire disturbances, and being replaced by savanna and grassland, because forests would no longer be able to regenerate in the very different climate conditions associated with this scenario.

Such potential impacts are seen not only at the ecosystem level, but also at the individual species level. Figure 12.6 (Plate 18) shows projections for changes in the distribution of sugar maple in the US, using scenarios generated by five different GCMs. In each case, the climatic conditions associated with a doubling of the atmospheric CO_2 concentration would result in sugar maple trees no longer being able to regenerate within its original range in the US. While the dynamics of such a change are not yet adequately modeled, the general pattern for ecosystem change is very robust across many species and many ecosystem types.

For the range of results described in the US National Assessment, regional sensitivities of ecosystems for each region in the US are summarized in Figure

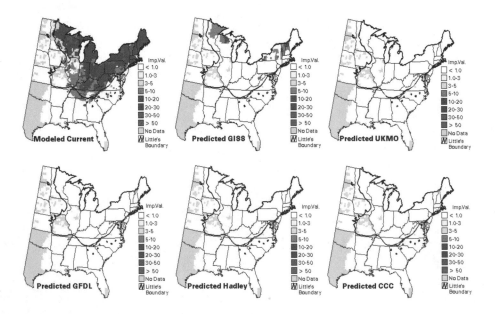

Figure 12.6 Present and projected distribution of sugar maple trees based on the results of five general circulation climate models assuming a doubling of the atmospheric CO_2 concentration (see Plate 18 for color version)

Source: Prasad and Iverson, 2007.

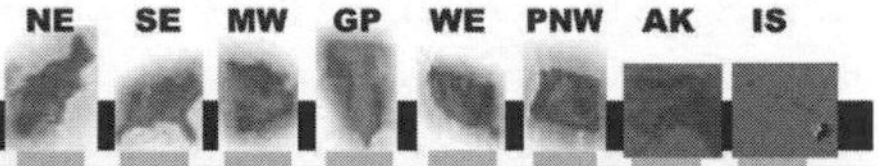

Ecosystem Type		NE	SE	MW	GP	WE	PNW	AK	IS
Forests	Impacts								
	Changes in tree species composition and alteration of animal habitat	X	X	X		X	X	X	X
	Displacement of forests by open woodlands and grasslands under a warmer climate in which soils are drier			X					
Grasslands									
	Displacement of grasslands by open woodlands and forests under a wetter climate					X			
	Increase in success of non-native invasive plant species				X	X			X
Tundra									
	Loss of alpine meadows as their species are displaced by lower-elevation species	X				X	X	X	
	Loss of northern tundra as trees migrate poleward							X	
	Changes in plant community composition and alteration of animal habitat							X	
Semi-arid and Arid									
	Increase in woody species and loss of desert species under wetter climate					X			
Freshwater									
	Loss of prairie potholes with more frequent drought conditions				X				
	Habitat changes in rivers and lakes as amount and timing of runoff changes and water temperatures rise	X	X	X	X	X	X		
Coastal & Marine									
	Loss of coastal wetlands as sea level rises and coastal development prevents landward migration	X	X			X	X		X
	Loss of barrier islands as sea-level rise prevents landward migration	X	X						
	Changes in quantity and quality of freshwater delivery to estuaries and bays alter plant and animal habitat	X	X			X	X	X	X
	Loss of coral reefs as water temperature increases		X						X
	Changes in ice location and duration alter marine mammal habitat							X	

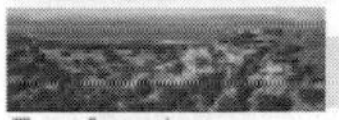

Figure 12.7 Types of impacts associated with various regions of the US based on studies done for the US National Assessment

Source: NAST, 2000.
Note: NE = Northeast; SE = Southeast; MW = Midwest; GP = Great Plains; WE = Western US; PNW = Pacific Northwest; AK = Alaska; IS = Islands.

12.7. Significant sensitivities for many ecosystems were noted for each region in the US.

The importance of thresholds and tipping points

Many impact analyses carried out in recent years have treated potential climate impacts as though they would occur more or less as slowly changing means in the delivery of ecosystem services or natural resources. The MEA (2005) points out the limitations of this assumption, which are evident in the many well-documented instances of ecosystems and natural resources changing rapidly, in a non-linear fashion, or in an irreversible way – i.e., behaving in a manner indicating that there are thresholds in species dynamics, beyond which very different conditions will be exhibited.

We are now beginning to see examples of threshold phenomena in ecosystem responses that are clearly related to climate variability and change. Coral bleaching has already been noted, as have the increases in fire frequency in western North America. But perhaps the most visible example at the present time is the interaction of drought stress, warm winters and pests in lodgepole pine forests of the western and northwestern forests of North America. The mountain pine beetle is the major pest, and, in part, because large areas of lodgepole pine are in drought stress and therefore weakened physiologically, and, in part, because winters have been too warm to kill off over-wintering larvae, infestations of this naturally occurring pest are more than an order of magnitude larger than ever before documented. Projections are for more than 90 per cent mortality of lodgepole pine in British Columbia throughout most of its range, which would make this infestation both an ecological and economic catastrophe for that region.

The potential for responding

The recent IPCC Working Group II report (IPCC, 2007b) raises a number of important points with respect to climate impacts and their consequences for human well-being. In terms of human vulnerability, the literature is clear that analyses of impacts at global and continental scales can mask significant regional vulnerabilities (i.e., there is great potential for significant variation in impacts and consequences at a regional scale). Working Group II identifies the major megadeltas, sub-Saharan Africa, the tropics and subtropics, small islands and the high northern latitudes as being at particular risk of important climate impacts. In part, this is because these geographic regions have ecosystems that exhibit particular vulnerability to expected climate change, and climate change impacts have already been detected in many areas, especially in the high latitudes (Arctic Climate Impact Assessment, 2005). In addition, many societies in these regions have limited adaptive capacity compared, for example, to more affluent regions in North America and Western Europe.

The Working Group II Fourth Assessment Report concluded that there is likely to be great variation in adaptive capacity among different societies. While adaptive capacity is thought to be generally related to the wealth of societies, this relationship is not straightforward. Even very wealthy societies can have significant vulnerabilities to the consequences of climate change, particularly among vulnerable segments of their populations. While there are beginning to be significant advances in knowledge relating to potential adaptive strategies, there are, so far, very few examples of proactive adaptation actions that would be applicable to natural ecosystems. The implications are clear: if climate change and its consequences turn out to be in the upper range of estimated probabilities, even the adaptive capacity of wealthy nations could be overwhelmed by the end of the century.

Conclusions

The US National Assessment, the MEA and now IPCC's Fourth Assessment Report all come to similar conclusions. Ecosystems, particularly those that are unmanaged to any great degree, are sensitive to the changes in the physical climate system that can reasonably be expected to occur over the next several decades to a century. Indeed, there are already many well-documented cases of impacts on marine and terrestrial ecosystems.

Such consequences are occurring and will occur on a background of already extremely rapid change in ecosystems, often driven by the extraction of goods and services in an unsustainable fashion by human societies. While some countries and economies are thought to have substantial adaptive capacity, many do not, especially in the developing world. Reasonable scenarios of ecological change due to climate change and other stresses could therefore result in overwhelming the adaptive capacity of even currently wealthy societies, although this is a conclusion subject to considerable uncertainty because of unknowns in the underlying science.

Continued preparation and purposeful adaptation will be necessary over coming decades. Successful adaptation will be dependent on both improvements in the underlying climate and ecological sciences and on actions by and improvements in institutions and policies that govern societal use of natural resources and ecosystem services.

References

Arctic Climate Impact Assessment (ACIA), 2005: *Arctic Climate Impact Assessment*, Cambridge University Press, Cambridge, 1042pp

Hoegh-Guldberg, O., 2005: Low coral cover in a high-CO_2 world, *Journal of Geophysical Research-Oceans*, **110** C09S06, doi: 10.1029/2004JC002528

IPCC (Intergovernmental Panel on Climate Change), 2007a: *Climate Change 2007: The Physical Science Basis*, Contribution of Working Group I to the Fourth Assessment Report of the Intergovernmental Panel on Climate Change (S. Solomon, D. Qin, M. Manning, et al (eds)), Cambridge University Press, Cambridge and New York, 996pp

IPCC, 2007b: Summary for Policymakers, in *Climate Change 2007:Impacts, Adaptation and Vulnerability*, Contribution of Working Group II to the Fourth Assessment Report of the Intergovernmental Panel on Climate Change (M. Parry, O. Canziani, J. Palutikof, P. van der Linden and C. Hanson (eds)), Cambridge University Press, Cambridge and New York, 976pp

Lepers, E., E. F. Lambin, A. C. Janetos, R. DeFries, F. Achard, N. Ramankutty and R. J. Scholes, 2005: A synthesis of information on rapid land-cover change for the period 1981–2000, *BioScience*, **55**(2), 115–124

MEA (Millennium Ecosystem Assessment), 2005: *Ecosystems and Human Well-Being*, Island Press, Washington DC

NAST (National Assessment Synthesis Team), 2000: *Climate Change Impacts on the United States: The Potential Consequences of Climate Variability and Change: Overview Report*, US Global Change Research Program, Cambridge University Press, Cambridge

Prasad, A. M. and L. R. Iverson, 2007: A Climate Change Atlas for 80 Forest Tree Species of the Eastern United States [spatial database], USDA Forest Service, Northeastern Research Station, Delaware, Ohio (see www.fs.fed.us/ne/delaware/atlas/index.html)

Wolf-Gladrow, D. A., J. Bijma and R. Zeebe, 1999: Model simulation of the carbonate chemistry in the microenvironment of symbiont bearing foraminifera, *Marine Chemistry*, **64**, 181–198

13

Increasing Vulnerability of Alaska's Boreal Forest as a Result of Climate Warming and the Changing Fire Regime

Eric S. Kasischke and F. Stuart Chapin III

The boreal region extends across the Earth's land surface between around 50°N and 67°N and covers some 15 million square kilometers. The biomes found in this region include forests, wetlands, peatlands and sub-alpine/alpine tundra. Most of this region has an average annual surface temperature around 0°C, with long, cold winters (average January low temperatures <-30°C) and short, warm summers (average July high temperatures >20°C). This temperature regime has resulted in the formation of permafrost (defined as any soil that has remained below 0°C for more than two years) throughout a significant portion of the boreal region. In turn, the presence of permafrost results in poor site drainage, low tree growth rates, and decreased rates of soil decomposition, leading to the development of deep organic layers lying on top of the ground surface.

A pronounced increase in the rate of summer-time warming (between 0.3 and 0.4°C per decade) began in the early 1960s throughout the western Arctic and Alaska (Chapin et al, 2005). While rates of precipitation have also increased, the rise in available soil water has not been sufficient to offset requirements for evapotranspiration, leading to lower tree growth in some regions due to moisture stress (Barber et al, 2000). Climate warming has also contributed to increases in insect outbreaks (Werner et al, 2006) and area burned as a result of lightning-ignited wildfires throughout the North American boreal forest (Gillett et al, 2004). Most scientists and federal and state land managers recognize that the recent warming in the high northern latitudes is likely to continue for the foreseeable future.

Fire is ubiquitous throughout the boreal region, with most of the burned area resulting from ignitions from lightning strikes (Dissing and Verbyla, 2003). Fire records show that during the 1990s, three million hectares of land surface were affected annually by fires in the boreal regions of North America (Kasischke and Turetsky, 2006), while satellite data show that between 10 and 15 million hectares per year have burned in Russia (Sukhinin et al, 2004) over the past decade. Depending on regional climate, sources of ignition and forest type, fire return intervals range between 50 and 200 years in boreal forests.

Paleoecological studies have provided insights as to how climate change has affected vegetation cover over the 12,000 years since the most recent recession of the Pleistocene ice sheets (Lloyd et al, 2006). The mosaic of forest cover in Interior Alaska – which is dominated by black spruce (*Picea mariana*), but also contains significant components of white spruce (*Picea glauca*), quaking aspen (*Populus tremuloides*), balsam poplar (*Populus balsimifera*) and paper birch (*Betula neoalaskana*) – has been present for the past 6000 years. Prior to that (6000 to 10,000 before present (BP)), warmer and slightly drier conditions resulted in white spruce being the dominant tree species. From 10,000 to 12,000 BP, warm and dry conditions resulted in a landscape where black and white spruce were only minor components of the landscape – during this period, vegetation was dominated by deciduous tree stands and shrub and grass-herb dominated ecosystems.

Given the above understanding of how past variations in climate shaped the composition of boreal forests it is fairly certain that the present mosaic of vegetation cover throughout interior Alaska, as elsewhere throughout the Arctic region, will change as temperatures continue to rise during the 21st century. However, a number of factors will influence the rate and direction of change, including variations in patterns of precipitation, changes to the fire regime, the degree to which insect outbreaks occur in different forest types, the rate of soil warming of areas underlain by permafrost, and the patterns of dispersion or human introduction of vegetation species not currently resident in this region. While some of these factors can be lessened through management intervention (for example, fire suppression, control of insects and pathogens, and prevention of the introduction of invasive species), many will remain outside of human control. Slowing the rate of climate change and influencing management strategies are the key priorities of those who depend on the many ecosystem services provided by Alaska's boreal forests, particularly Native Peoples.

Variation in fire severity and its effects on ecosystem characteristics

The community structure of upland forests in interior Alaska results from secondary succession following fires (Viereck et al, 1983; Van Cleve et al, 1996; Chapin et al, 2006). Ecosystem processes in these upland areas are strongly influenced by the aspect or orientation (which regulates the amount of solar insolation reaching a site), elevation (average temperature decreases with increasing elevation) and slope position (Slaughter and Viereck, 1986). Because of the role of topography, north facing slopes as well as sites at higher elevations (above 650 m) and sites located in

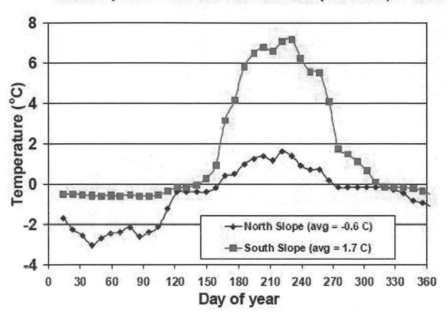

Figure 13.1 Seasonal soil temperature profiles collected from mature black spruce stands at an elevation of 650 m

Source: data courtesy of E. Kane, University of Alaska.

the bottoms of stream valleys are most susceptible to the formation of permafrost. The overall influence of permafrost on mineral soil temperature is illustrated in Figure 13.1. On the north-slope site, the mineral soil remains frozen for much of the year, thawing for only 120 days and reaching a maximum temperature of only 2°C. While the south-slope site only has an average temperature 2°C warmer, during the middle of the growing season, its maximum temperature is over 7°C.

For 10 to 60 years after the fire, deciduous forests (aspen and birch) dominate warmer and drier sites at lower elevations without permafrost; these are eventually succeeded by mature stands of white spruce 100 to 150 years after the fire. On cool, wet sites (often underlain by permafrost), deciduous tree species are unable to invade following fires, resulting in an initial domination (for 5 to 30 years after the fire) by herbs and shrubs that were present prior to the fire and are able to reproduce vegetatively. Black spruce seedlings that are established 1 to 10 years following a fire eventually grow into mature forest stands after 50 to 80 years.

Black spruce forests cover 50 to 60 per cent of the forested land of interior Alaska and are the most common forests that burn (see Figures 13.2a–c). Black spruce trees have relatively thin bark that does not provide protection from the heat

Figure 13.2 Typical mature black spruce forests found in interior Alaska

Note: (a) Black spruce-lichen forest with a 10–12 cm deep organic layer; (b) Black spruce-feathermoss forest with a 20–25 cm deep organic layer; (c) Black spruce-sphagnum moss forest with a 36–40 cm deep organic layer; and (d) Typical surface organic layer that sits on top of mineral soil in a black spruce-feathermoss forest. The top layer consists of live moss, which is underlain by the upper duff layer (light brown layer consisting of dead moss and fibric soil sub-layers) and the lower duff layer (dark brown, consisting of mesic and humic soil sub-layers).
Source: Photographs by E. Kasischke.

generated during fires (Johnson, 1992). Even surface fires with low to moderate intensity are hot enough to induce high rates of mortality in black spruce stands. As a result, most fires in these forests are stand-replacing events.

A key characteristic of black spruce stands in the North American boreal forest region is a deep layer of dead organic matter (see Figure 13.2d). The organic layer develops as a stand recovers after a fire because of the low rates of decomposition that occur on sites with cold and wet conditions (O'Neill et al, 2006). In mature stands, the organic layer depth in mature Alaskan black spruce forests averages 25 cm in depth (range of 7 to >40 cm) (see Figure 13.3, Plate 19). These surface organic layers represent a significant reservoir for terrestrial carbon, containing an average of 63 tC ha^{-1}. During fires, substantial levels of the surface organic layers in black spruce forests are consumed, primarily through smoldering combustion.

The amount of organic material remaining after a fire is highly variable (see Figure 13.3) and depends on the moisture level of the ground-layer organic

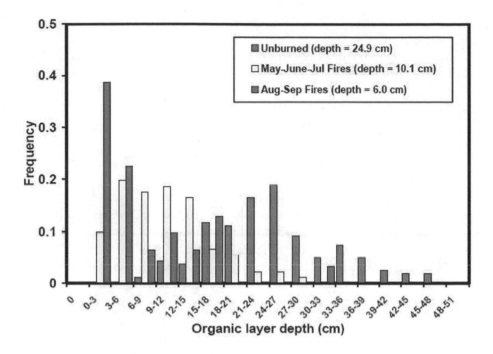

Figure 13.3 Distribution of organic layer depths measured in burned and unburned Alaskan black spruce forests (see Plate 19 for color version)

Note: The burned and unburned forest stands where these data were collected were 70 to 300 years old.
Source: Plot based on unpublished data from E. Kasischke and M. Turetsky (Michigan State University).

material. While the moisture content of the upper portion of the surface organic layer is controlled by climatic variables (precipitation, air temperature, wind and solar insolation), the moisture content of the deeper layers just above mineral soil is regulated by site drainage characteristics (mineral soil texture, slope and seasonal thawing depth where permafrost is present). On average, the depths of the surface organic layers are reduced by 64 per cent during fires, and 54 per cent of the carbon is consumed. Because depth of soil thawing increases over the growing season, sites with permafrost are better drained during late-season fires. As a result, depth of burning is 30 per cent greater during late-season (after 1 August) fires compared to early-season fires, resulting in a 40 per cent greater amount of carbon consumed (see Figure 13.3)

When considering the surface organic layers in black spruce forests, two measures are needed to assess fire severity. The first measure is the depth of the organic material remaining after a fire. The second measure is the depth of the organic layer prior to the fire. Together, this information can be used to assess the degree to which a site has been altered by the fire (fire severity). In turn, fire severity affects ecosystem processes in three ways. First, it regulates key pathways for exchange of water and energy between the land surface and atmosphere. Second, it affects vegetative reproduction. And third, it alters key site characteristics that regulate seed germination and seedling growth.

The deep surface organic layer in black spruce forests facilitates the formation of permafrost (Yoshikawa et al, 2002). The moisture and water present in the organic layer decrease thermal conductance and reduce the amount of downward energy transfer during the warm summer months. While the organic layer also serves as an insulating blanket during the winter, it is less effective when the water present in this layer freezes and increases thermal conductance. As a result, there is a net energy loss in surfaces covered by organic layers, with the degree of cooling being proportional to the depth of the surface organic layer.

The region where the soil layer thaws by the end of the growing season in sites with permafrost is called the active layer, because it is within this soil volume where above freezing temperatures allow biological processes (such as decomposition, water and nutrient uptake by roots) to occur. In sites with permafrost, soil temperature and the depth of the active layer are inversely proportional to the depth of the surface organic layer. In black spruce-lichen forests with shallow organic layers (see Figure 13.2a), the active layer is 200–300 cm deep. In contrast, the active layer in black spruce-sphagnum moss forests (see Figure 13.2c) may only be 25–35 cm deep.

By reducing the depth of the organic layer, fires result in a net warming of the ground layer for the first two decades following a fire. Within 5 to 10 years following a fire, in black spruce-feathermoss forests (see Figure 13.2b) the depth of the active layer can increase by 100–150 cm in sites underlain by permafrost.

The effects of fire on soil moisture are more complex. In killing the overstory trees as well as consuming most of the understory vegetation, fires cause a net increase in soil water because they eliminate losses from evapotranspiration. Decreases in surface albedo result in a warming of the surface and increase in evaporation. In areas underlain by permafrost, the depth of seasonal thawing increases slowly for the first several years after a fire. The net result is that soils in burned areas are as wet or even wetter than in unburned areas for the first several years after a fire, and gradually become drier than unburned stands five to ten years following the fire as the increase in depth of seasonal thawing results in better drained soils (Kasischke and Johnstone, 2005). In sites without permafrost, the warming of the ground following fires may be accompanied by an immediate drying of soils even with the elimination of evapotranspiration.

Vegetative reproduction is a common strategy for plant species in fire-prone ecosystems because it allows for rapid re-establishment following disturbance (Zasada et al, 1983). Herbs and shrubs in black spruce forests reproduce following fire through sprouting from roots and stumps. This strategy is successful in sites with shallow to moderately deep burning of the organic layers, but fails when deep-burning fire consumes the underground vegetative material.

Figure 13.4 presents examples of variations in the patterns of vegetation recovery that have been observed in black spruce forests in interior Alaska that were collected at sites that burned during a 1994 fire (see Johnstone and Kasischke, 2005; Johnstone and Chapin, 2006). The depth of the organic layers in these black spruce-feathermoss forests (see Figure 13.2c) sites was 25 cm prior to the burn (see Figure 13.2d). The data from these plots illustrate how patterns of regrowth vary as a function of fire severity. In the site in Figure 13.4a, only the upper part of the organic layer was consumed by the fire, and vegetative reproduction at this site resulted in the re-establishment of herbs and shrubs that were present prior to the

Figure 13.4 Patterns of post-fire regrowth in black spruce-feather moss forests that burned in July and August of 1994

Note: These photographs were taken in the summer of 2003 in areas that were adjacent to the unburned stand presented in Figure 13.2b. (a) Site with 15–20 cm of organic matter remaining after the fire; (b) Site with 4–6 cm of organic matter remaining after the fire; (c) Site with <1 cm of organic matter remaining after the fire.
Source: Photographs by E. Kasischke.

fire. At this time, recruitment of black spruce was 4 seedlings m^{-2}, a density that was 370 per cent of the stand density at the time of the fire. While aspen seedlings were present, their growth was low, with total aspen biomass being 9 g m^{-2}.

The site in Figure 13.4b experienced a more severe fire than that in Figure 13.4a, with only 4–6 cm of organic matter remaining. The vegetation at this site was dominated by seedlings, with little or no vegetative reproduction. Aspen seedlings were dense in this stand (4 stems m^{-2}), but their growth was modest (53 g m^{-2}), with most stems being less than 1 m in height. Spruce seedlings were present in lower levels than in the lightly-burned stand, 1.7 stems m^{-2}, which was 150 per cent of pre-burn stand density. Finally, the stand in Figure 13.4c experienced a severe burn, with less than 1 cm of organic matter left. The vegetation reproduction at this site was only from seedlings. While aspen density was low (2.2 stems m^{-2}), the growth was vigorous (323 g m^{-2}), with many stems being 2–3 m in height. Black spruce seedling density was low (0.5 stems m^{-2}), being only 50 per cent of pre-burn stand density. In summary, while the lightly burned site in Figure 13.4a is following a regrowth trajectory that is common in black spruce forests, the severely burned site in Figure 13.4c is following a different trajectory. This site will most likely develop into a mature, dense aspen stand with a very low-density understory of black spruce. Permafrost will eventually result in poorly drained soils in the lightly burned site as mosses regrow, the depth of the organic layer increases, and the ground layer cools. In the severely burned site, however, the ground layer will continue to warm until permafrost disappears.

In addition to depth of burning, site microclimate and moisture conditions are important for post-fire tree recruitment. Figure 13.5 presents photographs collected in 2006 of sites that burned during a June 1999 fire. The stand in Figure 13.5a differed from the examples in Figure 13.4 because it contained a mature black spruce-lichen forest prior to the fire (see Figure 13.2a) and had a much shallower organic layer and a deeper active layer. The area burned in the 1999 fire is located in a region that experiences frequent periods of high wind from an adjacent mountain pass, which causes much higher rates of surface evaporation and transpiration. As a result of deeper active layers and high winds, the post fire soil moisture in the sites in this region were lower than the sites in the 1994 burn (Kasischke et al, 2007), and resulted in conditions where seeds could not germinate and seedlings experienced higher rates of mortality. Because of these dry conditions, there was very little recruitment of aspen in the severely burned site (see Figure 13.5a) (0.06 stems m^{-2} compared to 2.2 stems m^{-2} in the site that was severely burned in 1994). The recruitment of black spruce seedlings in the site with the deeper post-fire organic layer (see Figure 13.5b) was 0.7 stems m^{-2}, which was only 15 per cent of the pre-burn stand density (compared to 4.4 stems m^{-2} and 300 per cent of pre-burn stand density in the lightly burned stand from the 1994 fire; see Figure 13.4a). This study illustrates that microclimate and soil moisture conditions at a site are also important in determining post-fire regeneration.

Figure 13.5 Patterns of post-fire regrowth from a fire event that occurred in June 1999

Note: These photographs were taken in the summer of 2006: (a) Black spruce-lichen stand with <1 cm of organic matter remaining after the fire (site adjacent to the unburned stand of Figure 13.2a, which had 10 cm of organic matter); (b) Black spruce-feathermoss stand with 10–12 cm of organic matter remaining after the fire (site had a 16 cm deep organic layer prior to the fire).
Source: Photographs by E. Kasischke.

Recent changes to the fire regime and permafrost

In addition to the warming of the climate over the past half-century, interior Alaska has also seen changes to the fire regime and a warming of permafrost. Figure 13.6 presents the annual burned area in the entire state of Alaska for 1950 to 2006, where over 95 per cent of the total occurs in the interior region. For the past 22 years (1985–2006), the average burned area increased by 70 per cent compared to the previous 35 years (1950–1984), reaching 520,000 ha y⁻¹. The increase in fire activity is the result of a significant rise in the frequency of larger fire years (i.e., years with large, very large or ultra-large areas burned) (see Figure 13.6, Plate 20). Prior to 1985, 1.7 larger fire years occurred per decade. Since 1985, 3.2 larger fire years have occurred each decade. During the record fire years of 2004 and 2005, nearly 4.5 million hectares of land was impacted by fire, which represents >10 per cent of the land surface of the interior ecozones of Alaska. Recent changes in the frequency of larger fire years have also been observed in western Canada as well (Kasischke and Turetsky, 2006).

Over the past two decades, the occurrence of fire in interior Alaska has been strongly influenced by the seasonal patterns of precipitation. During small fire years, the non-human fire season begins in early June, when enough moisture enters the atmosphere to result in late-afternoon, convective lightning storms. Precipitation during April and May averages less than 4 cm throughout most of the interior, which results in the low fuel moistures and relative humidities that create conditions that support the ignition and spread of wildland fire. During

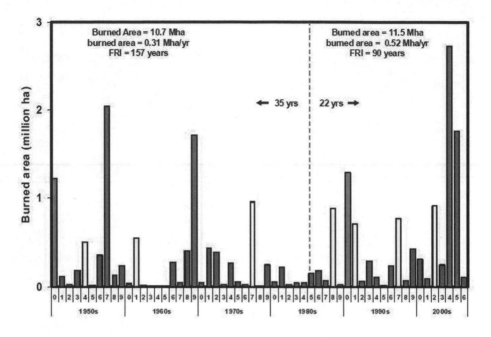

Figure 13.6 Historical patterns of annual burned area in Alaska (see also Plate 20 for color version)

Note: The blue bars represent small fire years, when <1 per cent of the land surface in interior Alaska burned. The yellow bars represent large fire years, when 1–2 per cent of the land surface burned. The orange bars represent very large fire years, when 2–3 per cent of the land surface burned. The red bars represent ultra-large fire years, when 3 per cent of the land surface burned.

Source: Based on fire records from the Alaska Fire Service, Bureau of Land Management.

low fire years, precipitation increases beginning in mid-July and August, raising both fuel moisture and relative humidity to the point where the ignition and spread of fires cannot be sustained. During larger fire seasons, however, stationary high-pressure centers interrupt seasonal precipitation patterns and create drought conditions that allow fires to burn longer, as well as leading to more fires being ignited. During larger fire years in the period 1985 to 2006, there was a substantial increase in the amount of late season burning (see Figure 13.7, Plate 21). These seasonal differences in burned area between smaller and larger fire years were not present during 1950–1984. As a result, there has been a doubling in the rate of burning in late-season fires, from 82,600 ha y^{-1} during 1950–1984 to 175,300 ha y^{-1} during 1985–2006.

Over the longer term, average air temperature directly controls average permafrost temperature. Because of this, long-term measurements show the temperature of deep permafrost (1–10 m) has been rising in interior Alaska at nearly the same rate as air temperatures since the beginning of the 1970s (Osterkamp, 2005).

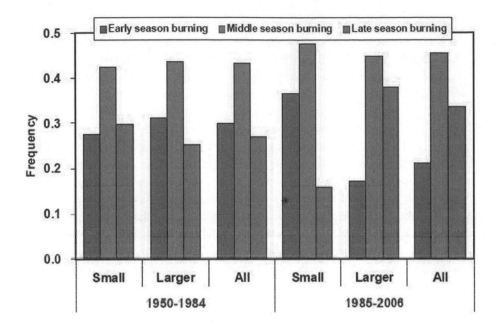

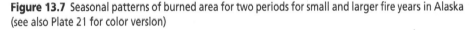

Figure 13.7 Seasonal patterns of burned area for two periods for small and larger fire years in Alaska (see also Plate 21 for color version)

Source: Based on fire records from the Alaska Fire Service, Bureau of Land Management.

Trends in surface temperatures of shallower soil layers in permafrost regions are more variable because inter-annual differences in snow depth and winter-time temperature can cause large variations in near surface temperatures. However, for the period from 1960 to 1999, model studies calculate an overall rise of about 2°C for near surface mineral soil temperatures in black spruce forests with permafrost (Hinzman et al, 2006), which matches the difference in annual average temperature between the north- and south-slope sites shown in Figure 13.1.

Vulnerability of Alaska's black spruce forests

Studies show that the variation in depth of burning of the surface organic layer and site moisture are critical factors in altering post-fire succession in the black spruce forests (see Figures 13.4 and 13.5). Black spruce can grow under a wide range of temperature and moisture conditions, and the presence of even a shallow (4–6 cm) surface organic layer restricts the invasion and survival of deciduous tree species (see Figure 13.4a, 13.4b and 13.5b). Thus, even in a warming climate, it is unlikely that the distribution of black spruce will be reduced unless deep burning of the surface organic layer occurs. Fire severity studies show that in sites with surface organic layers deeper than about 20 cm, the seasonal thawing of the ground layer controls the moisture of the deeper surface organic layers. Because of this, sites with deeper surface organic layers are only vulnerable to deep burning during fires that occur late in the growing season (i.e. after 1 August).

Recent changes to the fire regime in interior Alaska (see Figure 13.6) indicate that black spruce forests have experienced an increase in late season fires (see Figure 13.7). In addition, warming of permafrost since the beginning of the 1960s means that the upper soil layers of sites underlain by permafrost have experienced a deeper thawing and are therefore better drained late in the growing season. This would indicate that, at the same time Alaska's boreal forests have experienced an increase in late season burning, the sites have also experienced lower duff moisture later in the growing season because of warming permafrost. Thus, changes to the fire regime and a warming of permafrost have most likely increased the vulnerability of Alaska's black spruce forests to deep burning fires, and have combined to accelerate the rate of change.

Effects of forest cover change on ecosystem services and society

The ecological changes caused by fire have important societal consequences, which can be described in terms of ecosystem services (the benefits that society derives from ecosystems). Some of these services affect society globally through changes in the climate system and others affect society more locally through changes in local conditions.

Fire-induced changes in tree cover and carbon sequestration in boreal forest can have large effects on the global climate system through changes in energy exchange (Bonan et al, 1992; Foley et al, 1994), carbon emissions to the atmosphere (Kurz and Apps, 1999; Kasischke and Stocks, 2000; McGuire and Chapin, 2006), and other processes such as soot deposition on glaciers and changes in cloudiness or ozone concentrations of the atmosphere (Randerson et al, 2006). The largest of these climate effects are changes in carbon sequestration and energy exchange. The increased areal extent and severity of burning described earlier result in greater CO_2 release to the atmosphere, which acts as a positive feedback to global warming. Because CO_2 has a relatively long lifetime in the atmosphere, this warming effect is distributed globally by atmospheric mixing (McGuire and Chapin, 2006).

Fire also increases albedo (short-wave reflectance), which reduces the amount of solar energy absorbed by the land surface and transferred to the atmosphere. This occurs in spring due to removal of the tree canopy, exposing the more reflective snow-covered ground, and in the summer due to replacement of the dark complex black spruce canopy by the more reflective, less complex canopy of herbs, grasses and deciduous shrubs and trees (Chapin et al, 2000, Chambers and Chapin, 2002, McGuire and Chapin, 2006). Fire thus has a net cooling effect on climate through this change in energy exchange. Most of this cooling occurs locally, due to the short residence time of heat in the atmosphere (Chapin et al, 2000).

As a result of these counterbalancing effects of fire on climate from trace gas emissions (a heating effect) and energy exchange (a cooling effect), the net effect of fire on climate appears to be a modest cooling of climate, with this effect being concentrated near areas that burned (Randerson et al, 2006). This balance between heating and cooling is sensitive to burn severity (the amount of carbon released) and vegetation trajectory (the time required for late successional conifers to return to dominance). If fire severity or the areal extent of wildfire continue to increase, as projected, we expect this to increase both the positive feedbacks to warming (greater carbon emissions) and the negative feedbacks (longer time before return to the low-albedo conifer vegetation), with the net effect on climate feedbacks depending on the magnitude of these two effects. One thing that appears certain, however, is that the negative feedbacks to climate will predominate locally within the boreal forest. This is important because it is one of the few negative feedbacks that have been identified and that will limit the high-latitude amplification of warming caused changes in snow and ice cover.

Changes in fire regime also have important effects on society locally through changes in other ecosystem services. Rural Alaskan residents, the majority of whom are Alaska Natives, depend on subsistence hunting for both a large proportion of their meat supply and maintenance of cultural connections to the land (Magdanz et al, 2002). Changes in fire regime will probably be the major way in which climate warming will change the availability of these subsistence resources (Chapin et al, 2003). For example, caribou, which are among the major subsistence resources for many Athabascan communities, depend on lichens as their primary winter forage. Lichens recover slowly after fire, so caribou tend to avoid burned areas for 80–100 years before using them as winter habitat. Recent and projected increases in area burned are reducing habitat available to caribou and therefore the availability of caribou as a subsistence resource to local communities (Rupp et al, 2006; Nelson et al, in review). Moose, in contrast, are most abundant 15–30 years after fire (Maier et al, 2005), so the recent reduction in fire return interval from 160 to 90 years (see Figure 13.6) should increase moose abundance in interior Alaska. Availability of these and other subsistence resources to local communities depends not only on their abundance but also on accessibility. Wildfires burn remote trapping cabins and topple trees along traplines, making it more difficult and dangerous to hunt and trap (Huntington et al, 2006).

Although fire also affects availability of timber resources, there is currently only a local market for timber, primarily for rough-cut lumber and firewood, and these are harvested mostly where there is good road or over-ice river access.

White spruce, which is the main timber species, burns less frequently than black spruce, so fire has been a relatively modest concern, except where insect outbreaks have killed extensive stands of trees, as in the Kenai Peninsula of south-central Alaska.

Another fire-dependent ecosystem service that is becoming increasingly important and controversial in interior Alaska is the regulation of disturbance spread – specifically fire risk to communities. Early successional post-fire vegetation is less flammable than late successional black spruce, so recent fires act as fuel breaks that reduce the likelihood of future fires (Rupp et al, 2002). Climate warming has two counteracting effects on this fire-vegetation feedback. First, increases in fire extent reduce landscape flammability by increasing the proportion of non-flammable vegetation on the landscape (Rupp et al, 2002; Chapin et al, 2003). Second, these vegetation differences in flammability are least pronounced under hot dry conditions (Kasischke et al, 2002), which reduces the effectiveness of recently burned stands as fuel breaks. The net effect of climate warming thus appears to be an increase in fire risk (Chapin et al, 2003).

Conclusions

While the overall species diversity of boreal biomes is lower than found in most, if not all, temperate, subtropical and tropical regions, these biomes contain numerous species that are adapted to the region's harsh environment. In addition, the low abundance of predators combined with a high level of insect species whose life cycles are suited to the short, intense summers have resulted in the large numbers of a variety of bird species that migrate to this region each summer. This region is also unique in that a significant portion of Native Peoples who live in small villages scattered throughout the North American boreal region still employ traditional subsistence harvesting and hunting practices, and therefore depend on many of the services that the wildlife and ecosystems provide.

Given the recent rates of change to the sub-arctic climate and the boreal forest, and the projections for continuing or accelerated warming throughout the 21st century, there is little doubt that the ecosystems of this region will undergo dramatic changes. Based on dynamic global vegetation models, there is a consensus that there will be a northward shift in the extent of the boreal forest, with the northern boundary extending into areas currently occupied by tundra and the southern boreal forest being replaced by temperate forests or steppe/grasslands (Cramer et al, 2001). However, while such models present a broad overview of the patterns of vegetation cover change, they are problematic in terms of predicting specific changes at regional scales. These models predict changes of plant functional types based on assuming equilibrium states that are only achieved over longer time scales, and may not accurately predict the time it takes for species migration to occur. In addition, most models do not have realistic representations of permafrost dynamics and the impacts of and interactions between disturbance by insects, disease and fire. While modeling studies indicate there will be a continuing increase in the annual burned area across the North American boreal forest (Flannigan et al, 2005), particular attention needs to be paid to future changes in the frequency of large fire years at regional scales, seasonal patterns of burning, and variations in fire severity, including shifts between surface and crown fires and the depth of burning in ecosystems with deep organic layers.

In summary, while most scientists and resource managers accept the fact that dramatic changes are going to take place throughout the boreal region, given the complexity of processes that control ecosystem processes, the need for continuing research and monitoring is imperative. There is little doubt, however, that over the next few decades, there will be a continuing period of discovery as research and observations begin to answer some of the many unanswered questions that we now face.

Acknowledgements

The research in this chapter was supported by NASA through Grants NNG04GD25G and NNX06AF85G and the Bonanza Creek Long-Term Ecological Research program (USFS grant number PNW01-JV11261952-231 and NSF grant number DEB-0080609).

References

Barber, V. A., G. P. Juday and B. P. Finney, 2000: Reduced growth of Alaskan white spruce in the twentieth century from temperature-induced drought stress, *Nature*, **405**, 668–673

Bonan, G. B., D. Pollard and S. L. Thompson, 1992: Effects of boreal forest vegetation on global climate, *Nature*, **359**, 716–718

Chambers, S. D. and F. S. Chapin, III, 2002: Fire effects on surface-atmosphere energy exchange in Alaskan black spruce ecosystems: Implications for feedbacks to regional climate, *Journal of Geophysical Research*, **108**, 8145, doi:8110.1029/2001JD000530

Chapin III, F. S., W. Eugster, J. P. McFadden, A. H. Lynch and D. A. Walker, 2000: Summer differences among arctic ecosystems in regional climate forcing, *Journal of Climate*, **13**, 2002–2010

Chapin III, F. S., T. Hollingsworth, D. F. Murray, L. A. Viereck and M. D. Walker, 2006: Floristic diversity and vegetation distribution in the Alaskan boreal forest, in F. S. Chapin III, M. W. Oswood, K. Van Cleve, L. A. Viereck and D. L. Verbyla (eds) *Alaska's Changing Boreal Forest*, Oxford University Press, New York

Chapin, F. S., III, T. S. Rupp, A. M. Starfield, L. DeWilde, E. S. Zavaleta, N. Fresco and A. D. McGuire, 2003: Planning for resilience: Modeling change in human-fire interactions in the Alaskan boreal forest, *Frontiers in Ecology and the Environment*, **1**, 255–261

Chapin, F. S., III, M. Sturm, M. C. Serreze, J. P. McFadden, J. R. Key, A. H. Lloyd, A. D. McGuire, T. S. Rupp, A. H. Lynch, J. P. Schimel, J. Beringer, W. L. Chapman, H. E. Epstein, E. S. Euskirchen, L. D. Hinzman, G. Jia, C. L. Ping, K. D. Tape, C. D. C. Thompson, D. A. Walker and J. M. Welker, 2005: Role of land-surface changes in Arctic summer warming, *Science*, **310**, 657–660

Cramer, W., A. Bondeau, F. I. Woodward, I. C. Prentice, R. A. Betts, V. Brovkin, P. M. Cox, V. Fisher, J. A. Foley, A. D. Friend, C. J. Kucharik, M. R. Lomas, N. Ramankutty, S. Sitch, B. Smith, A. White and C. Young-Molling, 2001: Global response of terrestrial ecosystem structure and function to CO_2 and climate change: results from six dynamic global vegetation models, *Global Change Biology*, **7**, 357–373

Dissing, D. D. and D. L. Verbyla, 2003: Spatial patterns of lightning strikes in Interior Alaska and their relations to elevation and vegetation, *Canadian Journal of Forest Research*, **33**, 770–785

Flannigan, M. D., K. A. Logan, B. D. Amiro, W. R. Skinner and B. J. Stocks, 2005: Future area burned in Canada, *Climatic Change*, **72**, 1–16

Foley, J. A., J. E. Kutzbach, M. T. Coe and S. Levis, 1994: Feedbacks between climate and boreal forests during the Holocene epoch, *Nature*, **371**, 52–54

Gillett, A. J. Weaver, F. W. Zwiers and M. D. Flannigan, 2004: Detecting the effect of climate change on Canadian forest fires, *Geophysical Research Letters*, **31**, L18211, doi:10.1029/2004GL020876

Huntington, H. P., S. F. Trainor, D. C. Natcher, O. Huntington, L. DeWilde and F. S. Chapin, III, 2006: The significance of context in community-based research: Understanding discussions about wildfire in Huslia, Alaska, *Ecology and Society*, **11** (available at www.ecologyandsociety.org/vol11/iss11/art40/)

Johnson, E. A., 1992: *Fire and Vegetation Dynamics. Studies from the North American Boreal Forest*, Cambridge University Press, Cambridge

Johnstone, J. F. and F. S. Chapin, 2006: Effects of soil burn severity on post-fire tree recruitment in boreal forests, *Ecosystems*, **9**, 14–31

Johnstone, J. F. and E. S. Kasischke, 2005: Stand-level effects of burn severity on post-fire regeneration in a recently-burned black spruce forest, *Canadian Journal of Forest Research*, **35**, 2151–2163

Hinzman, L. D., L. A. Viereck, P. C. Adams, V. E. Romanovsky and K. Yoshikawa, 2006: Climate and permafrost dynamics of the Alaskan boreal forest, in F. S. Chapin III, M. W. Oswood, K. Van Cleve, L. A. Viereck and D. L. Verbyla (eds) *Alaska's Changing Boreal Forest*, Oxford University Press, New York

Kasischke, E. S., and J. F. Johnstone, 2005: Variation in post-fire organic layer thickness in a black spruce forest complex in Interior Alaska and its effects on soil temperature and moisture, *Canadian Journal of Forest Research*, **35**, 2164–2177

Kasischke, E. S. and B. J. Stocks (eds), 2000: *Fire, Climate Change, and Carbon Cycling in the Boreal Forest*, Springer-Verlag, New York

Kasischke, E. S. and M. R. Turetsky, 2006: Recent changes in the fire regime across the North American boreal region--spatial and temporal patterns of burning across Canada and Alaska, *Geophysical Research Letters*, **33**, L09703, doi:10.1029/2006GL025677

Kasischke, E. S., L. L. Bourgeau-Chavez and J. F. Johnstone, 2007: Assessing spatial and temporal variations in surface soil moisture in fire-disturbed black spruce forests using spaceborne synthetic aperture radar imagery - implications for post-fire tree recruitment, *Remote Sensing of Environment*, 108, 42–58, doi:10.1016/j.rse.2006.10.020

Kasischke, E. S., D. Williams and D. Barry, 2002: Analysis of the patterns of large fires in the boreal forest region of Alaska, *International Journal of Wildland Fire*, **11**, 131–144

Kurz, W. A. and M. J. Apps, 1999 : A 70-year retrospective analysis of carbon fluxes in the Canadian forest sector, *Ecological Applications*, **9**, 526–547

Lloyd, A. H., J. A. Lynch, M. E. Edwards, V. Barber, B. P. Finney and N. H. Bigelow, 2006: Holocene development of the Alaskan boreal forest, in F. S. Chapin III, M. W. Oswood, K. Van Cleve, L. A. Viereck and D. L. Verbyla (eds) *Alaska's Changing Boreal Forest*, Oxford University Press, New York

Magdanz, J. S., C. J. Utermohle and R. J. Wolfe, 2002: *The Production and Distribution of Wild Food in Wales and Deering, Alaska*, Technical Paper 259, Alaska Department of Fish and Game, Division of Subsistence, Kotzebue

Maier, J. A. K., J. Ver Hoef, A. D. McGuire, R. T. Bowyer, L. Saperstein and H. A. Maier, 2005: Distribution and density of moose in relation to landscape characteristics: Effects of scale, *Canadian Journal of Forest Research*, **35**, 2233–2243

McGuire, A. D. and F. S. Chapin, III, 2006: Climate feedbacks in the Alaskan boreal forest, in F. S. Chapin III, M. W. Oswood, K. Van Cleve, L. A. Viereck and D. L. Verbyla (eds) *Alaska's Changing Boreal Forest*, Oxford University Press, New York

Nelson, J. L., E. Zavaleta and F. S. Chapin, III, In review: Boreal fire effects on subsistence resources in Alaska and adjacent Canada, *Ecosystems*

O'Neill, K. P., D. D. Richter and E. S. Kasischke, 2006: Succession-driven changes in soil respiration following fire in black spruce stands of Interior Alaska, *Biogeochemistry*, **80**, 1–20

Osterkamp, T. E., 2005: The recent warming of permafrost in Alaska, *Global and Planetary Change*, **49**, 187–202

Randerson, J. T., H. Liu, M. Flanner, S. D. Chambers, Y. Jin, P. G. Hess, G. Pfister, M. C. Mack, K. K. Treseder, L. Welp, F. S. Chapin, III, J. W. Harden, M. L. Goulden, E. Lyons, J. C. Neff, E. A. G. Schuur and C. Zender, 2006: The impact of boreal forest fire on climate warming, *Science*, **314**, 1130–1132

Rupp, T. S., M. Olson, J. Henkelman, L. Adams, B. Dale, K. Joly, W. Collins and A. M. Starfield, 2006: Simulating the influence of a changing fire regime on caribou winter foraging habitat, *Ecological Applications*, **16**, 1730–1743

Rupp, T. S., A. M. Starfield, F. S. Chapin, III and P. Duffy, 2002: Modeling the impact of black spruce on the fire regime of Alaskan boreal forest, *Climatic Change*, **55**, 213–233

Slaughter, C. W. and L. A. Viereck, 1986: Climatic characteristics of the taiga in interior Alaska, in K. Van Cleve, F. S. Chapin, III, P. W. Flanagan, L. A. Viereck and C. T. Dyrness (eds) *Forest Ecosystems in the Alaskan Taiga*, Springer-Verlag, New York

Sukhinin, A. I., N. H. F. French, E. S. Kasischke, J. H. Hewson, A. J. Soja, I. A. Csiszar, E. Hyer, T. Loboda, S. G. Conard, V. I. Romasko, E. A. Pavlichenko, S. I. Miskiv and O. A. Slinkin, 2004: AVHRR-based mapping of fires in eastern Russia: New products for fire management and carbon cycle studies, *Remote Sensing of Environment*, **93**, 546–564

Van Cleve, K., L. A. Viereck and C. T. Dyrness, 1996: State factor control of soils and forest succession along the Tanana River in Interior Alaska, U.S.A., *Arctic and Alpine Research*, **28**, 388–400

Viereck, L. A., C. T. Dyrness, K. Van Cleve and M. J. Foote, 1983: Vegetation, soils, and forest productivity in selected forest types in Interior Alaska, *Canadian Journal of Forest Research*, **13**, 703–720

Werner, R. A., K. F. Raffa and B. L. Ilman, 2006: Dynamics of phytophagous insects and their pathogens in Alaskan boreal forests, in F. S. Chapin III, M. W. Oswood, K. Van Cleve, L. A. Viereck and D. L. Verbyla (eds) *Alaska's Changing Boreal Forest*, Oxford University Press, New York

Yoshikawa, K., W. R. Bolton, V. Romanovsky, M. Fukuda and L. D. Hinzman, 2002: Impacts of wildfire on the permafrost in the boreal forests of Interior Alaska, *Journal of Geophysical Research*, **107**, 8148, doi:10.1029/2001JD000438, 2002 [printed 108 (D1), 2003]

Zasada, J., R. A. Norum, R. M. Van Veldhuizen and C. E. Teutsch, 1983: Artificial regeneration of trees and tall shrubs in experimentally burned upland black spruce/ feather moss stands in Alaska, *Canadian Journal of Forest Research*, **13**, 903–913

14

Polar Bears in a Warming Arctic

Andrew E. Derocher

Surviving in the frigid Arctic through months of winter darkness and roaming vast areas over the frozen oceans, few species are as charismatic and photogenic as the polar bear (*Ursus maritimus*) (see Figure 14.1). Sitting at the top of the Arctic marine food web, polar bears provide insight on the status, health and functioning of marine ecosystems over a variety of spatial and temporal scales. Having evolved from a grizzly/brown bear (*U. arctos*) ancestor in a rapid burst of evolution (Waits et al, 1999), polar bears evolved a life history pattern dependent on the sea ice. With this specialization, numerous morphological and physiological adaptations followed.

Polar bears differ vastly from their land-bound cousins and have abandoned over-winter denning except for pregnant females (Watts and Hansen, 1987). Being active in the icy winter means the bears must contend with air that would cool their body core and have thus evolved a narrower skull that helps to warm cold air before it reaches the lungs. The elongated skull also allows for heightened olfactory sensitivity important for finding prey. The large body size of polar bears is a further adaptation to the cold: larger animals have less surface area relative to their volume than smaller animals and this means they are better able to keep body heat from escaping. Add in a fur coat and a thick layer of fat and you have an animal perfected to deal with cold but unsuited to the heat. The shorter and more curved claws are well adapted to a predatory way of life and assist with the seizing of slippery prey eager to slide back into its watery domain. To deal with the variable conditions of the Arctic and the periodic scarcity of prey, all polar bears have a facultative ability to enter a fasting mode to conserve energy, a state that their ancestors only entered during denning (Ramsay et al, 1991).

Polar bears evolved to exploit a vacant niche on the sea ice of the Arctic as an obligate predator of seals. The hallmark white fur of polar bears serves as camouflage given that the prey of polar bears – ringed seals (*Phoca hispida*) and bearded seals (*Erignathus barbatus*) – are wary and have evolved means of avoiding the bears (DeMaster and Stirling, 1981). Polar bears and their prey have

Figure 14.1 Four-month-old cubs snuggle up to their mother during research activities on the ecology of polar bears in the Beaufort Sea, Canada

Source: Photograph by A. E. Derocher.

co-evolved with the bears exploiting a variety of means to capture their prey and the seals evolving to avoid capture (Kingsley and Stirling, 1991). The sea ice is also crucial habitat for the seals. Both ringed and bearded seals rely on sea ice to give birth to and rear their young. Additional prey of polar bears includes harp seals (*Phoca groenlandica*), harbor seals (*Phoca vitulina*), walrus (*Odobenus rosmarus*), white whales (*Delphinapterus leucas*) and narwhal (*Monodon monoceros*). Polar bears are opportunistic and will sometimes feed on seaweed, berries, birds and other mammals although the energetic return is usually minimal (Smith and Sjare, 1990; Derocher et al, 1993; Derocher et al, 2002).

Polar bear survival

With a circumpolar distribution, the sea ice over the continental shelves is the primary habitat for polar bears and is used as the platform for traveling, hunting, mating and, in some areas, for denning (see Figure 14.2, Plate 22). Annual ice that forms during autumn and winter is the preferred habitat of the bears because the thicker multiyear ice found at higher latitudes has low primary productivity, and thus few seals. The key to the success of polar bears lies in exploiting the fat of other marine mammals and turning it into a portable food store for periods when food is unavailable (see Figure 14.3). When a seal is killed, the bears strip the fat from the carcass and then deposit it with little modification directly onto their own stores (Stirling and McEwan, 1975, Iverson et al, 2006). The bears are able to consume up to 20 per cent of their body mass in a single meal and for a

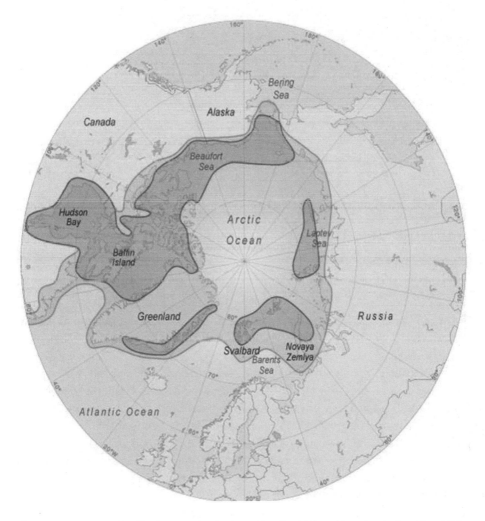

Figure 14.2 Circumpolar distribution of polar bears showing high and low density (see Plate 22 for color version)

Source: A. E. Derocher and Norwegian Polar Institute.

Figure 14.3 Partially consumed adult ringed seal killed by an adult male polar bear in the Beaufort Sea, Canada

Source: Photograph by A. E. Derocher.

500 kg (1100 lb) adult male this is a huge amount of energy. A bellyful of seal fat converted to a bear's own fat stores will help in the summer when seals are scarce or unavailable.

While superbly adapted to the highly variable conditions in the Arctic, polar bears live close to the limit of what is biologically possible. Pregnant females can successfully fast for over eight months while over-wintering in dens and rearing cubs, which weigh only 600 grams (1.5 lbs) at birth (Ramsay and Stirling, 1988). The tiny cubs are kept warm in snow dens and are fed rich milk containing up to 50 per cent fat. Success at rearing offspring, however, is tied to how much fat a mother bear is able to store and this, in turn, is linked to the dynamics of their sea ice habitat. If the sea ice melts earlier than normal, the bears lose the opportunity to add to their fat stores and are also forced to begin their fasting earlier. Delayed sea ice formation prolongs the fast and further depletes fat stores. If the fasting period is too long, mothers with cubs stop nursing and with little fat of their own, cubs can soon weaken and succumb to the harsh environment.

In addition, change in the sea ice can affect a bear's ability to hunt. Seal populations are dependent on specific ice conditions and if they are unavailable, the seals leave for other areas or fail to reproduce. Take away or alter the sea ice too much and the bears are pushed beyond their limits and populations decline through reduced recruitment.

Status of polar bear populations

Polar bears live in 19 relatively discrete subpopulations around the circumpolar north and the effects of climate warming are becoming evident throughout their range (IUCN/SSC Polar Bear Specialist Group, 2006) (see Figure 14.4). Despite the sense that many people think of polar bears as a species living in the far reaches of the Arctic, the southernmost bears live at the same latitude as London, England. Other bears live near the North Pole, but the densities at high latitudes are thought to be very low and virtually nothing is known about this area.

Research has shown that the effects of climate change are apparent in polar bear subpopulations in a myriad of manners. Most often, the first symptom is a decline in the condition of the bears when they have difficulty obtaining sufficient prey. While the Arctic is a harsh and variable environment, the whole life history strategy of polar bears is tied to trading off reproduction to ensure survival. Females have the potential to reproduce many times over a 25-year lifespan. Thus, if hunting conditions are poor and body condition declines, the reproductive output of females drops. Most notable are smaller litter sizes, smaller cubs and cubs with lower survival rates. If sea ice conditions do not improve, the low recruitment rates to a subpopulation result in a slow decline. If the conditions are severe enough, the survival rates of sub-adults and adults are lower and a precipitous population decline can follow. When coupled with the slow maturation of the bears and the prolonged mother–offspring period (normally 2.5 years), polar bear populations are naturally slow to change in numbers, but once depressed in abundance, they are very slow to recover if the conditions allow.

To date, the effects of climate change are most evident in three subpopulations. The body mass of bears has declined in the Southern Beaufort Sea, Western Hudson Bay and Southern Hudson Bay subpopulations (Derocher and Stirling, 1995; Stirling et al, 1999; Regehr et al, 2006; Obbard et al, 2006) (see Figure 14.4). The first two subpopulations have declined by 17 per cent over 20 years and 22 per cent over the last decade, respectively (IUCN/SSC Polar Bear Specialist Group, 2006; Regehr et al, 2007). Changes in sea ice conditions are clearly implicated. While these rates of decline may seem low, for long-lived mammals with low reproductive potential, the rates are a serious concern for the persistence of the populations. Changes in sea ice conditions are clearly implicated but making these linkages is very difficult. Most other subpopulations lack sufficient monitoring

Figure 14.4 Subpopulation boundaries for polar bears

Note: SB=Southern Beaufort Sea, NB=Northern Beaufort Sea, VM=Viscount Melville, NW=Norwegian Bay, LS=Lancaster Sound, GB=Gulf of Boothia, MC=M'Clintock Channel, FB=Foxe Basin, WH=Western Hudson Bay, SH=Southern Hudson Bay, KB=Kane Basin, BB=Baffin Bay and DS=Davis Strait. QE=Queen Elizabeth but is now considered part of the Arctic Basin subpopulation.
Source: IUCN/SSC Polar Bear Specialist Group, 2006.

data to determine their trends, but symptoms of climate change are chronic and increasing in regularity. So far, the changes that have been observed can be typified as gradual declines punctuated by unusual events. Of concern is the possibility of climate warming creating a year or two of very poor conditions that could result in rapid population declines. The strategy of polar bears to store body fat to buffer poor years and periods without food can only be pushed so far.

Recent observations of polar bears drowning can be related to the sudden changes in sea ice patterns (Monnett and Gleason, 2006). As the sea ice has retreated from the Alaskan coast, polar bears are unable to maintain contact with the ice and with more open water; larger waves that form due to the increased fetch on the water make it difficult for the bears to regain contact with their primary habitat or, alternatively, land. The effects of this loss are unknown, but it appears to be a recent development. Polar bears are excellent swimmers, but, unlike seals and whales, they rely on walking for most of their movements and cannot remain permanently in water.

Further, as the sea ice cracks and drifts more on wind and current, the bears are effectively on a treadmill that humans are steadily increasing in speed (Mauritzen et al, 2003). The more energy that is used for locomotion, the less energy there is for growth and reproduction. Signs are showing up in several populations that polar bears are shrinking, not only in mass, but body length as well (Atkinson et al, 1996; Derocher, 2005).

Additional indicators of change come from recent observations of intraspecific killing and cannibalism (see Figure 14.5). In the Southern Beaufort Sea subpopulation, four adult females were killed and partially consumed by other bears, presumably by food stressed adult males (Amstrup et al, 2006; Stirling et al, in review). Cannibalism has been observed to occur in polar bears before, but the clear suggestion of an increase in occurrence is cause for concern. During the same period as the cannibalism observations, polar bears were attempting to prey on seals by digging through ice rather than through snow due to changes in the habitat (Stirling et al, in review).

Changes in prey consumed by polar bears are already underway in Hudson Bay, where the bears are consuming more harbor seals that are normally associated with temperate waters (Iverson et al, 2006). In other areas, the number of problem bears has increased as food stressed bears seek alternate food sources (Stirling and Parkinson, 2006). New data show that polar bears off the Alaska coast that once commonly denned on the sea ice are abandoning the drifting ice and are shifting to denning on land (A. Fischbach, personal communication). Even on land, polar bears may not be safe inside their dens. Warm weather, particularly rain in spring, can lead to den collapse and result in the death of both mother and cubs (Clarkson and Irish, 1991).

Other changes are likely to be more subtle, but they are appearing. Changes in the home range sizes and movement rates of polar bears have been documented (Parks et al, 2006). Other changes are possible and could include shifts in subpopulation boundaries and new diseases. These sorts of changes are difficult to monitor given the dispersed nature of polar bears. There is no single definitive study that can link climate change and polar bears; scientists have to rely on numerous smaller research studies and work to 'connect the dots'. The collective experience of polar bear researchers and northerners who live on the land are

Figure 14.5 Partially consumed adult female polar bear killed by another polar bear, spring 2006, Beaufort Sea, Canada

Source: Photography by A. E. Derocher.

developing a clear picture of the situation and it does not look good for the Arctic ice bear.

Changes in polar bear habitat

Two of the great challenges facing polar bear conservation in the face of climate warming are the huge areas involved and the fact that their habitat is disappearing. The home range size of polar bears vary from fjord-living bears, which may use an area of only 5000 km², to pelagic bears, which use areas of over 300,000 km² (Garner et al, 1991; Mauritzen et al, 2001).

In terrestrial ecosystems, conservation biologists can look to habitat restoration or habitat protection measures to improve the conservation status for a species. In stark contrast, there are no such methods available for the conservation of polar bears. Supplemental feeding is one option open to sustaining food stressed polar bears, but sourcing the amounts of food that would be required would be a daunting task and harvesting seal populations that are also being affected by climate warming would seem unwise and unsustainable.

Relocating polar bears to higher latitudes may seem logical but there are few indications that these ecosystems have spare capacity to sustain more animals. Even as the sea ice begins to melt away at high latitudes, the solar radiation in these areas will not change and the short growing season will limit the primary productivity that drives the system. Some have suggested that climate change could improve habitat for polar bears in areas that are currently covered by thick multi-year ice. The problem is that these areas are small relative to the distribution of the bears, and while they may provide new habitat for a while, continued climate warming will eventually erode these areas as well.

The Arctic Ocean at the top of the planet is currently covered by permanent polar pack ice and is another area that could act as a refuge for the bears, but, unfortunately, those waters are deep, cold and biologically unproductive. Further, bearded seals would be unlikely to survive there because they are benthic feeders (feed on the ocean bottom) and cannot dive to the ocean floor in the deep waters of the Arctic Ocean. Predictions are now clear that the Arctic Ocean will become ice-free in summer and at a much more accelerated rate than earlier thought (Comiso, 2002; Stroeve et al, 2007). Populations from the Beaufort Sea westward to Svalbard, Norway all rely on the permanent polar pack ice as a summer refuge area. If the permanent polar pack ice melts away during summer, any animals in this area would be stranded far from land with possibly dire consequences.

More radical conservation measures, such as captive rearing, are useful for species that can be warehoused until their numbers are sufficient to be released in secure habitats. However, if the sea ice cannot support polar bears, it is unclear what conservation value these bears could provide.

Effects of future warming on polar bear populations and other Arctic species

If climate warming continues unchecked, the persistence of many polar bear populations is doubtful. Recently, the members of the IUCN/SSC Polar Bear Specialist Group, representing the scientific and management expertise of the five nations with polar bear populations (Russia, Norway, Denmark/Greenland, Canada and the US), unanimously raised the level of conservation concern for the species. Polar bears are now listed as 'Vulnerable', which means they are considered to be facing a high risk of extinction in the wild. The timeframe of concern varies for each population, but a global decline exceeding 30 per cent is possible within the next 35 to 50 years; if this were to occur, the world could lose over 8000 polar bears within three generations of bears. Faced with this prospect, future challenges for conserving polar bears and their Arctic habitat will be greater than at any time in the past because of the rapid rate at which environmental change is occurring.

One area that will likely enter conservation plans in coming years is the reduction of polar bear harvest by local people. While to some this may seem like a simple and logical solution, this response will victimize northern people who are already being severely affected by climate change. Inuit have lived with and hunted polar bears for thousands of years. Loss of harvest rights will have negative social, cultural and economic consequences. It is important to note that each subpopulation will show the signs of climate warming at different times and a blanket policy to close harvest is unnecessary as long as a sustainable harvest is available.

Some have naïvely suggested that polar bears will adopt a more terrestrial lifestyle and adapt back to the ways of their ancestral species. Unfortunately, for a species like the polar bear, the changes may be too fast. Evolution in large mammals with long generation times occurs over tens or hundreds of thousands of years, not decades or centuries. Further, the terrestrial niche for an Arctic bear is already occupied and there are indications that barren-ground grizzlies are already advancing northward. History has shown that large and highly specialized species generally do not fair well with rapid changes in their environment.

It is more than just polar bears that are threatened: all ice-dependent species are at risk. In particular, Arctic marine mammals that rely on sea ice are at risk of being negatively affected. Both Arctic seals and whales rely on the presence of sea ice. As the sea ice disappears, there will be a shift towards species from the north Atlantic and north Pacific oceans. If the ice retreats too far, ringed and bearded seals will be replaced by harbor and harp seals and the narwhal and white whales will slip away as killer whales (*Orcinus orca*) take over the top predator role. Northern baleen whales such as the abundant minke whale (*Balaenoptera acutorostrata*) would likely expand into the previously ice-covered waters. A new ecosystem will emerge but it will be one without polar bears.

Conclusions

The future of the polar bear remains uncertain. Unless the rapid changes to the sea ice are stopped, continued erosion of their habitat will continue to affect the species. Should these changes go unchecked, the distribution of the bears will shrink northwards and southern populations will be extirpated. As the sea ice disappears, so will the polar bears. Without climate stabilization, climate warming will eventually affect the last remaining populations at the highest latitudes and the most iconic of the Arctic species will blink out. With their passing, the biological diversity of the world would be impoverished and the Arctic would diminish in its mystery and magnificence.

References

Amstrup, S. C., I. Stirling, T. S. Smith, C. Perham and G. W. Thiemann, 2006: Recent observations of intraspecific predation and cannibalism among polar bears in the southern Beaufort Sea, *Polar Biology*, **29**, 997–1002

Atkinson, S. N., I. Stirling and M. A. Ramsay, 1996: Growth in early life and relative body size among adult polar bears (*Ursus maritimus*), *Journal of Zoology, London*, **239**, 225–234

Clarkson, P. L. and D. Irish, 1991: Den collapse kills female polar bear and two newborn cubs, *Arctic*, **44**, 83–84

Comiso, J.C., 2002: A rapidly declining perennial sea ice cover in the Arctic, *Geophysical Research Letters*, **29**, 1956 doi 10.1029/2002GL015650

DeMaster, D. P. and I. Stirling, 1981: Ursus maritimus, *Mammalian Species*, **145**, 1–7

Derocher, A. E., 2005: Population ecology of polar bears at Svalbard, Norway, *Population Ecology*, **47**, 267–275

Derocher, A. E. and I. Stirling, 1995: Temporal variation in reproduction and body mass of polar bears in western Hudson Bay, *Canadian Journal of Zoology*, **73**, 1657–1665

Derocher, A. E., D. Andriashek and I. Stirling, 1993: Terrestrial foraging by polar bears during the ice-free period in western Hudson Bay, *Arctic*, **46**, 251–254

Derocher, A. E., Ø. Wiig and M. Andersen, 2002: Diet composition of polar bears in Svalbard and the western Barents Sea, *Polar Biology*, **25**, 448–452

Garner, G. W., S. T. Knick and D. C. Douglas, 1991: Seasonal movements of adult female polar bears in the Bering and Chukchi Seas, *International Conference on Bear Biology and Management*, **8**, 219–226

IUCN/SSC Polar Bear Specialist Group, 2006: *Polar bears: Proceedings of the 14th Working Meeting of the IUCN Polar Bear Specialist Group*, J. Aars, N. J. Lunn and A. E. Derocher (eds), IUCN, Gland, Switzerland and Cambridge

Iverson, S. J., I. Stirling and S. L. C. Lang, 2006: Spatial and temporal variation in the diets of polar bears across the Canadian Arctic: Indicators of changes in prey populations and environment, in I. L. Boyd, S. Wanless and C. J. Camphuysen (eds) *Top Predators in Marine Ecosystems*, Cambridge University Press, Cambridge

Kingsley, M. C. S. and I. Stirling, 1991: Haul-out behaviour of ringed and bearded seals in relation to defence against surface predators, *Canadian Journal of Zoology*, **69**, 1857–1861

Mauritzen, M., A. E. Derocher and Ø. Wiig, 2001: Space-use strategies of female polar bears in a dynamic sea ice habitat, *Canadian Journal of Zoology*, **79**, 1704–1713

Mauritzen, M., A. E. Derocher, O. Pavlova and Ø. Wiig, 2003: Female polar bears, *Ursus maritimus*, on the Barents Sea drift ice: Walking the treadmill, *Animal Behaviour*, **66**, 107–113

Monnett, C. and J. S. Gleason, 2006: Observations of mortality associated with extended open-water swimming by polar bears in the Alaskan Beaufort Sea, *Polar Biology*, **29**, 681–687

Obbard, M. E., M. R. L. Cattet, T. Moody, L. Walton, D. Potter, J. Inglis and C. Chenier, 2006: Temporal trends in the body condition of Southern Hudson Bay polar bears, *Climate Change Research Information Note*, **3**, 1–8

Parks, E. K., A. E. Derocher and N. J. Lunn, 2006: Seasonal and annual movement patterns of polar bears on the sea ice of Hudson Bay, *Canadian Journal of Zoology*, **84**, 1281–1294

Ramsay, M. A., and I. Stirling, 1988: Reproductive biology and ecology of female polar bears (*Ursus maritimus*), *Journal of Zoology (London)*, **214**, 601–634

Ramsay, M. A., R. A. Nelson and I. Stirling, 1991: Seasonal changes in the ratio of serum urea to serum creatinine in feeding and fasting polar bears, *Canadian Journal of Zoology*, **69**, 298–302

Regehr, E. V., S. C. Amstrup and I. Stirling, 2006: Polar bear population status in the southern Beaufort Sea, *U.S. Geological Survey Open-File Report 2006-1337*, US Department of the Interior, US Geological Survey, Reston, VA

Regehr, E. V., N. J. Lunn, S. C. Amstrup, and I. Stirling, 2007: Survival and population size of polar bears in western Hudson Bay in relation to earlier sea ice break-up, *Journal of Wildlife Management*, in press

Smith, T.G. and B. Sjare, 1990: Predation of belugas and narwhals by polar bears in nearshore areas of the Canadian High Arctic, *Arctic*, **43**, 99–102

Stirling, I. and E. H. McEwan, 1975: The calorific value of whole ringed seals (*Phoca hispida*) in relation to polar bear (*Ursus maritimus*) ecology and hunting behaviour, *Canadian Journal of Zoology*, **53**, 1021–1027

Stirling, I. and C. L. Parkinson, 2006: Possible effects of climate warming on selected populations of polar bears (*Ursus maritimus*) in the Canadian Arctic, *Arctic*, **59**, 261–275

Stirling, I., N. J. Lunn and J. Iacozza, 1999: Long-term trends in the population ecology of polar bears in western Hudson Bay in relation to climate change, *Arctic*, **52**, 294–306

Stirling, I., E. Richardson, G. W. Thiemann and A. E. Derocher, in review: Unusual observations of attempted polar bear predation on ringed seals in the southern Beaufort Sea, *Arctic*

Stroeve, J., M. M. Holland, W. Meier, T. Scambos and M. Serreze, 2007: Arctic sea ice decline: faster than forecast, *Geophysical Research Letters*, **34**, L09501, doi: 10.1029/2007GL029703

Waits, L. P., J. Sullivan, S. J. O'Brien and R. H. Ward, 1999: Rapid radiation events in the Family Ursidae indicated by likelihood phylogenetic estimation from multiple fragments of mtDNA, *Molecular Phylogenetics and Evolution*, **13**, 82–92

Watts, P. D. and S. E. Hansen, 1987: Cyclic starvation as a reproductive strategy in the polar bear, *Symposia of the Zoological Society of London*, **57**, 305–318

Part 5

The Potential for Accelerating Action to Limit Climate Change

Introduction to Part 5

William A. Nitze

With the indications that climate change is accelerating and its impacts are intensifying, the need for aggressive and effective action is becoming increasingly clear. The longer that we wait to get started on the transition to a new energy system for the US and the world, the larger and more difficult the steps that we have to take will become. In Chapter 15 of this book, Sir Crispin Tickell, UK's former ambassador to the United Nations and former chairman of the Board of Directors of the Climate Institute, provides an overview of actions occurring on the international stage aimed at putting the community of nations on the path to meeting the objective of the 1992 Framework Convention on Climate Change, namely to 'prevent dangerous anthropogenic interference with the climate system'.

The US, which has been lagging in addressing the climate change issue, is also starting to take action. There are increasing signs that the public recognizes the need for action and, indeed, action is really beginning. In introducing the panel of politicians that addressed the Symposium, Claudine Schneider, Rhode Island's representative in the US House of Representatives from 1981–1990 and a member of the Board of Directors of the Climate Institute described her success in recruiting major corporations to participate in the EPA's Corporate Leaders program. She has also been working with four western states (California, Nevada, Arizona and New Mexico) to promote use of the bountiful solar radiation available in the southwestern US, which could provide enough electricity to meet the needs of the entire US.

Senator Bingaman of New Mexico, whose resolution to initiate action had recently won majority approval from the Senate, indicated that members of Congress have come to realize that climate change is one of the most important issues they face – and one that failing to act on will be unacceptable. The main challenges being faced are how to get started, and how to most effectively put a price on carbon.

Representative Sherwood Boehlert of New York, reflecting on his completion of 24 years in office, also suggested that minds were changing and not to despair – that the number of members committed to acting was rising as the realities of science were punching through the ideological objections. He argued for scientists to engage more with elected officials, being clear, accurate, responsible and upfront with their discussion of uncertainties. In urging people not to give up hope of addressing the problem, he quoted from an observation made by former New Jersey Governor Kean that helped lead to facing up to, rather than continuing to investigate, the risk of a critical environmental problem: 'If all we did were to continue to study acid rain, we would end up with the best-documented environmental disaster in history'. Soon after this statement, action was taken, and control of sulfur dioxide emissions proved significantly less costly than was feared. As William Calvin responded in the questions: 'The doctor who waits for certainty of the diagnosis will end up with a dead patient'.

So, what can be done? Representative Boehlert indicated that many did not have a sense of what was possible and felt that there were no good choices, as actor Woody Allen had once opined: 'We have arrived at a crossroads; one road leads to hopelessness and despair, the other to total extinction'.

As captured in the following chapters, those speaking at the Climate Institute's Summit had a much more optimistic view of what could be done – arguing that the crossroads does offer a more positive road forward. Chapter 16, authored by Climate Institute president John Topping Jr and Harvard student Erin Frey, provides an overview of this better choice, pointing to the positive signs indicating that change is possible and, based on actions being taken by leading corporations, concluding that we can indeed change our energy system, rapidly and cost effectively. They describe, for example, the important steps being taken by General Electric to produce products that use energy much more efficiently and by Wal-Mart to reduce their energy use by making use of renewable energy technologies. They also report on presentations at the Climate Summit by a number of industry leaders, including: William Gerwig, Western Hemisphere Director of Health, Safety, Security and Environment for BP America, describes the investments being made in clean energy by BP and other oil companies; Daniel Gross, who heads environmental policy and alternative energy investing for Goldman-Sachs, describes their commitment to promote energy efficiency and invest very substantially in renewable energy technologies; and Josephine Cooper, Toyota's group vice-president in North America for government policy, describes the efforts to date, including the hybrid synergy drive used in the Toyota Prius, and their vision for the future that encompasses heading for fuel cell vehicles.

The authors of the rest of the chapters in Part 5 describe an even wider range of possibilities and ways for moving forward; many are already well along. In

Chapter 17, Ólafur Ragnar Grímsson, the President of Iceland, describes his country's progress in using geothermal and other energy to replace virtually all of their energy from fossil fuels. International organizations, such as the World Bank, the United Nations Environment Programme, the United Nations Department of Economic and Social Affairs, the Organization of American States, and others are all assisting countries to get started in moving toward more efficient use of energy and production of energy from sources of renewable fuels. In Chapter 18, Nasir Khattak describes the goals and progress of the Global Sustainable Energy Island Initiative (GSEII), which is a partnership among seven international organizations, including the Alliance of Small Island States (AOSIS), the UN Industrial Development Organization (UNIDO) and the Climate Institute, aimed at helping individual island states promote the sustainable generation and use of energy. Activities are already underway with St Lucia, Grenada, Dominica and St Kitts and Nevis in the Caribbean, and with the Republic of the Marshall Islands in the Pacific. Since the Summit, activities are being expanded under an International Leadership Alliance for Climate Stabilization that is expanding to include leading officials from the Dominican Republic, Mexico and other nations.

Even though the use of energy is much greater in the US economy, significant progress is possible – if we just commit to it. In Chapter 19, Chris Flavin, president of the Worldwatch Institute, describes the potential for stimulating a clean energy revolution in the US as outlined in the insightful plan presented in 'American Energy – The Renewable Path to Energy Security'. In Chapter 20, Tom Casten, president of Recycled Energy Development, describes the tremendous potential for energy to be derived by co-generation, basically using the presently wasted heat from current industrial plants and electric power plants. Quite clearly, the problem is not the potential to generate energy without emitting any, or as much, greenhouse gases – the problem is one of attitude.

In Chapter 21, Denis Hayes, president of the Bullitt Foundation and co-founder of Earth Day, provides the framework for the presentation of religious perspectives and initiatives by seven leaders in the movement that is helping people understand that climate change needs to be recognized, most fundamentally, as a moral issue. The seven co-authors he brings together describe the basis for action that emerges out of Jewish, Muslim, Mormon, Catholic and Protestant traditions and the types of interfaith activities that are underway. In Chapter 22, Dan Worth, who is executive director of the National Association of Environmental Law Societies, describes his increasingly successful efforts to have the young people in colleges and universities take the initiative to save the world that they will be growing up in.

So, what can all of us do? In addition to using less energy generally, improving the efficiency of our energy use, and recycling the products we do use, we can each take actions that will help promote the more rapid development of green energy around the world. In Chapter 23, Alexia Kelly of The Climate Trust, which provided offsets to emissions associated with the Washington Summit on Climate Stabilization, describes the role of greenhouse gas offsets in helping to make this happen – buying credits to offset the fossil fuel energy we cannot avoid using and, through The Climate Trust, partnering with others to, for example, promote measures to reduce energy use or encourage movement to renewables. For years the Climate Institute has partnered with another climate offset group, Oxford, UK-based Climate Care, that has provided tens of thousands of energy efficient light bulbs for those in island nations seeking to reduce greenhouse emissions.

Together, we can all make a difference. There are exciting pathways out there that can lead us to a much less damaging energy system, and one that will help us to avoid climate catastrophes. The world can be a much better place – there are many already headed in that direction, getting cleaner energy cost effectively. Certainly, investments will be needed – but they will produce jobs, a cleaner environment and long-term savings. We simply must get started.

15

International Action to Buffer Against the Rapid Onset of Climate Change

Sir Crispin Tickell

Growing awareness of the possible consequences of rapid climate change has made people aware of the limited, ephemeral and precarious character of our present environment. We are tiny parts of a system of life whose complexity surpasses, and will always surpass, human understanding. The Earth system, however, is highly vulnerable to change; of the many environmental problems facing society, climate change is perhaps the greatest problem of all.

It is mainly because of the shortness of our lives and the narrowness of our perspective on the past that we are mostly unaware of the changes underway and their importance; until very recently, we had scarcely noticed the pressures on the environment. Yet, over the last 40,000 years, the human impact on the Earth has slowly, and then rapidly, increased. A periodic visitor from outer space would find more change in the last 200 years than in the preceding 2000, and more change in the last 20 years than in the preceding 200.

Increasing international awareness

Recent developments in climate science have stirred the international community of nations. Every week brings something new in the scientific literature, and every few months the results from new meetings point more strongly to the significance of changes being imposed on the planet. For example, in 2005, when the British government occupied the chairmanship of the G8 countries, a large scientific meeting was convened in Exeter to consider the potential for sudden abrupt change and to reflect on what might be considered 'dangerous anthropogenic change'.

Building on these results, international assessments and statements are indicating growing acceptance of the potential for very serious change. For example, there is now far greater precision and better understanding of how rapidly the climate is changing and the reasons why. The IPCC, which was set up to establish and communicate the consensus of scientific opinion on climate change to international leaders, is just now completing its Fourth Assessment Report. This report brings together the scientific evidence and vividly demonstrates the degree to which the uncertainties surrounding climate change and its consequences for the environment and society are being reduced with each round of IPCC assessment.

There is also a widening consensus across the scientific community. In 2005, there was a declaration by the national academies of science of 11 main countries in the world, including the US National Academy of Sciences, entitled 'Global Responses to Climate Change'. This statement made clear that the scientific evidence is very strong and the imperative for global action increasingly pressing.

While this was as strong a statement as was warranted given the state of the science in July of 2005, things have moved on in both the scientific and the public domain. For example, there have been major articles in leading newspapers and major newsmagazines. *The Economist* produced a major supplement on climate change in September 2005, an important and unexpected step for a business newspaper, and *Scientific American* published a special issue on the subject, the same month. This trend continued to accelerate during 2006.

Political acceptance of climate change

Important political progress was also made in 2005, including at a propitious, but rather unexpected, forum. In particular, the issue came up at the G8 summit in Gleneagles and a declaration was published afterwards. This statement (The Gleneagles Communiqué, 2005), signed by President Bush, states:

> *Climate change is a serious and long-term challenge that has the potential to affect every part of the globe. We know that increased need and use of energy from fossil fuels and other human activities contribute in large part to increases in greenhouse gasses associated with a warming of our Earth's surface. While uncertainties remain in our understanding of climate science, we know enough to act now to put ourselves on a path to slow and, as the science justifies, stop and then reverse the growth [in concentration] of greenhouse gasses.*

The recent book, *Collapse*, by Jared Diamond (2005) of the University of California has also galvanized the attention of international leaders. In it, Diamond identifies three stages for dealing with a major environmental problem. Stage one in the process is recognizing or acknowledging there is a problem that needs to be addressed. The next stage in the analysis is working out ways of coping with that problem. And the third stage, of course, is taking the necessary steps to address the problem.

At present, the world stands somewhere between stages one and two. Most nations, to differing degrees, agree there is a major problem. Some have ideas about how it should be dealt with and some governments are putting these ideas into practice. While much international action has, in fact, already taken place, beginning with the creation of the IPCC in 1988, the signing of the UN Framework Convention on Climate Change in 1992, the negotiation of the Kyoto Protocol in 1997, and the start of international negotiations for a post-Kyoto framework taking effect in 2012, the world community has not yet reached the point of taking the necessary action.

In some nations, the situation is advancing significantly. In the UK, for example, stage two is well advanced, and a recent MORI poll found that 91 per cent of the British public agrees that climate change is a problem.

A similar topical poll in the US might not even reach 75 per cent, although awareness is steadily growing as well. The lack of leadership and delay in action in the US has been a problem, but there are encouraging signs of movement at both the national and state levels. President Bush has referred to the US dependence on fossil fuels and the need to do something about it, and the administration is, to some degree, supporting research on new technologies that would reduce carbon emissions. California and Oregon have passed carbon emission regulations and the states in New England are also moving to cut emissions. The US business community, previously at the forefront in the phasing out of chlorofluorocarbons, is also showing substantial signs of change with companies such as General Electric starting to take action on their own. Things will likely be substantially different after the next presidential election in 2008. Senators McCain and Clinton have both made the long and difficult journey to Svalbard, the Norwegian archipelago in the high Arctic. That these candidates for president think it worthwhile taking the time to see for themselves the rapid changes happening in the Arctic environment is an encouraging sign for future climate legislation.

Addressing and slowing the consequences of climate change

Many of the policies proposed to address climate change have focused on mitigation or how we can reduce carbon emissions. The need for adaptation strategies, however, also should be underlined because we are now beyond the point at which mitigation of climate change will produce all the answers. We must recognize that adaptation to climate change will be necessary, and that this will require also looking at all of the related environmental problems. Climate change, described recently by the British Government's Chief Scientific Advisor as a threat to society greater than terrorism, may be the driving force behind most environmental change during the 21st century, but climate change does not act in isolation. Our ability to adapt to climate change is heavily dependent on solving other environmental problems, for example, bringing the human population increase under control. Other threats to society include the shortage of water and variations in rainfall already being felt in some areas of the world, the steady depletion of resources and continued existence of the consumptionist society, the accumulation of waste that we don't know what to do with, and the serious, irreparable damage to biodiversity.

Solving climate change and these other environmental problems will require a serious rethinking of economics and the way we value things in general. We need change in a value system that gives primacy to market forces, exploitation of resources and ever-rising consumption. Traditional cost–benefit analysis hardly answers any problems at all, and is, in fact, an important part of the problem. If indeed environmental problems are to be properly addressed, in addition to the traditional costs of research, process and production, prices need to reflect the costs involved in replacing a resource or substituting for it, as well as the cost of any associated environmental or human problems. As has been noted by many others, markets are superb at setting prices but incapable of recognizing costs. Future economics will require the kind of 'green accounting' now being pioneered in China, which moves away from simple measures of GNP and GDP toward an appreciation of human welfare. The aim of this approach is to create a 'well-rounded' society without extremes of poverty or wealth – a society that seems very different from the one we have at the moment.

Conclusions

We really need to keep in mind that climate change has critical implications for society. For this reason, it is essential that we keep on gathering more information, pursuing research programs, conducting assessments and convening regional study groups, always focusing on looking at all aspects of climate and related issues and the potential for changes over the decades ahead. We need to expand and improve our analyses, getting beyond simple cost–benefit approaches to consider the full range of implications for the near and distant future. Solutions will require participation of both the public and private sectors, both governments and business, and it is encouraging that some governments and industries are starting to take significant action.

I conclude with four ideas for communicating climate change that I believe can help to promote the needed movement to address the climate change issue:

1. We need a top-down as well as a bottom-up approach. This means that there needs to be full public communication on the significance of the issue, including the introduction of climate change into the school curriculum.
2. It is important to choose the right vocabulary when communicating with policy makers. Politicians, scientists and economists need to come together so that they can at least talk in the same language.
3. We need to insist upon interdisciplinarity. All the interrelated environmental issues mentioned above need to be seen within the framework of the climate change discussion.
4. We need to make sure that the most important reports are sent to the right addresses. We must make sure that the key people understand the importance of this issue.

Finally, we should always remember that we cannot rely on our survival as a species. Life on Earth, from the bottom of the seas to the top of the atmosphere, is so robust that the human experience could easily become no more than a short, but peculiar, episode in the history of life on Earth.

References

Diamond, J., 2005: *Collapse: How Societies Choose to Fail or Succeed*, Viking Press, New York

The Gleneagles Communiqué, 2005: http://news.bbc.co.uk/1/shared/bsp/hi/pdfs/g8_gleneagles_communique.pdf

16

A Moral and Profitable Path to Climate Stabilization

John C. Topping, Jr and Erin Frey

Energy is the lifeblood of the world. Energy travels through the veins of wires, pipelines, roads and sea routes, providing light, heat, food, water and power to most of the globe. Motor vehicles, vessels and planes, powered almost entirely from fossil fuels, under-gird the global economy and provide unprecedented mobility.

However, the implications of relying on fossil fuels are now beginning to be understood, and the long-term environmental, and then societal, consequences are likely to be dire. Higher concentrations of CO_2 in the atmosphere are causing the climate and environment to change at rates faster than most scientists were predicting even a few years ago. While some of the added effects can be attributed to the rapid industrialization of China, India and other booming Asian economies, feedback effects are causing sea ice retreat, glacial melting, sea level rise and ecosystem impacts that are greater than anticipated, as convincingly described earlier in this book.

The accelerating pace of environmental change, the failure of many governments to take strong measures to curb global warming, and the world's seemingly insatiable appetite for fossil fuels are convincing many that we are nearing a 'climatic tipping point'. Once that point is reached, if we are not there already, the resulting changes and impacts are likely to become irreversible and, eventually, globally debilitating.

James Hansen, one of the world's foremost climate scientists and director of the Goddard Institute for Space Studies, has said that the world has less than ten years to initiate dramatic steps toward reducing greenhouse gas emissions. 'We are not now on a path to do that, and if we do not begin actions to get on a different path within the next several years, we will pass a point of no return', he says (cited in Farrell, 2006).

Other scientists warn that to avoid the most serious consequences, we must cut global carbon emissions in half over the next 50 years (Eilperin, 2006). But the steps to cut emissions must begin in the next decade, before we cause irreparable damage to our planet.

Convincing those in the US to sharply reduce their emissions of CO_2 is proving particularly daunting because currently fossil fuels are fundamental to most aspects of American life. But that course must be taken – the US simply must become less dependent on coal, oil and natural gas. Available and emerging technologies make it clear that large changes are possible by greatly increasing efficiency of energy use and by embracing renewable technologies such as wind, solar and hydrogen power. In light of these advances, the task at hand is likely to be less difficult than it may have first appeared.

There is also a precedent for such a significant change. Americans have always been at the forefront in addressing technological challenges, creating new products and making existing technology smaller, faster, cheaper and more efficient. The first computers were agonizingly slow, room-sized, multi-million dollar machines. Today, they can be carried around in backpacks, disseminate information around the world in a fraction of a second, and cost a fraction of their original price. The computer transformation took less than 50 years. The energy transformation away from fossil fuels can be achieved in this time scale as well, but it must start now.

This chapter will focus on examples of proven, practical technologies that are already being used by industry, financial institutions, governments and civil society to produce a lower-carbon economy. It will examine how examples of corporate, state and national leadership can be used to spur and inform future US action on emissions reductions. The chapter will not, however, address some of the more uncertain and longer-term roles that may be played by nuclear power, carbon sequestration or geo-engineering.

Corporate involvement

In the last few years, many multinational corporations and US businesses have committed themselves to addressing climate change. Large companies are able to use their market power to influence the types of products consumers buy. Some companies have realized this, and are now leveraging their market power and offering increasingly environmentally friendly products to their customers. For example:

- Home Depot, one of the largest suppliers of lumber in the US, has decided to sell only certified wood (wood that has been harvested in a sustainable way) in its stores (Mangu-Ward, 2006).
- Wal-Mart is using its market power to educate consumers about climate-friendly approaches. For example, they are featuring more efficient electrical

products in their stores, and are significantly increasing the number of organic-ally grown cotton products they sell (Ruben, 2006).

Neither Home Depot nor Wal-Mart would have been able to produce such a large effect on the products consumers buy if they did not control such a large share of their respective marketplaces. Although not as large, hundreds of other businesses around the country are also voluntarily reducing emissions, using sustainable products and becoming more environmentally aware.

Perhaps most importantly, many corporations are now investing millions of dollars in alternative and renewable energy sources. Over US$48 billion was invested in renewables in 2005, and that number was expected to reach US$60 billion for 2006 (Wasik, 2006). Venture capitalists in the US invested over US$1.4 billion in clean technology markets in 2005, markets that produce global annual revenues of US$150 billion each year (Roosevelt, 2006).

The following examples give an indication of the many positive actions that are being initiated in the energy production, transportation, technology/industry and financial sectors.

Energy

BP was the first major oil company to acknowledge publicly that climate change is a serious threat. It is working to increase its efficiency and reduce its own greenhouse gas emissions (Hertsgaard, 2006). In addition, it has created an Alternative Energy Division and has pledged to invest up to US$8 billion in clean energy over the next decade (Roosevelt, 2006). Although some critics contend that BP's investments in green technologies have been aimed at improving their reputation rather than accomplishing anything substantial, the evidence proves otherwise. BP tops the list put together by Ceres (Investors and Environmentalists for Sustainable Prosperity) ranking multinational firms in their adoption of climate-protecting steps (Cogan, 2006).

Other energy companies are taking substantial steps: Shell has become an investment leader in hydrogen and is spearheading such efforts in the US and Iceland; Chevron currently invests more than US$100 million each year in alternative energy and has included clean technologies in its energy portfolio (Cogan, 2006). Others are following their leads.

Transportation

Toyota, the largest non-US auto company, has committed itself to meeting the emissions reductions called for in the Kyoto Protocol and is reducing greenhouse gas emissions at its facilities. In addition, it plans to offer hybrid options for all of its major models by 2010.

GM, the world's largest auto manufacturer, has also started to turn its attention to alternative energy and fuels. It has already invested more than US$1 billion in developing fuel cell technology and has increased its inventory of vehicles that run on bio-fuels (Cogan, 2006).

Technology and industry

IBM participates in the Chicago Climate Exchange, the only voluntary but legally binding greenhouse gas trading system in North America. It also purchases 4 per cent of its US electrical needs from renewable resources (IBM, 2005).

DuPont has been a corporate leader in addressing climate issues. It has reduced its greenhouse gas emissions by 72 per cent since 1990, and is developing energy-efficient building materials and low-emitting refrigerants. DuPont's energy conservation strategies have actually saved the company over US$3 billion. 'What started as an effort to address our carbon footprint has turned out to be financially a very good thing', explains DuPont Vice-President Linda Fisher (DuPont News, 2006).

GE recently introduced its 'ecomagination' campaign, and plans to invest US$1.5 billion in green technologies annually. The initiative generated revenues of US$10 billion in 2005 alone and the company expects to double this to US$20 billion by 2010. GE's wind power program appears to be especially promising; it operates over 7000 wind turbines worldwide already and the number is growing rapidly (GE, 2006). This US$2 billion program is expected to grow to US$4 billion shortly (Eizenstat and Kraiem, 2005; Deutsch, 2006; *The Economist*, 2006; Roosevelt, 2006).

Financial

J. P. Morgan, a leading provider of financial services, has established an 'environmental policy' that outlines the socially responsible conduct that the company will follow concerning the environment. In addition, it has pledged to invest US$250 million in wind power initiatives (Deutsch, 2006).

Goldman Sachs has also committed itself to combating global warming. In their 'Environmental Policy Framework', the company has committed to reducing greenhouse gas emissions from their offices by 7 per cent (the Kyoto Protocol requirement for the US) by 2012. It will also promote market formation for emissions permits and renewable energy credits, and will invest up to US$1 billion in renewable energy and efficiency programs (Goldman Sachs, 2005). According to a spokesperson for the company, it is 'well on its way' to reaching the US$1 billion investment goal (Deutsch, 2006).

Green companies do better

The wide variety and growing number of businesses contributing and the sheer amount of capital being invested in sustainable and 'green' technologies may seem surprising. These companies, however, are not acting solely out of concern for the environment. They are making sound business decisions and are finding that being green also means being profitable.

Many businesses readily express this mindset. As the Vice-President of Wal-Mart, Andrew Ruben, explained in testimony to Congress, 'we know that being an efficient and profitable business and being a good steward for the environment are goals that can work together' (Ruben, 2006). Companies will not generally undertake environmental initiatives at the expense of reducing their profits. Goldman Sachs, in its 'Environmental Policy Framework' statement, maintains that in pursuing sound environmental policies, 'we will not stray from our central business objective of creating long-term value for our shareholders' (Goldman Sachs, 2005). Robert Langert, director for environmental affairs at McDonald's, explains, 'we were willing to invest money into something, but if it is really going to be sustainable, it has to be economical as well' (Mangu-Ward, 2006).

All of these corporations are taking action because, as former Vice-President Al Gore describes, there is indeed no 'conflict between the environment and the economy' (Kabel, 2006). In fact, evidence suggests that greener and more sustainable companies do better than companies that disregard environmental concerns.

A recent study by Innovest Strategic Advisors, Inc. found that over the past 5 years the world's 100 most sustainable public corporations outperformed the Morgan Stanley Capital International index by 7.1 per cent (Holloway, 2006).

New market indexes for alternative energy are used to track the performance of alternative energy companies and can be compared to other market indices, such as the Dow Jones Industrial Average (Keehner, 2006). The numbers suggest that alternative energy indices (and companies) do better than many non-green indices. One index, Global Climate 100, increased 10 per cent over the first half of 2006, while the Morgan Stanley International World index was up 6 per cent. Another green index, Wilderhill Clean Energy, increased 24 per cent, compared to Standard & Poor's 500-stock index, which rose only 4 per cent (Keehner, 2006). As a whole, green companies are doing better than many other corporations, and many businesses are beginning to realize that being pro-environment can also be profitable.

This trend is likely to be reinforced by a shift in consumer attitudes as more of the public becomes conscious of the environmental consequences of their purchasing decisions. Many people are already willing to opt for more environmentally benign products, even if this requires paying a cost premium. Millions of Americans have purchased Energy Star appliances, computers and office machines; though these machines have slightly higher capital costs, the payback time of an Energy Star appliance in reduced energy costs is remarkably fast.

A sea of change in public attitudes may be setting in. A Campus Climate Neutral Network is springing up on many US campuses and students have been willing to impose modest additional levies on themselves to lower their campus' greenhouse emissions. In June, the General Assembly of the Presbyterian Church USA passed a resolution asking each of its 2.3 million members to bear 'a bold witness' by leading a carbon neutral lifestyle (Climate Institute, 2006).

As the idea that we are each responsible for cleaning up our own mess gains sway among religious and secular institutions, a powerful dynamic will be at play in the marketplace. For example, Land Rover will be including the cost of offsetting carbon emissions for the first 45,000 miles driven in the price of most of its models sold in the UK beginning in 2007. The company has clearly calculated that most of its consumers are prepared to pay a little extra in order to reduce their impact on the environment.

A role for government

Despite the rapidly increasing investment in renewable energies, the pace of the transformation from fossil fuels to alternative power is sluggish relative to the urgency of the problem. This lethargy arises from the fact that without a price reflecting the negative externalities caused by carbon emissions, coal, natural gas and oil are all still ultimately cheaper than wind, solar or hydrogen fuel cell power.

The fact remains that major environmental problems such as global warming, cannot be solved by voluntarism alone. Government involvement is essential in determining the degree of penetration – or lack thereof – that renewable energy has into American society. One study found that government subsidies of fossil fuels worldwide amount to over US$130 billion each year. These subsidies constitute a substantial barrier to newer energy sources because they artificially lower the cost of nonrenewable power, making clean energy alternatives relatively more expensive and less desirable. Simply removing distortionary government subsidies on fossil fuels would encourage the switch to renewable sources of power.

Further government action to subsidize wind, solar and hydrogen power would accelerate the transition to alternative fuels. Studies have found that tax credits on both wind and solar power significantly hastened the development of these technologies and increased their degree of market penetration in the past (Tietenberg, 2006).

Reducing fossil fuel subsidies and increasing tax credits for alternative energy will serve to eliminate many of the economic barriers to entry that new green technologies face. So far, however, the federal government has been reluctant to do this. Because emerging technologies such as wind, solar, biomass, tidal and wave energy are much smaller in scale than conventional power plants, the federal and state regulatory and approval process is relatively more onerous, creating an additional bar to competition. Generally these projects should not be exempt from environmental scrutiny, but the requirements should be carefully tailored to ensure that they are not simply a means of maintaining the status quo.

Unfortunately, economic barriers are not the only impediment to establishing alternative energy sources. Many new technologies, especially hydrogen power, face a 'chicken-and-egg' problem, whereby they need a substantial infrastructure in place before the energy can become economically feasible. Encouragingly, state governments are taking the initiative to remove the technological and regulatory barriers that stand in the way of widespread renewable power use. Not only are states creating legal limits on carbon emissions, they are also helping to create alternative energy infrastructure so that new technologies can flourish. Many states hope that their actions will be a model for the federal government to follow.

State initiatives

State and local governments are taking it upon themselves to promote cleaner technologies and stricter environmental standards in their areas, independently of the federal government. The largest of these initiatives is the Regional Greenhouse Gas Initiative (RGGI), which brings together 11 Northeastern and Mid-Atlantic states that have pledged to reduce CO_2 emissions by 10 per cent by 2010 through a cap-and-trade system. It is hoped that the RGGI initiative will become a model for future federal programs.

Some states are even creating coalitions with international leaders to address the climate challenge. For example, Governor Schwarzenegger of California signed a climate agreement with former British Prime Minister Tony Blair that recognizes the need for 'urgent action' in reducing greenhouse gas emissions. The agreement stipulates that the UK and California will work together to address climate change by sharing experiences, finding new solutions and even looking into a possible emissions-trading system (BBC News, 2006).

Texas too is pushing forward in the reduction of carbon emissions. It is actively promoting the development and use of renewable energy technologies, and is becoming a leader in the production of wind power. As of the beginning of 2006, Texas was the second largest generator of wind power in the US (AWEA, 2006), but by the end of the year it is expected to surpass California and become the largest producer in the country (SECO, 2007).

States are also making strides in transforming the transportation sector by encouraging and investing in hydrogen-powered vehicles. Florida, New York, Nevada and Washington DC are working on demonstration projects of this new technology (Birdsong, 2005; Kenworthy, 2005). But no state has gone further than California to incorporate hydrogen fuel cell technology into the transportation sector.

California and hydrogen power

California has always been a trendsetter for the US and the world, and its role in renewable energy production is no exception. California is the US' largest consumer of gasoline, but it has also taken the largest steps to incorporate hydrogen-powered transportation into the economy.

Only six months after taking office, Governor Arnold Schwarzenegger established the 'Hydrogen Highway Project', a program to develop the infrastructure for a hydrogen-powered transportation sector. This program's goal is to install roughly 100 hydrogen-fueling stations along the California interstate highway system and develop a fleet of 2000 fuel-cell vehicles by 2010 (CHH, 2004). In addition, a 'significant and increasing' percentage of hydrogen will be produced using renewable energy as the project continues (Birdsong, 2005). By developing both the fuel-cell fleet and the refueling infrastructure simultaneously, California is avoiding the 'chicken-and-egg' problem that has plagued other efforts to begin the transition to a hydrogen economy.

Public/private partnerships, such as the California Fuel Cell Partnership, currently provide input about both vehicle and infrastructure development to the Hydrogen Highway Project. Partnership members include many major domestic and international auto manufacturers, energy and oil companies, and energy and environmental agencies (CAFP, 2005). This collaboration between the automotive industry, energy suppliers and government agencies has already borne fruit: currently there are 22 hydrogen-fueling stations in operation and 143 fuel-cell vehicles in California (CHH, 2004). The encouraging results of this cooperation illustrate that business and environmental goals can be fulfilled simultaneously.

Although it has already made great strides, the California Hydrogen Highway has a long way to go. Some auto manufacturers hope to have hydrogen vehicles ready for widespread commercial use within the next decade, but ultimately the price of hydrogen must become competitive with gasoline before the technology will be widely adopted. An additional important concern will be ensuring that most of the hydrogen is produced from non-carbon energy sources; otherwise greenhouse mitigation benefits will be modest at best.

Nonetheless, California's leadership, in developing the infrastructure for a hydrogen economy, is helping to lower the barriers to entry for this alternative energy. The state's intelligent policy choice to promote cleaner technology will hasten the transition to renewable power and will make California the center of the booming green-energy industry, placing it in an enviable position as a market leader as other states scramble to catch up to its lead.

International efforts

Not only states, but also other nations are providing leadership and taking initiative on the climate issue. Countries on every continent are switching to alternative energy sources such as wind, biofuels and even hydrogen power. Other parts of the world, particularly Europe, are modifying current energy-generation practices to reduce their impact on the environment. Later chapters discuss in more detail ongoing efforts in Iceland and small island states. Here, we highlight other groundbreaking efforts taking place in the rest of the world.

Brazil

Brazil is one of the few countries that has already firmly established renewable power in its entire economy. In addition to deriving the vast majority of its electricity from hydropower, renewable biofuels comprise 40 per cent of the energy used by the transportation sector. Ethanol, a biofuel made from sugarcane (or in the US, from corn), is used to power automobiles and other vehicles. It can be mixed with gasoline, and Brazil now requires that all automotive fuel contain at least 20 per cent ethanol (da Silva, 2006).

Brazil produces over four billion gallons of ethanol each year, which are then sold at more than 30,000 service stations around the country. As a result of this extensive ethanol distribution network, 70 per cent of new cars sold in Brazil can run on pure ethanol or a combination of gasoline and ethanol (Lynch, 2006). Because consumers can choose between two fuels and use whatever is cheapest at a given time, introducing this option of using a domestic fuel source has helped to insulate consumers from fluctuating international oil and ethanol prices.

The success of ethanol is partially due to Brazil's ideal agricultural conditions: lots of rain, land and inexpensive labor. But the switch to ethanol still took time and investment; it was a 30-year process that was, at least initially, heavily government directed.

The oil supply shocks of the 1970s hit Brazil hard; at the time, the country imported over 80 per cent of its fuel as petroleum. As a result, the military leaders of the 1970s and 1980s decided to incorporate ethanol into the fuel infrastructure and began a series of government directives that included mandatory mixing of gasoline and ethanol, loans to sugar companies to build ethanol plants, guaranteed prices for companies that produced ethanol, dictated production levels, requirements for fueling stations to supply ethanol, and monetary incentives to car dealerships that displayed vehicles that would run on ethanol. It is estimated that between 1979 and the mid-1990s, the Brazilian government spent over US$16 billion on the promotion of this biofuel, mostly in the form of loans and price supports. These policies did have a substantial effect, however, as purchases of ethanol vehicles rose dramatically in the 1980s (Luhnow and Samor, 2006).

With the hyperinflation of the 1990s, however, Brazil was forced to cut ethanol price supports, causing ethanol-powered automobiles to become uneconomical; as a result, these vehicles all but disappeared from the roads. But the government still mandated that gasoline be mixed with ethanol, meaning sugar companies continued to produce the fuel and gradually the process became less expensive and more efficient. Now, rapidly rising oil prices and the widespread market penetration of flex cars have made ethanol a viable option again (Luhnow and Samor, 2006).

The country is also looking to double its exports of biofuel to over a billion gallons per year, and to help other nations begin ethanol projects of their own. Australia and India are two of the many countries that may follow the Brazilian example and establish biofuel facilities in the future (Lynch, 2006). Both India and China have sent officials to observe the Brazilian ethanol program, and India has begun requiring some of its states to add ethanol to gasoline (Luhnow and Samor, 2006).

The US also produces ethanol, but uses corn instead of sugar cane to create the fuel. As a result, the manufacturing process is more complicated, expensive and demanding of fertilizer generated using fossil fuels. As a result, in order to make domestic ethanol competitive, the federal government imposes a 54-cent tariff on each gallon of Brazilian ethanol that is imported, hindering the widespread adoption of competitive Brazilian ethanol in the US.

Europe

European countries have recently received a great deal of attention for their use of renewable energy – particularly wind power – to decrease their carbon emissions. Europeans have also embraced the diesel engine as a way to conserve oil resources. Currently, 25–40 per cent of all Western European vehicles run on diesel, and that number is expected to grow to 50 per cent by 2010 (Falk, 2000). Consumers are increasingly running these vehicles on biodiesel, an even cleaner and more environmentally sustainable fuel (Styles, 2005).

A lesser-known trend in European energy generation involves the increased use of combined heat and power (CHP) facilities. CHP involves the capturing of waste heat from a power plant and using this heat for nearby consumers. The details and economics of the process are discussed in more detail in Chapter 19, but it typically doubles the efficiency of a power plant, reducing carbon emissions and saving money at the same time (Marvin, 1991). CHP is currently being pioneered in Western Europe, in particular.

The amount of cogenerated power has been growing, and in some Western European countries, over 40 per cent of all electricity is generated this way (Smith, 2000). In Europe as a whole, CHP accounts for about 10 per cent of the electricity market and 10 per cent of the heat market. The EU hopes to increase those numbers to 18 per cent by 2010, and recent trends show that the goal may be reached (Blankinship, 2004). Many European electricity markets are undergoing deregulation and liberalization, which has increased the market for independently owned CHP electricity. Future deregulation is expected to boost cogeneration, particularly in Belgium (Smith, 2000).

Denmark is opening up its energy markets using different approaches than many other countries in Europe, thereby increasing, for example, the share of its power from wind turbines. In addition, Denmark continues to be the most advanced producer of CHP. The Danish government is using cogeneration as a major tool to improve the environment, and is giving subsidies and tax breaks to encourage the building of additional CHP plants (Smith, 2000). Germany, The Netherlands and Finland are other leaders in cogeneration. While there are some limits on the amount of CHP that can be sustained, it is likely that it will play an important role in helping the EU reach the 20 per cent reduction in emissions by 2020 target that it is committed to.

Conclusions

Countries all over the world are attempting to address the problem of global warming and are switching to alternative energy sources. These are encouraging trends, and the US should take note and consider following the examples of other nations.

There is no one answer to the energy crisis we face. Hydrogen alone is not the answer. Neither is ethanol, wind power, solar energy or cogeneration alone. There is no magic bullet, no one miraculous technology that will end our dependence on nonrenewable energy.

Rather, the solution to the carbon problem lies in quickly developing a diverse energy portfolio and a proactive policy on the part of the federal government. The US must utilize all energy options available, and can do this by following state and international examples of policies that reduce barriers to entry for new technologies. Development of infrastructure, lowering subsidies on fossil fuels, and reducing tariffs on clean energy from other countries are all actions that the US should pursue, in addition to developing incentives for more corporate investment in alternative energy. Only if there is a cooperative public–private effort to encourage renewable power will the US be able to move quickly enough to a sustainable, carbon-free economy.

To prevent the most serious consequences of climate change, many of which have been outlined in earlier chapters, the US and the international community need to take dramatic steps within the next decade to reduce carbon emissions. This may sound like a daunting task, but the corporate investment, state initiatives and international leadership that have begun indicate what is possible – but they are only beginnings. More work must be done to develop alternative energy sources and to improve energy efficiency, and much of that work must be encouraged, promoted, and even led by the federal government. It is time for Congress and the White House to take responsibility and show leadership for our future.

The US has accomplished extraordinary feats before and we can do it again. We can reduce our greenhouse gas emissions, we can stabilize atmospheric CO_2 concentrations, and we can avoid the most devastating consequences of climate change. We can increase corporate investment, we can produce effective and long-lasting government policies, and we can work with our international partners on this global problem. But, for environmental, moral, stewardship and long-term economic reasons, we all need to make the commitment and we need to make it now. If we rise to this occasion, we will make the world more stable, secure and prosperous, and future generations will appreciate that we had the wisdom and moral courage to meet the climate challenge.

References

AWEA, 2006: Annual industry rankings demonstrate continued growth of wind energy in the United States, *American Wind Energy Association News Release*, 15 March

BBC News, 2006: California and UK in climate pact, http://news.bbc.co.uk/2/hi/5233466.stm, accessed 23 March 2007

Birdsong, A., 2005: California drives the future of the automobile, *Worldwatch*, March/April, www.worldwatch.org/node/573

Blankinship, S., 2004: Greater CHP use cited as top blackout fighter, *Power Engineering*, March, 50

CAFP, 2005: California Fuel Cell Partnership, www.cafcp.org/, accessed 22 March 2007

CHH, 2004: www.hydrogenhighway.ca.gov/vision/vision.htm, accessed 23 March 2007

Climate Institute, 2006: Presbyterian Church USA asks its 2.3 million members each to become carbon neutral, http://www.climate.org/topics/climate/presbyterian_climate_neutral.shtml, accessed 23 March 2007.

Cogan, D. G., 2006: Corporate governance and climate change: Making the connection, *Summary Report*, Ceres, Boston, MA, March

da Silva, L. I. L., 2006: Fuel for thought, *The Wall Street Journal*, 14 July, A12

Deutsch, C., 2006: Investors are tilting toward windmills, *The New York Times*, v. 155, issue 53491, 15 February, C1–C8

Dupont News, 2006: USA Today highlights DuPont climate change efforts, *DuPont News*, 2 June, http://www2.dupont.com/Media_Center/en_US/daily_news/june/article20060602a.html, accessed 23 March 2007

The Economist, 2006: Can business be cool?, *The Economist*, 10 June, 69–70

Eilperin, J., 2006: Debate on climate shifts to issue of irreparable change, *Washington Post*, 29 January

Eizenstat, S. and R. Kraiem, 2005: In green company, *Foreign Policy*, September/October, 92–93

Falk, H., 2000: Diesel engine, as a 'ready for use' energy saving technology, *Energy Saving Now*, http://energy.saving.nu/biofuels/dieseltech.shtml, accessed 23 March 2007

Farrell, B., 2006: Political science, *The Nation*, 13 February

GE (General Electric), 2006: Wind energy at GE, www.gepower.com/businesses/ge_wind_energy/en/index.htm, accessed 22 March 2007

Goldman Sachs, 2005: Environmental policy framework, http://www2.goldmansachs.com/our_firm/our_culture/corporate_citizenship/environmental_policy_framework/docs/EnvironmentalPolicyFramework.pdf, accessed 22 March 2007

Hertsgaard, M., 2006: Green grows grassroots, *The Nation*, 13 July

Holloway, A., 2006: Sustain to gain, *Canadian Business*, **79**(3), 30 January, www.canadianbusiness.com/markets/article.jsp?content=20060130_73968_73968

IBM, 2005: IBM executes the 4th largest corporate purchase of certified renewable energy certificates in the US, 1 December, www.ibm.com/ibm/environment/news/rec_2005.shtml, accessed 22 March 2007

Kabel, M., 2006: Gore praises Wal-Mart for sustainability plans, *Environmental News Network*, 13 July

Keehner, J., 2006: Options grow for green investors, *The Wall Street Journal*, 20 June

Kenworthy, T., 2005: States get into the driver's seat of fuel-cell development, *USA Today*, 14 April, 4a

Luhnow, D. and G. Samor, 2006: As Brazil fills up on ethanol, it weans off energy imports, *The Wall Street Journal*, 16 January

Lynch, D. J., 2006: Brazil hopes to build on its ethanol success, *USA Today*, 28 March

Mangu-Ward, K., 2006: The age of corporate environmentalism, *Reason*, **37**(9), www.reason.com/news/show/36208.html

Marvin, S., 1991: Combined heat and power/district heating: A review, *Planning Practice & Research*, **6**(2), 31–35

Roosevelt, T., 2006: *Statement Regarding Climate Change: Understanding the Degree of the Problem and the Nature of its Solution*, submitted to the Government Reform Committee, US House of Representatives, Pew Center on Global Climate Change, Washington, DC

Ruben, A., 2006: Climate Change: Understanding the Degree of the Problem, written testimony before the United States House of Representatives, Committee on Government Reform, Washington DC

SECO, 2007: Texas wind energy, http://www.seco.cpa.state.tx.us/re_wind.htm, accessed 22 March 2007

Smith, D. J., 2000: The European Union promotes cogeneration, *Power Engineering*, May, 56–60

Styles, G., 2005: Europe's shift to diesel fuel, *Energy Outlook*, 6 October, http://energyoutlook.blogspot.com/2005/10/europes-shift-to-diesel-fuel.html, accessed 23 March 2007

Tietenberg, T, 2006: *Environmental and Natural Resource Economics*, Pearson Addison Wesley, Boston

Wasik, J. F., 2006: 'Green' companies likely to cost you, *Bloomberg News*, 16 July

17

Moving Toward Climate Stabilization: Iceland's Example

President Ólafur Ragnar Grímsson

I have believed for a number of years that the dialogue between scientists and public officials is the fundamental key to progress in the area of global debate about climate change. It is, in fact remarkable, when we look back even just five or six years, what enormous progress has taken place.

I had a conversation with an editor of one of the major American magazines in New York about five years ago, trying to entice him into doing a cover story about what was happening up north in the Arctic and surrounding territories. His answer was very frank and blunt: 'No, sorry, we are not going to do anything about it all. Our readers are not interested'. I was therefore very happy to see the same magazine only some months ago carrying a major cover story, with a polar bear on the front, warning the world in strong terms that time is very short.

We live, fortunately, in a very democratic global community, despite a certain number of dictatorships and difficult totalitarian societies in various parts of the world. By and large, we live in a time where the possibilities for an open, democratic, global debate have never been as strong and as promising. It is really up to us, quite frankly, all of us in the public world and the science world, to make use of those opportunities that have been created by technology, by the information revolution, by the fundamental changes in global media, and, above all, in the transformation of the mindset of people all over the world.

I think the fundamental positive result, the shift in the debate on climate change that has taken place in the last few years, is very strong evidence of what a democratic and open dialogue between people from different elements in society, science, media and public officials of various kinds, can achieve, irrespective of the opposition of a number of governments or their leaders to this cause. I find this tremendously encouraging.

I would even go so far as to say that we are now in a new era as far as this issue is concerned. We have now got the attention of the world. Of course, there are different levels of interest. There are challenging parts and difficulties ahead.

But we should not overlook the fact that we have entered a new era, so far as the global debate on climate change and what we can do about it are concerned. This creates a fascinating challenge for scientists; namely, to be at the same time fundamentally thorough and sound scientists, but also to be active citizens and democratic participants at the same time.

In the same way that the scientific community continues rightly to urge myself and my colleagues, presidents and other national leaders, to listen to the scientists, it is important for the scientists to also be active participants in the democratic process, without, of course violating the fundamental principles of scientific enquiry. Scientists need to both provide scientific results for public leaders, and also to press for attention to them in fulfilling their democratic responsibility.

Progress in Iceland

In my country, we have seen, in my lifetime, extraordinary progress in the fields of climate awareness and renewable energy. Many people who come to Iceland today marvel at what they see in terms of the use of renewable resources and praise our country very strongly. But I remember as a small boy that if you visited Reykjavik, the capital of my country was daily covered in smoke from the coal fires and the largest part of the harbor was taken up by the coal depot. Back then, the ships that most frequently visited Iceland were the coal ships from the UK and other parts of Europe.

To have predicted at that time that at the beginning of the 21st century, almost 100 per cent of our energy would come from renewable resources, that almost 100 per cent of the houses in Iceland would be heated by renewable resources, and that over 70 per cent of our total energy needs would be provided by renewable energy resources, would have been considered such a utopian prediction as to be completely wild in its framework and its thinking.

At that time, the prevailing view in my country was that we could only use geothermal resources for heating houses where we saw white steam coming up from the ground and, perhaps in some fortunate places, build a few swimming pools to create a leisure area for the people. Now we are drilling as deep as 3 km, and have recently enacted policy that calls for drilling down to 5 km; one of the fortuitous benefits that we have obtained from the oil industry is part of the drilling process that will enable this. Developing and demonstrating the capability to drill down to 5 km will completely transform the potential for geothermal energy all around the world.

The problem with the energy debate, not only today, but also in recent decades, is that it has been dominated by the pursuit of big solutions and big profits. This has been the case not just in the approach toward solving the energy challenges of Iceland and the US, but also of the world. Attention has focused on finding the big solution to the problem, whether it is nuclear power stations, big hydro dams or any other form of major solution. Geothermal power, however, is like a harmonica: it can be used on many different scales (for example, to heat a single house, a village, a region, a factory or a major city), depending on the particular requirements of the situation.

Progress across the North

In the last decade or so, our participation on this issue has been, to some extent, within the framework of what is happening in what I call 'the North', but what some people call the Arctic. I call the region 'the North' because I believe that we need a wider perspective and a wider geographical placement than just the Arctic. Perhaps no area in the world was as central as the Arctic during the nuclear confrontation of the Cold War, the region being in the path of bombers and missiles and the hiding spot of nuclear submarines. It is remarkable how, in the last ten years or so, we have seen various forms of cooperation in the Arctic and in the North, ranging from the creation of the Arctic Council (a body of intergovernmental cooperation), down to active institutions encompassing citizens, scientists and others.

As we all know, and as earlier chapters in this book document, the North is also a key area in terms of the debate on climate change. This is the case primarily, in my opinion, for three reasons. The first is that nowhere in the world are the traces of climate change as clear as in the North. The dramatic pictures, the scientific evidence, the territory, the melting of the ice, the transformation of the habitat for various species, the wildlife, the insects, the fishing stocks and all the other aspects of the Earth's biological existence – everything is changing. Second, experts estimate that about 25 per cent of the untapped energy resources in the world are in the North; depending on how we use the Earth's energy resources, the North could become, if not the new Middle East of the 21st century, certainly a major supplier of energy. The region has a great variety of such resources, not only gas and oil, but hydro, geothermal and others. Finally, the likely opening of the Northern Sea Route as a result of the melting sea ice might transform global trade even more than the Suez Canal did when it opened over a century ago.

While also an active participant in the debate on climate change and renewable energy, Iceland has strongly encouraged cooperation among scientists and public officials in the North. As one aspect of this effort, Iceland's Ambassador Gunnar Paulsson served as chair of the Arctic Council during completion of the Arctic Climate Impact Assessment, which summarized the environmental concerns and the evolution of what is happening in the Arctic. For the future, we will be encouraging even more active cooperation and links among the Northern Territories and the Arctic countries. We need to further draw Russia into the discussion, not only because of the vast energy resources in Russia, but also because of the Russian scientific community and the long tradition that the Russians have of studying ice and the Northern regions.

Iceland is taking actions to address climate change

I am reasonably optimistic that action to limit climate change can be taken in time. While it is my nature to be optimistic (otherwise I would not have survived in the business I am in for such a long time), I believe my optimism stems from more than this. I have seen a big change take place in the global debate and in my own country. Iceland is at the forefront in seven areas that we believe are of importance not only to us, but also to others. By showing what can be done in a very short time, indeed, in only one lifetime, imagine what we can do if we pool our resources.

Many say that Iceland is a special case, that it is blessed with volcanoes and geysers and so on – this is, of course, correct, as the Almighty was very generous when he created Iceland. I sometimes say that when we read the opening account in the book of Genesis about how the Almighty created the Earth in six days and then decided to rest because the work was finished, that account is not entirely accurate because when it came to the creation of Iceland, the Almighty became so fascinated by the possibilities that the creation has continued in my country up to the present day, with new volcanoes and lava fields and earthquakes, and other examples of continuing activities.

This still-active environment has affected the mindset of our people; geological creativity and the natural world have had an impact on our souls, and we have realized, perhaps because we grow up with this sense from early childhood, that we are not the masters of the universe, that there are forces stronger than ourselves, and, despite all the achievements and progress of science, technology and business, that the forces that dominate the Earth are still much stronger than our capabilities. That is why this issue is so important, and our seven efforts are so varied and intense. They are:

1. *Geothermal Energy.* The first applications of geothermal energy involved heating houses and, since then, geothermal energy has developed into a major resource. We are now building geothermal power stations that will produce electricity for large aluminum smelters, and these will be the first aluminum smelters in the world that will be driven by electricity from geothermal resources. We are now receiving a stream of visits from all kinds of corporations in different fields, corporations that want to come to Iceland to build stations or factories there because they want to be able to tell their customers and clients that they produce goods using clean energy. It is not only

the aluminum companies that are coming. There is also a group interested in building a research and development center that is powered by clean energy. I am sure that this type of experience is also happening in other parts of the world.

2. *Hydroelectric Power.* The second element is the development of hydroelectric power, including building large hydro dams. We are now producing almost 85 per cent of our electricity in this way.

3. *Hydrogen for transportation.* With heating and electricity now provided by renewables, the remaining challenge is transitioning to renewable fuels for transportation and shipping. In cooperation with Daimler-Chrysler, Shell and others, we initiated a hydrogen project a few years ago. The first public hydrogen station in Iceland has now opened, and a few buses and private cars are taking part in the early testing; indeed, I had the distinction of being the first person in Iceland to break the speed limit by driving a hydrogen car. This early success, coming within a decade of starting the project, has overcome early skepticism about hydrogen fuel. And Iceland is an ideal test case for determining how a nation and a community can transition to hydrogen-powered transportation. The results have been very positive – so positive that Reykjavik had to issue certificates to foreign tourists who wanted to come and ride on their hydrogen buses. So, hydrogen-fuelled vehicles have become not only an interesting element in our traffic system, but also a strong tourist attraction, which is yet another good sign of how mindsets are changing.

4. *Carbon sequestration.* In order to share in the global effort to get rid of CO_2, we have begun a cooperative effort involving the Reykjavik Energy Company and three universities to carry out sequestration experiments in the next three years at the new geothermal construction site close to Reykjavik. The experiment will evaluate the potential for taking CO_2 from the atmosphere and pumping it down into the basalt layers. If the experiment succeeds, it will represent a very important step. We have already entered into preliminary discussions with the government of India to undertake a second experiment with them in their country if the Icelandic experiment looks promising in two years time. This could lead, within five or six years, to an operating system in India. In addition, our experiment will be linked to an effort to take some of the exhaust stream from the aluminum smelters and pump it down into the ground. Working with the global scientific community, we are thus seeking to develop a new approach to the dramatic challenge that mankind faces in the coming years.

5. *International participation and leadership.* Our chairmanship of the Arctic Council, and the publication of the Arctic Climate Impact Assessment was one important step, but we are doing more. For example, the Global Roundtable on Climate Change, which was created by Jeff Sachs and others a few years ago and is based in New York, held its only meeting outside that

region in Iceland earlier this year, and we are trying to be even more active. We see international participation and leadership as our obligation and our duty, even though it is quite a challenge for a small country. With the end of the cold war, the importance of nations is not measured in military strength or financial power; the importance of nations is measured in what we can contribute to the solutions of some of the challenges that face people all over the world, and what we can offer in terms of ideas. In these areas, my small nation, and other small nations, can indeed play important parts.

6.   *Financing of clean energy solutions.* Our financial community, led by the Glitnir Bank, has decided to make global financing of clean energy solutions one of its major portfolios (and, if the banks have grabbed onto the need for renewable energy, we have indeed moved a long way). It is a confirmation of their serious intent that the leaders of that effort within the banks are actively participating in events around the world. I think their efforts are also sending the message to other financial institutions in different parts of the world that, if the banks have concluded that clean energy is good business, they better also face up to the climate change challenge.

7.   *Creating partnerships and cooperation with other countries.* Iceland has now entered into partnerships on firm projects with countries such as China, India, Russia and many European countries, and even with the State of California. We are in the process of expanding our efforts into Indonesia and Africa, because many countries in eastern Africa have huge geothermal potential, and it could be a very interesting aspect of the evolution of Africa and the need to develop Africa to combine economic development there with the use of geothermal and clean energy resources. The Geothermal Department of the United Nations University has been based in Iceland for 25 years, and we have educated over 300 experts from different parts of the world. These partnerships that we have now created and are in the process of creating in almost every part of the world are, I believe, a confirmation that governments, regional authorities and others have woken up to the fact that there is the possibility of creating renewable energy resources where people were not aware of them before.

Of course, all of these activities will never be *the* solution to the problem or *the* road we can travel to fully combat climate change, but I believe they can be a very important part of the solution. Our efforts are also a confirmation that a country that 60 years ago had its capital covered with coal smoke and a large part of its harbor taken up by the coal depot can, in the lifetime of one generation, become a global leader in the field of renewable energy, creating partnerships with countries as different as Russia and the US, India and China, and many others. If we can do it in my small country, the potential for others with greater resources is enormous.

18

Climate Impacts in the Developing World:
A Case Study of the Small Island States

Nasir Khattak

The disproportionate vulnerability of developing countries to climate change, the appropriate responsibility for both developing countries and those with high emissions in moderating and adapting to these impacts, and the appropriate role of developing nations in limiting future emissions are all highly contentious issues in global politics. As such, these issues tend to lead to protracted meetings and delays in any nation undertaking any sort of measures. Only by understanding and coming to agreement on these vulnerabilities, their causes and what actions need to be taken will international negotiations be able to move forward.

Developing countries are particularly susceptible to climate change because most lie in regions of the world where the most intense and damaging impacts are likely to occur, and because they lack the resources to prepare for and adapt to those impacts. To cite just one example of the vulnerability of those in the developing world, the 2004 floods in Bangladesh, which killed 600 people and displaced 20 million, showed how ill-prepared that region is for excessive monsoon rains (POST-UK, 2006). As storms become more intense and damages and loss of life mount, the increasing losses will make it more and more difficult for development to raise the standard of living in developing nations, unless aid and assistance from the outside rises as well.

With respect to the role of developing nations in contributing to the pace of climate change, it will be difficult to stabilize the Earth's climate without developing countries keeping their emissions very low. Though the average resident of a developing country emits only a small fraction of the greenhouse gases of the average person in a developed country, the massive and growing populations of the developing countries, coupled with their rising standards of living, will eventually render that fact irrelevant. Many argue, however, that demanding restrictions would be unfair, given that the already-developed countries had no similar restrictions on their historical development and growth (Najam et al, 2003). Any future climate policy must strike a delicate balance between these issues of equity and efficacy if it is to succeed.

Climate change and the small island developing states

The case of the small island developing states provides a number of important insights into how these issues might best be handled. These countries are among the most susceptible in the world to climate impacts, as even a small increase in sea level would submerge a significant proportion of their territories. Moreover, many lie in regions that are already susceptible to hurricanes and typhoons. In addition, severe weather events are likely to increase in frequency and intensity as climate change accelerates, causing further devastation in these countries.

The small island developing states are also, as a group, relatively poor countries, with limited ability to meet even the basic needs of their citizens, much less adapt to climate change. Historically, their primary fuel source has been imported diesel fuel that, when combusted, gives off a significant amount of pollution. As a result, these countries have limited capacity to generate electricity, and what electricity is available is often expensive, unreliable and environmentally damaging.

In November 2000, the Climate Institute and its partners including the Organization of American States, the Energy and Security Group established the Global Sustainable Energy Islands Initiative to assist the small islands states in developing and implementing comprehensive sustainable energy plans that would transform their energy systems from fossil fuels to a renewable energy base and reduce their reliance on imported diesel. This program is currently active in four Caribbean and two Pacific island nations with plans to expand to another three islands states in 2008–2009. The donors of this initiative include the Rockefeller Brothers Fund, the United Nations Foundation, the government of Italy, Austria and the US Agency for International Development.

GSEII in the Caribbean

One country in which the GSEII has been particularly successful is the Caribbean island of Saint Lucia. Six years ago, the Saint Lucian government drafted and approved a sustainable energy plan with the assistance of the Climate Institute and the Organization of American States. The plan aimed to achieve significant improvement in the electrical capacity of the island while cutting the projected business-as-usual increase in greenhouse gas emissions by 35 per cent.

Currently, many projects aimed at meeting the plan's goals have been completed, and several others are in progress. The former category includes: one project that is encouraging the use of compact fluorescent light (CFL) bulbs (which are far more efficient than traditional light bulbs) that is being implemented with the assistance of Climate Care, a British NGO; a second project aimed at educating the island's large and growing hospitality industry about energy efficiency measures that they could take; and a third project focused on designing and implementing a broad-based campaign for the general public on efficiency.

Three energy-generation projects are in the planning stage. These include: a wind farm on the eastern side of the island; a power generation facility intended to burn methane gas captured from a large landfill; and exploration and development of Saint Lucia's geothermal energy resources for power generation. Each of these projects is directed towards improving the electricity supply and efficiency of Saint Lucia while acting to limit potential climate impacts. The program as a whole, meanwhile, is tailored to suit the island's individual needs.

Another GSEII success in the Caribbean has been in the island of Dominica. Former Prime Minister Pierre Charles committed the country to increasing the share of sustainable energy sources as it develops. Currently, two projects have been implemented, and the country plans to investigate several additional large renewable energy projects in the near future. The two main projects implemented so far include one promoting widespread use of efficient CFL technology, similar to the aforementioned project in Saint Lucia, and a second focused on improving the efficiency of the grid system, seeking to reduce losses to 20–30 per cent of their current level. Other projects include a major geothermal energy project, construction of micro-hydroelectric facilities and/or wind turbines to supply additional generating capacity.

A third unique project currently underway in the Caribbean is being implemented in the country of St Kitts and Nevis. This program focuses on reviving the currently dormant sugar industry of the islands by using sugarcane for electricity and/or biofuels production. The project would allow for additional economic development in the country, but would do so without burning environmentally damaging fossil fuels.

GSEII in the Pacific

In the Pacific, the GSEII's greatest success story has been the Republic of the Marshall Islands. The islands' government is very concerned about the issue of global warming, as the average height of the entire territory of the islands is about 2 m above sea level. The Climate Institute has partnered with the government to help the country develop its energy capacity cleanly.

Three GSEII projects have been initiated to date. As with two of the aforementioned Caribbean countries, the Marshall Islands instituted a CFL project in partnership with Climate Care UK. A second project involves the development of photovoltaic solar power on the island as a substitute for imported fossil fuels; because the islands receive high levels of sunlight year round, they are well suited to this technology. The third project focuses on the development of coconut oil as a biofuel to replace imported diesel. Again, each of these projects is tailored to the specific needs of the islands, but works toward a sustainable energy solution for the future.

Implications for developing nations

The plans of these small island developing states highlight a way forward for climate policy in developing countries. If even small developing countries with fairly weak economies can take significant strides toward reducing their carbon emissions, surely larger developing countries with greater resources can do the same. The key will be to develop plans that play to each country's individual strengths, as the small island developing states have done.

For some countries, the best initial course will be to focus on efficiency improvements. Compact fluorescent lighting is certainly an important and cost-effective way to reduce electricity consumption, as the programs described above demonstrate. In some countries, upgrading the grid, as in the case of Dominica, will provide further efficiency improvements.

In other countries, a focus on renewable energy development will be more effective. As the experiences of the small island developing states demonstrate, renewable generation can be achieved in a variety of ways. Some countries will focus on biofuels from a variety of sources; others will focus on emerging technologies like wind and solar power to undergird their development. Either method will reduce potential fossil fuel consumption while countries work at the same time to further improve their standards of living, thus striking a balance between considerations of equity and efficiency.

References

Najam, A., S. Huq and Y. Sokona, 2003: Climate negotiations beyond Kyoto: Developing countries concerns and interests, *Climate Policy*, **3**, 221–231 (available at www.climate-talks.net/2006-ENVRE130/PDF/Najam-CliPol%20Climate%20and%20SD.pdf)

POST-UK (Parliamentary Office of Science and Technology), 2006: Adapting to climate change, *Postnote* (available at www.parliament.uk/documents/upload/postpn269.pdf)

19

Stimulating a Clean Energy Revolution

Christopher Flavin

The 'perfect storm' of climate change, political instability in key energy regions, and high oil prices has created a demand for a new energy path. The advent of promising new technologies capable of turning abundant domestic energy sources – including solar, wind, geothermal, hydro, biomass and ocean energy – into transportation fuels, electricity and heat offer a path to an unprecedented energy revolution. Renewable energy technologies, combined with substantial improvements in energy efficiency, have the potential to rapidly and economically transform the world's energy system.

Over recent years, mounting concerns about climate change as well as a sharp rise in oil prices have driven the demands around the world for dramatic policy changes. One vision increasingly shared among policy makers is that there is a real need to forge a new energy model, a practical vision that would be based on clean and efficient energy.

The current renewables boom

In an absolute sense, the world is heavily dependent on fossil fuels, which currently provide over 80 per cent of the energy on which global society depends. However, the annual growth rates of various energy sources show that change is on the way (see Figure 19.1). Since 2001, the growth rates of the solar photovoltaic (30 per cent), wind (26 per cent) and biofuel (17 per cent) sectors have been much larger than for the traditional sectors of coal (4.4 per cent), oil (1.6 per cent), natural gas (2.5 per cent) and even nuclear (1.1 per cent).

This trend is characteristic of a new dynamic, namely the growing role that renewable energy sources are playing globally and in the US. Many of the new technologies that harness renewables are, or soon will be, economically competitive with fossil fuels. Although renewable energy currently provides only about 6 per cent of total US energy, there are compelling reasons to put these technologies to

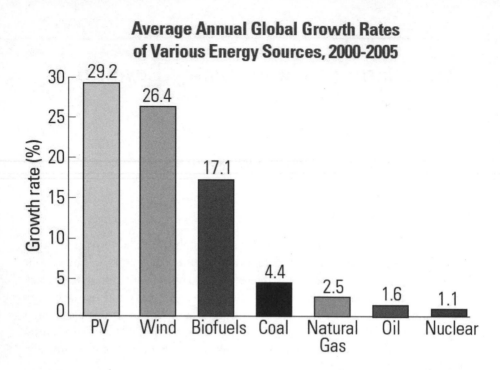

Figure 19.1 Percentage growth by technology sector of contributions to global energy generation from 2001–2005

Source: WI and CAP, 2006.

use on a larger scale, reasons that will become more and more viable as production levels increase.

These new technologies are increasingly attracting global investment from large corporations (such as Mitsubishi and Shell), venture capital and mainstream international banks. From 1995 to 2005, global investment in renewable forms of energy grew from about US$8 billion to over US$39 billion (see Figure 19.2). Current investment in wind power already greatly surpasses investment in nuclear (see Figure 19.3), showing that wind, like other renewables, must be taken seriously as a mainstream source of energy for the future.

Recent developments in the global marketplace demonstrate the potential for rapid growth in the renewables sector:

- Global wind energy generation has more than tripled since 2000, providing enough electricity to power the homes of about 25 million Americans. After lagging behind Europe for more than a decade, the US led the world in wind energy installations in 2005.

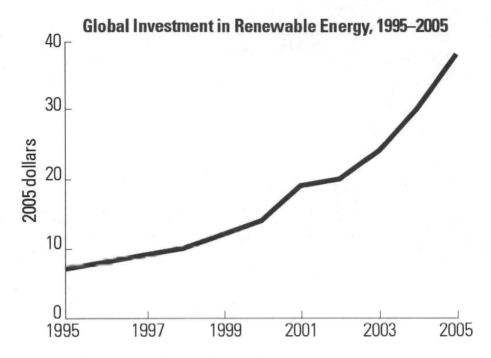

Figure 19.2 Global investment in renewable energy from 1995–2005

Source: WI and CAP, 2006.

- World production of electricity-generating solar cells is expanding rapidly, up 45 per cent in 2005, to six times the 2000 level. The solar cell industry is quickly becoming one of the world's fastest growing and most profitable industries.
- Production of fuel ethanol from crops more than doubled between 2000 and 2005, and biodiesel from vegetable oil and waste expanded nearly four-fold over this period.

European and Asian countries have led the development of most of these technologies over the past decade. The prominent positions that Germany and Spain hold in wind power, for example, and that Japan and Germany enjoy in solar energy, were achieved thanks to strong and enduring policies that their legislatures adopted in the 1990s. These policies created steadily growing markets for renewable energy technologies, fueling the development of robust new manufacturing industries.

The renewable energy boom can also be tracked through the emergence of renewable energy billionaires. In many countries, such as Germany (where the

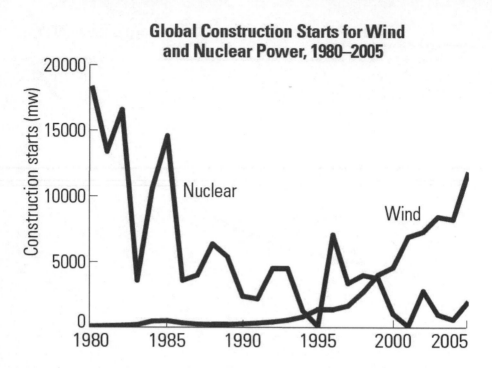

Figure 19.3 Global construction starts for wind and nuclear power from 1980–2005

Source: WI and CAP, 2006.

three richest men made their fortune on wind and solar energy) and China, entrepreneurs have rightly envisioned a rapid expansion of non-fossil energy and have made money in the process. A similar situation occurred in the first two decades of the 20th century during the beginning of the oil age when young entrepreneurs such as John D. Rockefeller made their fortunes investing in the oil business, which then represented only a trivial part of the nation's energy source.

US potential for renewable energy

In contrast those in Europe, US renewable energy policies over the past two decades have been an uneven and ever-changing patchwork of regulations and subsidies. Abrupt changes in direction at both the state and federal levels have deterred investors and led dozens of companies into bankruptcy. Embracing the path of renewable energy is not only an environmental necessity, it also makes good economic sense, allowing both companies and individuals to save money, and generating high-wage jobs in a rapidly growing technological industry.

Renewable resources are sometimes dismissed as serious options because it is argued their growth will be constrained by the underlying resource base. In fact, statistics show that the US has a very large resource base for wind, solar, geothermal and other renewables, and the land area required would be modest (see Figure 19.4). Recent studies show that if wind energy technology were to be fully implemented in only three states, it would generate enough electricity to power the whole nation. Similarly, solar energy fully deployed in seven states could supply *ten times* the nation's energy requirement, and much of this energy could be supplied using rooftop collectors.

If America is to become a world leader in reducing greenhouse gas emissions and achieving a low-carbon economy, it will need world-class energy policies based on a sustained and consistent policy framework at the local, state and national levels. Under the Bush administration, some progress has been observed over the last five years, particularly the proliferation of ambitious energy-efficiency programs at the state level. These efficiency projects are currently concentrated in four main regions: the West Coast, the Southwest, the Upper Midwest and the Northeast; other regions are poised to follow suit.

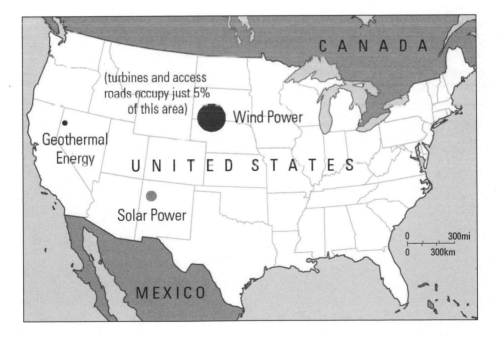

Figure 19.4 Comparative amounts of land area required to produce 30 per cent of US electricity using wind power, solar power and geothermal energy

Source: WI and CAP, 2006.

Conclusions

There are numerous reasons – economic, environmental and security-related – for the US to move rapidly to drastically shift its policies towards the support of renewable energy industries and initiatives. The current situation, in which the US trails both Europe and Asia in the implementation of renewable technology, can be reversed with a consistent and coherent energy policy that embraces renewables through long-term subsidies and the removal of perverse fossil fuel subsidies. This move is the first step on the long journey to the carbon-free economy that the US will inevitably have to adopt for the future, for, if not done soon, the US may not be able to catch up and assume the worldwide leadership in this area to which it aspires. Our recent report with the Center for American Progress (WI and CAP, 2006) describes the steps that the US must take to effect the fundamental transition to a 21st century energy system.

Reference

WI (Worldwatch Institute) and CAP (Center for American Progress), 2006: *American Energy – The Renewable Path to Energy Security* (available at www.americanenergynow. org)

20

Recycling Energy to Reduce Costs and Mitigate Climate Change

Thomas R. Casten

Al Gore's recent movie, *An Inconvenient Truth*, highlighted how climate change is a truth that most of us would like to ignore. Needed, however, is a spotlight on the convenient truth that efficient and effective options exist to reduce greenhouse gas emissions.

Conventional wisdom holds that battling climate change will cost enormous sums of money. Yet, this assertion rests on the questionable assumption that all present generation of heat and power, which accounts for 68 per cent of present fossil carbon emissions, is already economically optimal. Put another way, it assumes that no possible investments to improve energy efficiency can yield a profit.

This standard assumption, however, is wrong. Companies that I have managed – which installed 250 efficient combined-heat-and-power facilities, valued at more than US$2 billion – have generated substantial profits. According to a recent report by the American Council for an Energy Efficient Economy, 84 per cent of all new demand for energy services since 1996 has been met through improvements in efficiency (Laitner et al, 2007). Opportunities for additional efficiency abound, particularly by recycling wasted energy within the industrial sector.

Recycling energy

The manufacturing and electric-power industries, by and large, capture only a small portion of the potential energy in the fuel they burn, and then discard the rest as waste energy. Many cost-effective approaches are available to recycle these waste streams, generating incremental electricity and thermal energy without increasing pollution or burning additional fossil fuel. Recycled energy's unused potential may be society's best-kept secret.

Recycling waste energy can take two approaches. In the first case, power plants are sited at an industrial facility that produces a stream of waste energy, such as gas that is normally flared, hot exhaust or high-pressure gas or steam that must be decompressed back to atmospheric pressure. These plants, known in the literature as 'bottoming cycle cogeneration plants', convert the waste energy streams into electricity. The resulting electricity is typically sold back to the industrial host for use on site, thus avoiding the need for transmission and distribution wires and avoiding the losses associated with transmitting the same power over great distances. In the second case, explained in more detail below, power plants burn fuel to generate electricity and then recycle the inevitable waste heat to replace the supply of thermal energy from a separate boiler. These local power plant facilities convert 33–45 per cent of the fuel's potential energy to electricity, just like their larger centralized brothers. But instead of venting the remaining 55–67 per cent of the energy, these plants recycle the heat in order to supply the host with steam, hot water or process heat. These cogeneration units provide two energy services – heat and power – with one fire, saving money and pollution emissions.

Recycling industrial energy waste

Various industrial waste energy streams can be recycled into useful heat and power. These streams include hot exhaust, low-grade fuels and high-pressure steam and gas. High temperature exhaust can produce steam to drive turbine generators and produce electricity. Hot exhaust is available from coke ovens, glass furnaces, petrochemical processes and steel reheat furnaces. In other cases, presently flared flue gas from blast furnaces, refineries or chemical processes can be burned in boilers to produce steam. All pressurized gases, including steam, have the potential to generate electricity via backpressure (decompression) turbines. Industrial and commercial boiler plants produce high-pressure steam for distribution and then typically reduce pressure at points of use by means of valves. Nearly every college and university campus, as well as most industrial complexes, could produce some fuel-free electricity from such steam-pressure drops. Other opportunities abound. Consider the gas transmission companies that currently expend energy to compress natural gas, but then reduce that pressure with valves to feed local distribution systems. Recycling this discarded energy could supply 6500 megawatts, roughly equivalent to the output of nine coal-fired power plants.

Industrial energy recycling is well proven, with roughly 9900 megawatts in operation in the US. But this is only 10 per cent of the 95,000 megawatts of potential identified in a recent study for the US Environmental Protection Agency (Bailey and Worrell, 2004). Recycling waste energy could have produced 19 per cent of US electricity in 2003, displacing a quarter of the fossil fuel that was burned to generate electricity. In 2003, 22.9 per cent of US electricity was produced with renewable and nuclear energy, and recycling industrial energy would have raised the non-fossil total to 42 per cent.

At a smelter on the southern shore of Lake Michigan, more than 250 individual ovens bake metallurgical coal to produce blast furnace coke – expanded lumps of nearly pure carbon. The energy-recycling plant at this smelter converts the energy in the coke oven exhaust to produce 90,000 kilowatts and 500,000 pounds of low-pressure steam for Mittal's Inland Ispat steel complex. In 2004, this single plant generated more clean power than we estimate was produced by all of the solar collectors throughout the world.[1] The capital cost for the energy-recycling plant was US$165 million, compared with over US$5 billion invested in the world's solar photovoltaic arrays. Each dollar of investment in this energy-recycling plant produced 33 times more clean energy than a dollar invested in solar collectors and also produced 3.6 times more clean power than a dollar invested in wind generation and associated wires. These comparisons are not intended to disparage renewable energy, but to show the relative value of recycled energy.

Mittal Steel enjoys significant economic benefits from recycling wasted energy. Producing the same steam with natural gas and purchasing the same amount of electricity from the grid would have cost more than US$110 million per year at October 2005 prices. This project, therefore, illustrates how energy recycling satisfies both sides of the global warming debate, simultaneously reducing energy costs and CO_2 emissions.

Combined heat and power plants

The second way to recycle energy is to use waste heat from electric generation to provide thermal energy for heating, cooling and industrial processes. In 2003, the US power industry consumed 33 quadrillion British Thermal Units (quads) of raw energy in thermal power plants (excluding renewable energy) to deliver 11 quads of electricity, an average 33 per cent efficiency. Combined heat and power (CHP) plants sited near thermal users can achieve up to 90 per cent overall efficiency and can easily recycle half of the waste energy, doubling the conventional power-system efficiency. The US energy recycling potential is thus roughly 11 quads, or 13 per cent, of total US fossil energy consumption. This potential saving is in addition to the industrial energy-recycling potential noted above.

Roughly 92 per cent of the world's electricity is produced at remote generation plants, which discard, on average, two thirds of their input energy. To recycle the byproduct waste heat, a power plant must be located near thermal energy users because steam and hot water cannot be transmitted long distances without prohibitive losses. CHP plants, sited near thermal users, utilize all of the technologies and fuels used by central generation plants, but produce significantly more useful energy from each unit of fuel. The capacity of a single CHP plant ranges up to 700,000 kilowatts.

The *World Survey of Decentralized Energy for 2005* by the World Alliance for Decentralized Energy (2005) found that 7.5 per cent of worldwide electric generation was provided by CHP plants, but noted a great disparity among countries. The US and Canada generated respectively 7.2 per cent and 9.9 per cent of their power with CHP plants, while some countries generated between 30 per cent and 52 per cent of their power with more efficient CHP plants. Three US states reported no CHP plants, while California and Hawaii produced over 20 per cent of their power using CHP. Differences between countries in CHP use shown in Figure 20.1, as well as differences among US states, reflect local power industry governance. The actual amount of heat recycled using CHP plants is not captured in these macro data, which only report total electric production, not heat recovered and utilized.

The economics of decentralization

While acknowledging the efficiency advantages created by local generation that recycles waste energy, skeptics tend to assume that economies of scale make central generation more cost effective. Indeed, the reported average cost of all new central generation plants built in 2004, including base, intermediate and peak load plants, was US$890 per kilowatt of capacity, which was 25 per cent less than the estimated average cost of new decentralized plants. But this US$890 ignores the capital costs of required additional transmission, distribution and redundant generating capacity for emergencies. Transmission is already in short supply, and it is difficult to gain approval to site new transmission lines. Numerous power interruptions since 2000 have flagged problems with existing transmission systems in the US and Europe, and many developing countries experience daily blackouts as transmission capacity is rationed among users. Satisfying load growth

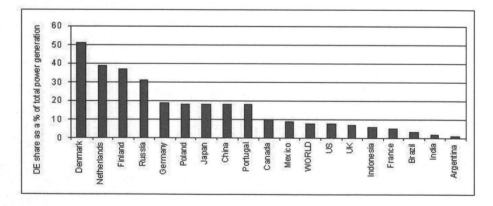

Figure 20.1 Combined heat and power production (or distributed energy – DE) as a percentage of total power, by country

Source: World Alliance for Decentralized Energy, 2005.

with new central generation requires additional investments in transmission and distribution that average US$1,380 per kilowatt of capacity (Little, 2002).

The cost of connecting local generation to the grid seldom exceeds 10 per cent of the cost for transmission and distribution (T&D) from new central generation facilities. Locally generated power flows directly to the user, freeing grid capacity. It should be noted that utility requests for standby rates typically claim much higher costs to connect a single local generator to the grid because these calculations assume that a single local generator will fail at the precise moment of system peak load, requiring the utility to build or dedicate sufficient grid capacity to supply 100 per cent of the user's peak load. Such analysis is of little relevance as any single local plant is likely to be lost in the noise. Policy considerations should focus on the costs of interconnecting multiple local plants inside each distribution system because the simultaneous failure of multiple independent distributed generators is highly unlikely.

Table 20.1 compares the total capital costs of new central and local generation facilities. The third data column shows that total capital costs to remotely generate and deliver one new kilowatt of peak load are 170 per cent of the total capital costs of locally generating the same power. Basically, the economies of scale created by large central plants are overwhelmed by the added transmission and distribution costs.

The fourth data column of Table 20.1 deals with another significant capital-cost difference. Line losses from remote generation to users averaged 9 per cent in the US in 2004, but peak losses are much higher because line losses tend to vary with the square of current flow and with ambient temperature, and are thus much higher during summer peak loads. Peak hour line losses from remote generation plants range from 20–30 per cent, depending on the system and the distance power must travel to users. Boston Edison's last application for a change

Table 20.1 *Capital required to provide an incremental kilowatt of peak load power*

	Generation	Transmission & distribution	Total/kW of new generation	KW per kW load	Costs/kW of new load
Central generation	$890	$1380	$2270	1.44	$3269
Local generation	$1200	$138	$1338	1.07	$1432
Savings (excess) of central versus local generation	$310	($1242)	($1068)	(0.37)	($1837)
Central generation capital as a percentage of local generation capital	74%	1000%	170%	135%	228%

in electric rates that was approved by the Massachusetts regulatory commission claimed losses from generator to consumer of 22 per cent. Using this estimate, one kilowatt of new load capacity will require 1.22 kilowatts of new central generation and distribution capacity. By contrast, net line losses from local generation seldom exceed 2 per cent. If a local plant generates power in excess of site needs, that power will flow backwards, towards central generation plants, reducing line losses.

Achieving system reliability also requires some redundant generation and grid capacity. An electric system composed solely of large central plants must have backup capacity for failure of the largest plant or for failure of the wires transmitting power from that plant to load centers. A recent Carnegie Mellon study found that a system of smaller generation units with 3 per cent to 5 per cent spare capacity would be just as reliable as the current central generation system, which has 18 per cent spare capacity (Zerriffi, 2004). Thus, as multiple distributed local generators come online, the overall need for spare generating capacity will diminish.

Considering all these factors, Table 20.1 shows that more than twice the capital cost is required to serve load growth with central generation as compared to serving the same load with local generation. Put another way, serving one year's US load growth of 14 million kilowatts with central generation will require US$21 billion more capital investment than serving that growth with local generation.

Energy markets are not free

If modern, distributed generation is more efficient and less polluting, requires half of the capital investment, and reduces system vulnerability to weather and terrorism, why do most countries continue to build central generating plants? The key factor seems to be a flaw in conventional thinking about the role of free markets. Most economists simply assume that market economies have optimized the production of goods and services, and that opportunities for additional efficiency do not exist.

Yet, markets work only when several preconditions exist, and the current market for heat and power is not free. One key attribute is the freedom of business entry. Despite some restructuring, many policies continue to block new firms and protect the monopoly position of franchised utilities. For example, it remains illegal in all 50 states for anyone but the utility monopoly to build an electric wire across a public street. You can construct a natural gas pipeline, an Internet wire, or a steam pipe over or under a street, but stringing an electric wire threatens the utility monopoly and will land you in jail. Being able to ship your end product only through the competitor's wires, of course, is a pretty strong barrier to entry and prevents an open market.

Utility regulatory commissions also effectively guarantee the financial return of centralized generation and its associated wires by including these investments in the 'rate base', on which utilities are guaranteed a profit. If sales of power do not materialize in amounts sufficient to provide the assured rate of return, commissioners simply raise rates in order to meet the targeted levels. Local generators, in contrast, enjoy no public guarantees, even though their dispersed plants can recycle the normally wasted heat, increase efficiency, cut pollutants and provide other public benefits. Power recycling entrepreneurs also face the risk that their manufacturer partner will cease or change operations and stop purchasing as much thermal energy, or will stop producing the expected amount of waste energy. In either case, the entrepreneur suffers reduced revenues and might not be able to pay back its investors and lenders.

Free markets also allow the freedom of business exit, or the freedom to fail. Yet, in the electricity business, no public service commission can stand by and allow its local utility to fail. Mistakes simply disappear into the rate base, raising rates for all consumers. As a result, the electricity business lacks the cleansing mechanism that is essential to functioning markets.

Efficient markets also require clear and accurate price signals, which allow both producers and consumers to make optimal choices about their investments and consumption, yet energy prices ignore an array of costs. Health and environmental expenses associated with power-plant pollution, for instance, are paid by taxpayers and healthcare consumers. The government of Ontario, Canada, estimates that the health and environmental costs of electricity from Ontario's coal-fired generation plants total C$120 per megawatt-hour. Yet, power in the province is sold for just C$60 per megawatt-hour, which covers only fuel and capital amortization. Selling power at one-third its full cost (which includes additional operating expenses, overhead and profit) obviously distorts the market and motivates both producers and consumers to make decisions that are suboptimal for society.

Environmental regulations, moreover, tilt the playing field against new power generators, even when they are significantly more efficient than existing plants. Today's weighted average age of US electricity generating plants is about 40 years, even though most plants have only 25-year design lives. The 1976 Clean Air Act 'grandfathered' emission rights to all existing electricity generators on the assumption they would be retired at the end of their planned lives. By contrast, a new plant must lower its emissions to the best control possible at the time it is built, requiring entrepreneurs to spend up to triple the cost of old plants, and then to compete against plants with grandfathered permits and no cleanup requirements. This regulatory approach effectively grants immortality to the old plants, perversely encouraging their owners to extend the lives of old, dirty and inefficient facilities.

Finally, markets do not work properly in the face of perverse incentives. All 50 states regulate electricity with a structure that magnifies the impact of changing electric sales on utility profits. The Regulatory Assistance Project recently found that a 5 per cent drop in sales of kilowatt-hours typically produced a 57 per cent drop in a utility's profits – nearly a 12:1 ratio. This flaw turns utility CEOs into fierce but hidden opponents of all efficiency improvements, including more efficient motors and light bulbs, because, by reducing electricity use, these improvements substantially threaten the profits of utilities. These CEOs may claim publicly to support improvements in efficiency, and they may even craft small efficiency programs advertised with large public relations budgets, but the 12:1 profit-to-sales ratio makes all regulated utilities the sworn enemies of local generation, regardless of its efficiency or societal benefit. Find an argument against local generation and it almost certainly can be traced to a utility author.

As a result of these deeply flawed policies and market distortions, the US electric system is not a free market and is therefore far from economically optimal. Ninety-two per cent of US generation is from plants in remote locations that burn twice as much fossil fuel and emit twice the CO_2 and other pollutants as would be required if local generation plants recycled the inevitable heat byproduct. A remote central plant and its associated T&D also require more than twice the investment per new kilowatt of peak electric load of a local generation plant.

Despite these economic realities, virtually every new power plant has been of the centralized type. There is now, however, strong evidence that alternative approaches can be quite profitable. Over the past 25 years, I have led companies that invested more than US$2 billion in 250 local generation plants in 22 states, Canada and Mexico. The worst of these facilities uses less than half the fuel and emits less than half the CO_2 of the average central generation plant. These energy-recycling plants contribute more than 10,000 megawatts of thermal and electric generating capacity. Every one of the plants saves money for its host and yields an acceptable rate of return to its investors.

These local plants achieve savings and emission reductions without any breakthrough technology by simply recycling normally wasted energy. In fact, the plants use the same technologies and fuels that are used by central plants, they are simply smaller versions, sized to meet the industrial host's requirement for heat or waste energy, doing the two jobs with one fire.

Policy options to encourage recycled energy

Despite the logic and long-term benefits, politicians tend to be nervous about eliminating energy subsidies or pricing power accurately. Those with special interests typically oppose anyone threatening their subsidy. Removing several of the policy barriers to clean energy technologies, however, could be enacted with relatively little political pain. While such small policy changes will not correct all governance problems, they can deliver appreciable benefits to the public and would begin unleashing market forces to improve the world's largest and most important industry.

Five policy changes would move the global power industry towards economic optimality and greenhouse gas emission reductions:

1. Allow local generators to build private wires to a limited number of retail customers, sufficient to transmit excess capacity. Alternatively, require commissions to set variable grid charges based on the distance the power will move and the relative tightness of the existing network. The 'postage stamp' rates employed in most jurisdictions charge all generators the average cost of moving power across the state, obscuring the locational value of generation.
2. Require grid operators to interconnect with backup generators in return for the right to obtain power from those generators during extreme system peaks and emergencies. The US standby generation fleet has a capacity equal to 12 per cent of system peak, but very little of that generation is interconnected with the grid. When the grid is approaching melt down, as happened in the Northeast and Midwest in August of 2003, several times in California, and more recently in France and Italy, interconnected standby generation could help avoid brownouts and blackouts and save lives.
3. Require regulatory commissions to pay local generators for the values their plants provide to the grid, including saved capital costs, saved line losses, reduced pollution and grid voltage support. Commissions rightfully expect local generators to pay for service provided by the grid, but seldom invert the analysis. A recent study conducted at the University of Massachusetts found that each kilowatt of new distributed generation installed in Boston would produce a *net* societal benefit of US\$351 per year, but is instead required to pay US\$114 per year for standby services. This represents a US\$465 penalty per year per kilowatt versus the net benefit to society created (Kosanovic and Ambs, 2005).
4. Make carbon savings from recycled energy eligible for 'green tags' and carbon trading credits. Many electric consumers voluntarily pay a premium for clean electricity but the choices are limited to renewable technologies. Including recycled energy will increase clean energy production and reduce its cost.
5. Base pollution control regulations on how much power was produced rather than how much fuel was used. Such output-based (rather than input-based) standards would more clearly reward the efficient generators and force the wasteful to pay higher costs for their increased pollution.

Conclusions

The stakes for energy efficiency may be much higher than generally realized. President Bush's assertion in 2001 that the US economy could not afford Kyoto may not have considered the vulnerability of the electric grid and other costs of hurricanes intensified by global warming (Ivan in 2004 was a 2500 year storm and was followed by an even more intense Katrina in 2005). Governments seeking to mitigate climate change without rewarding efficiency are increasing local energy prices and could well damage their own economies. Spending US$10.8 trillion to supply global electric load growth over the next 30 years with central generation will greatly worsen CO_2 emissions and will, according to the International Energy Agency, still leave over 1.4 billion people in energy poverty (IEA, 2002). The world would be better off deploying local generation with doubled efficiency, saving US$5 trillion in the process, and then using some of the savings to extend energy services to all people.

There is no reason to settle for current energy inefficiencies: energy recycling is already economically advantageous using existing technology. The best way to improve energy system efficiency is for governments to heed the lessons of economics and to fully expose the power industry to market forces, which would automatically improve economic and energy efficiency. Failing such full deregulation, performance can be improved by eliminating regulatory biases against local generation and by encouraging energy recycling. Once the public sees the benefits, support will grow for more comprehensive changes.

It should be emphasized that there is no need to eliminate existing central generation capacity. A great deal of new local generation is needed to just meet the world's expected electric load growth and retirement of the aging fleet of central plants. Nor is there any reason to weep for the established utilities. Nothing should prevent these organizations from participating in the inevitable (and profitable) new market for decentralized power plants that recycle energy.

Notes

1. At the end of 2004, 650 megawatts of solar collectors were installed worldwide, which, at an annual estimated 8 per cent load factor, would have produced 455,520 MWh (650*8760 hours*0.08). The 90 MW coke oven exhaust recycling plant produced 503,000 MWh in 2004, equal to an 8 per cent load factor of all solar collectors.

References

Bailey, O. and E. Worrell, 2004: *A Preliminary Inventory of the Potential for Electricity Generation*, Lawrence Berkeley National Laboratory, Berkeley, CA

IEA (International Energy Agency), 2002: *World Energy Outlook 3*, IEA, Paris

Kosanovic, D., and L. Ambs, 2005: *The Influence of Distributed Energy Resources on the Hourly Clearing Price of Electricity in a Restructured Market*, ACEEE Summer Study on Energy Efficiency in Industry, ACEEE, Washington DC

Laitner, J. A., K. Ehrhardt-Martinez and W. R. Prindle, 2007: *The American Energy Efficiency Market*, Energy Efficiency Finance Forum, ACEEE, Washington DC

Little, A. D., 2002: *Preliminary Assessment of Battery Energy Storage and Fuel Cell Systems in Building Publications*, National Energy Technology Laboratory, Pittsburgh, PA

World Alliance for Decentralized Energy, 2005: World survey of decentralized energy, www.localpower.org, accessed 4 May 2007

Zerriffi, H., 2004: *Electric Power Systems Under Stress: An Evaluation of Centralized Vs. Distributed Systems Architectures*, PhD thesis, Carnegie Mellon University, Pittsburgh, PA

21

Addressing Climate Change:
Religious Perspectives and Initiatives

Denis Hayes and panelists

Although the media are finally beginning to pay attention to climate change, this epoch-defining issue *never* ranks among the top ten news stories. Indeed, global warming is not yet judged by most news editors to warrant as much attention as the foibles of errant starlets and heiresses. Worse, most climate stories focus on the terrifying consequences likely to occur some decades hence when two lines cross on a graph, or they recount 'he said-she said' posturing by national politicians, including some who could use a remedial junior high school science course. This all makes for good theater and perhaps helps to sell newspapers. However, it does not help awaken American consumers and voters to their civic responsibilities.

A new chorus, however, is emerging. It is made up of the inner voices, generated by deeply held beliefs about the nature of humans and the responsibilities attendant on citizenship. In its simplest form, it is well represented by one of Benjamin Franklin's epigrams: 'It has been my opinion that he who receives an Estate from his ancestors is under some kind of obligation to transmit the same to their posterity'.

Among the strongest of these new voices are those who view the issue in moral terms. Not all of these moralists subscribe to organized religions. Some anchor their ethical concerns in secular reasoning. However, many of the most influential leaders are devout believers in various religious traditions.

In America, engagement by the religious community is often a sign that a social tipping point is approaching. The US is perhaps the most religious of the industrialized nations, and its religious leaders have often played crucial roles in successful social movements: the movement against slavery; the peace movement; the movement for justice in South Africa; the civil rights movement; the environmental movement. When such issues are discussed from the pulpit in moral terms, congregations begin to assign them a higher priority.

Political inertia is often the reflection of the resistance of vested economic interests to change. But, in American politics, morality can trump economics.

This chapter provides a dais for some leading voices in the religious community to summarize what they see happening (and are making happen) to address climate change. It shows how those with a moral perspective are finding ways to both lead and push the world toward a more respectful relationship with the environment.

An updated listing of a number of the official statements by religious groups, some of which are referred to by these authors, is posted at www.climate.org. The biographies of the contributing authors appear in the Appendix.

A Jewish response to climate change (Rabbi Warren G. Stone)

An ancient Jewish midrash (expository treatise) teaches that when God took Adam around the Garden of Eden and showed him its magnificence and splendor, God spoke to him saying, 'If you destroy it, there is no one else besides you!'.

Those words ring mightily today, for the very future of life as we know it is at stake. The destruction that climate change is wreaking on our fragile, sacred Earth has become the most profound religious issue of our times. Like Adam, we have been warned and cannot plead ignorance; like Adam, will we fail to heed God's words?

Who is responsible for responding to the challenge of global climate change? We tend to think that it is the scientist, the statesman and the environmentalist upon whom this responsibility lies. But climate change is an urgent moral and spiritual issue for all peoples of our world. We are witnessing its impact right now, and we can foresee the havoc it will wreak on the health and survival of future generations. The future will bring environmental refugees in numbers unknown in previous ages. As a result of climate change and habitat destruction, a myriad of species now faces a silent genocide.

As a Rabbi and religious leader, I am concerned about our common future, the quality of life for our families and the threatened species of our world, including our own. I join fellow religious leaders in that concern. But it is not enough to care about climate change, forest devastation and environmental threats to clean water, air and seas. It is incumbent upon every religious leader, religious institution and person of faith to serve as a beacon to our communities, illustrating by our actions and example our spiritual commitment to our Earth and its threatened and limited resources.

In a world where matters of faith seem so often and so tragically to divide us, there is no issue that aligns us more deeply than our shared dependence upon and sacred responsibility to this tiny planet, enfolded within its fragile atmosphere, spinning in the vastness of time and space. I experienced this shared conviction most profoundly, when, in 1997, I served as the Jewish NGO representative at the United Nations climate talks in Kyoto, Japan. I met with Catholic, Protestant, Muslim, Hindu and Buddhist leaders from around the world. We spoke at Kyoto's largest Buddhist Temple, and all concurred that our human actions, our sins, have damaged the environment. Each speaking from the voice of his or her own authentic spiritual tradition, we affirmed our religious responsibility to act. Amidst Buddhist chanting, I blew the shofar, a ram's horn, the blast of sound that has been Judaism's ancient call to action since the days we wandered, searching for our way, in the desert.

I carried this profound experience back to my own country and my own community. Here, too, I found that faith traditions can readily unite on issues of climate change. Working for many years with the National Partnership on Religion and the Environment, I have joined interfaith leaders to lobby on Capitol Hill and to meet with White House staff. Political leaders are eager to hear our religious point of view. Statements by Catholic bishops, Protestant leaders, rabbis and tribal leaders have symbolic power and carry political weight. Formal resolutions affirmed by hundreds of thousands of persons of faith help embolden our legislators to act. In 2006, religious leaders stood with sympathetic legislators on the US Capitol's steps, raising our voices to stop the drilling in the Arctic Wildlife Refuge. The opportunity to be heard is greater than in previous decades, and we have a prophetic responsibility to seize it. Bold initiatives are needed – and needed now – to protect species, to create incentives for the development of alternative energies, to protect endangered coastal areas and to mitigate our dependence on fossil fuels.

Of course, our collective, interfaith efforts gather their strength from the work each of us does within our own particular communities. As chair of the Environmental Committee of the Central Conference of American Rabbis, I have joined with many committed colleagues to use our faith tradition to increase awareness and encourage action in response to climate change and other environmental challenges. We have passed national resolutions on climate change and energy policy and have established environmentally conscious guidelines for our myriad congregations around the country. For example, we recently celebrated Chanukah, the Jewish holiday of light, renewal and commemoration of bold action that honors one's faith; during the holiday, we mounted a very successful national campaign – 'Let There Be (Renewable) Light! – or How Many Jews Does it Take to Change a Light Bulb?'. Thousands of congregations encouraged their members to install compact fluorescent light bulbs in their synagogues and homes and to add to their holiday ritual a ceremony that calls this generation to environmental action, in response to the moral imperatives of our own times.

I believe that our religious voice must be strongest closest to home, manifest in how we daily live. The congregation I serve, Temple Emanuel of the Greater Washington area, has worked on greening its agenda for 18 years. We believe that local action by religious communities can have a national and international impact. The congregation I serve has installed solar panels on the roof for our eternal light, added wind power from a regional collective, made use of energy efficient zoning, lighting and office equipment, and, in rebuilding, made use of passive solar throughout the building. We planted a sustainable garden to meet our annual ritual needs, growing grapes, horseradish and indoor olive and pomegranate trees. We regularly schedule environmental Shabbats and other opportunities for learning with our state representative and national leaders. We sell compact fluorescent bulbs and have information about climate change on our coffee tables. We have become an EPA energy star community and one of the nation's first 'zero carbon footprint' communities by supporting Carbonfund.org and their alternative energy investments. Our web page, www.Templeemanuelmd.org, includes our Green Shalom action guide, which is designed to educate and spur further community involvement and environmental action in our own homes and community. This community focus has borne fruit, with a good number of our young people choosing science, media, religion and public policy arenas that deal directly with environmental issues.

There is so much that each of us can and must do, within our own homes, congregations and communities, and beyond, as we work together, in common cause, to preserve and sanctify life. Religious communities have a crucial moral role in affirming the profound need to engage on the issue of climate change.

As Rabbi Tarphon of the second century reminds us: 'It is not your duty to finish all the work, but neither are you at liberty to desist from it'. May it be that years hence, our children and our children's children will look back with appreciation to this moment when we heeded one of the great moral imperatives of our time. May they know that we had the vision and the strength to fulfill our sacred obligation to preserve and protect the Earth in all of its majesty, this garden with which we have been entrusted, for those who will follow.

A Muslim perspective (Khalid Shaukat)

According to Islam, Man is the vice-regent on Earth of the supreme creator. As such, he is mandated to build civilization, but at the same time is held responsible for protecting the environment. Muslims, in particular, are duty-bound to make every effort to achieve sustainable development for the care of the environment and for the general well-being of everybody on this planet. The environment is a gift from God that individuals and communities must take care of in order to ensure the rights of every human being to a clean and sound environment.

The Qu'ran and the Hadith (sayings of the Prophet) are rich in proverbs and precepts that speak to the Almighty's design for creation and humanity's responsibility for preserving it. Many of the verses bear a striking resemblance to passages in the Bible, portraying a similar vision of Creation. Examples are: Q.

Ch. 64: v.3 'He has created the heavens and the earth in just proportions, and has given you shape, and made your shapes beautiful'; Q. Ch. 17: v.44 'The seven heavens and the earth and all therein declare His glory: there is not a thing but celebrates His praise'. These verses show that the Almighty created the world in a proportioned way that allows humans to live harmoniously and safely.

The interconnected aspects of the environmental crisis, including global warming, resource depletion, species extinction, pollution, population explosion and over-consumption, have been well documented. It is now clear that these environmental problems are both global in scope and local in impact. Islam teaches us that we should be cautious and on-guard against damages from pollution and global warming. From an Islamic point of view, protecting the environment and avoiding damaging climate change requires deepening awareness of the elements that affect life on our planet, ensuring the continuation of life by avoiding pollution, and using the power of religion to channel human activity into these productive areas. All these responses will be required in order to confront the challenge of climate change in a moral and responsible manner.

A Mormon perspective (Joseph Cannon)

The Mormon Church is a lay-leader church; it does not yet have an official position on climate change. Those of my faith believe that the Scriptures call us to fulfill our obligations to fellow man and to the environment. In writing his recent book, entitled *The Creation*, E. O. Wilson indicated that his purpose was to involve religious people in environmental issues. Our interpretation of the scriptures is that we have a duty to take care of the Earth; we do not believe there is a basis in the scriptures for taking the view that the end is coming so our stewardship responsibilities can be ignored.

Unlike other Christian religions, Mormons have modern-day Scriptures in addition to those from antiquity. One of the passages is particularly relevant, indicating that Man can make use of the environment, but with judgment, not going to excess, and avoiding extortion of it (i.e., not twisting resources from the Earth).

Mormon history also helps to explain our relationship with the environment. Mormons literally left the US when they moved west to Utah, which at the time was under the control of Mexico. The Salt Lake area was a barren place that the newly arrived Mormons worked to improve, as they had done to the region of Illinois from which they had come.

It is often not realized that more Mormons live outside North America than inside it. In the years that our young people serve overseas as missionaries, they come to better understand the world and its condition, and they often return with an environmental focus, recognizing that environmental degradation is both a social and a moral problem. This understanding is long lasting, and as a result, many in the Church are committed to the environment and their responsibilities of stewardship.

A Catholic perspective (Walt Grazer)

While some religious communities tend not to make public comments, the Catholic community tends to be more outspoken. Both within the Catholic community and operating through ecumenical and interfaith activities, the Church is frequently speaking out regarding the moral and ethical aspects of matters affecting society.

In preparing the statement that was eventually adopted by the US Catholic Bishops (see www.usccb.org/sdwp/international/globalclimate.htm), we recognized that we are not scientists, that instead we need to use science as a source of wisdom. In evaluating the significance of the scientific findings that have emerged, it is clear to us that prudence is the appropriate response to the increasing pace of change that science is finding and projecting. We see climate change as raising the 'Common Good' issue, that abuse of the environment is thus abuse of our fellow human beings and their best interests. In addition, the near permanence of the consequences and their irreversibility will affect future generations, raising significant issues of intergenerational equity, social justice, and, indeed, the place of humans in the environment. Fundamentally, therefore, climate change and issues relating to sustainability generally are being seen as raising two interconnected moral issues that we, indeed, must be responsive to: first, the increasing capability of Man to alter creation and the environment; and second, the calling to promote social good by being watchdogs for the poor, both in the US and internationally.

To deal with climate change, the Catholic community is endeavoring to have the issue integrated into everyone's life and thinking through their local parish. We are encouraging mobilization for advocacy at the local level, doing so by creating a small grants program. With its broad international presence, the Catholic bishops are increasingly engaging on these issues with their colleagues across the global community and especially in Latin America. Among other activities, a joint policy framework has been developed, entitled 'Looking Forward: Catholic Coalition on Climate Change', which is part of the Catholic effort in cooperation with the National Religious Partnership for the Environment. With 70 million members in the US and more churches than post offices, while the Catholic community can potentially be very important in effecting change, there is a lot more outreach and education to be done.

Green leadership in the religious community
(Rev. Sally Bingham)

The Regeneration Project (TRP) is a non-profit working to deepen the connection between ecology and faith. I serve as TRP's executive director. Our immediate and primary focus is on encouraging a 'religious response to global warming' through our Interfaith Power and Light Campaign. We ask our member congregations to serve as examples to their communities and congregants by practicing energy efficiency and conservation in their facilities. Where possible, we encourage our members to put solar collectors on the roofs of their facilities. We have numerous examples of congregations that have done this; by doing so, they are acting to save God's creation and are saving money too. For example, in Michigan, Father Charles Morris gets his electricity from a small solar array and a wind turbine that sit on the roof of his rectory. When the mid-Atlantic suffered through a week long blackout, St Elizabeth's was giving hot meals, showers and battery recharge to the neighborhood; the rectory was serving literally as a beacon of light in the otherwise dark city of Wyandotte, Michigan. Congregations have forever served as homes for the homeless, havens for refugees and food sanctuaries to the hungry. Through the Interfaith Power and Light movement, they will now serve as an energy resource that is clean and green.

At TRP we believe that climate change is the most important moral issue of our time. It will define what it means to be human today. We hear what the scientists are saying and we give them the honor of being today's prophets. The scientists are telling us that we have a potential catastrophic situation on the horizon and I believe them. How we respond will determine our children's future. We can begin to solve the climate problem or leave it to them, which may well be too late to take actions that would avoid catastrophic consequences for their environment and society.

Our call to serve one another is as strong as the call to love one another. We are asked to pay particular attention to the poor. Therefore, rising seas, crop disruption and more severe storms that harm the poor first are things we need to prevent. We must do our best to secure a future for every neighbor whether they are human, non-human or the next generation. Whatever we can do today to be good stewards of Creation will fulfill the commandment to 'love your neighbor as yourself'.

History proves that once the moral voice of religion enters the dialogue, things begin to change. Society cannot solve social dilemmas without involvement from the faith community. We have been the leading factor in cultural change in the past. Once the immorality of the slave trade was brought to the table by the religious voice, things began to change. The civil rights movement was led by a religious man who quoted from the Bible every time he spoke about injustice. We, the religious community, will once again be the voice that changes history.

We will show by example that the economy won't suffer, in fact, it will grow with new technologies, which will be on display in our congregations. And our congregations will also save money, which can be spent on responsibilities and new opportunities such as clean renewable energy.

Presbyterians move toward climate neutrality (Pam McVety)

At its General Assembly during the summer of 2006, the Presbyterian Church USA passed a resolution asking its 2.4 million members to each do their part to combat climate change impacts by going carbon neutral (see www.climate.org/topics/climate/presbyterian_climate_neutral.shtml). Carbon neutrality requires that energy use that releases CO_2 into the atmosphere be reduced and that carbon offsets be purchased to compensate for those CO_2 (or other greenhouse gas) emissions that could not be eliminated.

This appears to be the first time that a major religious denomination in any nation has called on each of its members to bear witness to their faith by becoming carbon neutral. Presbyterians believe that devotion to God and to the Word requires care for His Creation and that excessive energy usage is casting a shadow over all of creation and doing harm that is widespread and grave. It is therefore a test of Christian faith to recognize sins against Creation and make amends. Justice must be sought for Creation in everyday actions; reducing energy use is one important way.

For only pennies a day, each of us can take the following three simple steps to become carbon neutral:

- Calculate your carbon emissions. This can easily be done using one of many carbon calculators available on the Internet.
- Reduce your carbon emissions as much as possible by using less energy.
- Offset your remaining carbon emissions, specifically those that come from remaining electric usage and travel by car or planes, by purchasing carbon offsets.

As simple as these three steps are, their effects would be dramatic if millions stepped forward today to reduce their carbon emissions. Presbyterians and others who take these three simple steps are looking to the future and have positioned themselves to be leaders in the fight against climate change.

Evangelical actions to build climate protection into overseas ministry (Jo Anne Lyon)

World Hope International is a faith-based relief and development organization currently working in 30 countries to alleviate suffering and injustice through education, enterprise and community health. To the hungry, we offer life. To the forgotten, we give opportunity. To the outcast, we foster dignity. To the desperate, we bring hope. Our programs include Hope Enterprise – helping the poorest families learn new skills, receive small-business loans and launch small business ventures; Hope for Children – the child sponsorship arm; Community Health – providing health care services and education to developing countries by allowing communities to take charge of their own health; and Hope Corps, which facilitates short-term outreach opportunities for professionals, college students, families and individuals.

In most of the countries in which we operate, climate change presents a real threat to the well-being of the population, especially the poor. The adverse effects of climate change are likely to mount with time, so the very young and those yet to be born are likely most at risk. Recognizing this, I was a founding member of the Evangelical Environmental Network and served recently as spokesperson of the Evangelical Climate Initiative. In World Hope International's programs we hope to incorporate climate change considerations into our planning. We are heartened by efforts described earlier at the Washington Summit such as the International Leadership Alliance for Climate Stabilization and look forward to working with this effort and other similar climate protection initiatives to better the lives of those we seek to empower.

Concluding thought

What emerges from this testimony of broad, diverse, religious communities is a sense that religious organizations are becoming more and more engaged in the quest to halt global warming. It is difficult to exaggerate the importance of that development. It is impossible to effectively address climate change without confronting disparities in wealth, power, lifestyles and technologies. Individually and collectively, our choices will profoundly affect the options available to our children and grandchildren.

Technological and economic decisions that seemed rational 50 years ago now appear ethically irresponsible. Every major religious tradition carries an obligation of stewardship. It is appropriate, indeed it is essential, that religious leaders help guide us back toward a more sustainable future.

22

Climate Solutions on Today's Campuses: How Today's Students Must Drive a Modern Industrial Revolution

Dan Worth

The more than 4000 public and private four-year colleges and universities in the US are one of the least-often-mentioned byproducts of three centuries of successful US and global industry.[1] They have grown from humble beginnings to a powerful network of research centers, investment pools, and, in some cases, small cities, that collectively housed, fed, educated and trained more than 20 million students last year alone, while employing millions of university staff. Over the last 50 years, the percentage of the US population with a bachelor's degree increased five-fold. Today, nearly one in every four people in the US has a college degree and more than half have attended some college. The growth of the US university system over the past half century has greatly expanded the scope of the financial, intellectual and human resources that must be harnessed, but also gives an indication that there is historical precedent for rapidly changing the system.

Indeed, the breadth and depth of the current climate crisis require that today's 18–25 year olds oversee a dramatic national transformation to a low-carbon economy – locking in 70–90 per cent reductions in greenhouse gas emissions by the time they retire. History has shown that motivated students can and have organized and catalyzed national social movements – from civil rights, to Viet Nam, to the environmental movement, to fair trade, to anti-Apartheid campaigns – becoming societal change agents both before and after graduation. Energy Action, a diverse coalition of student and youth groups that have come together to launch the Campus Climate Challenge, are building on this history and current incarnation of student activism.

Responding to the current climate crisis is such a difficult and complex task that it will require today's students to go beyond their traditional roles as activists and social and political engineers. Today's students must not only *stop* carbon-intensive projects, but also *start* a modern industrial revolution that can support the demand for goods and services of a projected population in 2050 of 420 million in the US and 9.5 billion around the world. Armed with access to nearly open-source data and the academic freedoms won by students in the 1960s and 1970s, today's young leaders can provide the millions of hours of free and low-cost consulting work desperately needed to catalyze aggressive climate solutions. As described below, the National Association of Environmental Law Societies (NAELS), Harvard's Green Campus Initiative, Arizona State University's School of Sustainability, and CU Law's Energy and Environment Security Initiative (EESI) are all, along with other groups, started on this endeavor.

Historic context: University roots run deep

From 1946–1991, in constant dollars, the total budgets of colleges and universities increased by 20 times (see Box 22.1). Over that same period, the number of annual degrees awarded increased nine-fold, physical plant size increased by a factor of six, and full-time faculty compensation doubled. The Institute of Education Science reports that universities now receive more than US$36 billion in on-budget support for post-secondary education, more than US$30 billion of it for research and research institutions. Campus research has become big business.

This increased spending has led to a dramatic increase in the number of US graduates. From 1950–2007, the percentage of the population with a bachelor's degree jumped from more than 5 per cent to more than 25 per cent. This shift, combined with a doubling of population, has increased the number of college graduates in this country from 7.5 million to 75 million. Today, more than 50 per cent of Americans age 25 and up have attended some college.[2]

As they have expanded, US universities have also become major economic players. In 1999–2000 alone, public degree-granting institutions spent nearly US$238 billion.[3]Universities are also part of an enormous education sector, which occupies 10 billion square feet of space in 386,000 buildings and uses 820 trillion BTUs a year at an estimated cost of close to US$15 billion. As investors, 746 colleges and universities have combined endowment assets of more than US$298 billion; 56 of these institutions have endowment assets of over US$1 billion, and 334 other schools have endowments of over US$100 million.[4]

Taking action on energy: Stepping up to the challenge and driving a shift in power

The sit-ins were the main dynamo that powered the white movement, galvanizing the little nodes of opposition that had been forming in New York City, in the Boston and San Francisco Bay areas, in Chicago's Hyde Park, in Ann Arbor and

Box 22.1 Growth of the American education enterprise

1940: Federal funding for R&D at US$74 million (agriculture 40 per cent).

1946–1980s: Federal income formed 5–15 per cent of general academic revenues.

1950-2007: Percentage of Americans with high school degree jumped from 50 to 90 per cent.

Percentage with a bachelor degree jumped from 5 per cent to more than 25 per cent. US population doubled, from about 150 million to about 300 million.

1946–1991: In constant dollars college and university budgets increased by factor of 20. Physical plants increased by factor of 6. Average faculty compensation increased by factor of 2.5. Annual number of degrees increased factor of 9.

1951–1961: National Science Foundation budget rose from US$100,000 to US$100 million.

1961: 85 per cent of US$100 million went to universities and university research institutes.

1954–1997: Universities share of total federal expenditures for R&D rose from 5–22 per cent.

1968: 10 universities got 28 per cent of federal obligations for R&D.

1990: 10 universities got 24 per cent; 50 universities got 64 per cent.

1997: 50 largest recipients currently get US$60–500 million.

1997: 95 per cent of federal R&D goes to 10 per cent of four-year colleges/ universities.

Sources: Lewontin (1997); http://nces.ed.gov/programs/digest/d02/tables/dt343.asp; dt346.asp; dt345.asp; population figures from wikipedia, http://en.wikipedia.org/wiki/United_States.

Madison – wherever the booming universities, thick with students... Without the civil rights movement... [y]outh culture might have remained... the transitional subculture of the young... had it not been for the revolt of black youth, disrupting the American celebration in ways no one had imagined possible. (Todd Gitlin)

You know, you see these bums, you know, blowin' up the campuses. Listen, the boys that are on the college campuses today are the luckiest people in the world, going to the greatest universities, and here they are, burnin' up the books, I mean, stormin' around about this issue, I mean, you name it – get rid of the war, there'll be another one. (Richard Nixon, *The New York Times*, 2 May 1970)

From the beginning of World War II to 1960, American colleges and universities were uncharacteristically calm and disruptions were rare. By the late 1950s, however, a growing Civil Rights Movement began to spark campus activity. In February 1960, four African-American students from North Carolina Agricultural and Technical College sat in at a segregated lunch counter in Greensboro, North Carolina. These sit-ins and other civil rights activities spread, arousing the nation's consciousness and leading many students to take nonviolent direct action to express their support for civil rights (Carnegie Corporation, 1970).

A decade later, this activity had grown to encompass the peace and environmental movements as well. On 30 April 1970, President Nixon announced that American and South Vietnamese forces were moving against enemy sanctuaries in Cambodia. From 30 April–5 May, 20 new student strikes began each day, culminating with the infamous strike at Kent State where 4 students were killed. From 5–10 May, students launched 100 or more strikes each day. By May 10, 448 campuses were either still affected by some sort of strike or completely closed down. By the end of May, nearly one third of the 2500 US colleges and universities had experienced protest activity (Carnegie Corporation, 1970).

Since then, students have adapted this method of campus activism to address a large array of social issues, mounting successful campaigns to push this country towards increased guarantees of civil and human rights, environmental protection and an end to Apartheid and sweatshop labor. These campaigns have changed the practices of campuses, businesses and governments at the city, state, federal and global levels, and have empowered a new generation of rebellious, energetic, national and global leaders.

More recently, the leading student, youth and environmental groups from the US and Canada have come together to form Energy Action, a diverse, inspiring coalition dedicated to forcing this generation to address the impending climate crisis. In 2005, the Energy Action coalition launched its first project – the Campus Climate Challenge. The Challenge leverages the power of young people to organize on college campuses and high schools across Canada and the US to win 100 per cent clean energy policies at their schools. The Challenge is growing a generation-wide movement to stop global warming, by reducing the pollution from our high schools and colleges down to zero, and leading our society to a clean energy future.

In 2007, during the Climate Challenge's Week of Action, coalition groups flexed their collective muscles, organizing 50,000 students on 587 campuses in 49 states and 8 Canadian provinces and territories.[5] Students and campuses were also a central part of Step It Up,[6] a national mobilization with more than 1400 local actions from the most iconic places in the US calling for an 80 per cent reduction in greenhouse gas emissions by 2050 (see Table 22.1).

There is also evidence that today's youth are willing to follow in the footsteps of their more radical activist predecessors to engage in nonviolent, direct action. In

Table 22.1 *Energy Action's week of action by the numbers*

Number	Action
50,000	Students and youth involved in Climate Week activities worldwide
587	Campuses that took action
49 of 50	US states where actions took place
8 of 12	Canadian provinces and territories where actions took place
30	Organizations that provided direct support and outreach for the actions
71	Print, television, radio and online media hits reported
14	National media hits: Bloomberg, Washington Post, USA Today, The Associated Press, The Huffington Post

March 2007, several student activists joined local parents to sit in at the Governor of West Virginia's office to protest the siting of a new coal plant near Marsh Fork Elementary School. The result:

> *[E]leven parents, community leaders and student activists were arrested today while sitting in at the office of West Virginia Governor Joe Mancin. Their sit-in was spurred by a recent decision by the State Mine Board to approve a second coal silo near Marsh Fork Elementary School. Protesters were treated roughly and dragged through puddles of mud. About 40 protesters remain in the governor's office. Marsh Fork Elementary located near Sundial, WV currently sits 225 feet from a coal silo. Residents say Governor Joe Manchin is shirking his responsibility for the health and safety of the students.*[7]

In an example of how the Internet has transformed modern activism, a clip of students being dragged out of the Governor's office was posted on Youtube the following day.[8]

In October 2007, Energy Action will continue its evolution by bringing together 3000 students and youth in Washington DC to participate in Power Shift '07 – a launching point for the youth climate movement to take center stage. Attendees will meet with their representatives to try to influence Congress to pass a plan to cut CO_2 emissions. Powershift also hopes to strengthen and diversify the grassroots climate movement to push for national and local change.[9]

How climate-negative campuses will drive a modern industrial revolution

In the 1960s and 1970s, as undergraduates and youths were protesting and striking on campuses, graduate students were inventing whole new fields of study and pushing for increased academic freedoms. These graduate students taught the first seminars in African American studies, Latin American Studies and Women's Studies, expanded the university curriculum, and won future generations the freedom to supplement traditional learning with independent studies, directed research projects, internships and externships. Through these new freedoms, these fields of study have grown from small graduate lectures to mainstays on most of today's campuses, educating and training millions. Graduate students of 40 years ago are now established senior professionals.

More recently, the computer and Internet breakthroughs of the 1980s and 1990s have given students access to nearly open source information. In the modern Age of Data, these young minds will have a better view – a Google Earth aerial, if you will – of the enormous physical and social systems they are trying to change. By collecting, combining and crunching these data, today's college students can help create, sell and then implement a sophisticated, affordable, equitable vision of what their campuses, cities, states and nations should/could look like in 2012, 2020, 2030, 2050 and 2100.

Campus Climate Neutral

Over the past few years, today's law, engineering, design and business students have launched climate neutral and campus greening projects across the country.[10] Leading the way, NAELS launched Campus Climate Neutral (CCN) in 2004. CCN is a grassroots campaign to leverage the country's graduate student resources to pursue aggressive, for-credit, greenhouse gas reduction efforts on university campuses and in surrounding municipalities and counties. Through CCN projects, graduate students aim to help educate and connect the next generation of world leaders, training them and mobilizing them – across disciplines and political affiliations – in support of cost-effective, long-term climate solutions.

The model CCN project was launched in 2005 at the University of California Santa Barbara's Donald Bren School of Environmental Science and Management. Five students worked under climate expert and leading social scientist Oran Young. The students each received 12 credits for their year-long research project and delivered a final report, *Changing the Campus Climate: Campus Climate Neutral at UC – Santa Barbara*, in lieu of their senior thesis.[11] The student report found that the school could meet the California governor's 2020 climate targets and save several million dollars in the process, and it now serves as a national model for other campuses and students.

Most importantly, CCN showed the strategic benefit of using graduate students and collaborative research as an advocacy model. The project received glowing reviews from a diverse group of campus leaders as well as: Gus Speth, Dean of Yale's School of Forestry and the Environment; Mary Nichols, Director of the UCLA Center for the Environment; and UCSB Chancellor Henry Yang. NAELS is now pushing for 'climate negative' campuses that reduce their emissions, help their neighbors and cities to do the same, and invest human and financial capital towards further reductions around the globe.

National neutrality: American College & University Presidents Climate Commitment

A growing movement of international, national, regional, state and individual campuses and the champions who are driving change at these institutions are transforming their socially and physically complex campuses into climate neutral models of sustainability. Leading these efforts is the recently launched American College & University Presidents Climate Commitment (ACUPCC), a commitment by some 325 American colleges and universities who have pledged to eliminate their campuses' greenhouse gas emissions over time by:

- completing an emissions inventory;
- within two years, setting a target date and interim milestones for becoming climate neutral;
- taking immediate steps to reduce greenhouse gas emissions by choosing from a list of short-term actions;
- integrating sustainability into the curriculum and making it part of the educational experience;
- making the action plan, inventory and progress reports publicly available.[12]

Crimson & Platinum

Spurred by increased demand for climate and sustainability courses and offerings, campuses are dedicating significant funds to cross-campus efforts to create more sustainable institutions. One of the leading campuses pushing towards sustainability is Harvard University and its Harvard Green Campus Initiative (HGCI) — a cross-discipline center 'working to engage the Harvard community in becoming a learning organization and living laboratory dedicated to the pursuit of campus environmental sustainability'.[13]

The HGCI is run by Leith Sharp, a visionary who has been working in the field for more than a decade. After working in Australia on campus sustainability initiatives, Sharp wrote a paper on campus sustainability in 1999, *From Little Victories to Systematic Change*, which is a 'must read' for anyone working on campus sustainability and climate action on today's campuses.[14]

Sharp now runs the HGCI out of Harvard's historic Blackstone building in Cambridge, MA. The building was recently given a Platinum rating by Leadership in Energy and Environmental Design (LEED™). The project is not only the highest-rated historic renovation project to date, but is also the third highest scoring project ever in the country. According to Sharp:

the building was designed using an integrated design process which is why we came out of it at no added cost. You can certainly spend more on green buildings, but it is essential to understand that it is possible to minimize and even mitigate these additional costs using an integrated design approach, effective energy modeling, well-written specifications, a dedicated design team, and a strong client leader.

The HGCI also now uses the building as a learning tool, and Sharp declares that:

Students use the building and the site for class projects. Various faculty from the GSD [Graduate School of Design] and FAS [Faculty of Arts and Sciences] have hooked up student tours and projects using the innovations we've got here – geothermal, bioswale, energy performance issues. So it's become a really great teaching tool for the university.

Sending out an SOS: ASU's School of Sustainability

Elsewhere, campuses are developing entirely new programs to teach the new field of sustainability studies. Early in 2007, the largest campus sustainability gathering to date brought together leaders from around the country in Tempe, AZ to both catalyze the efforts of the ACUPCC and to launch Arizona State University's (ASU) revolutionary School of Sustainability (SOS).[15] SOS runs undergraduate and graduate programs to prepare students to address the complex, interdisciplinary challenges of building a sustainable future. The school and its research arm form the core of ASU's Global Institute of Sustainability.[16] As ASU sustainability guru, James Buizer, puts it, 'This is our way to make sustainability a basic tenet of everything ASU does. It has been a transformational exercise'.

What's law got to do with it?

Finally, individual graduate programs are stepping up to the challenge – training future leaders in the focused disciplinary (and related multidisciplinary) skills that they need to solve the current climate crisis. As part of the Energy and Environmental Security Initiative (EESI) at the University of Colorado in Boulder, Kevin Doran and visionary Professor Lakshman Guruswamy are leading law students on an interdisciplinary mission to use innovative legal and policy solutions to address climate change and energy security. Kevin explains:

What we do is help students see the impact of law on all the areas where progress is needed. Whether you're talking about basic science, applied R&D, market development and so forth, law either expands or contracts the universe of possibilities. Our students learn that good legal solutions can't be devised in the abstract. They need to be informed by the very environments and processes they're meant to deal with.

According to Guruswamy, 'We show students how to use law as an instrument for profound social change. We show them what the law can really do'.

Driving a modern industrial revolution (Project MIR)

In the process of using students to transform their campuses, universities will also create the leaders needed to drive a historically unprecedented modern industrial revolution (MIR). The word *mir*, in Russian, means peace. And the only way to build a global, sustainable peace (if that is really an achievable goal) is to help bring the prosperity we enjoy in the US to the Gaza Strip, to the Lebanese, to the Iraqis, to sub-Saharan Africa, and to the fast-developing Indian and Chinese populations. Today's campuses must churn out both environmental champions and modern industrial revolutionaries – today's Ghandis, Kings and Browers, but also today's Edisons, Rockefellers and Carnegies.

This generation must come together to retrofit 100 million US residences and build 50 million more; replace 500 million old, leaking windows; create 150 million cars that don't need much, if any, gas; transform the commercial and industrial sectors; and find massive, low-cost, low-carbon transportation solutions. These future leaders must literally build a new world. They must combine law, economics, business, environmental studies and engineering to energize a true modern industrial revolution.

In short, today's students must provide the soon to be 9 billion residents of planet Earth with enough food, energy and modern technology to keep global job rates up and mortality rates down. But they must figure out how to do this without breaking the backs and rich diversity of cultures around the world and without the annoying byproducts of CO_2, SO_2 and other industrial externalities that threaten humanity's very existence.

Although this may seem like a daunting task, history is full of young industrial revolutionaries who – in times of crisis – took the reins and changed the world. We need to change the world again. US colleges and universities must lead the charge – and, indeed, many are stepping forward (see Box 22.2).

Conclusions

Beginning in September 2007, there will be more than 20 million budding environmentalists and industrialists flooding back to the more than 4000 US campuses. These students will have access to a nearly limitless open source of human knowledge and the academic freedom to pursue whatever aggressive climate solutions they choose.

Like their parents of four decades ago, who have just celebrated the 40th anniversary of the Summer of Love, these students are ready for action. They have

Box 22.2 Selection of colleges, universities and educational associations stepping forward to take action

Professional efforts

Leading campus sustainability efforts

- Arizona State University Office of Sustainability Initiatives: www.asusustainability.asu.edu/ , Executive Director, James Buizer
- Brown Is Green: www.brown.edu/Departments/Brown_Is_Green/, Environmental Coordinator, Kurt Teichert,
- University of Buffalo U B Green: http://wings.buffalo.edu/ubgreen/, Walter Simpson, University Energy Officer & Erin Cala, Environmental Educator
- University of California Office of the President (UCOP) Facilities Administration Sustainability: www.ucop.edu/facil/sustain/welcome.html, Sustainability Specialist Matthew St. Claire
- Cal Climate Action Partnership: www.sustainability.berkeley.edu/calcap/index.html, Project Manager, Fahmida Ahmed
- University of Colorado Boulder Environmental Center: www.ecenter.colorado.edu/index.html, Director, Dave Newport
- Cornell Sustainable Campus: www.sustainablecampus.cornell.edu/, Director of Sustainability, Dean Koyanagi
- Dartmouth Office of Sustainability: www.dartmouth.edu/~sustain/, Sustainability Coordinator, Jim Merkel
- Environmental Sustainability @ Duke: www.duke.edu/sustainability/, Environmental Sustainability Coordinator, Tavey McDaniel Capps
- Emory University: www.emory.edu/sustainability.cfm, Director of Sustainability Initiatives, Ciannat Howett
- University of Florida Office of Sustainability: www.sustainable.ufl.edu/, Director, Dedee DeLongpre
- Harvard Green Campus Initiative: www.greencampus.harvard.edu/, Director, Leith Sharp
- University of Maine Sustainability Office: www.umaine.edu/ofm/sustainability/, Scott Wilkerson, Sustainability Officer
- Michigan State University: web.mit.edu/environment/commitment/eptf.html, Director, Terry Link
- Middlebury College, The Sustainable Campus: www.middlebury.edu/administration/enviro/, Jack Byrne, Campus Sustainability Coordinator
- MIT Sustainability: http://sustainability.mit.edu/, Steven Lanou
- University of New Hampshire Office of Sustainability: www.sustainableunh.unh.edu/, Tom Kelly, Chief Sustainability Officer
- Sustainability at University of North Carolina: http://sustainability.unc.edu/, Director, Cindy Pollock Shea
- North Carolina State U's Sustainability Team: www.ncsu.edu/environmental_sustainability/

- Penn State University Center for Sustainability: www.engr.psu.edu/cfs/index.aspx, Director, David Riley
- Tufts Climate Initiative: www.tufts.edu/tie/tci/, Director, Sarah Hammond Creighton
- Green.tulane.edu: http://green.tulane.edu/, Liz Davey, Environmental Coordinator
- Vermont University Greening UVM: www.uvm.edu/~envcncl/, Gioia Thompson, Environmental Coordinator
- Yale University Office of Sustainability: www.yale.edu/sustainability/, Director, Julie Newman

National efforts
- Association for Advancement of Sustainability in Higher Education (AASHE)
- Association of University Leaders for a Sustainable Future (ULSF): www.ulsf.edu
- Focus The Nation: www.focusthenation.org, Director Eban Goodstein
- Higher Education Associations Sustainability Consortium (HEASC): www.heasc.org
    - American Association of Community Colleges (AACC)
    - American Association of State Colleges & Universities (AASCU)
    - ACPA-College Student Educators International (ACPA)
    - Association for the Advancement of Sustainability in Higher Education (AASHE)
    - Association of College & University Housing Officers International (ACUHO-I)
    - Association of Governing Boards of Universities & Colleges (AGB)
    - Association of Higher Education Facilities Officers (APPA)
    - National Association for Campus Activities (NACA)
    - National Association of College & University Business Officers (NACUBO)
    - National Association of Educational Procurement (NAEP)
    - National Intramural-Recreational Sports Association (NIRSA)
    - Society for College & University Planning (SCUP)
- National Wildlife Federation Campus Ecology Program: www.nwf.org/campusEcology, Director Julian Keniry
- Second Nature: www.secondnature.org
- Sustainable Endowments Institute: www.endowmentinstitute.org/ College Sustainability Report Card: www.endowmentinstitute.org/sustainability/Director, Mark Orlowski
- US Partnership for Education for Sustainable Development (USPESD)

State and regional efforts
- Environmental Consortium of Hudson Valley Colleges and Universities: http://environmentalconsortium.org/consortium.cfm

- New Jersey Higher Education Partnership for Sustainability (NJHEPS): www.njheps.org/
- South Carolina Sustainable Universities Initiative (SUI): www.sc.edu/sustainableu/
- Green Campus Consortium of Maine: www.megreencampus.com/
- New England Schools for Campus Sustainability (NESCS)

International efforts
- Alliance for Global Sustainability: www.globalsustainability.org/
- Europe: Copernicus Campus: www.copernicus-campus.org/index.html
- University of British Columbia: www.sustain.ubc.ca/, Director of Sustainability, Charlene Easton
- World Student Community for Sustainable Development: http://wscsd.org/index.php

Student efforts

Campus efforts
- MIT Energy Club: http://web.mit.edu/mit_energy/about/index.html
- MIT Generator: http://sustainability.mit.edu/Generator

National student efforts
- Campus Climate Neutral: www.nael.sorg/projects/ccn/index.htm
- Campus Climate Challenge: www.campusclimatechallenge.org

Regional and state efforts
- California Student Sustainability Coalition (CSSC)

grown up with the immense cataclysmic threat of climate change as part of their worldview. Global warming is their generation's nuclear bomb. Today's young generation is scared, frustrated with a lack of concrete action, and ready to work towards solutions.

They are a generation that has watched the world change in unimaginable ways. They were not alive when Kennedy was shot, but they remember where they were when the Towers went down. They have not grown up with the impending threat of communism, but they know the impending threat of terrorism. They have never seen a world war, but they have come of age during the Cold War.

In 2007 and beyond, this generation will work with the various efforts described above – and others – to find details about every trustee, chancellor, president, professor, graduate program, facilities manager, energy manager, investment manager, alumnus and student in the US university system. They will combine these data with detailed physical and financial data about every building, bus, car, appliance and person in the system. They will then use these data to envision 4000 new campuses that provide the same goods and services with less than a fifth of the associated carbon emissions.

In the process, they will transform their institutions of higher learning into moral leaders in the global battle to address climate change, the laboratories for the technologies and management processes to neutralize emissions of greenhouse gases, and the breeding grounds for future climate-conscious world leaders, professionals and citizens. With the right tools, support and inspiration, they can follow in the mold of students of the past, pushing for social and political change.

If you are a student reading this, I urge you to join the modern industrial revolution and take on the exciting challenge of transforming your campus to a climate negative institution. If you are not a student, I urge you to motivate, mobilize, empower and inspire the students you know to get involved.

The impending climate crisis can either be framed as the biggest potential catastrophe that humanity will ever face, or as the dawning of a beautiful new world. This generation must choose the latter if we are to have any hope of preserving life as we know it. The future is in their hands. Let's hope this Greatest Generation is up to the task.

Notes

1. Cornelius Vanderbilt (1873); Leland Stanford (1885); John Rockefeller - University of Chicago/ Rockefeller University (1889/ 1901); Carnegie and Mellon brothers, Carnegie Institute of Tech (1900); the Mellon Institute of Industrial Research (1913), Washington Duke (1924), etc.
2. http://en.wikipedia.org/wiki/United_States
3. http://nces.ed.gov/programs/digest/d02/tables/dt343.asp; dt346.asp; dt345.asp
4. www.endowmentinstitute.org/resources.html
5. http://climatechallenge.org/the_story
6. http://stepitup2007.org/
7. http://itsgettinghotinhere.org/1216
8. Marsh Fork Protests Lead to Capitol Arrests: www.youtube.com/watch?v=3jq ENyow0cQ.
9. www.climatechallenge.org/powershift07
10. See Net Impact's Campus Greening Initiative (www.netimpact.org), USGBC's Emerging Green Builders (www.emergingbuilders.org/), Engineers Without Borders' work (http://ewb-usa.org/), and NAELS' Campus Climate Neutral (www. naels.org/projects/ccn/index.htm).
11. www.naels.org/Assets/naels_documents/CCN/Bren/bren_final_report.pdf
12. www.presidentsclimatecommitment.org/
13. www.greencampus.harvard.edu/

14.   www.greencampus.harvard.edu/about/documents/green_universities.pdf
15.   http://schoolofsustainability.asu.edu/
16.   http://sustainability.asu.edu/gios/

References

Carnegie Corporation, 1970: *Report of the President's Commission on Campus Unrest*, Carnegie Corporation of New York, US Government printing Office, Washington DC

Lewontin, R. C., 1997: The cold war and the transformation of the academy, in N. Chomsky, L. Nader, I. Wallerstein, R. C. Lewontin, R. Ohmann, H. Zinn, I. Katznelson, D. Montgomery and R. Siever *The Cold War and The University*, I. B. Taurus, London and New York

23

Strategies for Greenhouse Gas Emissions Reductions: The Role of Greenhouse Gas Offsets

Alexia Kelly

The science is in. Global warming is real, it is happening now, and humans are the primary drivers behind it. It has been a decade since the IPCC, the largest assemblage of scientists ever to address a single issue, first concluded that the Earth's climate is changing, and that there is a 'human fingerprint' on this change. Each year since, scientific evidence about human impacts on the climate has become more convincing and more concerning. In 2001, the National Research Council, in response to a request by President Bush to review the IPCC work, reaffirmed its conclusions. By 2001, national academies of science from 19 countries totaling over one-half of the world's population and greenhouse gas emissions issued a statement that 'the balance of scientific evidence demands effective steps now to avoid damaging changes to the Earth's climate'.

In 2005, and again in 2006, the majority of these academies issued a much more forceful statement, citing 'strong evidence' that human activity is already changing the climate, and stating that without prompt action now, 'long term global efforts to create a more healthy, prosperous, and sustainable world may be severely hindered by changes in the climate'. Significant, near-term action is needed to slow the pace of global warming and stabilize the climate at safe and sustainable concentrations of greenhouse gases.

Early actions

A number of regulatory regimes, including the Kyoto Protocol, the EU Emissions Trading Scheme, the Regional Greenhouse Gas Initiative in the Northeastern United States, Assembly Bill 32 in California and the Western Climate Initiative, have all emerged in response to the growing threat that climate change poses to the world. Moreover, increasing numbers of corporations, businesses and individuals are taking action to reduce their climate impact voluntarily.

The most important near-term actions that an organization or individual can take to reduce their impact on the climate are lowering their consumption of energy and increasing the efficiency of their energy use, ideally trying to derive none of their energy from fossil-fuel carbon (i.e. becoming 'carbon neutral'). Because so much of the US economy uses fossil-fuel carbon for energy, it is, however, nearly impossible to independently reduce carbon consumption to zero. One means of bridging the gap between carbon savings achieved through reduced consumption and increased energy efficiency, is through the use of 'greenhouse gas offsets' that are derived from greenhouse gas reduction projects. Such greenhouse gas offsets can provide a practical, cost-effective means of reducing greenhouse gas levels safely and sustainably.

Greenhouse gas offsets and their benefits

What are greenhouse gas offsets, and why are they an important part of a comprehensive climate policy? A greenhouse gas offset project is a project implemented specifically to reduce the level of greenhouse gases in the atmosphere, either by reducing the need for emissions or by sequestering a significant amount of a greenhouse gas such as CO_2. Thus, a greenhouse gas offset displaces, avoids or sequesters greenhouse gas emissions through the implementation of a specific project.

Offset projects can take advantage of a wide variety of technological approaches to achieve greenhouse gas reductions, including:

- promoting cogeneration of electricity from industrial waste heat;
- sequestering CO_2 in forests and in agricultural soils; and
- shifting from high-carbon energy sources to lower-carbon energy sources, for example, from coal to natural gas or biofuels.

The essential promise of a greenhouse gas offset is the achievement of a real and verifiable reduction in atmospheric greenhouse gas levels that is equal to reductions that would have been realized by on-site mitigation measures by emitters. Due to their long lifetimes and the ways in which greenhouse gases accumulate in the atmosphere, the location of a greenhouse gas emission reduction is essentially immaterial to its atmospheric impact. From the atmosphere's perspective, a reduction that occurs at a power plant is no different than a reduction that occurs in a remote African village. Figure 23.1 (Plate 23) illustrates this point graphically.

In addition to reducing the atmospheric concentrations of greenhouse gases, such reduction projects can also offer important benefits to the communities

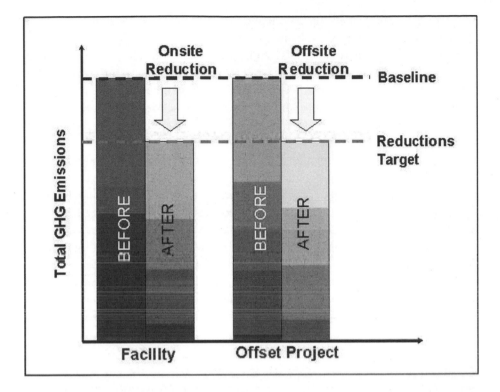

Figure 23.1 Equivalence of greenhouse gas reduction projects to onsite reductions (see Plate 23 for color version)

and regions in which they are located. These benefits can be both environmental and economic. For example, greenhouse gas reduction projects can reduce air pollution, improve habitat, watersheds and water quality, reduce soil erosion, and/or preserve biodiversity and endangered species. Economically, reduction projects can create jobs, stimulate demand for clean energy products, save money on energy and enhance energy security by reducing oil imports. Finally, they can channel funding into new sectors, stimulating innovation and the development of new technologies to help the world transition to a lower carbon economy.

Greenhouse gas offsets and regulatory policy

Greenhouse gas offsets are an established climate policy option. The market for project-based carbon emission reductions has been under development for the past 15 years. The Kyoto Protocol, the European Union Emissions Trading System, the Regional Greenhouse Gas Initiative and Oregon's Carbon Dioxide

Standard are just a few examples of regimes that are using carbon offsets as part of an overall greenhouse gas reduction strategy.

In the US, greenhouse gas offsets have begun to play a substantial role in existing and proposed regulations. Oregon began requiring new power plants to offset part of their CO_2 emissions in 1997. California's Assembly Bill 32 requires regulations be promulgated by 2012 that mandate emission reductions from the electrical, industrial and commercial sectors. At the regional level, RGGI allows an entity to use offsets to meet approximately 50 per cent of the required emissions reductions (or 3.3 per cent of total emissions). At the national level, the Climate Change White Paper issued by Senators Domenici and Bingaman includes a discussion about an offset pilot program, and the reintroduced McCain-Lieberman Climate Stewardship Act allows entities to use offsets for up to 30 per cent of their required reductions.

The first regulation of a greenhouse gas in the US occurred with the state of Oregon's Carbon Dioxide Standard, passed by the Oregon Legislature in 1997. The Oregon Carbon Dioxide Standard requires that new power plants built in the state offset a portion of their CO_2 emissions in order to obtain a site permit. To accomplish this, the power plants pay money on a fee-per-ton basis to The Climate Trust, a Portland-based non-profit that uses the money to buy offsets from greenhouse gas reduction projects. The Climate Trust has assembled one of the largest portfolios of regulatory grade carbon offsets in the country, and has earned a national and international reputation as a leader in offset quality.

The voluntary greenhouse gas market

Because the US is not a signatory to the Kyoto Protocol, it is not legally bound by that international accord to reduce its greenhouse gas levels. However, in the absence of federal regulation of greenhouse gas emissions, a rapidly evolving voluntary carbon market has emerged. This market is developing mainly: (1) to help counteract climate change; (2) as a means to earn 'early actor' status or credits for participating entities; (3) in anticipation of future governmental regulation of greenhouse gas emissions; and (4) to set the groundwork for future participation in international markets. This voluntary market is experiencing dynamic growth and is evolving rapidly as more and more individuals and organizations take action to reduce their climate impact.

The number and type of sellers of greenhouse gas offsets in the voluntary market has increased substantially over the past five years. Consumers can now offset their greenhouse gas emission by purchasing credits from projects ranging from light bulb replacement in Africa, to jungle reforestation in Ecuador, to sophisticated retrofits of large manufacturing plants in the US. Some organizations offer credits from only one or two types of projects while others, including The Climate Trust, offer offset credits from a diverse portfolio of projects.

When properly implemented, greenhouse gas offsets are a practical, cost-effective means of addressing climate change. Moreover, they are one of the most accessible and affordable means, after reduced energy consumption, for consumers to mitigate their individual impacts on the climate and to send a message to regulators that global warming is an issue they care enough about to voluntarily spend money on.

However, caution should be exercised when purchasing offsets in the voluntary market. Because a greenhouse gas offset is an intangible commodity that is based on a hypothetical projection of what emission levels would have been in the absence of the project, it is important to ensure that purchased offsets result in a real, verifiable reduction in greenhouse gas emissions. Currently, there is no one standard or certification for the offset credits that are being sold in the voluntary market. Therefore, it is especially important to purchase greenhouse gas offsets from a reputable source. Several standards are currently under development at the national and international levels and should be operational within one to two years. Until that time, consumers should ensure that greenhouse gas offsets meet the minimum principles discussed in the next section of this chapter; Clean Air-Cool Planet (2006) provides useful guidance and ranks several of the top providers in the industry.

The importance of offset quality

Project-based emissions reductions, when properly implemented, are a high-quality environmental commodity. They must be equally as effective in reducing atmospheric greenhouse gas levels as an on-site reduction by an emitter. Offsets that do not meet this test do not deliver on the basic promise that an offset makes: to reduce atmospheric greenhouse gas levels to what they would have been if the emissions being offset had not occurred in the first place.

To ensure that actual emissions reductions are achieved, in the jargon of the offset world, it is necessary to prove a project's emissions reductions are 'additional'; that is, that the project would not have occurred irrespective of greenhouse gas considerations, or under a 'business-as-usual' scenario. If the project underlying the offsets would have occurred anyway, then atmospheric greenhouse gas levels will not actually be reduced from what they would have been, and the emissions go unmitigated. For this reason, project-based emissions reductions should come from projects that are clearly beyond the business-as-usual scenario. Additionality, as the primary determinant of the beyond business-as-usual case, can only be assured through the application of stringent project review processes, procedures, standards and criteria.

There are several means of determining whether or not a greenhouse gas reduction project is effective in reducing CO_2 levels. Critical metrics include: *realistic project baselines*, *additionality* and *ongoing monitoring and verification*.

These criteria are intended to ensure that the emissions reductions resulting from a greenhouse gas reduction project result in a real and verifiable reduction in atmospheric greenhouse gas levels. In more detail:

- *Additionality.* Additionality is an essential determinant of the effectiveness of an offset project and one of the most important factors in assessing project quality. Additionality is a policy term by which an assessment is made regarding whether or not a project's emissions reductions are in addition to a business-as-usual scenario. The Climate Trust utilizes a project-specific additionality assessment, in which a project proponent must demonstrate that it faces barriers to implementation that can be addressed through carbon funding. These barriers can be institutional, technological or financial. Additionality is the metric by which a project demonstrates that it is resulting in a real, measurable reduction in atmospheric levels of greenhouse gases.
- *A realistic baseline.* A realistic baseline must be established in order to assess the effectiveness of a project's reduction of greenhouse gas levels. The baseline is intended to demonstrate what the greenhouse gas emission levels would have been in the absence of the greenhouse gas reduction project. Credible greenhouse emissions reductions can only be assessed if the baseline upon which the calculation is based is an accurate and realistic reflection of the business-as-usual emissions scenario.
- *Ongoing monitoring and verification.* Emissions reductions from greenhouse gas reduction projects must be accurately quantified. Each project must have a monitoring plan that defines how, when and by whom the quantification will be done. All emissions reductions must be verified by an independent third party, certification program or agency.

Conclusions

Greenhouse gas offsets are an important component of a comprehensive climate change mitigation policy. Offsets provide a means to achieve near-term, real reductions in greenhouse gas levels in a cost-effective and efficient manner. Participating in the voluntary greenhouse gas reduction market is a powerful means of taking action to reduce organizational and individual contributions to global warming. Project-based emissions reductions can also provide an important means to slow the increase in atmospheric concentrations of greenhouse gases during the transition to a lower carbon economy, and can help drive funding toward innovation and the development of new technology. In addition, greenhouse gas offsets can make important contributions to the communities in which they are located. Although greenhouse gas offsets cannot fully stop global warming, they can be a valuable and effective step forward on the long path to climate stabilization.

References

Clean Air-Cool Planet, 2006: *Consumers Guide to Carbon Offsets*, www.cleanair-coolplanet. org/ConsumersGuidetoCarbonOffsets.pdf

Appendices

List of Contributors

John Ashton

Mr Ashton, Chief Executive of E3G (Third Generation Environmentalism), was appointed in 2006 to be the UK Foreign Secretary's Special Representative for Climate Change. In this role, he is assisting the UK Foreign Secretary and other ministers to build a stronger political foundation for international action on climate change. Ambassador Ashton has been working closely with other government departments as well as national and international stakeholders to create the conditions for an accelerated shift in investment towards a low carbon global economy, including through the Gleneagles Dialogue on Climate Change, Clean Energy and Sustainable Development, which was launched at the Gleneagles Summit in 2005.

Robert Bindschadler

Dr Bindschadler is a Chief Scientist of NASA's Hydrospheric and Biospheric Sciences Laboratory, a senior fellow of the Goddard Space Flight Center (GSFC), a fellow of the American Geophysical Union, and a past president of the International Glaciological Society. His research focuses on the dynamics of glaciers and ice sheets, investigating how remote sensing can be used to improve understanding of the role of ice in the Earth's climate. As the leader of 14 Antarctic field expeditions, he has extensive first-hand knowledge of the hazards and challenges of working in the Antarctic environment. Other research has taken him to Greenland and various glaciers throughout the world. During his 28 years at GSFC, he has developed numerous unique applications of remote sensing data for glaciological research, including measuring ice velocity and elevation using both visible and radar imagery, monitoring melt of ice sheets by microwave emissions, and detecting changes in ice sheet volume by repeat space-borne radar altimetry. He has testified before Congress, briefed the US Vice President on the issue of ice sheet stability, and served on many scientific commissions and study groups as an expert in glaciology and remote sensing of ice. He has over 145 scientific publications and numerous review articles.

Rev. Sally G. Bingham

The Rev. Sally Grover Bingham is a native of California. She is Priest in the Diocese of California, currently working as the Environmental Minister at Grace Cathedral in San Francisco. She is the founder and executive director of The Regeneration Project (TRP), a non-profit ministry dedicated to deepening the connection between faith and the environment. Currently, the primary focus of TRP is the Interfaith Power and Light Campaign. This mission is a 'religious response to global warming' and TRP has taken a leadership role in that effort. Many organizations have recognized the importance of Rev. Bingham's work: in November 2000, the World Wildlife Fund recognized Interfaith Power and Light as a Sacred Gift to the Planet at a ceremony in Katmandu, Nepal; in July 2001, Rev. Bingham received the Green Power Leadership Pilot Award from the Center for Resource Solutions, the US Environmental Protection Agency, and the US Department of Energy; TRP received the international Global Energy Award 2002, which was presented to Rev. Bingham in Austria by President Gorbachev; in 2005, the Interfaith Power and Light Campaign was recognized in 2005 at the Clinton Global Initiative; in July 2007, Rev. Bingham and the Interfaith Power and Light Campaign were given the Senator Barbara Boxer 'Conservation Champion Award'; in May 2007, Rev. Bingham was awarded the US EPA Climate Protection Award; and in 2007, Rev. Bingham is a finalist for a 'Purpose Prize' award.

Malcolm Bowman

Dr Bowman obtained his B.S. and M.S. degrees in physics and mathematics at the University of Auckland, New Zealand, and his Ph.D. in engineering physics at the University of Saskatchewan, Canada. He is currently Professor of Physical Oceanography and Distinguished Service Professor at the Marine Sciences Research Center, Stony Brook University. He is principal investigator of the Stony Brook Storm Surge Research Group, which develops and tests coupled meteorological-ocean models to predict coastal flooding from extreme weather events, focusing particularly on the threat to the New York area from global climate change and rising sea level. Between 1996 and 1999, Dr Bowman returned to his native New Zealand to act as founding head of the School of Environmental and Marine Sciences at Auckland University. He is a Director of the Environmental Defence Society (NZ), an honorary Professor of Physics at Auckland University, the Founder and current President of the Stony Brook Environmental Conservancy, and a Distinguished Member of the National Society of Collegiate Scholars.

Virginia Burkett

Dr Burkett is the Chief Scientist for Global Change Research at the US Geological Survey (USGS). She had formerly served as Chief of the Forest Ecology Branch at the National Wetlands Research Center and subsequently as Associate Regional Chief Biologist for the USGS Central Region. Prior to becoming a Department of Interior employee in 1991, Dr Burkett was Director of the Louisiana Department of Wildlife and Fisheries. She has published extensively on the topics of global change and low-lying coastal zones. Nominated by the US government, she was a lead author of the coastal and marine impacts section for the Third (2001) and Fourth (2007) Assessment Reports of the IPCC. From 1998–2000, Dr Burkett was a member of the National Assessment Synthesis Team and coordinated both the Coastal and Southeast synthesis chapters of the US National Assessment of the Consequences of Climate Variability and Change. She received her B.S. in zoology and M.S. in botany from Northwestern State University of Louisiana. Her doctoral work in forestry was completed at Stephen F. Austin State University of Texas in 1996.

Joseph A. Cannon

Mr Cannon is Editor of the *Deseret Morning News* in Utah. Just before assuming this position he served as a partner at Pillsbury Winthrop Shaw Pitman, LLP, in the firm's Environment, Land Use and Natural Resources practice, and was Co-Leader of its Public Policy & Political Law practice. Prior to rejoining the firm, he was the Chief Executive Officer and Chairman of Geneva Steel from 1987 to 2001. He formerly served as Assistant Administrator for Air and Radiation, and Associate Administrator for Policy and Resource Management at the US Environmental Protection Agency. In the past, Mr Cannon has also served numerous organizations in the following capacities: member of the Board of Trustees of the American Enterprise Institute; member of the Administrative Conference of the US; member of the Board of Trustees of the Salt Lake Olympic Organizing Committee; Chairman of the American Bar Association's Natural Resources Law Section, Air Quality Committee; Vice Chairman of the Committee of Interagency Radiation Research and Policy Coordination; US Representative to the Environment Committee, Organization for Economic Cooperation and Development; and member of the US Holocaust Memorial Council and capital campaign committee.

Thomas R. Casten

Mr Casten has spent 30 years developing and operating combined heat and power (CHP) plants as a way to save money and reduce pollution. He serves as Chairman of Recycled Energy Development LLC. He founded and served as Chair and CEO of Primary Energy Ventures LLC, and Primary Energy Recycling Corp, which developed, owned and operated 14 projects that recycle waste energy in 5 states. He formed Cummins Cogeneration Company, a division of Cummins Engine Co., in 1977 to develop on-site combined heat and power plants and in 1986 founded Trigen Energy Corporation. Under his leadership, Trigen produced energy at 57 plants in 19 states, Canada and Mexico, and became a market leader in developing profitable district energy and on-site combined heat and power. Mr Casten is a nationally recognized expert on energy and environment issues. In 1998 he published *Turning Off the Heat*, a book explaining how the world can save money and reduce pollution by removing regulatory barriers to efficiency. He is the co-founder and former Chairman of the World Alliance for Distributed Energy (WADE) and also serves on the Board of Directors/Advisory Boards of the Carnegie Mellon Electric Industry Center, and the Center for Inquiry. He has served as President of the International District Energy Association, received the Norman R. Taylor Award for distinguished achievement and contributions to the industry, has been named a 'CHP Champion' by the US CHP Association and was the initial inductee into the Hall of Fame of the World Alliance for Decentralized Energy. He has served as an adviser to senior government officials, participated with President Clinton and Vice President Gore in the White House conference on global climate change, testified before Congress, State Public Service Commissions and State legislative committees, and has advised Indian, Chinese and Brazilian government officials on power industry governance.

F. Stuart Chapin III

Dr Chapin is a faculty member in the Department of Biology and Wildlife at the University of Alaska Fairbanks, where he directs the Bonanza Creek Long-Term Ecological Research (LTER). He received his B.A. in biology at Swarthmore College in 1966 and his Ph.D. in Biology at Stanford University in 1973.His research focuses on ecosystem ecology and on the resilience of social-ecological systems. His ecological research addresses the consequences of plant traits for ecosystem and global processes, particularly vegetation effects on nutrient cycling, fire regime and biodiversity. He also studies vegetation-mediated feedbacks to high-latitude climate warming, as mediated by changes in water and energy exchange. His research on social-ecological systems emphasizes the resilience of northern regions to recent changes in climate and fire regime. This research entails studies of human and climatic effects on fire regime, the resulting effects on ecosystem services, wages and cultural integrity, and the effects of local opinions about fire and national fire policy on the fire policies developed and implemented at regional scales. Most of his current research focuses on Alaska and eastern Siberia.

Robert W. Corell

Dr Corell is currently Director of the Global Change Program at The H. John Heinz III Center for Science, Economics and the Environment, and also a Senior Policy Fellow at the Policy Program of the American Meteorological Society. He is actively engaged in research on the sciences of global change and the interface between science and public policy. He is currently also serving as Chair of the Arctic Climate Impact Assessment, as co-chair of an international strategic planning group that is developing programs and activities designed to harness science, technology and innovation for sustainable development, and as the lead for the 'Global Hydrogen Partnership', which is an international partnership seeking to better understand and plan for a transition to hydrogen for several nations. Prior to January 2000, Dr Corell was Assistant Director for Geosciences at the National Science Foundation, where he had oversight for the Atmospheric, Earth and Ocean Sciences and the global change programs of the National Science Foundation (NSF). Dr Corell is an oceanographer and engineer by background, having received his degrees at Case Western Reserve University and MIT. He has held appointments at the Woods Hole Institution of Oceanography, the Scripps Institution of Oceanography, the University of Washington, Case Western Reserve University, and the Belfer Center for Science and International Affairs at Harvard University's Kennedy School of Government.

Judith Curry

Dr Curry is Professor and Chair of the School of Earth and Atmospheric Sciences at the Georgia Institute of Technology. She received her Ph.D. in atmospheric science from the University of Chicago in 1982. Prior to joining the faculty at Georgia Tech, she held faculty positions at the University of Colorado, Penn State University and Purdue University. Dr Curry's current research interests include air/sea interactions, climate feedback processes associated with clouds and sea ice, and applications of satellite data to interpreting recent variations in the climate data record. She currently serves on the Climate Research Committee and the Space Studies Board of the National Academies, and on the NOAA Climate Working Group. She is author of the book *Thermodynamics of Atmospheres and Oceans*, editor for the *Encyclopedia of Atmospheric Sciences*, and author of over

130 refereed journal articles. Her research has been recognized by receipt of the Presidential Young Investigator Award from the National Science Foundation and the Henry Houghton Award from the American Meteorological Society. Dr Curry is a Fellow of the American Meteorological Society and the American Geophysical Union.

Devra Lee Davis

Dr Davis is a visiting professor at Carnegie Mellon University's Heinz School, an honorary professor at London's School of Hygiene and Tropical Medicine, and an expert advisor to the World Health Organization. Her research focuses on environmental health and chronic disease. She was appointed to the Chemical Safety and Hazard Investigation Board (1994–1999) by President Clinton and has also served as Senior Advisor to the Assistant Secretary for Health in the Department of Health and Human Services. She has authored more than 170 publications in books and journals and has written for *The New York Times*, the *Los Angeles Times* and other mass media outlets. Her book *When Smoke Ran Like Water* was a National Book Award finalist in 2002. She co-chaired an expert workshop on assessing the public health implications of climate change sponsored by the OECD, IPCC and EPA. Dr Davis holds a Ph.D. from the University of Chicago as well as an M.A. from the University of Pittsburgh and a M.P.H. from Johns Hopkins University.

Andrew E. Derocher

Dr Derocher is Professor of biological sciences at the University of Alberta. His research group focuses on the ecology, conservation and management of large carnivores with the aim to improve our understanding of how they are affected by human activities. Over the past 25 years, his primary research has focused on polar bears in both the North American and European Arctic. His research group works closely with territorial and federal government agencies. He holds a Ph.D. from the University of Alberta and is currently the Chair of the IUCN/SSC Polar Bear Specialist Group.

Bruce C. Douglas

Mr Douglas has been a Research Professor in the Laboratory for Coastal Research at Florida International University since 2000. Prior to that he was Director of NOAA's National Oceanographic Data Center, and Senior Research Scientist in the Geography Department at the University of Maryland. His special research interests are global sea level rise and coastal impacts of sea level rise. He has published many widely-cited papers on these topics, and is co-editor of the 2001 book *Sea Level Rise: History and Consequences*.

Christopher Flavin

Mr Flavin is President of the Worldwatch Institute, a Washington-based research organization known for its path-breaking work on the connections between economic, social and environmental trends. In his long career at Worldwatch, Mr Flavin has guided the Institute's development as Vice President of Research and as Senior Vice President before being appointed President in 2000. He is a regular co-author of the Institute's annual report, *State of the World*, which has been published in 36 languages and is read by decision makers around the world. Mr Flavin is widely known for his writing on energy strategies and policies, including prospects for oil, strategies for reducing CO_2 emissions, and potential of new and renewable energy technologies. He is co-author of three books on energy, including *Power Surge: Guide to the Coming Energy Revolution*, which presciently described the need for a post-petroleum energy economy and laid out a roadmap for achieving it. Mr Flavin is active in international policy circles and has participated in several historic international conferences, including the Earth Summit in Rio de Janeiro in 1992 and the Climate Change Conference in Kyoto, Japan in 1997. He is a lecturer to business, university and policy audiences and meets frequently with the leaders of governments, international agencies and corporations. He has also written for a wide range of popular and scholarly periodicals, including *The New York Times*, *Technology Review*, *The Harvard International Review* and *TIME Magazine*. Mr. Flavin is a graduate of Williams College, where he studied economics, biology and environmental studies.

Erin Frey

Ms Frey is a member of the class of 2008 at Harvard University, where she is majoring in Environmental Science and Public Policy with a minor in Economics. Especially interested in economic solutions to energy and environmental problems, she is currently writing her senior honors thesis on the intersection of economic incentives, government regulations and the abatement of greenhouse gasses. After graduation, Ms Frey plans to attend graduate school and pursue her doctorate in environmental economics or science and technology policy. She co-authored and provided the principal research for the *Background Paper* for the Washington Summit, which was adapted to form Chapter 16 in this volume.

Walter E. Grazer

Mr Grazer retired from his position as Director of the Environmental Justice Program and Policy Advisor for Religious Liberty, Human Rights and European Affairs for the United States Catholic Conference in June 2007. Formerly, he served as Deputy Director for Migration and Refugee Services, and as Policy Advisor for Food, Agriculture and Rural Development at the Conference. He has worked for the US Catholic Conference for 25 years. Prior to his service at the USCC, he directed the Social Ministry Program of the Diocese of Richmond after working for the City of Richmond's Commission on Human Relations and the Richmond Community Action Program. He is co-editor with Rev. Drew Christiansen of *And God Saw That It Was Good: Catholic Theology and the Environment*. Mr Grazer holds an M.A. in International Relations, an M.S.W. in social work and a B.A. in philosophy.

President Ólafur Ragnar Grímsson

Mr Ólafur Ragnar Grímsson was elected the fifth President of the Republic of Iceland on 29 June 1996 for a four-year term. He was re-elected for additional four-year terms in 2000 and 2004. He holds a Ph.D. from the University of Manchester in Political Science and has been a professor at the University of Iceland where he studied the evolution of the Icelandic political system and helped to build up the Social Science Department of the university. Mr Grímsson was elected to Althingi (parliament) as a representative for Reykjavik in 1978 as a representative of the People's Alliance Party. He was re-elected in 1979, 1991, 1995 and served as an alternate in 1984, 1985, 1987, 1988, 1989 and 1990. He was the Minister of Finance in the Government of Mr Steingrímur Hermansson from 1988 to 1991 and was elected leader of the People's Alliance Party between 1987 and 1995. He has been a member of various public bodies, including the Economic Council (1966–1968), the Icelandic Broadcasting Service (1971–1975) and the Icelandic Social Sciences Commission (1979–1990). Mr Grímsson was also chairman and later president of the International Association of Parliamentarians for Global Action, an association of 1800 parliamentarians from about 80 countries and he accepted the Indira Gandhi Peace Prize on behalf of the association in 1987.

Denis Hayes

Mr Hayes is President of the Bullitt Foundation, a US$100 million environmental philanthropy located in Seattle. He is also the immediate past chair of the Energy Foundation – a joint project of the Hewlett, Packard, MacArthur, McKnight and

Mertz-Gilmore Foundations to promote energy efficiency and renewable energy in the US and China. In 1970, Mr Hayes was National Coordinator of the first Earth Day and he still chairs the board of the Earth Day Network. He was head of the National Renewable Energy Laboratory during the Carter administration and from 1983 to 1988 was an adjunct professor of energy engineering at Stanford University. In 1979, Mr Hayes received the national Jefferson Medal for Greatest Public Service by an individual under 35. In 1985, he was given the John Muir Award by the Sierra Club. He has also received the highest honors awarded by the National Wildlife Federation, the Natural Resources Council of America, the Humane Society of the US, and the Interfaith Center for Corporate Responsibility. *Time Magazine* selected Mr Hayes as one of its 'Heroes of the Planet', and the National Audubon Society included him in its list of the 100 Environmental Heroes of the 20th Century. He has been profiled as 'Newsmaker of the Week' by ABC News and as 'Today's Person in the News' by *The New York Times*.

Anthony C. Janetos

Dr Janetos is Director of the Joint Global Change Research Institute, which is a joint endeavor between the Pacific Northwest National Laboratory and the University of Maryland. Prior to accepting this position in 2006, he had been a Senior Fellow and Vice President of The H. John Heinz III Center for Science, Economics and the Environment, where he was responsible for promoting new directions in their global change program. He has written and spoken widely on the needs for scientific input and scientific assessment in the policy making process. His prior positions include Vice President for Science and Research at the World Resources Institute and Senior Scientist for the Land-Cover and Land-Use Change Program in NASA's Office of Earth Science. He also was Program Scientist for NASA's Landsat 7 mission. His research and policy interests in the area of ecology and the environment include air pollution effects on forests, climate change impacts, land-use change, ecosystem modeling and the global carbon cycle. He was a co-chair of the US National Assessment, and an author of the IPCC Special Report on Land-Use Change and Forestry, the Global Biodiversity Assessment, and the Millennium Ecosystem Assessment. Dr Janetos received his B.S. in biology from Harvard College and M.S. and a Ph.D. in biology from Princeton University.

Eric S. Kasischke

Dr Kasischke is a professor in the Department of Geography at the University of Maryland College Park. He has an adjunct appointment of Senior Research

Associate at the University of Alaska, Fairbanks, where he serves as Senior Investigator on the Bonanza Creek Long-Term Ecological Research Program. He spent his early career working for the Environmental Research Institute of Michigan in Ann Arbor, where he conducted research on airborne and spaceborne remotely sensed data. His doctoral research focused on developing approaches to using imaging radar data to assess variations in forest biomass. Since the early 1990s, his research has focused on studying the impacts of fires on ecosystem processes and biogeochemical cycling in boreal forests. His specific focus is on how variations in the fire regime are interacting with the climate to drive changes in terrestrial carbon cycling, permafrost dynamics and post-fire succession in this region. He is currently a member of the US Carbon Cycle Scientific Steering Group. Dr. Kasischke received his Ph.D. from the University of Michigan in 1992, where he also received his B.S. and M.S. degrees.

Michael S. Kearney

Dr Kearney is a professor in the Department of Geography at the University of Maryland College Park. His research interests include coastal processes and ecology, climate change and remote sensing. He is author or co-author of numerous papers, chapters and books on coastal ecology and sea-level rise, including: *Large-Scale Decline of Coastal Marshes in Chesapeake Bay and Delaware Bay, USA, Determined from Landsat Imagery* and *Sea Level Rise: History and Consequences*. He received his Ph.D. in geography and geomorphology from the University of Western Ontario.

Alexia C. Kelly

Ms Kelly joined The Climate Trust in 2006. The Climate Trust is an independent non-profit organization that is dedicated to the purchase of high quality greenhouse gas offsets and the advancement of sound offset policy; it currently holds a diverse portfolio of 17 offset projects, accounting for US$8.8 million and 2.7 million tons of greenhouse gas emission reductions. As The Climate Trust's Policy Analyst, Ms Kelly's responsibilities include tracking and analyzing developments in the climate change policy arena and in the greenhouse gas offset market, preparing policy statements, comments and white papers on a range of topics, and providing information and advice to policy makers. In addition to her policy activities, she assists with a variety of consulting projects and participates in the acquisition and contract management of the Trust's offset projects. Ms Kelly holds a B.A. in Planning, Public Policy and Management from the University of Oregon, and a Master of Public Administration and a Master of Community and Regional Planning from the University of Oregon.

Nasir Khattak

Mr Khattak is Director of Global Environmental Programs at the Climate Institute and has over 12 years of experience in working on a variety of international environmental and renewable energy policy projects. He is spearheading the Institute's International Leadership Alliance for Climate Stabilization, which includes development and implementation of sustainable energy and climate protection plans for participating small islands states and states within populous developing nations. He also manages the Climate Institute's Global Sustainable Energy Islands Initiative, which involves a half dozen small island states in the Caribbean Sea and Pacific Ocean. Mr Khattak has a master's degree in Engineering Management from George Washington University in Washington DC. He got his bachelor's degree in Civil Engineering from Pakistan and also has a bachelor's degree in law and political science from the University of Peshawar in Pakistan.

Stephen P. Leatherman

Dr Leatherman is Director of the International Hurricane Research Center (IHRC) as well as the Director for their Laboratory of Coastal Research. His major research focus is storm impacts on coastal areas, including high-technology mapping with airborne lasers. He served for many years on the National Academy of Sciences Post-Storm Disaster Field Team that was dispatched from Washington DC to survey hurricane damage and thus has considerable first-hand experience with these disasters. Dr Leatherman has authored or edited 15 books and authored more than 200 refereed journal articles and technical reports. He has provided expert testimony to the US Senate and House of Representatives committees ten times during the past decade on important science policy issues, especially coastal storm impacts and federal response. Dr Leatherman has given hundreds of invited talks at professional conferences and public workshops and his research has also been widely reported on television programs and in newspapers.

Admiral James M. Loy

In 2005, Admiral Loy completed a 45-year career in public service, retiring as the first Deputy Secretary of Homeland Security. In this capacity, he was involved in all aspects of consolidating 22 separate agencies into one unified cabinet department as well as managing the day-to-day activities of the agency. Prior to the establishment of the Department of Homeland Security in 2002, Admiral Loy served in the Transportation Security Administration as Chief Operating Officer and Under Secretary for Security. He retired from the US Coast Guard in 2002, after a distinguished career, including as Commandant (1998–2002) and

Commander of the Atlantic Area (1994–1996). A career seagoing officer, Admiral Loy has served tours aboard six Coast Guard cutters, including commander of a patrol boat during the Vietnam War and commander of major cutters in both the Atlantic and Pacific Oceans. His military and civilian honors are numerous and include four Coast Guard Distinguished Service Medals; the Defense Superior Service Medal; the Combat Action Ribbon; and the Naval Order of the US' Distinguished Sea Service Award. Admiral Loy graduated from the US Coast Guard Academy in 1964 and holds masters degrees from Wesleyan University and the University of Rhode Island.

Michael C. MacCracken

Dr MacCracken is Chief Scientist for Climate Change Programs at the Climate Institute in Washington DC. His activities focus on improving scientific and public understanding of climate change and its impacts. From 2003 to 2007, he also served as the president of the International Association of Meteorology and Atmospheric Sciences, and an international panel that he served on recently completed the report *Confronting Climate Change: Avoiding the Unmanageable and Managing the Unavoidable* (http://www.confrontingclimatechange.org). From 1997 to 2001, he served as executive director of the US Global Change Research Program's National Assessment Coordination Office, which coordinated the efforts of 20 regional assessment teams, five sectoral teams, and the National Assessment Synthesis Team that prepared national-level reports that were forwarded to the President and to Congress. From 1993 to 1997 he served as the first executive director of the Office of the US Global Change Research Program. His earlier research with the Lawrence Livermore National Laboratory focused on application of climate models to evaluate natural and anthropogenic causes of climate change. He holds a B.Sc. in Engineering degree from Princeton University and a Ph.D. in Applied Science from the University of California Davis/Livermore.

Pamela P. McVety

Ms McVety has a master's degree in zoology from the University of South Florida and has worked for the State of Florida's Department of Environmental Protection for over 30 years. She began her career in dredge and fill permitting and worked for the first four Secretaries of the Department of Environmental Protection in policy development and coordination. She was the Director of the Division of Marine Resources and Executive Coordinator (Deputy Secretary) for Ecosystem Management and Water Policy. She finished her paid career in the Florida Park Service in July 2003 and currently does volunteer work for the Presbyterian Church on climate change and energy issues, frequently lecturing on the science of global climate change and energy. She also helped found the Big Bend Climate Action Team, a citizen group of scientists and writers working with local governments, businesses and citizens to abate climate change by reducing fossil fuel use and promoting energy conservation, efficiency and renewable fuels in power plants, buildings and vehicles.

Frances Moore

Ms Moore is now a staff researcher at the Earth Policy Institute in Washington DC. Prior to joining EPI, she worked as a researcher at the Climate Institute where she helped to prepare this volume for publication. Ms Moore holds a B.A. (*summa cum laude*) in Earth and Planetary Sciences from Harvard University, where her studies focused on climate change and its physical and social effects. She has traveled to Svalbard to study the effects of climate change in the high arctic and has undertaken research into carbon cycling in the Cretaceous ocean.

William A. Nitze

Mr Nitze has been working on energy and environmental issues for most of his career. He currently serves as chairman of two companies that are developing clean energy technologies: GridPoint, Inc., which designs, manufactures and markets intelligent energy management systems; and Oceana Energy Company, which is developing an innovative technology for converting tidal energy into electricity. He also serves as Chairman of the Board of the Climate Institute, and serves on the board of the Galapagos Conservancy. Mr Nitze has served as Assistant Administrator for International Activities at the EPA during the Clinton Administration and as Deputy Assistant Secretary of State for Environment in the Reagan and Bush administrations, where he played a key role in creating and organizing the IPCC in 1988. After leaving the State Department in early 1990, Mr Nitze was a Visiting Scholar at the Environmental Law Institute, where he wrote a monograph entitled *The Greenhouse Effect: Formulating a Convention*. Many of the elements discussed in this monograph were subsequently incorporated into the Framework Convention on Climate Change, signed in 1992. Mr Nitze holds B.A. degrees from Harvard College and Wadham College, Oxford, and a J.D. degree from Harvard Law School.

Claire L. Parkinson

Dr Parkinson is a climatologist at NASA's Goddard Space Flight Center, where she's worked since July 1978 and where her research is focused on polar sea ice and its connections to the rest of the climate system and to climate change. Since April 1993, she has additionally been Project Scientist for the Aqua satellite mission, which launched in May 2002 and is transmitting data on many atmospheric, oceanic, land and ice variables from its suite of six Earth-observing instruments. Most of her research has involved the analysis of sea ice from satellite data, although she has also developed a numerical model of sea ice and has done fieldwork in both the Arctic and the Antarctic. Dr Parkinson is the lead author of an atlas of Arctic sea ice and a co-author of two other sea ice atlases, and she has written books on satellite Earth observations and the history of science. She has been awarded a NASA Exceptional Service Medal, a NASA Outstanding Leadership Medal and the Goldthwait Polar Medal from the Byrd Polar Research Center. She is a fellow of both the American Meteorological Society and Phi Beta Kappa and holds a B.A. in mathematics from Wellesley College and a Ph.D. in climatology from Ohio State University.

A. Barrie Pittock

Dr Pittock has been an active researcher on topics including stratospheric ozone, patterns of climate change and variability, the El Niño-Southern Oscillation, solar-weather relations, the environmental effects of nuclear war, and the greenhouse effect. He has been on the editorial board of several scientific journals, and remains on that of the journal *Climatic Change*. He has over 250 scientific publications. He was Leader of the Climate Impacts Group in CSIRO Atmospheric Research until his retirement in 1999, and edited the book *Climate Change: An Australian Guide to the Science and Potential Impacts*, for the Australian government's Greenhouse Office in 2003. In 2005, he published a book covering the science, impacts, adaptation, mitigation and policy issues of an enhanced greenhouse effect entitled *Climate Change: Turning Up the Heat*. He holds a Ph.D. from Melbourne University. Dr Pittock was awarded an Australian Public Service Medal in 1999 for his work on climate change.

Paul C. Pritchard

The renowned conservationist, Michael Frome, described Paul Pritchard as one of the most influential conservationists of modern times and the Smithsonian Institution recognized him in its book, *Conservation Leaders*. Founder of the National Park Trust and President of National Parks and Conservation Association, he has been a significant force in the addition of over half of the US' national parks, the first estuarine and marine sanctuaries, state heritage programs, the saving of Canada's St Catherine Islands, the protection of China's national parks, and the fight for the Earth's delicate climate. A decorated career officer in the US Department of the Interior, Mr Pritchard has chaired a Presidential task force and was instrumental in the addition of Alaska national park units. He has published more than 100 articles, including 1 celebrating the 75th anniversary of the National Park Service in *National Geographic*. He was also the creator of the March for Parks Earth Day event and the founding chair of the Climate Institute. He holds a B.A. in Humanities and an M.Sc. in Planning and is a decorated Vietnam veteran.

Eric Rignot

Dr Eric Rignot is a Senior Research Scientist at the Jet Propulsion Laboratory's Radar Science and Engineering Section, a Professor at the University of California Irvine's Earth System Science Department, an Adjunct Researcher at the Centro de Estuios Cientificos' Glaciology and Climate Change Branch, a Visiting Scientist at the University of Colorado, Boulder, and a Team Leader at the University of Kansas' CreSIS NSF center for ice sheet research. His research in the last 15 years has focused on the determination of the mass balance of glaciers and ice sheets, and on studying the relationship between ice motion, mass balance and climate. He has led many NASA projects and survey campaigns to study the mass balance of Greenland, Antarctica and Patagonia glaciers, ice shelf–ocean interactions, and changes in ice dynamics using satellite radar remote sensing techniques (interferometry, polarimetry) combined with other methods. He is currently developing new ice sheet numerical models coupled with remote sensing data and novel radio echo sounding techniques for the probing of outlet glaciers. He received NASA's Award for Exceptional Scientific Achievement in 2003 and 2007, the Ed Stone Award in 2002 and 2004 and the Lew Allen Award in 1998. He has over 75 scientific publications and numerous book chapters. He is a member of the American Geophysical Union and the International Glaciological Society, and Editor of *Geophysical Research Letters*.

Tom Roper

The Honorable Tom Roper retired after 21 years service in the Victorian (Australia) Parliament, half as a minister. He currently serves on the board of the Climate Institute and acts as project leader for the Small Islands Green Energy

Initiative. He has been involved in a variety of projects concerning climate change, including representing the Climate Institute at the Kyoto, Buenos Aires and Hague Conferences. Mr Roper has been involved in environmental policy and issues at all levels – local, state, federal and international. His wide-ranging ministerial experience has included Treasury, Planning and Environment, Aboriginal Affairs, Health and Transport. During his term at Planning and Environment, he helped to develop programs to protect the stratospheric ozone layer, oversaw the State Conservation Strategy, funded the first local government conservation strategies, and was instrumental in legislation to establish two major national parks and to stop unrestricted tree clearing.

Kahlid Shaukat

Dr Khalid Shaukat was born in India in 1943, migrated to Pakistan with his parents in 1956, and continued his college education in Karachi, Pakistan. He has bachelor's degrees in physics and civil engineering from the University of Karachi. He obtained his graduate degree in civil engineering from Georgia Tech in 1970. Since migrating to the US in 1969, he has been involved in scientific and engineering research, especially in physics, mathematics and astronomy. Over the last three decades he has published articles in various journals and publications on earthquake engineering, seismic design of structures, pump seals, scientific aspects of moon-sighting (a scientific as well as religious global issue) and the global Islamic calendar. He has given over 90 lectures on various subject of his expertise in many countries of the world, including at the American Muslims Social Scientists (AMSS) Convention, the Climate Stabilization Conference (Washington DC), Islam in America Conventions, and Islamic Society of North America (ISNA) Annual Conventions.

Rabbi Warren G. Stone

Rabbi Warren Stone has served as rabbi of Temple Emanuel in the Washington metropolitan area in Kensington, Maryland since 1988 when he arrived in the Washington area after serving congregations in California and Texas. He is known nationally for his work on religion and the environment: he is the founding and current chair of the Central Conference of American Rabbis' Committee on the Environment; he was the sole Jewish UN delegate to the Kyoto conference in 1997; he has led delegations on environmental issues to the Congress and the White House and has co-chaired a Senate conference with Senator Lieberman calling for protection of the Arctic National Wildlife Refuge. Rabbi Stone has served on many boards, including the Coalition on the Environment and Jewish

Life and the advisory board for the District of Columbia Green Faith Initiative. He has had articles published in the *Washington Jewish Week, Reform Judaism Magazine* and the *Central Conference of American Rabbis Journal*. Rabbi Stone holds a B.A. in Near Eastern and Judaic Studies from Brandeis University, a M.A.H.L. from Hebrew Union College-Jewish Institute, and a D.Min. in Religion and Psychotherapy from Andover Newton Theological School. He received an honorary Doctorate of Divinity from Hebrew University College-Jewish Institute of Religion in March 2003.

Sir Crispin Tickell

Sir Crispin Tickell is currently Director of the Policy Foresight Programme in the James Martin Institute for Science and Civilization at Oxford University. From 1996 to 2006 he served as Chancellor of the University of Kent. His principal interests are in the fields of the environment and international affairs. Most of Sir Crispin's career has been in the UK's Diplomatic Service. He has been Chef de Cabinet to the President of the European Commission (1977–1980), Ambassador to Mexico (1981–1983), Permanent Secretary of the Overseas Development Administration (1984–1987), and British Permanent Representative to the UN (1987–1990). In 1990 he became Warden of Green College, Oxford and served in that capacity until 1997. Among other things, he has been President of the Royal Geographical Society (1990–1993), Chairman of the Board of the Climate Institute of Washington DC (1990–2002), Convenor of the Government Panel on Sustainable Development (1994–2000), and an Inaugural Senior Visiting Fellow at the Harvard University Center for the Environment (2002–2003). He is the author of *Climatic Change and World Affairs* (1977 and 1986); has contributed to many books on human population problems, conservation of biodiversity and other environmental issues; and has been a member of two government task forces, one on urban regeneration and the other on potentially hazardous near-Earth objects.

John Topping

Mr Topping is President/CEO of the Climate Institute, a non-profit that he founded in 1986 to promote global climate balance. Under his leadership, the Climate Institute, the world's first environmental organization focused on climate protection, organized the first Symposium on Climate Change for UN missions, has carried out Country Studies in nations with a quarter of the Earth's population, and has carried out activities in over 40 nations. Prior to establishing the Climate Institute, he was staff director of the Office of Air and Radiation of the Environmental Protection Agency and a lawyer with the US Department of Commerce, the President's advisory council on minority business enterprise, and the US Air Force. He is the co-author of a book on US air pollution control law and editor of two volumes on climate change, *Preparing for Climate Change* and *Coping with Climate Change.* He edited the portions of the IPCC First Assessment Report on Impacts of climate change on human settlement, transport, industry, energy, human health, air quality and UV radiation, and was lead author of the sections on human settlement, industry and transport. He is currently a director of Oceana Energy Company, which is developing tidal energy in San Francisco Bay and a number of other locations. Mr Topping received an A.B. in international relations from Dartmouth College and a J.D. from Yale University. In 2002, he received Dartmouth College's Martin Luther King, Jr Social Justice Award for Lifetime Achievement.

Dan Worth

Mr Worth is the Executive Director of the National Association of Environmental Law Societies (NAELS), a coalition of environmental law student groups that is seeking to mobilize the university community in support of public interest environmental solutions. He also currently serves on the Steering Committee for the Energy Action Network, a coalition of student and youth groups working on climate and energy issues. Prior to joining NAELS, Mr Worth was a Harvard Law School Environmental Fellow, where he coordinated the Environmental Working Group – a team of Harvard Law School administrators, professors, alumni and students working to develop a comprehensive environmental law program. While at Harvard, he volunteered for the Law Offices of Matthew F. Pawa, PC, where he conducted research on the recent tort-based global warming cases. He graduated from Boston University School of Law and has clerked for Earthjustice Legal Defense Fund in the organization's DC and Juneau, Alaska offices.

Acknowledgements

John C. Topping

This book is the result of a remarkable conference that marked the 20th Anniversary of the Climate Institute. The Washington Summit on Climate Stabilization had two principal objectives – to provide an accurate picture of the risks that climate change might accelerate past the point at which humanity and ecosystems could reasonably adapt, and to outline the beginnings of a public–private partnership to pioneer in comprehensive, pro-active Climate Protection Strategies that might provide humanity and other living things breathing room.

Key to the success of the International Leadership Alliance for Climate Stabilization, which is a public–private partnership that the Climate Institute has stimulated, is a broad-scale recognition of the international and intergenerational equity issues posed by climate change. The International Leadership Alliance draws on these ethical concerns to link leaders in vulnerable island nations and states or provinces of more populous nations with research institutions, universities, religious groups, voluntary carbon offset groups and corporations that share an interest in climate protection.

The seed money for the Summit came from the Evergreen Foundation whose benefactor, Bert Kerstetter, has been at the forefront of efforts to examine the ethical dimensions of global environmental issues. Bert Kerstetter's generosity has enabled his alma mater, Princeton University, to develop innovative programs in ethics and to enhance its own sustainability practices. The Climate Institute's Chief Scientist, Michael MacCracken, the driving force behind our 19 September 2006 Science Symposium and also an alumnus of Princeton, contacted Bert Kerstetter, who arranged for the funds to enable us to organize what proved to be a rarely matched presentation by world class scientists of the increasing risks of large-scale disruption posed by climate change. The Evergreen Foundation has also generously provided resources as we have sought to distill the Summit's message for a broader audience.

For the content of *Sudden and Disruptive Climate Change: Exploring the Real Risks and How We Can Avoid Them*, we are indebted to the authors of the individual chapters, whose biographies are provided in the list of contributors, and to two remarkable editors, who both served on a pro bono basis. Mike MacCracken was a driving force behind the US National Assessment on Climate Change, served on the synthesis team for the *Arctic Climate Impact Assessment*, and on the author team for Sigma Xi/UN Foundation report, *Confronting Climate Change: Managing the Unavoidable and Avoiding the Unmanageable*. A few months before finishing his four-year term as President of the International Association on Meteorology and Atmospheric Sciences, Mike had the almost unprecedented distinction of having a page and a half of his affidavit on risks associated with climate change quoted and relied upon by Justice Stevens in the US Supreme Court's majority opinion in the historic case of *Massachusetts v EPA*. Frances Moore, a 2006 *summa cum laude* graduate of Harvard College working as an intern with the Climate Institute, served as co-editor. Fran has a remarkable grasp both of paleoclimatology and of climate change in the Arctic. At the same time she was serving as co-editor, she also prepared papers available online at our website www.climate.org: *Putting Climate Change in a Geological Context: Are Models Under-predicting Future Changes in Sea Level?* and *Debunking Urban Legends of Climate Change.* The first article collects evidence from the last major deglaciation that suggests it resulted in rapid rise in sea level around the world, while the second eviscerates arguments advanced by climate skeptics that human influences on climate are minimal and that all or most observed climate change is attributable to natural factors.

In addition to Bert Kerstetter, we are grateful to several individuals, families and organizations whose generosity and foresight made it possible for the Climate Institute to celebrate its 20th Anniversary as the world's first environmental organization focused on climate protection. We are especially grateful to our board member, Jason Elliott, and the entire Wyly family for general support funds in 2006 and 2007 that have been crucial to our success. Sam Wyly, a pioneer in computer software and communications revolutions, brought this same insight to green power marketing as he spearheaded Green Mountain Energy. As the Keynoter of the Seattle Summit on Protecting the World's Climate convened by the Climate Institute in April 2000, he set out a vision of the information revolution as a model for a potentially sweeping transformation of the global energy system. Seven years later, Sam Wyly's vision seems to be shared by industrial and financial leaders in the US and abroad, and tens of billions of dollars worth of clean energy investments are made each month. Through the Communities Foundation of Texas, Michaels Stores, and other groups with which the Wyly family has been associated, the Climate Institute has received vital and generous support over the past eight years.

Another family, the Thomas H. and Barbara W. Gale family of Eastern Shore, Maryland, has played a similarly vital role. Tom and Barbara Gale were instrumental in funding the Symposium on Climate Change for United Nations Missions organized by the Climate Institute in June 1988, and provided crucial seed money for the Cairo World Climate Conference convened by the Climate Institute in December 1989. Their daughter, Wendy, was the Climate Institute's first intern and about 150 individuals, including her sister Jennifer, from over two dozen nations, have followed in Wendy's footsteps. Tom and Barbara provided vital support first through the William Bingham Foundation and, in more recent years, through the Thomas H. and Barbara W. Gale Foundation.

Melinda Kimble has also played a vital role in our success, even before becoming Vice President for Programs of the United Nations Foundation. As a senior official of the US Department of State she had the vision to see the value of what was to become the Global Sustainable Energy Islands Initiative (GSEII). The United Nations Foundation has been a major supporter of GSEII as well as a sponsor of the Washington Summit. Support from Rockefeller Brothers Fund has also been crucial to GSEII's success, and for this we are especially grateful to Michael Northrop.

Additional support for the Washington Summit came from firms that have had little previous linkage to the Climate Institute, but that have in the past few years, embraced an energy transformation goal akin to that advanced by the Climate Institute. Especially notable is Goldman Sachs, which has begun to invest billions of dollars of its own funds into renewable energy and efficiency ventures. We were pleased to recognize Goldman Sachs and its Managing Director, Alan Waxman, who is spearheading his firm's energy transformation effort, through a Financial Stewardship Award presented at our 20th Anniversary Dinner. We also deeply appreciate the support of Toyota Motor Company and its Vice President Josephine Cooper, who spoke at the Summit on Toyota's success in commercializing gas/electric hybrids and in marketing fuel-efficient vehicles and who, on behalf of Toyota, accepted the Climate Institute's Transportation Leadership Award. We very much appreciate the participation and sponsorship of BP and congratulate them for their first place ranking among major multinationals on climate protection in the 2006 CERES ratings, an achievement for which they were recognized at the 20th Anniversary Dinner. We are also grateful for the sponsorship of the PG&E Corporation and would like to thank their CEO, Peter Darbee, and President, Tom King, who have both been working to vault their firm into leadership in clean energy.

We deeply appreciate the generous sponsorship of the Casten Family Fund and the brilliant presentation of Tom Casten, who has been both a very successful builder of Combined Heat and Power (CHP) facilities and a persuasive advocate of steps to remove regulatory barriers to such innovations. We appreciate the generous co-sponsorship by Glitnir, an Icelandic bank that has emerged as the world's leader in geothermal energy financing, and the Icelandic Tourist Board. We also would like to thank Duraflame, the leading manufacturer of firelogs, for their sponsorship, which has helped us to publish this book, and also congratulate them for the steps they have taken to transform their firelogs to a carbon neutral basis.

Several other institutions that provided tangible financial support and informational materials also deserve recognition. These include ICF International, a pioneer in greenhouse emissions inventory methodologies and a driving force behind the Green Lights and Energy Star programs; thanks especially go to Michael Barth who spearheaded ICF's first work in climate protection. We were delighted to have the sponsorship of Energy Conversion Devices (ECD) and the participation of its Founder and Chairman, Stan Ovshinsky, who has been aptly described as 'the Thomas Edison of clean energy', and its Vice President, Nancy Bacon, who has made ECD a real factor in clean energy policy formation in the US. The US Geothermal Energy Association also provided welcome sponsorship. We are grateful for the sponsorship of the Southern Alliance for Clean Energy and would like to congratulate its Chairman, John H. Noel, for receipt of the 2007 Conservation Award of the Daughters of the American Revolution. His speech accepting this award before 3500 attendees in Constitution Hall on 30 June 2007 was one of the finest talks ever given on the need for the US to act on climate change; it drew a standing ovation. We also appreciate the generous support of the Summit by Bill Nitze, Lee Huebner, Michael Brewer, Hal Rabner, Hans and Sabrina Weger, Robert Raymar, Scott Sklar, Devra Davis and Dick Morgenstern, and Paul and Ellen Hoff.

Deep thanks are also owed to several US and international leaders whose messages evoked hope that we might act effectively to avert some of the potential high-end disruptions of the climate and society. John Ashton, British Special Ambassador for Climate and a Member of our Board of Advisors, noted efforts of Her Majesty's Government to explore the risks of irreversible damage from climate change and to take decisive steps to limit UK greenhouse emissions. Sir Crispin Tickell, Chairman Emeritus of the Climate Institute and a driving force behind Global Environmental Protection efforts for the past three decades, discussed international actions that might buffer humanity against some of the most adverse effects of climate change. President Ólafur Ragmar Grimsson of Iceland mesmerized us with his insightful description of how Iceland leveraged its clean energy transformation to move from being the poorest nation in Northern Europe to become one of the world's most prosperous nations.

The Summit also engaged US political leaders, despite the fact that it was occurring just as Congress was wrapping up a contentious and busy session. On 20 September, a large crowd assembled at 8 am to hear from two of the most thoughtful US legislators: Senator Jeff Bingaman of New Mexico, now Chair of the Energy Committee, and F. Sherwood Boehlert of New York, Retiring Chair of the House Science and Astronautics Committee, and a spearhead of the Summit's success. The Climate Institute's Board Member Claudine (Schneider) Cmarada, Member of the House of Representatives from Rhode Island from 1981–1991, during which time she was the leading House champion of action on climate protection and renewable energy, organized that session. One came away from this discussion with the distinct impression that the US was near a political tipping point on climate change. A strong congratulatory joint letter from Connecticut Senator Joseph Lieberman and Arizona Senator John McCain was distributed at the 20th Anniversary Dinner attended by Wisconsin Congressman Thomas Petri and a number of Congressional staff and numerous other conferees.

Bringing the Summit to fruition took a tremendous amount of organizational work. Alexis Sloan Nussbaum was the driving force behind the Summit, working tirelessly from early 2006 and in a remarkably insightful and professional manner and with quite modest resources to make the Summit a success. Working beside her with the same diligence and resourcefulness was Lina Karaoglanova, who served as Summit Registrar. Nine remarkably talented and industrious interns worked under their skillful direction. Erin Frey, Harvard 2008, worked closely with me developing the Summit Background Paper adapted to be Chapter 16 in this book. Holly Johnson, MIT 2007; Joe Roy-Mayhew, MIT 2008; Susie Chung, Dartmouth 2007, and three graduate students – Nalin Srivastava, a former Indian Forester studying at the Yale School of Forestry and Environmental Studies; Mariam Ubilava, a Muskie Fellow from the Republic of Georgia and graduate student at Evergreen State University; and Marie-Claire Munnelly, a student at the Bren School at the University of California Santa Barbara, all did wonders, editing *Climate Alert*, preparing the 20th Anniversary Report, helping prepare the Summit website, recruiting potential attendees, coordinating with speakers, procuring in-kind donations and more. Even before their arrival, Nina Rinnerberger, an Austrian national studying at American University, was preparing the Endangered Islands Campaign website; she recently has been chosen as Director of Operations and Director of our Intern Program. Starting just before the Summit, Courtney Wilson, a student at Hobart and William Smith, provided crucial assistance at the Summit and subsequently.

Several other Climate Institute staff and close allies played a key role as well. Nasir Khattak was the driving force behind the launch on 20 September of the International Leadership Alliance. He also oversaw successful workshop sessions on 18 and 21 September at the Climate Institute. Jack Werner oversaw the Registration Tables at the Summit and was assisted by Rob Arner, Courtney Wilson, Susie Chung and Holly Johnson, the latter three all Climate Institute interns. Ata Qureshi, who played a key role in the Climate Institute's success for nearly a decade, led our efforts to recruit embassy participants and did this with spectacular results. Nina Robbins and Sam Sherer provided sage counsel throughout our Summit planning.

Luis Roberto Acosta produced what was ultimately to prove the greatest single breakthrough at the Summit – the invitational letter from the Director of Mexico's Astrophysics Institute for the Climate Institute to build a High Altitude Climate

Observatory atop Sierra Negra, about 15,000 feet above sea level in a science park housing a radio telescope. Carlos Diaz Leal skillfully arranged for Televisa to provide extensive coverage of the Summit. For several days, the Summit was one of the two leading stories on Mexican television, along with their hotly contested presidential election. Our thanks also go to several US groups for publicizing the Summit – especially the Environmental and Energy Study Institute (Carol Werner, Fred Beck and Leanne Lamusga) and Worldwatch Institute (Darcey Rakestraw).

We are also grateful to several individual honorees for getting the 18 September opening Workshop on Climate Communications off to such a great start. Susan Joy Hassol, recipient of the Nancy Wilson Memorial Award for her work on many fronts – writing the Synthesis Report of the Arctic Climate Impact Assessment, writing the script for the HBO movie, *Too Hot Not To Handle*, etc. – described how to communicate with full effect, as did fellow Award Winner, Karen Coshof, producer of the widely acclaimed movie *The Great Warming*. Karen has gone on to organize a US–Canadian Coalition for Climate Action from this great film.

Two high points of our 20th Anniversary Dinner were the great anecdote about our first Science Award Winner, Roger Revelle, by Robert Corell, recipient of our First Revelle Memorial Award, and a stirring tribute to our beloved *Climate Alert* Founding Editor, the late Nancy Wilson, by Mark Goldberg, our Vice Chairman. With Nancy's determination we may yet achieve climate stabilization.

Index

Page numbers in *italics* refer to figures, tables and boxes